Anatomy of Post-Communist
European Defense Institutions

Anatomy of Post-Communist European Defense Institutions

The Mirage of Military Modernity

Thomas-Durell Young

BLOOMSBURY ACADEMIC

LONDON • NEW YORK • OXFORD • NEW DELHI • SYDNEY

BLOOMSBURY ACADEMIC
Bloomsbury Publishing Plc
50 Bedford Square, London, WC1B 3DP, UK
1385 Broadway, New York, NY 10018, USA

BLOOMSBURY, BLOOMSBURY ACADEMIC and the
Diana logo are trademarks of Bloomsbury Publishing Plc

First published in Great Britain 2017
Paperback edition published 2018

A catalogue record for this book is available from the British Library.

ISBN: HB: 978-1-3500-1239-4
PB: 978-1-3500-9580-9
ePDF: 978-1-3500-1240-0
eBook: 978-1-3500-1241-7

Names: Young, Thomas-Durell, author.
Title: Anatomy of post-communist European defense institutions :
the mirage of military modernity / Thomas-Durell Young.
Description: New York : Bloomsbury Academic, an imprint of
Bloomsbury Publishing Plc, [2017] | Includes bibliographical references.
Identifiers: LCCN 2016046329| ISBN 9781350012394 (hb) |
ISBN 9781350012417 (epub)
Subjects: LCSH: Europe, Eastern–Armed Forces–Reorganization. |
Former Soviet republics–Armed Forces–Reorganization. |
Europe, Eastern–Armed Forces–History. | Former Soviet republics–Armed
Forces–History. |
Former Soviet republics–Defenses. | Former communist countries–Defenses. |
Europe, Eastern–Defenses. | Military assistance.
Classification: LCC UA646.8 .Y68 2017 | DDC 355.00947/09049–dc23
LC record available at https://lccn.loc.gov/2016046329

Typeset by Integra Software Services Pvt. Ltd.

To find out more about our authors and books visit
www.bloomsbury.com and sign up for our newsletters.

For Earlene

The difficulty lies not so much in developing new ideas as in escaping from old ones, which ramify, for those brought up as most of us have been, into every corner of our minds.

John Maynard Keynes[*]

[*] John Maynard Keynes, preface, *The General Theory of Employment, Interest and Money*, in *The Collected Writings of John Maynard Keynes, Volume 7*, edited by Elizabeth Johnson and Donald Moggridge (Cambridge: Cambridge University Press, 1978). © The Royal Economic Society 1973, 2007, 2013, published by Cambridge University Press, reproduced with permission.

Contents

Illustrations

Figures

Tables

Preface

It is with no small amount of humility that I have endeavored to write this book concerning what I perceive to be failures in many aspects of the Western approach to assisting communist legacy defense institutions in Central and Eastern Europe reform themselves. I have had the great fortune of having been professionally engaged in working in the defense institutions of every Central and Eastern European country (save one). It has been as a result of these interactions over many years, research, analysis, and conversations with officials, academic experts, and consultants that I came to fathom the almost limitless depth of the problem the West collectively and myself personally have faced in helping these institutions adopt Western democratic defense governance concepts. It is with a sincere *mea culpa* that the work will proceed to throw around considerable criticism of the assumptions, concepts, and approaches the West has adopted, one supposes by default or simply by inattention, to the challenges facing these institutions.

I confess I made many of the mistakes critiqued in this work, at least until around 2011. It was at that stage after an intensive period of engagement in Bulgaria assisting the reform-minded minister of defense Mr Anyu Angelov to undertake that defense institution's most profound reforms to date that the true nature of the challenge slowly became clear. I am greatly indebted to Glen Grant, Vladimir Melinski, and Celeste Ward Gventer, in particular, as we collectively tried to figure out why our patients are not responding to the conventional protocols, such as technical assistance, education, and training. Over the following years, with each new project and problem set, I have been able to refine my thinking to answer the following question: *In the almost twenty-five years since the end of the Cold War why have defense institutions in the region either largely gone unreformed or are continuously struggling to adopt what I refer to as Western democratic defense governance concepts?* To be sure, there are some instances of apparent qualified success (e.g., Poland, Slovenia, and Romania), but despite the provision of training, equipment, education, and advice, most of these institutions have largely atrophied, losing their Cold War operational focus, if not complete meaning. Something in the Western approach to helping them reform is simply not fit for purpose. To wit: these defense institutions are, by and large, not capable of conducting even rudimentary defense planning and are oversized in terms of personnel, yet contain empty units. An examination of units in the field, aircraft on hardstands, and ships at docks demonstrates that these legacy defense institutions are literally rusting and wasting away. Indeed, when a senior official of the International Staff, in a private capacity, can refer to one of the new NATO member's defense institution as almost "un-reformable," it is well past time for serious self-reflection.

It was approximately at this point that fortuitously I became reacquainted with Keynes's admonition (referenced in the book's epigraph) of the difficulty of escaping from old concepts, and the germination of a different way to assess the lack of reform took place. The reflection, reading, analysis, and debates with officials and experts made me rethink from first principles the challenge of escaping from communist legacy concepts to adopt those based on Western democratic values. The result of this period of contemplation and thought is this book. It was written almost exclusively in my private time due to the demands of my official duties, and hopefully this cathartic exercise may benefit the professional understanding of all involved in addressing the challenges of reforming legacy defense institutions. In fact, it is incumbent that I acknowledge the unique opportunity I have enjoyed to work closely with the defense institutions in this region in a variety of capacities. I would like to state most emphatically that no classified, restricted, or privileged information has been used writing this book. Moreover, this work does not reflect the policy or position of the US Department of Defense, Department of the Navy, or the Naval Postgraduate School. I have also been judicious, *in extremis*, not to use sensitive information gained from working with client defense institutions. As the extensive use of citations will attest, the data cited in this work are all from unclassified published sources.

Now that I have explained what the book addresses, it is equally incumbent that I explain what the book does not. Most importantly, this is not a work that addresses the whole of government concept of Security Sector Reform. Rather, this work limits itself to the defense institutions of these countries. I feel it is helpful to use a typology to serve as a heuristic in understanding these organizations. This is a typology of former Soviet, former Warsaw Pact, and former Yugoslav republics. It is my contention that this typology allows comparison across time and space, which leads to recommendations to guide policy the better to leverage strengths and control for challenges in each. The acorn does not fall far from the oak tree, and this work will argue that officials and experts would be well advised to think of these countries more in terms of their communist provenance than as simply being new allies or partners. Moreover, it allows me to offer observations gained from experience within each typology, which provides a richer understanding of the underlying operating nature of these defense institutions, by recounting the unique nature of these groupings of defense institutions at the end of the Cold War. Younger generations of Western officials and officers have little, or no, knowledge of these communist armed forces' value system and mental paradigm, let alone the degree to which their legacies continue to retain their gravitational grip on their successor defense institutions. That an intelligent US officer serving in a former Yugoslav republic could claim in 2014 never to have heard of the Yugoslav Peoples' Army (JNA), let alone not appreciate its still extant influence, speaks to the need for the detailed explanation of these armed forces.

The reader will note that Albania is not addressed in this work, nor is Kosovo. Despite being familiar with both countries, I have chosen not to address either in this work as they do not fit within the typology. Albania, albeit profoundly communist, was outside of the Eastern bloc's military alliance and structures. To be frank, it requires its own treatment. Equally, Kosovo is not studied as it, too, is a one-off. It has only recently started to transition to a formal armed force. This case, too, deserves its own treatment and assessment. Note that neither Russia nor Belarus is addressed for reasons that should be obvious.

It is recognized that some will be perplexed and others possibly annoyed with the book's argument that the alliance should adopt a policy of "Honest Defense" in the same spirit that it has adopted "Smart Defense," "Defense Institution Building," and "Defense Capacity Building." The data, alas, point to complacency on the part of officials, both from the East and West, as to the true state of underdevelopment of legacy defense institutions, accompanied with either resignations or overly optimistic prognoses for reform. Simply stated, as long as new NATO countries and NATO aspirants were keen to support operations far afield, Western and NATO officials consciously, or not, have held these countries' defense institutions to a much lower standard than long-standing allies and now are experiencing, according to Edward Lucas, strategic incoherence.[1] This has been a mistake and must be reassessed in the short term. If nothing else, in light of Russia's new muscular foreign policy, the West has precious little time to develop effective new policies and assumptions to assist new allies and partners develop greater degrees of *policy and capability coherence*. The creation of such capabilities is essential to deter any potential adversary and prove that NATO nations are committed to, and capable of an, effective and unified response if necessary.

Acknowledgments

It would be specious of me to argue that this work is of complete originality, as the literature on the evolution of defense institutions in Central and Eastern Europe is extensive. As such, it is my ambition to do justice to the body of work that has been published in this field since the end of the Cold War. I have benefited greatly from reading and studying the impressive literature authored by scholars such as Timothy Edmunds, Andrew Cotty, Anthony Forster, James Sherr, Donald Abenheim, Jeff Simon, Philipp Fluri, David J. Betz, Zoltan Barany, Marybeth Peterson Ulrich, Christopher Donnelly, Jake Kipp, and David Glantz (and the latter three having founded and continue to edit the superb *Journal of Soviet/Slavic Military Studies*). I have endeavored "to stand on the shoulders of these giants" in order to move forward our understanding of the challenges facing the reform of post-communist defense institutions in Central and Eastern Europe. In particular, I was strongly influenced by two works that have not received the credit their authors so deserve: that of the Hungarian scholar and government official, Reka Szemerkenyi, who observed as early as 1996 that PfP was wrongly being militarized, and Brigadier Michael Clemmesen, whose 2000 work I requested on the challenge of educating legacy officers for a special edition of *Security and Defense Analysis* on NATO that I coedited with Andrew Dorman. As the founder of the Baltic Defence College in Tartu, Estonia, Michael is one of the very few who has written so perceptively about the communist officers' mind-set and values. I have relied heavily on the impressive work that the Geneva Centre for the Democratic Control of Armed Forces continues to produce on civil-military relations and the status of defense reform in the region. Frankly, all of them, to my mind, have not received the credit that they so greatly deserve for their original work in helping us comprehend the challenges of reforming legacy defense institutions.

Over the years, I have been incredibly fortunate to learn from the wisdom and insights of a number of colleagues, and their efforts to reform these defense institutions need to be acknowledged: Jay ("Hoss") Ballard, Antonius Bernards, Kent Davis, Gordon Grant, Celeste Ward Gventer, Walter Holmes, Martin Hurt, Eric MacArthur, William O'Malley, Tiffany Petros, Robin ("Sak") Sakoda, Kristina Soukupova, Ken Strain, and Gino Wessan. Jaan Murumets and Vladimir Milenski have been particularly instrumental in helping me understand the nuanced challenges legacy defense institutions face and determining more effective reform techniques. I am particularly indebted to Glen Grant, with whom I have spent innumerable hours debating the actual causation of impediments to change and developing innovative approaches to these intractable challenges.

Numerous US officials have labored for many years to make a difference despite all the challenges that I document in this work, and for their often unrecognized efforts, credit is due: Nathan Bein, David Cate, Rick Dyer, Rachel Ellehuus, David Gouin, Kay

Judkins, Jessica Kehl, Thomas Keithly, James McDougal, Stephen Peterson, Judith Reed, "Oz" Sanborn, Ed Shelleda, and Sandra Sherman. I have received sage advice and encouragement from colleagues in the NATO International Staff, including Frank Boland, Jean-Claude Gagnon, Mari Tomingas, and Brendan Wilson. British defense advisers to Ukraine Stephen Glover, Phil Jones, and David Jones have typified the example of what it is to be an effective expert adviser to legacy defense institutions.

I have also had the pleasure of working closely with a bevy of world-class US military officers who have performed outstanding work in Central and Eastern Europe in assisting defense institutions reform and, critically, furthering Western allied interests: the late and dearly missed Ihor Balaban, Erik Bauer, Jeremy Bobeck, Paul Brotzen, Thomas Butler, Phil Chechowitz, Greg Cook, Mark Davis, Robert Dorsey, Douglas Faherty, Ryan Fayrweather, Lee Gabel, Dave Galles, Byron Harper, Fred Jessen, Glen Lawson, Sean Long, Brendan McAloon, Mathew Manning, Robert Mathers, Jay Mathews, Cindy Matuskevich, Tom Melton, Vincent Mucker, Bruce Murphy, Todd Scatini, Paul Schmidt, John Smith, Jeffrey Snell, Marek Strosin, Scott Sweetser, Robert Timm, "Dash" Wilmot, Ray Wojcik, Al Zaccor, and James Zink.

Sincere recognition is warranted to defense officials and analysts in Central and Eastern Europe with whom I have had the pleasure to collaborate. They have all bravely attempted, often in the face of considerable opposition, to reform their defense institutions: Lauri Almann, Yordan Agov, Anyu Angelov, Drago Babic, Svetožar Braković, Ljubomir Bojovic, Liliana Brozic, Iryna Bystrova, Tamas Csiki, Ştefan Dănilă, Sanela Dozgic, Jovica Đjuretic, Bozidar Forca, Agnieszka Gogolewska, Nusret Hanjalić, Szymon Hatlas, David Humar, Tomas Jermalavičius, Ihor Kabanenko, Victor Korendovych, Tomasz Kowalik, Aleksandar Miscevic, Bence Nemeth, Ilyia Nalbantov, Mihael Neydanov, Ivan Mikuž, Nikola Pekec, Rajko Pešić, Boris Pittner, Zdravko Ponos, Dragan Samardžić, Boyko Spassov, Trayko Stoykov, Georgi Todorov, Hannes Toomsalu, Valari Saar, Kristina Soukupova, Tomislav Vibovec, and Stefan Yanev.

Additional thanks are offered to my colleagues who have been encouraging of this endeavor in many critical ways: Stephen Blank, Laurie Chavez, Melanie Craig, Mike Crouch, John Feeley, Daniel Fields, Lindsay Fritz, Carolyn Halladay, Shay Hochsteder, Rich Hoffman, Eric Leyte, Cris Matei, Jennifer Moroney, Misha Tsypkin, Donald Stoker, Thomas Szayna, Nick Tomb, Matt Vaccaro, and Jim Wirtz.

A number of colleagues have generously given their time to read and review drafts of the manuscript, whose wisdom I have eagerly accepted to make this book much stronger. Mark Davis, Chris Donnelly, James Horncastle, Vladimir Milenski, and Paul Rich (my long-suffering coeditor of *Small Wars and Insurgencies*) freely gave their time to read carefully drafts of the manuscript, for which I am most grateful. Notwithstanding their superb comments, advice, and suggested changes, I remain responsible for any errors and omissions.

Sincere gratitude is also expressed to Amanda Wilman and Professor Denise Osborne, general secretary of the Royal Economic Society, as well as Svetlana Shadrina of Cambridge University Press for granting permission to use the epigraph for this book from the preface of John Maynard Keynes's masterly work *The General Theory*.

Lastly, but most importantly, to my dear Earlene—partner in all of life's important endeavors: to which this work is sincerely dedicated.

List of Abbreviations

ACO	Allied Command Operations
BiH	Bosnia and Herzegovina
C2	command and control
CHOD	Chief of Defense
COA	course of action
DIB	Defense Institution Building
E-IMET	Expanded International Military Education and Training
FMF	Foreign Military Financing
GDP	gross domestic product
HNS	host-nation support
HRM	human resource management
IMET	International Military Education and Training
IPAP	Individual Partnership Action Plan
ISAF	International Security Assistance Force in Afghanistan
JNA	*Jugoslovenska Narodna Armija* (Yugoslav Peoples' Army)
MAP	Membership Action Plan
MDMP	military decision-making process
NATO	North Atlantic Treaty Organization
NCO	noncommissioned officer
NSWP	Non-Soviet Warsaw Pact
NVA	*Nationale Volksarmee* (National Peoples' Army)
PARP	Planning and Review Process
PfP	Partnership for Peace
PG	Partnership Goal
PME	professional military education
PPBS	Planning, Programming, and Budgeting System
SDR	strategic defense review
SOF	Special Operations Forces

1

Introduction

Everything has been thought of before, but the problem is to think of it again in ways that are appropriate in one's current circumstances.

Johann Wolfgang Goethe

It is a truth, universally acknowledged, that the "West" won the Cold War. But what is the status, precisely, of the consolidation of this victory, that is, specifically, the reform, or indeed the transformation, of the defense institutions in these post-communist nations? Intimately tied to this issue is the related question of how successful has the West been in assisting its former adversaries, a plurality of which are now allies, in adopting Western democratic defense governance concepts so that collective defense is possible? These are not idle musings of mere academic relevance. The Russian invasion of Crimea in winter 2014 and its subsequent support for "separatists" in Eastern Ukraine should add immediacy to ascertaining the precise status of these reform efforts. Moreover, it is conversely a truth not universally acknowledged that due to the lack of consistent political pressure, from both Western political officials and politicians within these countries, the armed forces of many of these post-communist countries are slowly, but literally, disintegrating. In those countries in which the military is not in an active state of decline (e.g., the Slovenian, Polish, and Romanian armed forces), the civil defense institutions remain underdeveloped by Western democratic standards, which hinders achieving greater operational effectiveness and their financial sustainability. But the fact remains that Soviet, Warsaw Pact, and Yugoslav-sourced military, naval, and aerial platforms and systems are coming to the end of their respective operational lives. Due to very limited institutional awareness, ongoing efforts to undertake force management and force development are episodic at best. Yet, it was never the West's plan completely to disarm these armed forces; but for the reasons that will be recounted in this work, this is precisely what *is* occurring. For instance, almost in despair, Slovak defense officials publicly acknowledged in 2013 that some 70 percent of Slovak ground equipment was past its life cycle and admitted that there were doubts that the armed forces could defend the country, not to mention meeting Slovakia's NATO commitments.[1]

What is maddening is that there seems to be little effective political attention being given to this reality, by either Western or Eastern political officials; albeit writing in the shadow of Russia's new adventurism in Syria and Ukraine, some officials are apparently growing aware of this problem. This lack of appreciation could very well be due to the fact that where attention is being paid, it is almost exclusively focused to the diminished military capabilities of long-standing NATO members in the West. For instance, the otherwise prescient columnist "Charlemagne" of *The Economist* did not even mention, let alone assess, the shrinking defense capabilities (as opposed to the size of armed forces) of new members of NATO in a 2013 article lamenting the decline in resources dedicated to defense by Western European governments.[2] This is troubling on three levels. First, the decline in military capabilities in post-communist legacy armed forces has been more accelerated compared with those in the West. Modernization efforts in Western forces may be modest, but these nations still possess world-class lethal and sustainable capabilities. This is largely not the case with the armed forces of new NATO members, heavily burdened with time-expiring communist-designed equipment. Unreformed, they cannot contribute significantly in crisis or war, while requiring Western resources to support them, which could be better used elsewhere. Second, surely it must be of concern that the diminution in military capabilities and the continued weakness of communist legacy defense institutions to manage effectively their armed forces are occurring in close geographic proximity to a Russia that continues to act as an active spoiler in European affairs in the best of times, and now as an aggressor ignoring agreed post–Cold War norms of international behavior. One can ponder the wisdom of bringing these Cold War security "orphans"[3] into the Western alliance, but by allowing their armed forces to devolve into an unsanctioned state of atrophy, the West has unwittingly created an "unfunded" liability. As the Ukrainian crisis has demonstrated, countries whose militaries are not reformed are at serious risk of invasion or destabilization. Third, and finally, most if not all of these nations have been very supportive of Western, and particularly US, campaigns both within and outside of Europe and have loyally provided troop deployments. That they are disarming by default should cause alarm bells to be set ringing. From all angles, therefore, the immediacy of assisting legacy defense institutions more effectively is clear.

The fact that these defense institutions have faced challenges to reform at best, and atrophied in the worst cases, must be tempered by the fact that there has been no lack of effort by them to reform their defense institutions and armed forces by adopting Western democratic defense governance concepts. This effort took on greater import and immediacy following the establishment of NATO's Partnership for Peace (PfP) program in 1994, when the alliance's policy toward these nations was agreed and later their membership within the alliance became possible. In consequence, from the Baltic to the Balkans, and from the Oder to the Caucasus, "defense reform," and after 2004 Defense Institution Building, has become the mantra of essentially all of the defense policies of these former communist countries.[4] Certainly, within the context of modern history, this development must be assessed as constituting the most geographically widespread effort to reform defense institutions. From the Baltic States, which had to establish armed forces *ab ovo*, to Poland[5] and Romania,[6] with their tradition of professional, and by regional standards, effective *national* defense institutions, great efforts have been made to create operationally effective, and (in time) financially efficient, institutions. Moreover, the reform endeavors of these states have not been executed without significant advice and assistance from NATO and its member nations. Indeed, NATO's transformation from a strictly collective defense treaty to what is now an organization with global relevance[7] remains extensively associated with encouraging defense reform among PfP partners and indeed beyond.

However, the ability of post-communist legacy defense institutions to transform themselves to develop and maintain forces in accordance with Western concepts has been modest at best. An effort to assess the capability of any state to produce defense outcomes in a simple objective manner would be complex and would miss crucial information from many highly important factors, some of which could be construed as being subjective and which continues to befuddle their defense officials. As such, one cannot reliably measure progress on a single chart or graph, let alone the fact that this task does not lend itself to capture by a simplistic checklist so beloved by bureaucrats. As presciently observed by Bebler when assessing the degree of the Westernization of the ministries of defense of these former communist countries, they "should not be assessed through a mechanical application of the arrangements which have gradually developed and spread in the West under Anglo-Saxon influence."[8] Rather, a review of befuddled concepts, unbalanced structures, and meager defense outcomes paints a nuanced picture of troubling ineffectiveness. To wit, the principle of *fixed* territorial defense remains the de facto if not de jure predominant operational (and mental) concept for a number of legacy defense institutions, arguably unintentionally undermining the principle of collective defense and the cornerstone of the North Atlantic Alliance, that is, Article 5.

Confusion can be found throughout the region as to what constitutes viable operational formations and professional standards. The Serbian Army has a total of 13,250 personnel but is structured around *thirty-five* regular battalions. The Lithuanian Army of 3,200 soldiers is organized into *eight* battalions. The Moldovan Army of 3,250 is organized into *five* brigades and *four* battalions. Conversely, the Belgian Army has 11,950 personnel organized into the equivalent of approximately *twelve* battalion-equivalents (a battalion constituting approximately 400 to 700 assigned personnel). The Bosnian defense budget in 2012 was approximately US$228 million but the country is assessed by the International Institute for Strategic Studies as possessing little capability to mount combat operations. This dismal state of affairs exists despite a US$100-million train-and-equip program launched after the Dayton Peace Accords to enable the new Bosnia-Herzegovina Federation (BiH) to defend itself, underwritten by the United States (and carried out by a private firm) with approximately 200 retired US military personnel.[9] Bulgarian Air Force pilots can expect to fly only 30 to 40 hours per annum at best, while before the conflict with Russia, their Ukrainian counterparts were averaging around 40 hours, whereas NATO considers 180 hours per annum to constitute the floor in order to maintain basic proficiency.[10] These representative and disparate data paint a picture of not only underfunded and hollow units, but more importantly the inability of officials to bring themselves to ensure that defense *fits* their existing budgets, in order that they produce measurable defense outcomes and field armed forces that could operate and survive on the modern battlefield. There is an incomplete appreciation, or even ignorance, in many of these countries of the need to achieve *capability coherence* in national defense in accordance with Western democratic defense governance concepts. Clearly, emotive and atavistic thinking continues to dominate defense policy and planning: *res ipsa loquitur.*

How is military innovation adopted in countries? This question is addressed elegantly by David Ralston in his book *Importing the European Army.*[11] It not only is a significant intellectual question, but rather also has profound contemporary practical relevance and wide policy implications. As witnessed by the mixed record, at best, of the United States and its coalition partners in their combined efforts to rebuild indigenous police, paramilitary, and armed forces in Iraq and Afghanistan, the creation of defense institutions to govern state-controlled means of violence presents no small challenge. Clearly, it is not difficult to train army infantry battalions, and equally it is clear NATO armies are quite adept at executing this task. However, the US and other NATO nations' records of success in creating national-level defense structures and implementing basic Western concepts in these two countries have been much more problematic.[12] As the decline of military capabilities in new members has not been a stated objective of the alliance, what this work will argue is that there can be no other conclusion than, notwithstanding the efforts of many Western countries, both the national efforts of new members and partners with assistance from old NATO states have not been successful. Indeed, it will be argued that any dispassionate, objective cost–benefit analysis of Western efforts to encourage, finance, and/or cajole these defense institutions to reform would suggest that the West has received meager returns on its considerable investments. This can only lead to the sensitive observation that current Western policies and the designated organizations to manage defense reform programs need to be reassessed from their basic policy assumptions and programmatic first principles.

The less than convincing record of the Western governments in overseeing the creation of new civil defense institutions and armed forces in Iraq and Afghanistan speaks clearly to the need for an examination of how the West in general *approaches* the issue of reforming, or creating *ab ovo* defense institutions and armed forces.[13] To be sure, every country, let alone each region of the world, has their own unique peculiarities in governance. However, it is the rare defense institution that has not been touched or influenced by either Western democratic-derived or communist concepts. It will be argued that the military equipment countries procured from abroad, if they are fully integrated into the armed forces, perforce will affect the management of that national institution and in fundamental ways. One would like to assume that the Western world has a strong understanding of their own defense institutions, which can be used effectively in dealing constructively with similar counterparts. Understanding the nature of reforming defense institutions created, or heavily influenced by communism, is another issue. During the Cold War, Soviet security assistance spanned the globe[14] and while Russia is no longer governed by the Communist Party, communist-inspired military concepts, planning assumptions, and institutional *logic* still permeate the Russian defense institution, not to mention the People's Liberation Army of China, the Cuban armed forces, and those of North Korea, all of which have assistance programs to allies and client states and groups. The point being that a strong understanding of the legacy characteristics of communist defense institutions continues to have relevance in terms of adjusting both the West's approach to assisting its allies and partners in Central and Eastern Europe and potentially many other defense institutions the world over which have comparable traits. Fortunately, or not, there remains a data-rich series of communist legacy civil defense institutions, from which upon examination can provide useful insights to enable Western policy to readjust reform approaches to only those that are most relevant *and* effective.

This book constitutes a modest attempt to provide a better understanding of the challenge presented to Western and Eastern officials when contemplating the reform of legacy defense institutions. Clearly, both officials and analysts need such a resource to provide a deeper understanding of the problem and its causation.[15] In so doing, this work addresses five key questions. First, in a documented and comprehensive fashion, what is the current state of the institutional capabilities of defense institutions in Central and Eastern Europe? There have been many excellent studies undertaken that assess individual states, but to date, no work has taken on the ambitious task of looking at essentially *all* of them. In effect, by drawing together many disparate sources on all of these countries, this work endeavors to weave a narrative that allows the reader to gain a macro understanding of the state of functionality of these defense institutions within their proper typology. Second, in light of this analysis, what have been the key impediments to enabling these countries to create anew when necessary, or reform existing legacy civilian defense institutions and armed forces, in accordance with Western democratic defense governance concepts? As an unsubtle act of foreshadowing, this book's epigraph citing John Maynard Keynes's *General Theory* presciently speaks to the multitudes of unseen communist concepts that continue to this day to "ramify" throughout these defense institutions. Third, when assessing current Western policy and management of assistance efforts in these countries, what might be considered to be effective reform techniques employed to date, and by inference, what have been the least useful? Fourth, contextualizing this problem from a different perspective, how well has NATO and its nations' policies and its implementing organizational management practices performed in assisting these allies and partners adopt Western democratic-derived defense and military concepts? Finally, which policies, concepts, assumptions, and *logic* need to change in both Western and Eastern capitals to facilitate reform of these institutions in a more timely manner?

The research, analysis, and on-the-ground experience of this author in defense institutions throughout the region have resulted in the following theses that will be argued in this work. First, notwithstanding the efforts of Western nations, when examining the underdeveloped state of the defense institutions in the region and the slow disintegration of their military capabilities, one can only conclude that the return on investment of these efforts has been modest. Farrell and Terriff helpfully identify three pathways by which military change occurs (i.e., via innovation, adaptation, and emulation).[16] Yet one is hard-pressed to find many successful examples of such change that can be manifested in outcomes among these countries. There are some in the case of individual formations (e.g., developing Special Operations Forces (SOF) to American/British standards) or new Western platforms (e.g., multi-role fighters: F-16 Fighting Falcons to Poland and Romania, and JAS 39 Gripens to Hungary and the Czech Republic), but across an entire organization is rare. As will be documented, since PfP was initiated, the US government alone has invested some *US$2.5 billion* in just one key defense assistance program to reform these defense institutions, yet one continues to witness a persistent decline in military capabilities. As observed by no less an expert than Chris Donnelly in 2001,

> we in the West have not actually been very good at analysing the situation [of civil-military relations], either in our own countries or in Central and Eastern Europe. Therefore we have found it difficult to cross the cultural divide and lend a hand to the new democracies in their task of transformation. A lot of our well-meant efforts has been wasted because it was inappropriate, inapplicable or just plain wrong. We overestimated the competence of Central and Eastern Europe governments to draw up and implement plans in this sphere. We underestimated the impact of corruption and vested self-interest as obstacles to change.[17]

Second, Western assumptions of the state of development and professionalism of officials in these defense institutions have proven to be erroneous. As dispassionately observed by Clemmesen, Western officials greatly underestimated the state of rot within these armed forces, and given that national defense concepts, assumptions, and logic have not fully changed, this rot continues its destructive metastasis. Third, much of the causation for the lack of progress to reform can be traced to a continued widespread use of legacy concepts which remain in place throughout these defense institutions. An easily observable example of this is found in the continued hyper-concentration of power (complicated in many cases by collective decision-making) within these institutions that has obviated against the development of a strong policy framework and its necessary supporting planning and management tools.[18] The lack of fully appreciating the continued widespread use of legacy concepts presents Western nations that provide advice and assistance one of the most significant impediments to the development of more effective reform techniques. Fourth, this has been a direct result of the decision by Western officials to define the reform of communist legacy armed forces as a *military problem* that can be addressed largely by using their armed forces. This approach has been at the expense of reinforcing emerging and/or weak ministries of defense; *civil* ministries that perforce perform important roles of raising, training, and equipping their armed forces, and, critically, engaging in the mundane day-to-day tasks to ensure effective civilian control of armed forces. Albeit written in a different geographical context, Pion-Berlin's observation of the transition of Latin American countries to democracy that "[t]he balance of power has unquestionably tilted in favor of civilians ... *the balance of competence has not*"[19] very much holds true in the case of Central and Eastern Europe. The failure of Western officials to understand this distinction has hindered a more cohesive approach to assisting these defense institutions to reform themselves. It is troubling that the essence of this problem was first brought to light in a prescient monograph published in 1996 which regrettably went ignored.[20]

Fifth, in so deciding that defense reform should be delegated to their armed forces; by default, Western officials have defined the challenge of effecting change as requiring a *technical* approach to be addressed with *training* and (perforce) at the *tactical* level (the "three Ts," so to speak). Western officials have yet fully to appreciate the need to confront the persistent existence of communist legacy defense concepts that continue to *drive* these defense institutions, but in the *wrong* direction. The lack of appreciation of the powerful gravitational nature of these persistent legacy concepts has been accompanied by the widespread failure to understand fully the malignant persistence of totalitarian norms in these societies:

> When thinking about the fall of any dictatorship, one should have no illusions that the whole system comes to an end like a bad dream with that fall. The physical existence of the system does indeed cease. But its psychological and social results live on for years, and even survive in the form of subconsciously continued behavior. A dictatorship that destroys the intelligentsia and culture leaves behind itself an empty, sour field on which the tree of thought won't grow quickly. It is not always the best people who emerge from hiding.[21]

Kapuscinksi's "subconsciously continued behavior" has allowed Western models, and indeed concepts, to be carelessly applied atop existing legacy foundations, which has produced a multitude of negative externalities. Sixth, as such, *causation* of the continued inability of these countries to adopt Western democratic-derived defense governance concepts has been ignored in the planning of many Western assistance programs. Finally, effective reform of these defense institutions will only be accomplished through the adoption of different policies by Western *and* Eastern officials, as well as the introduction of new management concepts and programs by Western governments and NATO that must define the problem differently. This needs to change from one that sees the problem as being addressed in a technical fashion with tactical training to a new *mentalité* that recognizes the political context of this problem and uses change management principles to guide advice and assistance, but tempered by a profound understanding of organizational cultures and existing disincentives to change within them.

It will be argued in this work that only by defining the problem *differently* will Western efforts be capable of understanding and addressing the *antithetical* nature of persistent and pernicious communist legacy concepts, defense planning assumptions, and *logic*. On the basis of this new understanding, governments in the region can develop solutions that effectively replace these "ramifying" concepts with a more nuanced understanding of Western democratic defense governance concepts. If one accepts the work's theses, by inference, it is essential then for *all* NATO nations to change their own policies, concepts, assumptions, programs, and indeed institutional *logic* when designing and managing reform projects in allied/partner's defense institutions. This is essential as previous experience over the past twenty-five years demonstrates that existing Western approaches have not produced envisaged change. Furthermore, this suggested new approach is also applicable to the whole process of transformation that is at the core of NATO as an organization and of defense change management in each of its member states. Albert Einstein reportedly observed that the definition of insanity is doing the same thing repetitively while expecting different results: Western practice is dangerously close to fitting this troubling diagnosis.

The literature on this subject of the diffusion of military innovation is not bereft of serious analytical studies. A recent and well-received compendium edited by Emily Goldman and the late Leslie Eliasen systematically presented a wide array of case studies[22] to ascertain the conditions on which military innovation can be transmitted. Their thesis is, *en bref,* "The process of diffusion appears far less deterministic and much more vulnerable to local conditions than the system view suggests." Additionally, organizational research shows that the adoption and assimilation of foreign models is not easy.[23] Indeed, historical research reveals no clear explanation of why the diffusion of military innovation and technology was successful in some countries and periods (e.g., Meiji Japan) but a failure in others (e.g., nineteenth-century Ottoman Empire). "These puzzles demonstrate the contingent nature of the diffusion process and suggest the need to search for factors that explain the remarkably wide range of responses to innovation across societies, organizations, cultures, contexts, and historical epochs."[24] Supporting this interpretation, Goldman and Eliasen argue that "military innovations requiring significant changes in sociocultural values and behavioral patterns spread more slowly, less uniformly, and with more unpredictable outcomes."[25]

The results of this work's analysis of the uncompleted record of reforming post-legacy defense institutions reinforce the literature that change agents are necessary to enable the adoption of *technical* solutions. Schein, for example, argues that culture is the most difficult organizational attribute to alter and that will surely survive any organization's outputs: products, services, founders, and leadership, and even physical organizational manifestations.[26] One should not infer that such observations on the importance of culture have not been addressed in the context of defense. In addition to the Ralston case studies, the eminent military historian Richard Millet in his analysis of the record of US efforts to reform the Guardia Nacional de Nicaragua in the interwar period concluded that "while technical expertise can be created, altering political behaviour and institutions are much more difficult, if not impossible."[27] The results of this work's research findings and supporting analysis clearly underscore the theses of Millett and Ralston that cultural norms are either impediments or enablers to the acceptance of Western military innovation. Ralston's historical survey uncovers that "The reformers were to learn, often to their dismay, that the introduction of European forms and methods into their military establishments would sooner or later oblige their societies to undergo internal adjustments which were by no means trivial."[28] That Western policy, to date, has yet to take notice and learn from historical experience has been remarkably shortsighted.

This work is organized accordingly. First, it is important to provide an accurate description of the basic institutional, command philosophy, and overarching conceptual characteristics of these communist legacy armed forces, circa the end of the Cold War. This is discussed in Chapter 2. Of critical importance is the fact that notwithstanding that the antecedents of these institutions were firmly rooted in the defense of communist/totalitarian regimes, these armed forces were quite different from each other in many fundamental ways, thereby suggesting the need for a deeper understanding of their legacy inheritance when attempting to assist them in adopting Western democratic defense governance concepts. Thus, a differentiated typology is used and it will be argued that this sub-aggregation of defense institutions constitutes a useful means to appreciate the provenance of these different communist armies. It is only with a full appreciation of the *conceptual* foundations of these defense institutions circa 1990 that one can understand of how little has actually *changed* in many key and fundamental areas of these defense institutions. Second, in contradistinction within the same chapter, a description will be briefly provided of what constitutes Western democratic defense governance concepts. In effect, this section will endeavor to present a synthesis of what constitutes the basic and fundamental elements of Western democratic nations' philosophy of commanding, planning, and conducting military operations, thereby providing the *aspired* conceptual model against which one can compare progress made by legacy armed forces. At its most basic, Western armed forces are deliberately designed, raised, trained, and equipped to be collective *thinking* organizations at the tactical level. This is in contrast with dominating concepts found in communist armed forces (save arguably to some extent in the JNA). To be sure, there are some differences and nuances in how, for example, old NATO nations conduct the military decision-making process (MDMP) at the tactical level. However, it will be argued that these are not conceptually contradictory in logic and nature so as to cause significant dissonance, or impediments to effecting *intellectual interoperability*.[29] Indeed, the amalgamation of these concepts has been accumulated into the ever-expanding nature of NATO doctrinal publications. In fact, this corpus of doctrine has come to constitute what has become the global gold standard as regards the most effective approach to planning and executing military operations.

Of critical importance is the need for the reader to appreciate the most basic building blocks of Western military operations: the military decision-making process. This section will argue that these processes (mission analysis, course of action development, operational planning, etc.), along with the important concept of training to standard and seeking military excellence (vice blindly training to time), are essential elements of how Western armed forces organize themselves to plan and conduct operations at the tactical and operational levels. That said, these processes also are critically important for effective national-level planning, management, and oversight of the defense institutions. In fact, without such a process that can create and transmit bottom-up data, this chapter argues that the adoption of Western democratic national-level defense planning and management concepts is impossible. This section also has the objective of discerning principles against which one can measure the progress of defense reform in Central and Eastern European countries. It will also make the case for both the need for the systematic adoption of delegating authority to commanders to implement these tactical-level processes and also for senior officials to break from their power-based top-down thinking and to accept those junior to them as professional equals in order to enable the adoption of the Western defense and military concepts.

Chapter 3 addresses how the Western alliance has approached managing its relations with its new partners in Central and Eastern Europe. Three general points will be discussed. First, it is essential to describe, briefly, the numerous policy cooperation vehicles devised by the alliance to assist PfP members to become closer militarily to the alliance and its members. The programs and review processes established by the alliance are, indeed, quite extensive, if not comprehensive. In fact, there is no other regional, or international, body that can compare to what the alliance has developed both to manage, in a structured fashion, its military cooperative programs with its PfP partners and to assist the latter to effect defense reform. Second, the chapter will argue that Western policy has been based on a number of false premises and assumptions, not the least of which has been to direct their armed forces to take the *lead* in developing peacetime relationships with their communist legacy counterparts. What has been largely missing from these policy directives is fully informed guidance to direct such interaction and cooperation that recognizes the actual state of these legacy armed forces, while addressing the reform of ministries of defense came almost as an afterthought. Consequently, cooperation has been based on the erroneous assumption that both soldiers from long-standing democracies and those from legacy institutions enjoyed a common conceptual understanding of what constitutes military professionalism and that both enjoy a common basis of competence. Time has shown that nothing could be further from the truth, but policy and *behavior* in particular have not appreciably changed. The chapter will detail the characteristics that typify officer corps spawned by communism and whose long half-life continues to impede their adoption of Western democratic defense governance concepts. As a means to explain why the adoption of these concepts has been challenging, the work uses the superb cultural dimensions methods developed by the Dutch social psychologist Geert Hofstede to explain how and why some cultures are more amenable to certain forms of change, while others simply are not.

A representative sample of the countries assessed in this work is presented to provide a general, objective, and *comparative* understanding of the underlying cultural realities of these former communist countries. It is proposed not to use these data as necessarily presenting a comprehensive or exhaustive analysis of these societies, but rather they should be used by Western and Eastern political and defense officials as a *starting* point in attempting to come to understand the inherent cultural characteristics in these countries which can either impede or enable change; and such an understanding needs to be reflected in donor nations' policies and support programs. The chapter concludes with an argument that these countries are still in the very early stages of (re) creating distinct strategic cultures, the lack of which is impeding reform, presenting conceptual, linguistic, and indeed institutional false cognates, as well as providing an analysis of the current state of civil-military relations in the region. While there is a general consensus among scholars that holds that these states have moved beyond the basic stages of civilian control of armed forces, by not having inclinations to become involved in domestic politics, this work will demonstrate that this judgment is true, but only in its most general sense. A deeper analysis of the inherent weaknesses in these defense institutions demonstrates that there are, indeed, few positive, let alone effective, instruments of positive control.

Chapters 4, 5, and 6 address in detail the current state of institutional development of, respectively, former Soviet republics, former Warsaw Pact republics, and those of the successor republics of the former Yugoslavia. The analysis presented in these chapters presents data on the state of transformation of these defense institutions that is essential to determining their level of (re)development, upon which one can determine prevailing impediments to reform, as well as creating the most effective reform techniques. To this author's knowledge, this is the first time such a broad analysis of all of these countries' defense institutions has been assembled in one work in order both to provide an analysis and to enable a comparative understanding and appreciation of the status of their development. Indeed the chapters are structured in a similar manner in order to facilitate cross-analysis and comparisons. To be sure, management and organizational pathologies are almost universally the same, yet there are variations in their intensity and indeed presence in each of the individual countries, as well as within the typologies under examination.

Furthermore, there are in each of these chapters a series of charts that, based on the analysis presented, represent this author's *judgment* of the status of the progress of conceptual transformation in these countries as they relate to critically important policy, planning, management, and execution capabilities. For explanation, the judgments are denoted as: (1) legacy, (2) in transition, and (3) extant. The term "NATO" is defined as constituting a country using NATO concepts, assumptions, and content, as an extension of membership in the alliance. In a small number of cases, "unknown" is listed, as well as some minor qualifying comments. It is stated, without qualification, that these judgments are inferences based on research and observations, if indeed some are *sharp*, they have been informed by public documents, many years working in these civil defense institutions and armed forces, and by discussions with experts and officials. As such, the reader is advised to read these observations *addito salis grano*. But, these conclusions reflect this author's view that these defense institutions have, with varying degrees, made only modest success of replacing legacy concepts with their Western counterparts. Indeed, it is suggested that rather than serving as a focal point for disagreement, these judgments should be seen as presenting a basis for questioning how the book's analysis has led to these stark judgments on the state of development of these institutions and in adopting Western democratic defense governance concepts. Finally, the information and assessment presented in these chapters will provide an essential comparative and cross-regional understanding of the performance of defense reform in each country, as well as in an aggregated fashion in the three typologies. It is against these baselines that Western advice and assistance performance can be assessed.

It is in Chapter 7 that the aggregated Western response and approach to reform is analyzed in a critical light. This is indeed a lengthy chapter and it is organized to address four key issues. First, a brief synthesis of commonality in pathologies that exist across the three typologies is developed, which have consistently inhibited these defense institutions from adopting deeper democratic reforms. Second, looking at the challenge from a different perspective, derived from literature, reports, and personal experience, another synthesis will be developed that seeks to capture common approaches, models, and (critically) the *assumptions* that have guided Western advice and assistance efforts. Third, in light of the arguably significant gap between legacy defense institutions and the requirements to produce change, this section argues the case for using different approaches that employ completely different concepts and assumptions to provide more appropriate and effective advice and assistance. Fourth, and finally, in order to complete the circle of presentation of facts and analysis, the work assesses how these new defense concepts should be applied specifically to each of the three typologies of legacy defense institutions and armed forces. It is in this section that the reader will be able to judge whether the book's use of the three typologies has value in refining and developing more focused approaches to providing change management advice and assistance.

Chapter 8 addresses current NATO and key NATO nations' policy guidance and managerial practices that have been used to guide Western efforts to assist legacy defense institutions adopt key Western democratic defense governance concepts. The chapter argues that while the West has been quite effective in providing world-class assistance to aid in the reforming of these armed forces, there have been correspondingly problematic results in providing effective advice to help develop new, or reform existing, defense institutions. It is argued that this has created a condition that has encouraged long-term dependency on Western nations to provide capabilities and support in areas that one would expect allies to provide for themselves. In effect, Western efforts have endeavored to introduce Western defense and military concepts (e.g., special operations forces and deployable units) that are bereft of a fundamental policy understanding within these defense institutions.

Chapter 9 is the conclusion where in addition to providing a summary of the five questions posed in this chapter, it will also make some specific recommendations for changes in policy. This chapter will argue, *inter alia*, that both Western and Eastern political officials need to take a hard look at their respective policy assumptions and expectations if there is any expectation that effective change in their defense institutions is to take place. By this, it is long past due that NATO return to the golden age of blunt talk when burden-sharing was the daily issue of debate and complaints. Much has been made of the recent initiative to adopt "Smart Defense." This is all well and fine, but *ceteris paribus*, both Western and Eastern officials should adopt a new basis for constructive debate: "Honest Defense." That is to say, that it is time for Eastern officials to recognize that their defense institutions are all in serious need of change, while Western officials need to end the practice of communicating unwarranted compliments with insincere politeness. In the final analysis, this work endeavors to convince the skeptical reader that Western donors' best intentions, as expressed in policies and programs, failed to address adequately the seriously underestimated challenge of reforming their partners and allies' defense institutions. In this respect, perhaps the West overestimated the threat of these armed forces becoming modern praetorian guards, and underestimated the difficulty of creating defense institutions capable of preforming the mundane requirement of basic accountable public administration of the defense institution.[30]

Given the nuanced lexicon used in this work, it is appropriate at this stage to define specific meaning in the work's terminology in order to avoid confusion. The author has chosen to use the term "West/Western" nations to designate old NATO members, that is, long-standing democracies. This is not implied to suggest any pejorative connotation that these nations are superior, or always correct, but simply to facilitate shorthand comparisons. The work refers continuously to the differences between Western democratic defense governance concepts with their communist legacy counterparts. This is an important point argued in this work. All too often, the underlying rationales for behaviors, incentives, and attitudes are founded in, or subsequently framed by, concepts, assumptions, and their ensuing organizational logic. As such, these distinctions can be best defined as constituting a diagnostic tool to assist in understanding better the challenges to achieving defense governance based on Western democratic values.

Directly related to this distinction is the term "conceptual coherence." This term is defined as matching policy objectives and priorities with the correct conceptual means to achieve them across the whole defense organism, not just in limited parts. Perforce, this implies extracting obstructionist legacy concepts and their replacement with their modern counterparts. It will be argued that communist legacy and Western democratic defense governance concepts are antithetical in their logic and value sets; and as such, they are incompatible and simply cannot coexist. Ergo, there is a need for greater conceptual coherence based on Western defense and military concepts within a reforming defense institution. That said, there is a nuance in pursuing this objective. It is acknowledged that communist armed forces were exceedingly coherent in terms of their *daktrina*, equipment, and intellectual understanding of war. As such, one may suspect that many legacy officers look upon vague Western defense and military concepts that require interpretation to meet different conditions as being *incoherent* to them, which only further underscores the depth of this ongoing misunderstanding.

An essential tool to achieving coherence in any defense institution is the need for a strong, "policy framework." This implies that the entire defense institution is responsive to the direction and priorities of the minister of defense and the elected government. Thus, no actions, or money spent, should take place outside of that which is sanctioned by policy. Perhaps this distinction is self-evident to the Western reader, but it is an all but unknown concept in legacy governance. The work employs the term "defense institution." It is an important choice as the civil governance of armed forces has too frequently been assumed away by Western nations and alliance officials either to be extant or functional. As the findings of the work demonstrate, there is an urgent need for all officials to focus attention on thinking of these organizations as what they should be: a more coherent whole, absent legacy concepts, assumptions, and logic. The nuanced term "professionalism" is employed and this author selects to use the definition provided by Anthony Forster as "a process [that] involves defining the military's role, revising its force structure to be consistent with the redefined role and adopting professional standards—in particular in the areas of expertise, responsibility and promotion—so that armed forces carry out their missions."[31] Finally, the term "militarized" is employed emphatically not as a pejorative, but rather simply to describe how officials have defined the approach and organizations to assisting legacy institutions reform.

The State of Communist Defense Institutions and Armed Forces, circa 1990

Notwithstanding the general Western public's perception during the Cold War that Warsaw Pact forces were uniform in nature and aligned lockstep vis-à-vis NATO forces in Central Europe, it would be counter productive not to differentiate among Soviet and Eastern European armed forces. They were not the same, if for no other explanation than communistic mind control was introduced only after the Second World War. Moreover, as this analysis aims to include addressing the evolution of former Yugoslav republics' armed forces, a clear distinction of their conceptual base among these institutions is required. Whereas they might well have had common equipment, and in some case, similar operational concepts, their individual and different institutional histories, societies and indeed foreign policies had profound influences on the conceptual frameworks of these armed forces. Thus, despite some important commonalities, it is essential that they be described and analyzed separately. As a result, it is best to address these communist defense institutions based upon their political provenance: (1) Soviet, (2) Warsaw Pact, and (3) Yugoslav. An important point of clarification is that given the many differences in Warsaw Pact armed forces, this chapter will take pains to present fundamentally important differentiations as these are keys to appreciating their subsequent successes, and more often failures, in subsequent reform efforts.

While admittedly largely more descriptive than analytical, the purpose of this chapter is to provide an understanding of the conceptual foundations of these armed forces circa 1990. This is essential in order to discern and measure progress made in their ability to adopt Western democratic defense governance concepts. As this chapter is envisaged to provide a standard comparative basis upon which one can measure differences with their Western counterparts, the final section of this chapter will present a generic description of Western/NATO nations' general approach to organizing their armed forces to conduct operations. A fundamental difference between Western/NATO forces and their communist counterparts is the basic fact that these institutions are explicitly designed, organized, trained, and equipped with the ability, and indeed expectation, to act as *thinking* organizations at the tactical level and to be able to deploy quickly from home station to areas of operation. In contraposition, communist models and most of their legacy armed forces were intentionally designed to be incapable of allowing such freedom of thought, and critically, freedom of action at the tactical level and were often reduced to the strength of cadre in peacetime, thus never improving or developing. These basic differences need to be remembered and controlled when Western/NATO officials and forces have dealings with new NATO allies and partners with legacy defense institutions. Such fundamental differences, one is finding, are simply not easily reformed in these former communist institutions. The inability of these armed forces, or their governments, to adopt Western democratic defense governance concepts has left many of them unstructured for the modern battlefield, or at worst, they have devolved into bloated social welfare organizations. This situation is arguably the most intractable obstacle to achieving reform and effectively integrating them into NATO. But, as armed forces are reflections of societies and their historical experiences, one should not be surprised with such a finding. As observed by Goldman and Eliason regarding the adoption of new ideas, "software generally does not travel as well as hardware."[1]

Legacy of the Soviet armed forces

"What can be stated with relative certainty is that in the years following the Second World War, Soviet military culture had three important characteristics: emphasis on space as an immense defensive barrier, emphasis on mass, and an ambiguous attitude to military professionalism."[2] Tsypkin's prescient description of the influences of the Second World War on the subsequent conceptual basis upon which the Red Army was developed is still very much observable in the heirs to the Red Army. The newly independent post-Soviet republics shared this initial starting point, but evolved quite differently due to exogenous and indigenous factors and all have progressed at different velocities. One additional point needs to be added to this list that continues to spread its influence throughout all defense institutions of successor post-Soviet armed forces: the assumption that all planning, managerial, and indeed military problems can be solved using the Soviet understanding of science. Schneider defines this as follows:

> The Soviet scientific approach to war is firmly rooted in the dialectical materialism of Friedrich Engels. This world view readily lends itself to the support of rigorous scientific inquiry and impinges on all sectors of Soviet society. At the same time the Soviet military historian provides the scientist with a rich empirical data base. Together, military history and science provide a solid foundation for an effective military doctrine that is at once rigorous and dynamic.[3]

At the end of the Cold War, the following observations can be expressed of the characteristics of the Soviet General Staff and armed forces. Note that to facilitate comparative analysis, a standard organizational format is used for all three typologies.

Defense institution

The Soviet armed forces were commanded and directed by the General Staff of the Soviet Union. There simply was no civilian ministry of defense.[4] As presciently described by Yanokyan, "communist party direction of the armed forces was neither democratic nor truly civilian but it was real, and in most cases quite effective."[5] As such, political control was directed from the Politburo, but the Western democratic concept of standardized and formatted procedures to provide graduated and effective direction of the force (defined command authorities, rules of engagement, the concept of escalation, etc.) were all but nonexistent. Given that communism and capitalism were fated to be in an ideological intractable struggle, Western democratic concepts of civilian control of escalation of state-authorized violence simply could not exist. In consequence, the general staff enjoyed a privileged position within government structures and dominated discussions regarding defense and international security issues. It should come as no surprise with the subsequent establishment of ministries of defense in these republics, over which they were envisaged to control general staffs, that they were initially organized similarly to a general staff—and manned by officers, in all areas of responsibility. And indeed, the most powerful organization within these General Staffs was (and remains, in fact) the Main Operations Directorate. The subtlety should not be missed: operational requirements, as defined by this directorate, largely established *national* defense requirements.

Policy framework

There was no hint of a policy framework. Soviet thinking did not distinguish between national-level defense policy and its subordinated and hierarchical levels of policy implementation. Indeed, both conceptual and linguistic conditions simply did not support such an institutional understanding. "Military doctrine" (*Vayennaya daktrina*) was considered to be at the highest level of policy formation—a use of nomenclature which immediately confuses the Western military mind, as the latter defines "doctrine" as a corpus of concepts and procedures, vice national-level policy.[6] In the Soviet mind, these concepts were, in effect, conflated.[7] This lack of linguistic and conceptual differentiation reinforced the isolation of the execution of military operations from the Western democratic principle of civilian oversight, which to the communist mind would have seen as being both unwanted and unneeded. Moreover, one sees a continuation of Soviet practice that treats *daktrina* not as suggestive, or as providing guidelines to aid critical thinking, but rather as prescriptive, addressing *all* aspects of defense/military affairs and indeed having the force of *law*.[8] In a Huntingtonian sense, this is the positive control of the armed forces taken to its illogical conclusion. In short, the Western democratic concept of the overarching role played by the establishment of a "policy framework" to guide all defense governance, with a hierarchy of implementation documents *that directs money in the defense budget* and requires critical thinking and interpretation, was unknown and still is largely underdeveloped in these defense institutions. The existence of a positive law juridical system, perverted by the legacy of the communist contempt for the rule of law, has produced an unholy conflation of policy with law, a legacy that still impedes the development of a constructive policy framework in all of these countries.

National-level command of armed forces

The Soviet national command system was highly centralized and command resided in the Soviet General Staff where *all* decisions, of any consequence, were made. Nothing too mundane and routine could escape decision-making at the national level. Moreover, the general staff did not possess the post of staff director or chief of staff. Consequently, all decision-making was deferred to the highest level commander, that is, Chief of the General Staff. Stalin incentivized referring decision-making upward since responsibility carried with it a potential death sentence or service in a penal battalion. National command, as defined in the West as constituting discrete, legally defined and sanctioned command authorities which are mutually exclusive, and created with the view to their hierarchical and integrated execution,[9] was (and essentially remains) nonexistent under this model. Whereas the primacy of the Communist Party to establish national-level policy was not in question, and the party maintained strict control over the armed forces, the execution of the defense of the revolution was seen as solely a military responsibility due to their expertise, over which even party control and micro-management was seen as unnecessary, unwanted, and problematic. That said, it must be recognized that the senior Soviet officer class was highly politicized and "intertwined with the communist party through the establishment of party cells and the oversight of indoctrination throughout the armed forces." Notwithstanding this tight control by civilian party officials, the general staff was given wide berth in the areas of military (i.e., defense policy), strategy, and force development.[10] What was extremely odd to the Western observer, however, was the lack of an in-being command and control structure, which would be the same in peace and wartime. Rather, Soviet *daktrina* held that the peacetime structure was more an administrative one, whereas in wartime, already designated and practiced battle staffs would be established to exercise command and effect coordination.[11]

Military decision-making process

In consequence of this highly centralized command structure, the military decision-making process, at least as defined by Western armed forces, was nonexistent. Notwithstanding the Soviet recognition of a form of levels of war (strategic, theater, operational, and tactical), command was highly centralized and all subordinated formations fell under the command of the Main Operations Directorate of the General Staff. In the Soviet system, all such organizations were seen as solely executionary bodies, vice possessing thinking and adaptive command organizations. Emanating from practices developed during the Second World War, the Soviet Army developed an operations research-type capacity to study in great technical depth the results of their operational experience.

Studies of "battlefield performance" have continued without respite since the 1950s, though it should not be forgotten that in 1942 the Soviet command ordered OR [operations research] teams to evaluate operations in the wake of combat units.... The result was a whole series of operational typologies, embracing weapons holdings, structures, expected effectiveness, anticipated losses, and measurement against operational reality. This has also given rise to one of the richest tactical-technical military literatures in the world.[12]

Plans were developed by the general staff to be executed in accordance with scientific exactitude. Therefore, subordinated headquarters' staff, by Western practices, were and remain comparatively miniscule and incapable of effectively executing operations on a 24/7 basis, providing mission analysis, course of action development, and so on (i.e., the development of the Estimate for the commander's approval). There simply was no trained staff (let alone second command posts) to provide a tactical-level commander with such products, because such a capability was seen as both unneeded and, indeed, unwanted. Donnelly presciently describes why this is the case:

It is hard for a western officer to appreciate what a difficult concept this is to reconcile with a normal Soviet upbringing. There has never been a native Russian word for initiative. The idea of an individual initiating unilateral action is anathema to the Soviet system. The Soviet Army has always considered as one of its strengths its iron discipline and high-level, centralised command system combined with a universal tactical doctrine. The run-of-the-mill officer, particularly a sub-unit officer, has never had to do other than obey orders.[13]

As noted by Stone, given the conscript nature of the Tsarist Imperial and Soviet Red armies, and the low level of education and training of soldiers, no consideration was given to assuming these forces' ability to undertake exploitive independent action under the command of junior officers, let alone professional noncommissioned officers (NCOs).[14] Soviet operational planning by the general staff, informed by the aforementioned analytical studies of the Second World War, took the form of algorithms, that is, for each operational move, there was only *one* quantifiable and therefore one *scientifically* derived solution from which tactical-level commanders were never to deviate.[15] Initiative, such as it existed, was conceived as constituting a decision taken by a junior officer that could only be executed if his superior officer would know intuitively the pattern of action that was made.[16] Or, as in the case of employing airborne or air-assault forces in Afghanistan, there are recorded instances of junior officers taking initiative, but this was not the case with motorized rifle units.[17] That such conventional solutions were likely to be dear in lives and equipment was of little concern to a political system that placed no value on individual lives, let alone financial costs.[18]

Concept of operation

At the most basic level, as identified by Tsypkin, Soviet operational concepts stressed the essential importance of mass, as well as surprise.[19] While the Russian record of operations in the August 2008 war with Georgia, and since 2014, war in Eastern Ukraine, demonstrates a continuum of Soviet operational doctrinal principles in the Russian armed forces, it is the degree to which mass is stressed that so distinguishes the Soviet approach from its Western counterparts.[20] In Soviet military thinking, it is communist society's *requirement* to provide the armed forces with the necessary human, matériel, and financial resources to fit the needs of the Soviet model of operational mass. And, to the Soviet General Staff's credit, such a principle proved itself effective in the offensives against German forces; for example, Operation Bagration in 1944 to clear German forces from Belorussia.[21] That said, such operational principles are, perforce, extremely costly and are, arguably, antithetical to the Western democratic defense governance concepts of executing operations by balancing military efficiency with minimizing the loss of human life. However, in an era of increasing civilian political and financial oversight of the armed forces, and declining demographics, such a concept of operation is simply not financially and politically sustainable in successor Soviet republics. That said, structures, procedures, and the basic conceptual approaches to operations of many post-Soviet armed forces largely remain premised on these faulty assumptions.

Logistic support

The Soviet concept of logistics, or perhaps better to use its more specific nomenclature, procurement, acquisition, defense industry, and supply, was completely reconceptualized by the Soviets during the 1930s in order to align the Soviet economy to protect and spread the Revolution internationally. It is an important distinction to make early that the legacy communist concept of logistics continues to exist throughout the three typologies of defense institutions examined in this work, and it has been extremely hard for these countries to retire them. Schneider argues that the Soviet concept of logistics has no counterpart in the West as it is emblematic of the cohesiveness of the Soviet concept of warfighting. He argues that the Soviets defined logistics as larger than the management of the support of forces, but rather conceptualized it in a much broader expanse to encompass the entire nation. At the first level, Soviet planners examined comprehensively the military aspects of the nation's economy. Through a rigorous analysis of the foundations of war and the economy, principles of "Military Economic Science" were developed. The second level examined through the use of elaborate tools and techniques from central economic planning to determine how all of these economic inputs (commerce, industrial production, labor, and capital) could be mobilized to support military operations. The third and final level combined these factors into a core theory of military economic logistics: how the armed forces could mobilize the resources of the state. In practical terms, these factors are integrated into what was and is still called in many post-communist legacy defense institutions "Rear Area" ("Rear Security" in the context of Yugoslavia), which contained and managed all military support and sustainment.[22] To aid in a Western understanding: one should think of Soviet legacy logistics as wartime host-nation support (HNS), but on a hefty dose of steroids.

The Soviet concept of Military Economic Science, in essence, turns the Western counterpart of logistics essentially on its head. The general staff determined what the nation was to contribute to create and support the armed forces. In consequence, completely *absent* in the Soviet understanding is the basic Western democratic principle that the armed forces are an extension of, not apart from, society and a nation's economy. A further distinction is that in the West it is operational commanders who determine logistical requirements of their forces to meet assigned missions. This is completely antithetical to the Soviet and indeed many post-communist armed forces. Soviet and communist legacy armed forces deploy with extremely limited logistics (ten to twelve days) as replenishment is envisaged to be pushed forward from static support depots controlled by the Rear Area, while equipment and battle-casualties are recovered rearward to these same facilities. In sum, the Rear Area was and remains as centralized as physically possible.[23] In contradistinction, whereas Western armed forces employ the principle of "pull" logistics, the Soviet logistic concept (determined by mass effects) is based on the principle of centralized operational planning and execution to support a short, quick campaign, that is, "push" logistics, via a forward distribution system.[24] This tradition has its antecedents in Tsarist times when one considers the realities faced by military authorities: the immense size of the country and the huge differences between the small, educated, professional officer corps and masses of peasant soldiers meant that centralized control was the only functional option.[25]

It is important to stress the fundamental conceptual differences between Western and Soviet "logistics" in the context of this work for a number of reasons. Most importantly, Military Economic Science in most of these countries remains largely untouched by Western thinking. Given the antithetical nature of these two concepts (i.e., logistics and Military Economic Science), it is all but impossible to enable mutual understanding between Western and communist legacy military officers and defense officials. Indeed, it can be just short of comical to watch such exchanges given the antithetical nature of the two systems as regards their most basic concepts of logistics. It is little wonder, therefore, that in a classical Soviet-model general staff, there is no G-4, Directorate of Logistics, as logistics planning is subsumed by operational planning and is, therefore, not even seen as needed. Supply, procurement, acquisition, and defense industry are all controlled in ministries of defense.

Professionalism

As defenders of the *rodina* and, critically, the Communist Party, the Soviet officer corps enjoyed an elevated position in society. Officers, even twenty-five years after the fall of the communist system, continue to enjoy an enhanced status in post-Soviet republics as regards their authority over what they consider to be issues of national security and the concurrent attitudes concerning their essential authority and expertise. Within the context of the officer corps it is necessary to clarify that there was, and remains, only a modest professional NCO corps. Unlike their counterparts in the West, they were and continue to be used as technicians and are not entrusted with command, management, and leadership responsibilities. While greater openness and adoption of some Western democratic defense governance concepts now place the officer corps under new scrutiny and public critiques of performance failures, an officer's career still has practical advantages. Importantly, one needs to recognize that the Soviet armed forces were not just a military institution, but rather, they were also a social institution, and a highly privileged one at that.[26] Officers had access to dispensation not available to the general public, for example, an apartment. This was no small advantage in an economy with limited, and consequently expensive, housing, in addition to access to a parallel social support structure. The downside of these social arrangements is that they have a tendency to attract what liberal economists describe as rent-seekers. Thus, the Western concept of professional norms of service to nation is often missing from the Soviet officer corps and its legacy successor armed forces. In short, the concept of what constitutes professionalism in a liberal democracy is not directly applicable to these armed forces. The issue of the differentiation of what constitutes professionalism between Soviet and Western concepts will be addressed extensively *infra*.

Legacy of Warsaw Pact armed forces

As designed by Moscow, Warsaw Pact armed forces, to varying degrees and with one major exception, were closely modeled after their Soviet Red Army counterparts. However, there were important exemptions, particularly as they related to social, vice strictly military, characteristics. For instance, whereas the Czechoslovak and Hungarian armed forces were perceived by the populations of these countries as oppressors and not seen as legitimate institutions of the nation, conversely the armed forces of Poland and Romania were seen as legitimate. In the case of Romania, by the 1970s there were no permanent political officers, which only reinforced Ceausescu's mistrust of the armed forces.[27] Particularly after the 1968 Soviet invasion of Czechoslovakia, the Romanian Army underwent renationalization. Soviet models were rejected, which led to the complete overhaul of the political control of the armed force.[28] To be sure, service in this armed force was seen as honorable and patriotic, notwithstanding their role in defending the oppressive communist regimes for which they served. And one has to admire some of their institutional strengths. Romanians could argue that their defense institution and the state educational structure were the only institutions in Romanian society that Ceausescu was unable completely to subvert for his own political purposes. This social view of the armed forces was reflected in its high public approval rating.[29] The Polish people saw the armed forces as a welcome manifestation of the nation's sovereignty.[30] The subsequent problem with these admittedly positive characteristics of these armed forces is that after the dissolution of the Warsaw Pact and growing democratization, these institutions were not necessarily seen as needing to be reformed, unlike in Hungary and the Czechoslovak Republic which saw extensive purges of the their senior military leadership.[31] Thus these defense institutions do not lend themselves always to broad generalizations. Nuances and differences abound and, therefore, require detailed explanations where appropriate.

Defense institution

At the end of the Second World War and the subsequent consolidation of Soviet power in Eastern Europe, Soviet policy was simple: to rebuild these armed forces, to the highest degree possible, as mirror images of the Soviet Red Army and ensure that the officer corps was manned solely by communists and preferably those with proletarian backgrounds. It was envisaged that these characteristics, in addition to their all but complete dependence on the Soviet General Staff for planning, logistics, and doctrinal orientation, would provide Moscow with compliant and reliable allies. In consequence, national defense institutions in Warsaw Pact countries were essentially appendages of their Soviet counterpart, albeit lacking in most of the aforementioned critical areas. However, in parallel with the development of more technologically based societies, the generation of officers that subsequently replaced the original Soviet-installed officer corps was increasingly selected for technological and managerial competence, that is, "the red versus expert dilemma," also known as "loyalty versus expertise." The recognition of the need for greater technical expertise was apparently never equated to the concomitant need for the reform of defense institutions.[32] What is important to recognize is that after 1989 all of them were singularly ill-prepared and poorly suited to undertake national-level civil responsibilities within their emerging defense institutions.[33] As in the case of Hungary, for example, one of the reasons for its poor performance in reforming its defense structures, planning, and managerial processes was that the organization simply did not possess any experience or expertise in national-level defense planning (and equally, nor did the Polish Ministry of Defense).[34] Given the relatively large Red Army's physical presence in the country, and the fact that Hungarian forces were integrated into these larger Soviet formations, Hungarian officers consequently suffered from a lack of experience in high command which left them unprepared to exercise national command following the fall of the communist government, let alone provide expert advice on defense policy to democratically elected governments.[35] Civilian ministries had to be created from whole cloth while general staffs had little experience in command or management, let alone force development.

Policy framework

Like their Soviet counterparts, Warsaw Pact defense institutions were not policy-driven institutions. National-level defense policy, in the form of military doctrine, was largely dictated by Moscow from the Soviet General Staff. The Soviet-inspired creation of the Warsaw Pact in 1955, in effect, brought these nations into "Soviet notions of fraternal security obligations and coalition warfare."[36] Like their Soviet counterparts, Warsaw Pact countries did not recognize the distinction between defense policy and military operationally oriented doctrine. Operationally driven requirements served as the basis for military doctrine, which substituted as defense policy. In consequence, as in the case of the Soviet Union, elements of defense activities became the driver in the defense institution. For example, there was a heavy emphasis on defense industry in these countries, but there was an absence of a national defense armaments *policy* to determine requirements to ascertain competitive advantages in platforms and systems, and so on. Again, as appendages of Soviet defense industry, such national policies were simply not necessary.

A nuanced exception to this norm of the lack of a policy framework was the special case of Romania. In the early 1960s, Romania succeeded in seeing off all Soviet forces, an end to intelligence cooperation with the KGB and GRU, and it stopped participating in external exercises with the Red Army after 1968.[37] These successful acts of independence, coupled with the Ceausescu government's public opposition to the Warsaw Pact's invasion of Czechoslovakia, resulted in producing a unique communist defense organization as outlined in the 1972 Defense Act. While remaining a formal member of the Warsaw Pact, Romania alone within that alliance, inspired by the heretical Yugoslavia (*vide infra*), developed a national defense orientation based on the concept of the struggle of the entire people (i.e., Total Defense). This policy publicly excluded the armed forces from preparing for, or participating in, external operations, which resulted in proscribing "the presence of foreign troops or advisers on its territory and ended sending Romanians to Soviet military educational establishments."[38] The obvious result of this new orientation was to impede Soviet efforts to control the Romanian armed forces.[39] Regrettably, this independent stance did not survive long, as although these reforms raised the status of officers in society, a key externality of this new policy was the degradation in the quality of professionalization in the officer corps. Ceausescu became increasingly suspicious of the armed forces and shifted resources from it to the newly created Patriotic Guards (*Gărzile patriotice*) over which he had unquestionable control.[40]

National-level command of armed forces

The concept of national command (Romania being the key exception) was all but unknown in Warsaw Pact countries. Indeed, even after independence, many military officers from these countries strongly opposed the concept of civilian officials intruding into their respective areas of competence, command of the armed forces probably being the most sacred in their view. To an officer raised within a communist legacy armed force, command was synonymous with pure, unbridled power. Whoever possessed it could do essentially anything. Officially, the national command of Warsaw Pact forces was invested in the Warsaw Pact's secretariat in the Soviet General Staff in Moscow. Thus, the armed forces of Warsaw Pact countries fell under the direct command of the Soviet General Staff. The exception to this state of affairs being Romania after the introduction of its Total Defense doctrine which, after studying the lessons of Czechoslovakia, resulted in creating the Defense Council of Socialist Republic of Romania that included all the key military and political leadership under the commander-in-chief. This body was seen as being capable of reacting quickly in the event of imminent attack. Moreover, this command arrangement did not allow national command to be transferred to an outside authority.[41] According to new post–Cold War research, the Soviets instituted in 1980 what was called its

Statute system, which envisaged the Soviets seizing operational control of the armed forces of its satellites due to their perceived untrustworthiness.[42] Not surprisingly, at independence, none of these armed forces, save Romania, had any concept of what constituted the actual and effective national command of their armed forces; and traces of these legacy concepts, policies, and structures remain in all of these countries to this day.

Military decision-making process

Shortly following the advent of communist rule in these countries, the Soviet Union conducted a concerted effort to purge all these countries' officer corps of socially and politically undesirable individuals. This resulted in all but complete application of the Soviet Red Army model on the armed forces of these countries (to include Romania until 1972, if not before). Warsaw Pact tactical formations existed, therefore, solely to execute orders, emanating from the Main Operations Directorate of the Soviet General Staff. Officers were not to question orders, nor interpret them, no matter what the potential physical cost to their forces were. In short, the military decision-making process, as known in the West, simply did not exist. It is little wonder, therefore, that the Soviet-imposed military and educational systems did not address leadership and collaborative problem-solving; indeed, it would have been seen as constituting a direct threat to its iron discipline.[43] The point must be stressed, as well, that the lack of the ability of the individual to act on one's own initiative must not be misconstrued to apply solely to tactical army commanders. Even Soviet aircraft were specifically designed so as not to enable the pilot to undertake multi-roles. Combat aircraft were strictly designed to carry out only specified tasks under the command and direction from ground-based control centers.

Concept of operation

Warsaw Pact countries' approach to operations was largely defined strictly in accordance with Soviet concepts, Romania being a later exception. One would expect the adoption of the Soviet concept of mass and surprise given that these armed forces were essentially completely dependent upon their Soviet counterparts for everything: most of their equipment, education, training methods, logistics, exercise support, and so on. If anything, it would be surprising (*à la Roumanie*) if they were different in any significant manner given the complete dominance that the Red Army had over these armed forces.[44] A legacy that needs to be acknowledged is that as with the Soviet Red Army, they included negative attributes. The Soviet concept of centralized planning and execution had the negative effect of strongly discouraging the development of leadership skills in officers at all levels, let alone the ability to think critically. Since thinking individuals were not needed at the tactical level, the quality of officers was low and this caste became highly resistant to change, and while perhaps technically proficient (a result of their communist-inspired scientific/technical training), they suffered from what in the West would be considered to be low professional competence by Western, or indeed international, standards.[45]

Logistic support

Support of the armed forces, once again, was molded in the exact image of these organizations' Soviet counterparts. In other words, logistic concepts and structures were established to support the centralized operational concept of mass and surprise, that is, "push" logistics based on a highly analytical approach to operational planning that used algorithms to produce scientific solutions to operational objectives, with the added complication that much of the armed forces' matériel requirements were either supplied by the Soviet Union or produced in-country under agreement with Moscow.[46] The only difference between Warsaw Pact and Soviet forces in terms of logistics is that in the former, their stocks were lower than possessed by Soviet forces. As in the case of military decision-making processes, tactical formations were all but bereft of logistics planning and execution staffs (i.e., S-4 staff).

Professionalism

The imposition of communist cadres into the armed forces of the Warsaw Pact resulted in the creation of an officer corps of individuals largely coming from modest social backgrounds, but possessing the all-important qualification of party loyalty. Depending on the country (e.g., Poland, Czechoslovakia, and Romania),[47] at various periods in the 1950s through the 1960s, the introduction of modern and technically complex platforms and weapon systems necessitated the recruitment, education, and training of a better educated officer corps, thereby introducing new norms of professionalization, albeit only in a technical sense of education. Most mid-level and all senior officers in Warsaw Pact armed forces were members of the communist regime; and as such, they enjoyed considerable social and economic privileges, to the point that in some countries, they were a state within a state with their own social support structures, resorts, and so on. To quote Szayna and Larrabee,

> Throughout the Warsaw Pact countries, party control of the military, through the establishment of party cells, systematic political education within the military and the exercise of surveillance and penetration of the military by party organs, was combined with co-optation of the military by giving its members access to special privileges.[48]

They were also very well paid. On average, one source states that the officer corps of the Warsaw Pact armed forces enjoyed a salary of 30–50 percent higher than their civilian equivalents, in addition to priority for housing (a major incentive to join as there was always a short of apartments), access to Western goods, and probably the best medical care within their nations. In most of these countries, even after independence (Slovakia providing a good example), officers were provided with an apartment during their period of service and were allowed to keep it on retirement, which resulted in a shortage of housing for younger officers.[49] Pensions were also generous; twenty-five years of service would result in being vested in a defined benefit pension entitlement of anywhere from 60 to 90 percent of an individual's final active duty salary. Little wonder that it was highly popular to become an officer. Given that there was no NCO corps with leadership and management responsibilities, the officer corps had to assume these low-level responsibilities, thereby bloating its size.[50] The communist parties offered a combination of career mobility and material rewards that had the desired effect of co-opting the officer corps of the Warsaw Pact armed forces, except in the case (once again) of Romania. In contradistinction to the prevailing norm of the Warsaw Pact, the Romanian officer corps was poorly treated. As a result of the Ceausescu regime's inability thoroughly to compromise the armed forces, the Patriotic Guards were lavished with resources at the expense of the armed forces. Officers in the armed forces were paid 25 percent below their civilian counterparts, while the Patriotic Guards and *Securitate* officers (secret police) were paid considerably more.[51] That said, the relationship between soldier and state in the Warsaw Pact did evolve during the period of 1945 until 1990. In the case of Romania, Zulean notes three distinction periods which were, it must be acknowledged, case-specific: from 1945 to 1965, intensive Sovietization; 1965–1979, a period of professionalization brought on by, *inter alia*, the introduction of new sophisticated weapons and a requirement for higher intellectual abilities; and between 1979 and 1989, de-professionalization.[52] More emblematic of the issue of the status of the soldier in the communist state is his typology of professionalism as it can be related across the region.

(1) Low levels of professionalization due to low levels of training and technical expertise
(2) Tradition of politicization
(3) Legacy of mass conscription
(4) Centralized decision-making by the Secretary General of the Communist Party
(5) Tradition of promotion based on patronage and party membership.[53]

Despite its problematic "professionalism" by Western standards, the officer system did meet its political requirements. As Gitz presciently observes, "a combination of material rewards and career mobility appears to have been at least partially successful in coopting a large portion of the officer corps in the other NSWP [non-Soviet Warsaw Pact] states."[54]

Legacy of the Yugoslav People's Army

Yugoslavia's[55] defense institution differs in some rather significant and nuanced ways from the characteristics of their communist brethren.[56] From its creation during the Second World War, it was initially called the People's Liberation Army of Yugoslavia. It was forged as a partisan force during the Second World War and dominated by Marshal Josip Broz Tito and the League of Yugoslav Communists. "It is not exaggerating to say that a virtually symbiotic relationship between the Yugoslav party and the armed forces developed during the partisan struggle itself,"[57] as "the institutional roots of party and army are the same."[58] The country's postwar strident nonalignment on the international stage led to an orientation of defense from all directions, and an almost paranoia of possible Western aggression, which is quite difficult to fathom.[59] But, in the immediate postwar era, due to Tito's early and vehement disagreements with Stalin, the Yugoslav armed forces were truly a hybrid of East and West. Of all the armed forces assessed in this work, it is the only one that was largely transformed by Western assistance. The United States established a large military technical assistance program that spanned the 1950s and constituted a major step toward its modernization.[60] A US American Military Assistance Staff, Yugoslavia (comprising some thirty officers and commanded by a general officer) was responsible for providing matériel to the Yugoslav armed forces, as well as for its training on the use of these modern weapon systems (e.g., F-86 and F-84 Thunderjet fighters, M-36 Jackson tank destroyers). Beginning in 1951, Yugoslavia's personnel also attended military education and training courses in the United States. This assistance continued on a grant basis until 1958 and was formally terminated by an exchange of notes between the American ambassador and the Yugoslav under-secretary of state for foreign affairs on August 25, 1959.[61] Nor can the scope of this assistance be considered in anyway *de minimis*. Its total cost was approximately US$750 million.[62] Starting in the early 1960s, the Yugoslav People's Army was gradually reequipped with Soviet, and increasingly until the breakup of the federation in 1991, with indigenous platforms, organizational structures, and systems. But not completely; as late as the disintegration of the Yugoslav Federation in 1992, the JNA possessed some state-of-the-art Western weaponry, for example, Maverick air-to-surface missiles, radars, and Rolls Royce engines in their indigenous-produced fighter aircraft.[63] Elements of the Western approach to the organization and command of armed forces remained and can still be observed, to varying degrees, in the armed forces of the former Yugoslav republics. Dimitrijevic writes that all of this equipment came with extensive documentation and manuals: "[The] Yugoslavs were truly overwhelmed with the task of translating various sorts of technical documentation. The quite simple Soviet style of technical documentation was now replaced with a new style, where each piece of equipment possessed its own users' technical manual."[64] Of the three services, the army and air force benefited the most from the program. In fact, the intensive training program and need to introduce Western concepts, navigational aids, and safety standards for the Yugoslav Air Force put it in conformance with prevailing NATO air forces' standards.[65]

In addition to the Western provenance of so much of its early modern weapon systems, another important difference between the JNA and its other communist counterparts was the professionalism of JNA personnel. Although it was a conscript-based armed force, and the hand of the party was *never* far away, the highly technically trained officer corps was complemented by a professional cadre of NCOs. These individuals were specially recruited at the age of thirteen and underwent a Spartan and rigorous four years of training in a number of academies, with the principal training facility located in Sarajevo, which graduated approximately 400 NCOs a year. These graduates were posted to junior command positions in tactical formations (deputy platoon commanders, commanders of specialized platoons, e.g., mortars and anti-tank platoons)[66] The very best NCO graduates were given the opportunity to attend one of the officer-cadet academies and become commissioned. Unknown in other communist armed forces, following reforms in the early 1970s, NCOs were granted the new title of junior officers, and procedures were established enabling talented NCOs to apply for officer commissions with a career path that could lead to the rank of lieutenant-colonel.[67] That all said, the JNA trained its officer-cadets to the standard of being the best *soldier*. In other words, an officer's training was based on mastering some technical field of specialty, as well as soldiers' tasks, as opposed to being educated and utilized to become a manager and senior leader of soldiers. As will be seen in later chapters, this legacy concept of rigorous technical education, balanced with mastering soldiers' skills, continues to impede the further development of the armed forces of successors of the JNA.

Defense institution

The Yugoslav defense institution underwent a number of significant institutional changes through its fifty-plus years of existence. Starting as a partisan force, it was dominated by Bolshevist political commissars. From 1945 to 1948, the Soviet defense model was adopted wholesale, but this abruptly changed during the period of confrontation between Tito and the Communist Information Bureau (COMINFORM), when the partisan model was reintroduced to a skeptical officer corps and politicians who wanted conventional forces. Tito's reconciliation with both Greece and Turkey brought Yugoslavia to the forecourt of NATO. This also resulted in Western assistance to turn the JNA into a force capable of assisting in anchoring NATO's southern flank against the Warsaw Pact. The reestablishment of party-to-party relations with the Soviet Communist Party in the mid-1950s allowed a renewal of military cooperation with Moscow. Notwithstanding this open view toward cooperation with both the communist East and democratic West, both the Yugoslav government and particularly the JNA fiercely remained autonomous. The Warsaw Pact's invasion of Czechoslovakia in 1968 had a profound effect on the Yugoslav government. Any pretense that the Warsaw Pact held benevolent and fraternal feelings toward its southern Slav communist brethren was shattered. Although pressures for political and economic liberalization were building in Yugoslavia before the 1968 invasion, and planning was under way to develop a smaller and less expensive standing force, this action resulted in greater impetus to reorganize and reorient the JNA under what became the Total National Defense concept. This concept was applied in six republics and Territorial Defense Forces of two autonomous provinces.[68] These were *not* small forces. At the time of the breakup of the Yugoslav Federation, Territorial Defense Forces comprised 885,000 personnel in wartime and were equipped with small arms and supported with some armor, anti-armor, and air defense weaponry.[69] Yet, their respective defense secretariats were modest with an estimate establishment of some fifty personnel, albeit supported with command elements at the local level.[70] Providing them with an even greater degree of independence from Belgrade, they were financed by the individual republics and local governments.[71] Significantly, and unique to the European communist world, in 1975 academic programs in defense studies were created in five republic universities (Belgrade, Zagreb, Skopje, Sarajevo, and Ljubljana) that led to the creation of a class of civilian defense officials to run these secretariats and headquarters and educate a large cadre of reserve officers.[72] While political and security officers remained in the JNA, thus ensuring the party's direct control of the officer corps, an embryonic corps of civilian defense officials with not inconsequential expertise in defense emerged during this period—a development (admittedly holding reserve commissions in the JNA) that would stand some, but not all, republics in good stead when Yugoslavia dissolved in 1991.[73]

There is one additional characteristic of the Yugoslav defense institution which must be addressed and explained as the practice of collective decision-making through the organization of *collegia* continues to be used throughout the successor republics (save Slovenia). It is exceedingly difficult to find detailed information on these bodies; however, one can review abbreviated terms of reference of the general staff *collegium* of the *Vojska Srbije i Crne Gore* (Armed Forces of Serbia and Montenegro):

- Analyze the outcome of the General Staff's monthly work plan
- Analyze the combat readiness and determine causation of shortcomings
- Assess the regional intelligence/security situation and determine any implications for the country
- Assess the regional security situation of the Federal Republic of Yugoslavia and analyze its possible implications for the combat readiness of the armed forces and the defense of the Federal Republic of Yugoslavia
- Analyze the financial situation in the armed forces
- Determine whether there is a need for organizational changes within the armed forces
- Manage personnel issues:
  o Regulate the condition in the service, promotions, termination of service, and retention in the service of the professional soldiers of the generals rank
  o Review/approve the promotion list to colonel
  o Select candidates for professional military education (PME) courses
  o Assign postings for officers completing PME
  o Assign postings for colonels and lieutenant colonels
  o Manage regular promotion in the rank of colonel and all extraordinary promotions for all professional soldiers
  o Oversee the condition of the service for colonels who are assigned to mobilization units
  o Determine who should be retained in service as distinguished experts who meet the requirements for retirement
  o Approve release from service
  o Analyze the personnel management of the armed forces
- Propose other issues for the attention of the Chief of the General Staff at his request.[74]

From interviews discussing these bodies, these terms of reference (which, it must be stressed, addresses essentially all aspects of the management of the armed forces) are generally in line with legacy general staffs' *collegia* in the region. What is surprising to a Western observer is the extent of their oversight over essentially all aspects of the planning and management of the armed forces in fora which have had the effect of producing collective decisions thereby exculpating officials from any accountability or responsibility of their actions. They also enabled the arbitrary meddling at the level of experts, but with anonymity and complete immunity from responsibility. Moreover, all decision-making is limited only to colonels and general officers, and the views or recommendations of all others are not considered. It must be mentioned that many other communist legacy typologies still employ *collegia* (e.g., Ukraine and Moldova) in their ministries of defense and general staffs.

Policy framework

Notwithstanding the fact that Yugoslavia was ruled by the League of Communists, the relationship between soldier and the state was considerably different from other communist armed forces. Within the JNA, albeit with great deference paid to the advice and position of senior military leaders, there was an element of a policy framework that progressively dominated the governance of the armed forces. During the 1950s, the party allowed for decentralization and liberalization on a scale unmatched by Yugoslavia's communist counterparts in Central Europe and the Balkans. As a result of this liberalization, by the mid-1960s, public scrutiny of the defense budget and officers' special privileges was taking place.[75] By the end of that decade, this embryonic policy framework determined that Yugoslavia would be best served by the decentralization of defense and the division of the armed forces into the JNA and Territorial Defense Forces. The JNA's mission was redefined with a formal mandate in the 1974 Constitution to defend the Yugoslav Federation and socialist system.[76] It was these republic-based Territorial Defense Forces that were to enable the armed succession of some republics after 1991.[77] In comparison with the other typologies, the JNA leadership uniquely played an active political role within the country. In response to liberalization in the late 1960s, there was a conservative backlash generated by a perceived threat to the party from policies initiated by Croatian leaders. Liberal political leadership in all republics was ousted with support from the JNA. Moreover, Belgrade began the policy of posting ethnic Serbs to Slovenia and Croatia's Territory Defense Headquarters,[78] an act that was to have ominous consequences for the latter when it broke away from Yugoslav. To ensure the protection of the party, by mid-decade the JNA was represented in the Central Committee and composed 12 percent of its membership, up from only 2 percent a few years before.[79] Yet, after Tito died, there was a move to devolved more and more governance to the republics, which left the JNA as one of the few federal institutions left in Yugoslavia.

National-level command of armed forces

Like so many other areas in Yugoslavia, decentralization led to a uniquely Yugoslav blend of communist and Western traditions and concepts. The League of Communists, via the State Presidency, authorized the minister of defense to command the JNA and, ultimately, territorial forces.[80] Early manifestations of the Total National Defense concept held that partisan and territorial forces would remain "firmly within the organization of the Yugoslav People's Army and under the command of the central state and military leadership, even though command headquarters were also set up in individual republics for specific aspects of resistance."[81] Yet, the 1969 General People's Defense Act defined the JNA and Territorial Defense Forces as co-equals, and ended the practice of placing the latter under the command of the former and Belgrade. Henceforth, under the 1974 new Defense Act (which the JNA leadership insisted be passed), command of Territorial Defense Forces was clarified with their subordination to the JNA's chain of command, while limiting delegation of command to Republic Communist Party civilian officials[82] only in the extreme case of foreign aggression.[83] Notwithstanding this backlash against devolution, the fact remained that defense was the responsibility of not only the JNA but also these Territorial Defense Forces.

Operationally, it was party officials who had the responsibility to "direct the general people's resistance on their territory." It was envisaged that these reserve forces would fall under JNA command only when engaged in combined operations with the JNA.[84] Officially, then, they did not fall specifically within the command structures of the JNA. Nevertheless, they were always commanded by a JNA officer, and all the reserve officers had undergone JNA training.[85] Thus, it was envisaged that should an enemy occupy the soil of Yugoslavia, individual Territorial Defense Forces could command JNA and its territorial units.[86] Bringing these arrangements full circle back to party control, it was the president of each republic who appointed and dismissed commanders of these republic territorial forces; the fundamental distinction with other communist armed forces being that Yugoslavia did not possess an all-powerful Main Operations Directorate of the General Staff, which dominated *all* aspects of the armed forces, as was strictly the case in other communist countries. That said, it would be a mistake, according to Anton Bebler, to conclude that the JNA was in any way in accord with this arrangement. "For about two decades [following the creation of Territorial Defense Forces] the Yugoslav military leadership tried to obtain the federal government's support for either disbanding or disarming the Territorial Defence, absorbing it into the federal army's reserve forces or placing it under federal military control."[87]

Indeed, throughout the 1970s, the JNA argued for the need of unity of command, and by 1980, the Council for Territorial Defense was formed under the control of the Federal Secretary for National Defense. Uniquely, elements of "command" were defined, for example, in 1983 following the adoption of the policy of *Jedinstvo* ("unity"): to include planning, preparation, realization, execution, and control, and even principles of command that to a Westerner appear to be more like principles of war (unity, consistency, flexibility, efficiency, and security).[88] In 1988, on the basis of a ruling by the Yugoslav Federation's Presidency to attempt to recentralize control, a new National Defense Law eliminated republic districts, and subordinated republic and provincial Territorial Defense Forces to JNA district corps commanders in wartime. The position of JNA leadership was that in this manner duplication of strategic, operational, and tactical commands was to be avoided.[89] But in political reality, this was a desperate attempt by party officials in Belgrade and JNA leadership to remove Republican political leader from the chain of command. Due to these reforms, writes Horncastle, "The institutional connection between the republics and defense issues was being systematically broken down by the YPA [JNA]."[90]

Military decision-making process

It is perhaps inevitable that JNA operational concepts, based on Total National Defense, necessitated the devolution of command of units. That said, JNA leadership faced the challenge that such devolution would perennially collide with the military precept of unity of command, as well as the insatiable communist obsession with centralizing power. Thus, the challenge of meeting military conceptual objectives and politics produced a tortured record of delegation of command. It is difficult to trace the provenance of how the JNA, and Territorial Defense Forces, came to enjoy an understanding of the Western style of the military decision-making process. Indeed, according to Patrick, the JNA's force structure was specifically designed for flexibility.[91] But what is certain is that from its earliest days, decentralization and independent action by the JNA were recognized as being essential to the successful defense of the country. In 1953, writing in *Foreign Affairs*, Yugoslav lieutenant general Dusan Kveder outlined Yugoslav concepts of defense thinking by writing that territorial warfare perforce would be more political and ideological in character than conventional, maneuver combat: "All battalion and even company commanders, and especially the leaders of partisan detachments, must independently solve many political problems; their military actions cannot be otherwise intelligent or efficient."[92]

Whether it was a holdover from the Royal Yugoslav Army, decentralized partisan warfare, or the influence of Western weapon systems and platforms, the JNA had traces of this Western process. Absent from any of the typologies of communist armed forces, JNA commanders had budgets and a high degree of autonomy to manage their formations in peacetime. A motivating factor, interestingly enough, was the adoption of the emerging Total National Defense concept. An effective territorial defense capability would be, perforce, predicated on the ability of tactical units to being able to assess the enemy's strength and intentions, and to select appropriate courses of action for the requirements.[93] Various former JNA officers informed this author that while battalions on operations were largely executionary in nature (and internal staffing procedures were stove-piped), brigades and corps had more independence in their tactical planning, even if such efforts did not produce formal estimates in the Western sense. Yet, the basic concept of tactical formations being thinking organizations was sufficiently familiar to officers' training as to make it observable in the armed forces during the Yugoslav Wars. Not to be discounted, in addition was the JNA's large cadre of professional NCOs, which according to Niebuhr exercised tactical leadership and command, and a majority of which were ethnic Serbs, which gave Serbian forces an initial advantage in the subsequent wars of succession.[94]

Concept of operation

Operational concepts evolved over the existence of the JNA, but one common theme remains predominant throughout its existence: the security of Yugoslavia was based on mobilization, culminating in the execution of the Total National Defense concept. Depending on the relationship between Belgrade and its communist counterparts in the Warsaw Pact, the intensity and structure of the concept of Total National Defense responded in kind. One clear trend beginning in the late 1950s was the refinement of the concept based on decentralization at the tactical level and the later efforts to develop Territorial Defense Forces and defense *institutions* at the republic level. Mirroring the reform of the federation itself, which saw greater liberalization and devolution of power from Belgrade to the republics, so, too, were resources, units, and command authorities to flow downward. In fact, after 1969 and the passage of "General People's doctrine" was formulated with the objective of creating viable armed forces in all of the republics that would provide the federation with a defense in-depth, vice a linear, concept of operation to defending the country. The resulting concept of operations drew on Soviet Army, US Army, and uniquely Yugoslav interpretations of their operational experience to produce a concept that employed the regular JNA and Territorial Defense Forces in brigade-sized formations. The JNA would fight a conventional conflict for as long as possible, and if necessary, to devolve into long-term guerrilla warfare throughout the entire country: a policy and operational concept at considerable variance with NATO and Warsaw Pact armed forces.[95] Republic Territorial Defense Forces were organized around state enterprises, communes, and so on,[96] which were designed to be decentralized and organized to be independent without any standard force structure. They were designed to fight at the company and squad level depending upon requirements.

> The FY armed forces [JNA] were divided among four military regions. Each military region was intended to be a separate, self-sufficient war economy, able to sustain its subordinate armed forces in combat long after the national capital of Belgrade had been overrun. Each region was divided into districts, with each district responsible for administrative issues.[97]

What is perhaps ironic is that the efforts of JNA's leadership to maintain the federation by removing republics from the chain of command was seen by the JNA as a critical move toward creating a more modern and maneuver-oriented army. Yet, before it could achieve that goal, Yugoslavia dissolved and the JNA suffered a humiliating defeat at the hands of the small but well-motivated Slovenian Territorial Defense Force, using largely Total National Defense operational concepts and tactics.[98]

Logistic support

The JNA logistical system was named "Rear Security," which contained all elements of logistic support for the JNA and the Territorial Defense Forces. In addition to traditional logistics, Rear Security included considerable institutional elements of the defense institution (e.g., musical, legal, geodetic services, and even military police).[99] There appears to have been a unique Yugoslav approach to logistics that was a hybrid of communist legacy central control, with some elements of the "pull" logistics concept. The JNA had considerable trouble using US-provided equipment as it tried to understand the Western logistics (particularly supply concepts) in the 1950s.[100] But some Western logistics traditions and concepts continued even as more

Soviet equipment was progressively introduced after the early 1960s. In time, like other communist countries, logistics were highly centralized and essentially became conflated with all aspects of defense infrastructure, all tied to the nation's economy. It should be noted, however, that a "push" logistics system is not inherently negative. In an armed force where missions are limited (e.g., territorial defense), a "push" logistics system might well be quite appropriate given the limited mission set in a prescribed geographic area of operation. And, given that this was the case of the JNA, and particularly for the Territorial Defense Forces, it could be argued that such a system could be appropriate for Yugoslavia's needs. Additionally, as Herrick notes, latent logistic support for territorial forces is less expensive than for a professional, standing force,[101] not an insignificant consideration in economically troubling times. Territorial Defense Forces, as they were created in 1969, possessed their own headquarters and were completely independent in terms of operations and possessed decentralized logistics planning and depots.[102] However, the quid pro quo for such autonomy on the part of these republic forces included the accompanying financial cost that came with needing to provide for their logistic support.[103] This was not inconsiderable. It was estimated that the cost of Territorial Defense Forces was the equivalent of 1 percent of Yugoslavia's gross domestic product (GDP).[104] Finally, what does distinguish the Yugoslav case from many Warsaw Pact members was its extensive indigenous armaments industry. For example, circa 1973, Yugoslav armaments industry provided approximately 55 percent of the country's own requirements, largely from licensing agreements with the Soviet Union, as well as platforms and systems based on Yugoslav indigenous design.[105]

Professionalism

The character of the armed forces, despite its officer corps being almost exclusively party members, could still be considered as a professional force by some Western criteria. Edmunds argues that while admittedly its officer corps was dominated by ethnic Serbs,[106] "the JNA had fulfilled an explicitly *pan-Yugoslav* rather than pro-Serbian role in the old Socialist Federative Republic of Yugoslavia." The JNA struggled to balance the need and desire of professionalism within the realities of a communist system. By the breakup of Yugoslavia, it had developed a distinctly Yugoslav variant of professionalism and institutional autonomy which in the end, according to Edmunds, "made it resistant to manipulation by the Milosevic regime."[107] But it is clear from a review of the evidence that the JNA did not fully succeed in achieving the degree of professionalism that is taken for granted in the Western democracies. The reason for this conclusion is that the communist regime never relinquished the strong institutions within the JNA of political commissar and security officers. Moreover, notwithstanding unparalleled public scrutiny of the armed forces in a communist political system, the JNA enjoyed an elevated social and financial status, thereby making them a state within a state.[108] A combination of these perverse forces was strongly reinforced by a human resource management system (HRM) heavily dominated by *colleagia* that judged professional performance largely on security and ideological rationales.

The principles of selection were arbitrary, to be sure, and depended on one's superior who could apply them discretionarily with respect to personal preference, town of origin, national/ethnic or self-interest reasons. This is why negative selection and careerism prevailed in the personnel policy. Over time rank lost its functional characteristics and increasingly took on social and corruptive features.[109]

Differentiating communist from Western defense institutions

In light of the analysis of the three typologies, it is extremely challenging to make meaningful generations. Each of the models has their own distinct characteristics. Nevertheless, what these defense institutions do share is, in some ways, a negative case. That is to say, where they are similar is that they are not, to varying degrees, comparable to Western democratic defense governance concepts. The Yugoslav model, due to considerable Western security assistance provided to the JNA in formative development, obviously comes closest to its Western counterparts. However, it needs to be recalled that although Yugoslavia did subsequently produce copious quantities of defense armaments, many of its systems were still Soviet/Warsaw Pact inspired if not in provenance. Such systems are inherently designed on the Soviet principles of needing only rudimentary training, narrow mission sets, mass effects, and with a clear design orientation that discourages individual initiative and tactical-level problem-solving. But, to complete this analysis, what are the key elements of the antithesis of communist models?

Generic Western armed forces' model

In comparison with communist military models, generic Western democratic defense governance concepts are essentially antithetical in all key areas. At its heart, the Western approach to military art stresses the essential importance of the individual, *the citizen*, in the execution of military tasks. The Western military process of the preparation and prosecution of operations and war must strike *Homo Sovieticus* as dangerously decentralized and therefore, in this myopic view, quite disorganized. The latter being a characteristic that most in Western armed forces certainly would embrace with alacrity. In its most basic form, the modern Western military model is built upon a number of critical factors which are often not present in Eastern European/former Soviet republic societies, historical experience, and cultures.

(1) Citizen soldier: Western military establishments are made up of citizens, *voting*-citizens to be precise, who are largely not living apart from civil society. They are subjects, as well as objects, of statecraft. Even professional soldiers, let alone conscripts, are not seen as mere cannon fodder and cannot be treated as such. An incompetent disregard of human loss can have long-standing negative effects on a political class and the institution of the armed forces. The ability of the Soviet Union to execute the war against, for example, Nazi Germany, with complete disregard for human suffering followed with no political repercussions

stands in stark contrast to, for example, British commanders' caution in taking operational risks in the Second World War in light of the nation's horrific losses from 1914 to 1918.[110]

(2) Tactical units as *thinking* organizations: In consequence of the first point, Western countries expect all officers, NCOs, and soldiers to be capable of *critical thinking* and contribute to the successful solution of an operational problem. Legacy officers marvel in wonder at the relatively large size of a Western army's battalion headquarters and are largely at a loss to understand what all of these individuals could be possibly doing. While each country is slightly different, it is not unusual for a Western infantry battalion to have thirty to forty officers and a much larger body of professional NCOs. This is in contrast with a typical Soviet battalion that had a staff of approximately five or fewer officers. The reason for this relatively large number in Western militaries is due to the large number of tasks expected of commanders to fulfill, up to and including planning and executing continuous operations (i.e., 24/7). While guidance for a mission, or even tactical movement, is provided by a brigade commander, the battalion commander, with the assistance of his staff, is expected to develop a solution that best meets prevailing conditions (e.g., Mission, Enemy, Terrain, Troops available, Time, and Civilian considerations—METT-TC). Equally important is the fact that training requirements are determined at the company and platoon level by junior officers and NCOs. Their analysis determines which assigned tasks to the battalion cannot be met to given standards (based on the training concept of tasks, conditions, and standards). In this case, Western militaries should be thought of as autonomous thinking bodies that are quite capable of adjusting to changing missions and challenging conditions. For instance, it is interesting to observe that recent research conclusively demonstrates that the US Army's tactical formations in Iraq began adapting and changing to combat realities (i.e., the need to carry out effective counter insurgency operations) well before the publication of the highly publicized US Army counterinsurgency doctrine in 2006.[111]

(3) Yeomanry: The majority of countries in the West have the historical tradition of a society containing large numbers of literate and numerate farmers and urban craftsmen. While not quite lower nobles, and definitely not the rural or urban poor, this class was to provide armed forces for centuries with robust junior leaders and technical experts; in other words, professional NCOs. Given their own secured and established status within these societies, NCOs have come to provide armed forces with continuity and unparalleled leadership qualities at the tactical level. This societal class, while extant in Central and Eastern Europe, was not as large and has long had to struggle to attain the levels of command responsibility enjoyed by their Western counterparts.

(4) The product of the staff's critical thinking: The Estimate. This work postulates that the major distinction between Western armed forces and their post-communist counterparts (with some qualified exceptions) is the former produces thinking, problem-solving, and optimal tactical formations, organized to meet the realities of a range of operations. To be sure, every NATO armed force organizes and approaches tactical planning in accordance with their own unique history,

organizational structure, traditions, and cultural characteristics. Until recent years, due to all of these differences, it has been difficult to find a corpus of a generic Western approach to military operations. However, with the end of the Cold War, NATO has expanded considerably its organizational focus on combined and joint tactical and operational-level and planning procedures. Such alliance attention during the Cold War was seen as largely unnecessary, particularly for ground forces, given that states, with some notable exceptions (e.g., Multinational Corps LANDJUT),[112] organized their armies within national army corps, with combat, combat support, and combat service support elements organic to the structure. NATO naval and air forces, on the other hand, have long enjoyed specific planning and operational procedures (e.g., for maritime, Allied Tactical Publications; and for air, the all-encompassing Air Tasking Order). The end of the Cold War resulted in the rapid diminution in the size of allied armies and the need for allied/coalition forces to operate alongside each other in smaller tactical formations which has resulted in the development and publication of an extensive corpus of Allied Joint Publications, Bi-Strategic Command planning guidance, and procedural manuals. The documents of such a body of procedures can now essentially be considered as constituting the gold standard of military procedures and concepts. In consequence, it is now possible, by examining and using these documents, to be able to generalize a Western style of organization, command, and planning procedures.[113] The documents which probably best encapsulate the general Western approach to the planning and execution of military operations are Allied Command Operation's (ACO) *Comprehensive Operations Planning Directive*, and *Allied Joint Doctrine 3.0, Operations*.[114] Simply stated, NATO nations' armed forces generally follow the same methodology at the tactical level which produces an Estimate process and, as it is more or less similar, these various estimates will fit into and support allied planning at the operational level. Its essential procedures consist of rigorous Mission Analysis (in light of the higher commander's intent, limitations, etc.), statement of Factors and Deductions, the development of Courses of Action (COAs), producing a Comparison of COAs, and the staff's recommended COA. At the tactical level this may be in the form of a Battlefield Estimate, but it is likely to be more sophisticated and detailed at the brigade and divisional levels. NATO nations' tactical formations must produce an Estimate, which supports the Western style of the military decision-making process.[115] In sum, at its most basic, the Estimate is a manifestation of the formation's ability, collectively and organically, to think its way through meeting its assigned missions and tasks.

Finally, the actualization of these concepts at the national level in Western defense institutions comes together in the defense planning process. This is an important point, as will be seen later in this work; very few, if arguably *any*, legacy defense institutions can conduct the most basic aspects of defense planning. To be sure, plans are *written*, though sadly often in great profusion. But, as will be argued, very few of them have been actualized due, *inter alia*, to the continued existence of legacy concepts that preclude their implementation. As such, in each typology the record of defense planning efforts is assessed to discern if there are elements of Western defense planning concepts that exist and are used, and by extension, which are not employed. While there is likely no definitive agreement on what constitutes a comprehensive list of basic Western defense planning tools, the following list encompasses its most basic aspects:

(1) Contingency planning guidance from the government to the chief of defense (CHOD), which is absolutely necessary to ensure that the armed forces are organized, trained, equipped, and oriented to meet government-directed contingencies.

(2) Cost models that reflect accurate costs of formations, organizations, activities, and capabilities within a peacetime and operational framework. Many legacy defense institutions have such models, but they frequently are basic and are only capable of calculating static and fractional unit costs, vice determining the inclusive costs to produce a capability.

(3) Operational planning analysis, from which is produced both core capability requirements and capability gaps. It is one of the theses of this work that such objectively determined capability gaps can only be developed through a Western approach to the military decision-making process which encourages problem-solving at the tactical level, and which produces objective data to determine capability requirements.

(4) Capability trade-off analysis, based on cost models and the results of operational planning analysis, which can compare capabilities across the services and assess their financial costs.

(5) Force management to ensure that units and capabilities have all the resources necessary to meet their assigned missions as determined in contingency planning guidance, all the while attempting to effect efficiencies throughout the entire armed forces.

(6) Establishment of institutional responsibilities/functions to ensure that they are formally identified, de-conflicted, reconciled, exercised, and documented, and regularly updated to reflect changes in policy, law, the strategic environment, and technological advancements.

(7) A formal, structured, transparent, and responsive budgetary execution system that is responsive to policy, as expressed in defense plans. In recent years, one has seen the unfortunate and inaccurate conflation of such a system with programming, that is, Planning, Programming, and Budgeting System (PPBS). For the purposes of this work, such sloppy shorthand, which has even afflicted NATO/PfP documents, will be eschewed. The issue of the confusion caused by the introduction of PPBS and its implicit endorsement by Western defense officials will be addressed at length in Chapter 7.

Conclusion: Antithetical comparisons and applications

There should be no question that a comparison of communist armed forces and their Western counterparts could not result in more stark contrasts and fundamental differences.[116] To focus specifically on the former, one can make the general observation that as one moves from West to East, communist legacy influences become more pronounced, albeit Georgia being a major exception to this observation. In other words, the development of typologies does serve an important objective in manifesting key differences among their defense institutions. That said, there is one key characteristic that does typify, to varying degrees to be sure, these defense institutions. That characteristic is that they cannot be considered to be "thinking" tactical organizations. To be sure, the JNA comes closest to NATO armed forces due to its extensive decentralized Total National Defense concept, Territorial Defense Forces, and Western equipment and training provided at a critical juncture in its development. But it should not be forgotten that notwithstanding the existence of a robust domestic armaments industry, due to financial reasons, most of the JNA's kit was overwhelmingly acquired from the Soviet Union.[117] As argued in this chapter, Soviet/communist equipment inherently emphasized the Soviet concept that tactical formations and platforms performed solely execution functions and were not expected, empowered, resourced, or simply *allowed* to do otherwise. In consequence, one must consider the successors of the JNA to be more than slightly influenced by such factors. In addition, one must state emphatically that these distinctions are neither superficial nor unimportant.

The significance of these dissimilarities can be seen as Western democratic defense governance concepts were adopted by legacy defense institutions. Unless the underlying logic of the legacy concepts are addressed in a mutual-exclusive manner, one runs the serious risk of producing "conceptual spaghetti" as Western and communist legacy concepts overlay each other while struggling against the other for dominance. This is simplistically represented in Figure 2.1. As will be shown in a number of instances, the export of Western concepts and procedures has been, more often than not, "bolted" atop their legacy counterparts, thereby causing a new level of dysfunctionality as the two antithetical logic sets struggle

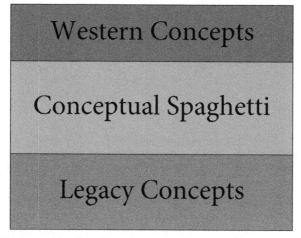

Figure 2.1 "Conceptual Spaghetti."

for supremacy. This has not infrequently resulted in creating new problems without solving identified needed reforms.

Finally, in order to demonstrate the depth of differences between Western and legacy defense institutions, in Table 2.1, the most fundamental element of any military organization, the concept of command, is compared between these two systems.[118] Without *any* doubt, it can be concluded that the differences between communist and Western armed forces are simply *conceptually antithetical* in their most basic assumptions, content, and logic. In short, communist legacy armed forces, at a conceptual level, could not be *more different* than their Western counterparts. As these key aspects of these armed forces are so fundamental to their constituted structures, one can very easily discern their contemporary manifestations throughout all three typologies.

It is for this reason that Table 2.2 is used to establish in a graphic (if indeed imperfect) broad generalization of these models laid across the areas of analysis with informed judgments the author assigned to each category. What the matrix demonstrates is three critically important points. First, it displays in stark terms the differences among the three different communist defense institutions and makes the point graphically; while their institutional pathologies vary, *there remain* critical conceptual differences from a Western perspective. Second, the chart gives pause to those Western officials who have the task of working cooperatively with these civil defense institutions and armed forces with the objective of integrating them into allied military structures, particularly as regards to improving their ability to achieve interoperability with NATO nations. To be sure, NATO has become more sophisticated over the years and now differentiates among the various levels of

Table 2.1 Understanding Western and Legacy Command Concepts

Mission command	*Versus*	Detailed command
Unpredictable	*Assumes war is*	Predictable
Disorder/uncertainty	*Accepts*	Order/certainty
Decentralization Informality Loose rein on subordinates Self-discipline Initiative Cooperation Ability at all echelons Higher tempo	*Tends to lead to*	Centralization Formality Tight rein on subordinates Imposed discipline Obedience Compliance Ability only at the top
Implicit Vertical/horizontal Interactive	*Types of communications*	Explicit Vertical Linear
Organic Ad hoc	*Organization types fostered*	Hierarchic Bureaucratic
Delegating	*Leadership styles*	Directing
Art of war	*Appropriate to*	Science of war

Table 2.2 Comparison of Communist and NATO Nations' Defense Governance Concepts, circa 1990

	Defense institutions	Policy framework	National-level command	Military decision-making process	Concept of operations	Logistics	Professionalism
Soviet	General Staff dominated	Weak	Rigid	Nonexistent	Mass	"Push"	Weak
Warsaw Pact	Moscow/General Staff dominated	Weak	Nonexistant/underdeveloped and directed by Moscow	Nonexistent	Mass	"Push"	Varying from weak to extant, albeit compromised
Yugoslav	Extant	Extant	Mixture of centralized (federation) and decentralized (republics)	Extant, but basic	Territorial defense	"Push", with traces of push	Extant, but compromised
NATO nations	Robust civil-military organizations	Highly developed	Robust and largely defined	Highly developed and used	General Defense Plans/deployment in select countries	"Pull" based on commanders' requirements	Highly developed

"interoperability."[119] However nuanced these definitions might be, major *conceptual* impediments stand in the way of making progress. In fact, in its most primary form, the challenge to achieve closer interoperability is clearly *conceptual* as recognized some years ago by David Glanz:

> The term interoperability itself has numerous facets and is still ill defined. Nevertheless, at a minimum it involves the ability of national forces to operate effectively with NATO forces, to be able to assume their NATO-assigned staff responsibilities, and most important, but less recognized, *to understand and implement Western military concepts.*[120]

It is appropriate to posit the question of how countries with conceptually different defense and military systems can hope to achieve even basic operational compatibility when fundamental organizational concepts are *antithetical*? Third and lastly, in light of these striking institutional differences which impede cooperation with Western nations, not to mention the fact that these countries do not constitute a common data set, one could assume, therefore, that NATO and NATO nations' officials have designed their respective advice and assistance policies to reflect particularly the need for a nuanced and differentiated approach. This line of enquiry is to ascertain if indeed this did take place. And, if it did not, then to answer the question: what have been the consequences? The following chapters will address this issue directly.

NATO Exports Its "New Model Army": Why It Did Not Take

The end of the Cold War produced a confluence of a commonality of interests between Eastern and Western Europe rarely witnessed before in European history. For once, almost all of the principal and minor powers were in close accord that the previous NATO and Warsaw Pact policies of collective defense needed to transition to one more inclusive of collective security. While some analysts naively contemplated the demise of NATO and the ascendance of the Conference on Security and Co-operation in Europe (CSCE) (later the Organization for Security and Cooperation in Europe [OSCE]),[1] soon-to-be former Warsaw Pact countries and newly freed former Soviet republics were far less keen to contemplate the conceptual possibilities of a new collective security organization when a proven collective defense organization was literally at, or near, their borders. Moreover, the troubling news coming from the increasingly violent dissolution of Yugoslavia had the additional effect of focusing the minds of these emerging democracies. And, finally, not to be discounted is the seemingly reachable allure of joining the European Union with all of the political, cultural, financial, and economic benefits that would accrue to those countries fortunate to gain admittance.

For the Western alliance, it took time for consensus to develop a common policy to deal with these new security orphans in Central and Eastern Europe. Political timidity on the part of a number of states is more than understandable. Bonn was managing the first unification of Germany without bloodshed in its long and troubled history. Other states (e.g., France) were equally reluctant to support any initiatives that could even remotely stir the reeling Russian government into a resolute and possibly violent response. Yet, in a relatively short period of time, a virtual *Augenblick* in terms of Europe's long history of instability and bloodshed, a NATO policy emerged and a systematic common project was initiated of assimilation of willing states into the Western alliance. Led largely by the Clinton administration, and in the face of much skepticism,[2] a common policy emerged on how the alliance would respond to membership expansion, as well as develop support programs to assist reforming defense institutions. Any significant skepticism to join NATO was sidelined by the argument that although there was no official policy as such, alliance membership was perceived as the antechamber to the European Union.[3]

It would appear that there emerged a confluence of interests and objectives among old NATO countries and the soon-to-be aspirants to press for membership. Both wanted to remove any perception of a security glacis vis-à-vis the east, and in so doing, the newly democratic states were to be presented with a formal process by which they could reform their defense institutions, thereby establishing their bona fides to prepare for NATO membership. On the surface, there could not have been more complementarity of intersecting interests. The West wanted these countries, once reformed, to be within the European security umbrella, and shortly in time these young democracies considered membership as an insurance policy to underwrite their independence. It was often only after gaining membership that it became clear to officials that membership is but an enhanced vehicle by which national political objectives are to be advanced, and certainly not an end unto itself.

This chapter addresses five major issues. First, it is necessary to provide historical context behind the eventual policy of what became NATO enlargement *and engagement*, as well as lay out the processes and approaches Western nations came to adopt to assist its new partners to become allies. Second, while a number of themes will be teased out in later chapters, it is appropriate to describe and assess critically the policies, approaches, and the underlying assumptions of the West's perceptions and understandings of the defense institutions of its aspiring allies and partners. Third, by examining the state of these legacy defense institutions in the aftermath of the end of the Cold War, this chapter will argue that the West made a fundamental error by defining the mission as necessitating the use of military diplomacy, vice professional military honesty, in the development of relationships with these communist legacy defense institutions. In lieu of deliberately designing reforms, objective progress has often been sacrificed for the nebulous objective of relationship-building, based on the dubious principles of mutual respect and equality. At the heart of the matter, the West's approach was founded on the erroneous premise, so presciently described by Clemmesen and Peterson Ulrich, of the existence of a commonality in their respective definitions of military professionalism.[4] Fourth, general impediments to reform are identified and assessed, which will demonstrate the shear enormity of the challenge faced by legacy defense institutions to adopt Western democratic defense governance concepts. These impediments are identified as including the continued use of antithetical concepts, the cultural characteristics and realities of post-communist societies, embryonic strategic cultures, and the confusing nature of various false cognates: linguistic, conceptual, and even institutional. Fifth, a brief assessment of the state of civil-military relations follows that argues that, notwithstanding progress, many governments, still lack effective positive, and not just negative, controlling mechanisms of their armed forces.

Rationales for Western integration

In light of Europe's long turbulent, troubled, and bloody history, what is remarkable is that such a seismic change in the balance of power took place at all, let alone without any bloodshed between the two blocs. And perhaps what is even more surprising is that this happened so quickly. To be sure, there were many skeptics in Western countries and capitals that simply could not accept that Moscow, no matter how prostrate, would allow its former Eastern possessions to slip into a perceived Western orbit that would be inimical to Russian vital interests. Whatever reluctance that existed on the part of Eastern European political elites was quickly assuaged, particularly when a distracted Russia appeared more concerned with maintaining its own internal cohesion and stability than reasserting its *droit du seigneur* in the lands to its west. No matter how perilous it might initially have appeared to Western officials, particularly those in Germany who were still assisting the removal of the Soviet Western Group of Forces in what was, since October 3, 1990, a unified Germany, the integration of this heterogeneous group of countries simply would have to be managed with a much less threatening Russia.[5]

If political and economic integration of these countries to Western Europe was the policy eventually adopted by Western European and North American governments, it made little sense not to address formally the question of their security.[6] Early efforts to initiate a dialogue with Eastern armed forces was purposefully designed to be nonthreatening and addressed such seemingly benign subjects as peacekeeping, doctrine, and general familiarization visits and contacts. Support for the reform and restructuring of defense institutions was also seen as being mutually beneficial. The West was motivated to transform these countries from seemingly security consumers into security producers.[7] Ergo, their policy was to support these armed forces (and, remarkably, less so their civil defense institutions) in developing dedicated peacekeeping formations.[8] However, the means by which any such cooperation could take place was only if these armed forces and their NATO counterparts could develop basic levels of interoperability. In essence, Eastern armed forces needed to transform themselves, or elements thereof, so that they could operate, if only at a basic level, alongside Western forces. The motivation on the part of Eastern countries was that NATO nations' technical assistance and resources could be used to reform bureaucratically bloated and underperforming defense institutions.

Creation of engagement policy and cooperative support programs

The West, as could be expected, began its discussions and engagement contacts with former communist armed forces in a rather disaggregated, if not disorganized, fashion. Countries like the United States initiated bilateral contact programs and projects to expose their Eastern counterparts to the nature of its armed forces. In and of themselves, these were critically important contacts as these orientation visits, seminars, and conferences had the effect of delegitimizing prevailing communist ideology which portrayed the world in a continuous struggle between it and capitalism, which could only be resolved by violence which would be instigated by the West. At their independence there was still a view in former communist countries that NATO had hostile intensions against them. That the Soviet Union and Warsaw Pact governments possessed copies of NATO's General Defence Plans (which were not offensive in orientation) was made known to at least one newly elected democratic government, which had the interesting unintended effect of destroying the credibility of communist officials who attempted to remain in a state of confrontation with the West or at least to develop a policy of neutrality.[9]

Formal NATO policy toward these orphans was announced in the "Rome Declaration on Peace and Cooperation," which declared the alliance intended "to develop a more institutional relationship of consultation and cooperation on political and security issues."[10] This policy was expanded in February 1994 when heads of state and government announced the creation of the PfP program.[11] From its modest beginnings, PfP has enabled the alliance formally to engage partners in areas of mutual interest and concern. Importantly, membership in PfP demonstrated that countries were intent to achieve closer ties with NATO and its members, as well as providing the political basis by which Western technical assistance projects could be initiated.[12] Interestingly enough, the creation of PfP forced the NATO International Staff and Military Authorities to reorient themselves away from planning solely for collective defense to developing generic content and programs in the area of defense planning and management that could be applicable to partners keen to develop closer military ties with the alliance. Within the context of PfP and using the alliance's defense planning review process, nations and the International Staff launched in 1995 the biannual Planning and Review Process (PARP) which enabled NATO and partner defense officials to engage in a detailed, if not always meaningful, structured dialogue of how the latter could declare forces to alliance collective security missions as well as discuss how their defense institutions could be reformed.[13] Edmunds writes that in the case of Croatia, PARP had the beneficial effect of obliging and motivating officials to adopt more transparent, and systematic defense planning techniques.[14] Greater explanation of this newly agreed common policy by which NATO could engage its former enemies, and in time, former Yugoslav republics, was via an arrangement agreed in 1997 to create the Euro-Atlantic Partnership Council. This body has overseen the Euro-Atlantic Work Plan, which contains specified chapters where nations could engage in dialogue to encourage the diffusion of Western democratic defense and military concepts eastward.[15] While PARP has remained the Defense Planning Directorate of the International Staff's engagement method, with its annual/semi-annual reporting cycle, the political side of the International Staff has developed an extensive series of consultative programs and arrangements to meet the political aspirational levels of partner countries.

These fora became necessary after the alliance released its Enlargement Study in 1995.[16] For the first time, the alliance stated publicly that it would entertain the politically delicate question of allowing former communist countries to become members in the alliance.[17] Shortly thereafter, the International Staff developed the Membership Action Plan (MAP) which provided a formal road map by which countries were encouraged to follow if their objective in PfP were to obtain membership. "The MAP is a tailored program for aspirants, designed to help build a roadmap to future membership, by offering active advice, assistance and practical support to strengthen their candidacies."[18] And, as time went on, for those countries whose geopolitical position was too delicate to allow membership (e.g., Ukraine and Georgia), new consultative arrangements were established to enable the degree of political dialogue that realities would allow, for example, Individual Partnership Action Plan[19] and Intensified Dialogue.[20]

What this combination of processes, guidance documents, and policies has produced is essentially a dynamic list of what is perceived to constitute "best practices" in defense institutions, management, and planning of armed forces. To be sure, a very close examination of these documents (which are generally not made available to the public) and the occasional weak assessment and report reveals a predictable unevenness. The tones of these narratives are often more diplomatic than accurate, analyses can be superficial and repetitive from previous reports, and recommendations are not always meaningful or relevant, let alone adequately explained. Moreover, at times, alliance officials find themselves in the unenviable position when they are asked to assess the progress of reforms in areas which are considered national responsibilities among NATO members. As such, there can be no NATO standards, for example, regarding policies related to national defense planning, budgeting, HRM, and so on.[21] Matser and Donnelly have argued that such norms would be an anathema to democracies as there are many ways to create armed forces.[22] However, to the credit of the NATO International Staff, despite these challenges, officials have developed, over time, a corpus of what could best be described as constituting Western *norms* that addresses these critical areas of defense organization and management. When combined with the efforts by ACO, the creation of Allied Joint Publications, ACO Directives, and so on, this emerging alliance corpus, when used appropriately, can provide nations with many critical guidelines that are founded on commonly agreed concepts, assumptions, principles, definitions, and procedures. Yet what is often misunderstood is that few of these procedures and documents can be adopted wholesale in order to produce national policies and procedures, as they can provide only basic direction for the development of national concepts, policies, structures, and procedures. It is also arguable that these NATO norms are merely manifestations of the lowest common denominator. But, as applied to these former communist defense institutions, if adopted judiciously, and in a mutually exclusive manner with existing concepts, assumptions, and logic, they could constitute major advances over their legacy counterparts.

Little understood outside of the alliance is the fact that NATO, qua NATO, is penurious at best. While there is NATO common funding, financial resources are quite finite and are jealously managed by nations.[23] In the area of providing matériel and nonmatériel assistance to partners, aspirants, and nonaspirants alike, it has been largely the United States and the United Kingdom which have provided most, but not all, of the resources to assist countries reform their defense institutions along Western lines.[24] For instance, US funding in the form of the Department of State's Security Assistance program began as early as fiscal year 1991 for Poland and Hungary, the Cooperative Threat Reduction program after the passage of the Soviet Threat Reduction Act in November 1991,[25] and finally in fiscal year 1994, Warsaw Initiative Funds were authorized with the explicit aim to help these nations become NATO members, or for partners to become closer to the alliance.[26] Elsewhere, since the United Kingdom's 1998 Strategic Defence Review, defense diplomacy has become one of the defense estate's core missions.[27] The Ministry of Defence's Directorate for Central and Eastern Europe initiated a formal outreach program "to assist in the development throughout the region of stable, sovereign and democratic states through the reform of their military institutions." Its Directorate for Central and Eastern Europe launched an initiative in 1994 to provide technical assistance through its outreach program to reforming post-communist countries in the region. "Militarily [the program] aims to promote efficient, democratic practices in central and eastern Europe; increase interoperability between the forces of NATO and its eastern partners; and develop training and exercise opportunity for UK forces in the region."[28] The Norwegian Ministry of Defense has been very active in the Baltic States and in former Yugoslav republics.[29] But in the end, notwithstanding these examples, it has been the focus on tactical proficiency that has largely dominated the vast majority of technical assistance being provided to these countries. In Appendix 2, there is a representation of US code Title 22 funding support to the countries being addressed in this work. In two funding categories alone, some US$2.5 billion has been provided to purchase education, services, and defense items. This matrix represents an incomplete,[30] but illustrative, example of just *two* funding authorities, but it speaks to the extent to which substantive US government funds have been directed to the reform of the defense institutions of these countries since the initiation of formal cooperative relations among these armed forces.

In sum, one can make a very strong argument that the West's response to the entreatments of the successor states of its former enemies and nonaligned Yugoslavia has been unparalleled in both scope and depth of engagement. There are few other modern cases where a collective has set out in a highly systematic manner to assist a large number of countries to undertake the reform of key government structures in such a fundamental manner. Yet, notwithstanding these good intentions, these efforts have produced only minor successes.

Problematic Western assumptions

At the abrupt end of the Cold War, NATO nations' knowledge of communist nations' orders of battle and performance of weapon systems and platforms did not seem to be matched with a full understanding of the communist concept of professionalism of their legacy officer corps, let alone the prevailing systemic incentives in these institutions. While there were extant general staffs of varying orders of competence, their respective civil defense institutions were either nonexistent or simply in their early embryonic stages of creation. In short, Western officials could argue justifiably that they were operating in *terra incognita*. However, that rationale was quickly contradicted once the scandalous state of disrepair of the armed forces became known following their first submission of the Defense Planning Questionnaires by the first tranche of new members (i.e., Poland, Czech Republic, and Hungary).[31] Cooperation with, and supporting the reform of, legacy defense institutions was very much a new challenge to NATO and its member nations. However, as astutely argued by Andrew Michta, there was one very early instance when Western officials were offered a ground-floor view of the actual state and conditions of legacy defense institutions which should have made them better aware of the immense challenge with which they were faced.[32] On October 3, 1990, the German Democratic Republic ceased to exist following the unification of Germany under the constitution of the Federal Republic of Germany. Immediately, the East German Army (*Nationale Volksarmee*, NVA) and its personnel fell under the command of the Federal Armed Forces of Germany (Bundeswehr). No less a senior official than the General Hans-Peter von Kirchbach (CHOD, 1999–2000), who took command of the 9th Armored Division of the NVA stationed in Eggesin on that date, wrote passionately of the need for understanding of the Eastern military experience and the need for patience before such individuals could be judged using traditional objective Western norms.[33]

In effect, this approach to the integration of post-communist individuals and, by extension, their defense institutions into Western structures rested on a key assumption. That is, that the military professionalism these individuals possess was equivalent to that of their Western counterparts and consequently could produce similar defense and military outcomes. Indeed, such an assumption has become a given among some officials, as it was argued how else could either party engage in a meaningful dialogue if the basis upon which all discussions was not founded on equality? This is an extremely important point as the acceptance of this assumption has greatly complicated not only how the two defense models have interacted and inter-related, but also raises serious and delicate political questions. And, to be fair to the legacy officer corps, there is a body of literature that argues that the growth in military technology in the 1960s made conditions more favorable for the development of a new kind of technology-proficient officer in communist armed forces, as distinct from their predecessors who were selected solely on the basis of political loyalty and reliability. The "red versus expert dilemma" could not be ignored. As Gitz relates,

> Provided after World War II with an almost unique opportunity to remake the Eastern European military establishments, the Soviet/NSWP leaderships were able to ensure that those forces were led by officers who were thought to be ideologically sound (i.e., pro-Soviet/communist) and in possession of social credentials (i.e., working class/peasant backgrounds) in keeping with their status as "people's armies". Over time, however, doubts were expressed by a number of Western analysts as to whether ideological considerations could maintain their priority in NSWP armed forces at the expense of technological and managerial competence.[34]

Indeed, in the case of Hungary, Dunay argues that as the minister of defense was never a full member of the Politburo of the Hungarian Socialist Workers' Party, there was space for the creation of military professionalism ethos in the Hungarian armed forces.[35]

Two outstanding Western general officers with deep experience with officers and soldiers from communist backgrounds have written strongly that their deep professional and command exposure to this cadre demonstrated that the gaps between their respective concepts of professionalism were all but irreconcilable. In light of their experience, one as a commander of a former NVA motorized division (*Himatschutz Brigade* 38, Wissenfels) and the other the first Danish defense attaché to the Baltic

States and later founder of the Baltic Defense College (in Tartu, Estonia) have posited that there were few, if any, common professional norms to enable achieving "intellectual interoperability." To Major General Christian Millotat (German Army), the simple fact of the matter was that the former NVA officers whom he found in the Bundeswehr's newly renamed home defense brigade universally were products of a system that made them unprofessional from a Western military perspective.[36] Albeit with exceptions, his general assessment was that former NVA officers in his brigade were incapable of carrying out the most basic leadership tasks that would be taken for granted in any Western armed force. It should not be forgotten that the NVA was considered by some Western military analysts to be the most capable of all Warsaw Pact armed forces.[37] Upon closely working with those NVA soldiers, NCOs and officers who were allowed to join the Bundeswehr, Western Bundeswehr soldiers

> were also astonished to find that these officers lacked almost everything considered by the *Bundeswehr* to be basic elements of leadership: the axioms of every leader's obligation tirelessly to care for his subordinates, to stand up for each other as fellow soldiers, to lead by mission-oriented command and control (*Auftragstaktik*), the readiness of all ranks to take responsibility, the feeling for what leaders can ask from their subordinates, a lack of fear of superiors in case of mistakes, and the courage to report to superiors when it is impossible to fulfill a particular task.[38]

Nor did these weaknesses and pathologies end quickly once selected officers and soldiers were invited to remain in the Bundeswehr. In what should have been an important lesson for Western nations, German defense officials found a popular narrative that once the political officers were released from service and communist indoctrination ended, a regime of Bundeswehr education and training would produce Western soldiers "who could adapt quickly to the military and ethical standards of *Bundeswehr* leaders by instruction and further training in the armed forces. This turned out to be wrong." Finally, as the Bundeswehr quickly discovered to their irritation, a great many routine and mundane tasks were carried out by officers and not NCOs, yet another critical indication of the fundamental dissimilarity found between some communist and Western armed forces.[39]

Brigadier Michael Clemmesen is even more damning of *Homo Sovieticus* in his manifestation as officer and leader. He provides a comprehensive and reflective account of all of the pathologies of the communist legacy officers from Central and Eastern Europe that he encountered in the region.

1. Individuals were universally trained never to question premises; they had to memorize facts and were actively discouraged to "think outside of the box."
2. Individuals growing up in communist societies learnt early never to take the initiative or accept responsibility. Interestingly, perhaps the only exception to this rule being when one was in command, as commanders were held personally responsible for what happened in, and the performance of, their formation.

3. As a corollary to never taking the initiative was the widespread norm to distrust subordinates and never delegate authority, except when needing to find someone to blame for any mishap.

4. The system taught from an early age that all military problems had to be defined properly, thereby enabling the officer to refer to some military scientifically founded book of norms, or database, to find the *one and only* correct solution. In other words, any military problem could only be solved basically using the right algorithm, based on the Soviet concept of military *science*.[40]

5. The communist concept of military-civilian relations was completely antithetical to its Western counterpart. In the latter's case, the armed forces exist to protect the state, or nation, and are fully subordinated to the rules of democratic society. The communist concept was that given that the armed forces existed to protect a society that was under ideological siege, it was the duty of society to provide it with all the resources it deemed needed to enable them to execute their respective missions (i.e., via Military Economic Science).

6. The officer cadre considered their unique privileges in society to be a given and not as a reward for diligence and dedication to service to the state and its citizens.

7. The officers of communist forces almost universally perceived the status of conscript soldiers to be on par with slaves.[41] Training was basically drill by rote, corporal punishment and hazing were the norm, and their role in peacetime was to serve as an all but slave labor force. Little time was given to making them an effective fighting force as they were seen largely as expendable if ever used in combat.

8. Staffs were treated as a collection of narrow specialists whose sole purpose was to serve the commander, as opposed to providing the basis for educated, forward, critical thinking.

9. These individuals led organizations that were bereft of a tradition of undertaking critical self-evaluation of structures, or procedures, with the view toward improving them.

10. A unit was considered to be high performance by virtue of manifestations of masculinity, as opposed to the execution of complex tasks under trying conditions, relying on soldiers and officers using creative thinking under stress.

11. The officer corps of these armed forces was, and remains, highly officer-heavy. As NCOs are largely relegated to specialized technical tasks, junior officers execute what would be sergeants' tasks in the West. There remains no consistent relationship between rank and responsibility. Promotion was limited and often dependent upon an individual's complete conformity to the organization's norms (or in some countries, simply based on time-in-grade).

12. To these individuals, the concept of becoming a professional soldier was devoid of the Western norm of the necessity of rotational assignments among demanding field assignments, staff postings, and professional schooling, all with the objective of growing the officer. Rather, mastery of the military scientific solution to an operational problem was considered to be the manner by which one should become a professional officer.

13. Finally, the formal education of officers was either based on highly technical training (e.g., mechanical engineering) or military-specific, very theoretical training that would produce the *one* possible answer to an operational problem.

To Clemmesen's mind, the fall of communist regimes in Eastern and Central Europe resulted in a widespread loss of social status, morale, and leadership within these armed forces. The result of this combination of negative events was to lead these organizations to devolve into "bloated, self-serving bureaucracies." Because of their insular nature, Clemmesen concludes that the rot in these armed forces developed faster and was more widespread than one otherwise might have predicted.[42] In effect, the result of the dissolution of communist regimes left a large body of officers whose selection, education, and training unsuited for the tasks and responsibilities expected of professional military officers in the West. To apply the metaphor used by Golts in describing the Russian armed forces, the communist system trained and produced officers who were craftsmen with deep but limited knowledge of their wider profession.[43] Moreover, as much of their formal education was, and still continues to be, technically focused (the Polish Military University of Technology in Warsaw constituting an excellent example),[44] this has only reinforced their predisposition to look for seemingly scientific solutions to all military challenges and problems.

Gulfs, divides, chasms, dissonance

It is essential to address in general the forces that continue to divide these two blocks of armed forces in order to present a clearer understanding of the sheer magnitude of the gulf that continues to exist between Western defense institutions and their legacy counterparts. As such, this section will address a number of impediments that have yet to be fully addressed in policy and practice that if understood better would collectively increase the mutual understanding of the challenges that face both Western and legacy defense officials. The issues to be addressed include the antithetical nature of Western and communist-inspired concepts, the role that culture plays in institutional reform, the implications of the lack of national strategic cultures, policy frameworks, the confusing nature of institutional names, and linguistic dissonance.

Table 3.1 complements Table 2.1 on differences in command philosophies. It is a general and admittedly hardly scientifically based representation of some of the key dissimilarities of how Western and legacy cultures continue to condition individuals to operate within their institutions' norms. Upon its review, it is not an overstatement to observe that these two conceptual models are unquestionably *antithetical*. By being antithetical, this is to state emphatically that they cannot coexist. Whereas Western officers and soldiers are selected, educated, trained, and utilized with the view to making them thinking agents in the execution of national policy, their counterparts continue to be plagued by communist social norms and organizational concepts which remain incompatible with basic liberal democratic values. As so perceptively observed by Mamardasvili, "A Soviet man is a product of invisible

Table 3.1 The Conceptual Divide

Western norms and democratic defense governance concepts	Legacy norms and defense governance concepts
• Practical	• Theoretical
• Decentralized execution	• Centralized execution
• Commanders are empowered	• Commanders only execute
• Results oriented	• Process oriented
• Future oriented	• Past obsessed
• Low social context	• High social context
• Serve the troops	• Mistreat soldiers
• Low power distance	• High power distance
• Low uncertainty avoidance	• High uncertainty avoidance
• Lying is unacceptable	• Lying is not a sin
• Failure is part of learning	• Failure is never an option

changes, degradation, and progressive deformation. Breaking the chain of those changes is hard. Perhaps they are irreversible."[45] The causation for the continuation of these deeply held, and to the Western eye perverse, values and behaviors is likely found in a number of explanations.

Critically, one should never underestimate the overwhelming influence played by a country's history and culture, particularly in the context of nations which have been long dominated and suppressed by foreign powers and where national institutions have been able to develop a high degree of resiliency to exogenous pressures as an essential mechanism for survival. In the particular case of Central and Eastern Europe, it is clear that most of these societies continue to struggle to overcome their recent history where a culture of distrust was pervasive. Despite some twenty-five years passing since the fall of communism, Branko Milanovic calculates that only 10 percent of the population of these countries has experienced economic prosperity greater than they had at independence. It should be little wonder, therefore, that failed transitions have resulted in messy politics and ineffectual governance.[46]

It is surprising that after 1990 there does not appear to have been any concerted effort (or indeed even recognition of the need) by the West to gain a greater understanding of the cultural conditions of the countries in Central and Eastern Europe, thereby informing Western policy. For solely illustrative purposes, Geert Hofstede is one among many experts who has developed methods by which one can study the difference between cultures.[47] There are other methods that could be selected, but a brief review of some of the data developed by Hofstede can be used simply to illustrate the *variance* of key cultural norms between Western nations and their counterparts in Central and Eastern Europe. To be sure, countries in this region are hardly homogenous, but those variations argue still for a *more* informed and nuanced understanding of those key cultural norms. As imperfect as the Hofstede data is (at the time of this writing, it did not contain entries for Armenia, Azerbaijan, Moldova, Bosnia, Macedonia, and Montenegro), a review of this data in Appendix 3 reveals some important and useful insights of the degree to which Western and Eastern cultural norms are significantly different (data for the United States is represented for comparative purposes). If one reviews just two cultural criteria, power distance[48] and uncertainty avoidance,[49] one can immediately observe where a better understanding of these differences should be extensively employed when developing/reviewing Western policy and advice/assistance planning assumptions. First, if some Western cultures (e.g., Nordic countries) can be typified as having low power distance, those in the East (particularly after the experience of communism) conversely have generally a high degree of power distance (i.e., Bulgaria, Poland, Romania, Slovakia, Croatia, Serbia, and Slovenia). For instance, in the case of Slovakia where power distance is scored to be at a maximum high of 100, a report by a Slovak think tank advocated the need for *regular* consultations between the president and the CHOD, as well as the minister of defense's *collegium* to enable more informed decision-making.[50] In other words, power is centralized at the top of an organization and delegation of authority is rarely allowed, and if so, only to a few trusted agents. This has direct applicability for defense institutions in many ways. Western-style mission-command and MDMP (the foundation stones on which Western democratic military concepts are based) are incomprehensible both to legacy officers and to soldiers from cultures with high power distances. Moreover, all of these armed forces have weak, and in some cases nonexistent, force management capabilities due to the fact that force management requires an ongoing institutional *dialogue* with those in tactical formations accurately reporting problems, proposing solutions, and arguing requirements via an ongoing institutional dialogue, where truth must be spoken to power. Finally, as regards this reality, in cultures with high power distance, only the most carefully reviewed and considered advice and assistance programs should be considered that wish to introduce concepts that necessitate the devolution of power and authority, for example, the introduction of professional NCOs. Second, Hofstede's other highly relevant cultural characteristic is uncertainty avoidance. Cultures with a high incidence of this norm are the three Baltic States, Bulgaria, the Czech Republic, Hungary, Poland, Romania, Croatia, Serbia, and Slovenia. In these cultures, individuals are self-limiting when confronted with challenges outside a societal norm out of fear of losing status and stature within society. Thus, problem-solving on one's own initiative, which would be a self-evident task of a Western armed force, will be difficult to encourage out of fear by individuals of unknown reactions by the group.

The purpose of examining these data is not to make sweeping or broad generalizations that hold for all cases. Rather, the point is that the data show significant societal and cultural divergences between Western and Central/Eastern European cultures. Where the data are sufficiently different speaks to the need for even a deeper understanding of each particular country's cultural foundations. It should be clear that adopting successfully Western defense and military concepts by legacy armed forces would be greatly enhanced with a full understanding of, *inter alia*, how to overcome, or perhaps even *co-opt*, these ingrained cultural traits. From a strictly NATO perspective, there should be seen a practical need for such an effort. Goldman and Eliasen support such an approach:

> A concerted effort to broaden and deepen "intellectual interoperability" within
> the context of NATO and other institutions of the growing democratic security

community, while beneficial, may require finding common ground culturally as well as politically and militarily.[51]

Directly related to the issue of a nation's culture is a concept that has emerged in the literature referred to as strategic culture.[52] It is essential to understand that as a result of their communist legacy, many of these countries lack a nationally determined military intellectual heritage. Those countries in the Warsaw Pact were all but completely subordinated to the Soviet High Command, and therefore, their societies did not directly inherit legitimate national strategic cognizance. For example, "The concept of strategic culture has been almost completely absent from both academic and political discourses in the Czech Republic."[53] Duny writes that during the communist period, Hungary was strategically subordinated to the Soviet High Command and hence was simply denied any strategic culture of its own for at least four decades.[54] In the case of the former Yugoslavia, there is a more nuanced explanation. The decision in 1968 to create Territorial Defense Forces in the republics allowed the development of unique defense institutions, albeit with limited responsibilities and functions. That said, in some cases (e.g., Slovenia) these were sufficiently capable organizations to serve as a firm basis for the development of embryonic strategic cultures.[55] Finally, with the exception of the Baltic States, newly independent former Soviet republics possessed no such recent historical legacy, tradition, or institutions that they could use as the basis to create such unique conceptual understandings.[56] At their birth as independent republics, there was little in the way of constructive Soviet inherence from which they could select. The all but nonexistent state of a strategic culture in the Soviet Union can be seen in the inability of Soviet officials to come to terms with the politico-military realities of nuclear weapons in the postwar era due to the experiences of the Second World War. In effect, Soviet military officials simply treated nuclear weapons as artillery since there was no community of independent think tanks that could ponder their politico-military implications and accordingly argue the need to adjust national-level policy.[57] Indeed, after twenty-five-plus years of independence, one could make a strong argument that all of these post-Soviet republics are still struggling to achieve such strategic self-understanding.

The lack of such strategic self-awareness should not be considered as an intellectual luxury without practical meaning, let alone importance. It could be argued that the absence of a national *Weltanschauung* among these countries has had the practical implication of contributing to the unawareness of the necessity of a policy framework that is essential to drive the most basic operations of the entire defense institution. Simply put, in these countries there has been no recent history of making defense *policy* within the context of an independent democracy, the direct result of which has been to set these defense institutions adrift, bereft of direction. Thus, these armed forces suffer from a state of possessing ageing operational capabilities, of varying degrees of effectiveness, and governing defense institutions which are, in terms of policy and functionally, almost comatose. Csiki and Talas could not have encapsulated the dilemma better than as it relates to Hungary: "contemporary strategic culture in Hungary has remained in a state of transformation, stuck between outdated structural-institutional remains of the (post)

Cold War era and the pressing need [for] modernization within a multinational Euro-Atlantic security framework."[58] It is little wonder that many armed forces have become rent-seeking bureaucracies, thoroughly incapable of shedding themselves of legacy practices, attitudes, and values. For these institutions to experience some form of collective renewal and determine how they are to function in a democracy as society's protectors, there is a need for a collective realization of such needs. In short, strategic culture and creating a policy framework still have to be (re)discovered and embraced in most of these countries. As will be seen *infra*, this process is proving itself to be challenging at best and almost insurmountable at worst.

As Edmunds, Cottey, and Forster postulated in 2006, one of the most significant challenges facing reforming defense institutions in Central and Eastern Europe is the "distinct problem of establishing effective control over defence policy."[59] The obvious place to initiate efforts to close this gapping policy framework was the creation of a proper ministry of defense, which exists almost exclusively to develop policy.[60] But the case of Hungary is illustrative of a common problem that was faced by every newly independent post-communist country:

> Hungary as a new democracy could not immediately install a competent class of civilians in the Ministry of Defense to support the civilian political leadership directly after the system change. The armed forces were suspicious of the few civilians who had acquired expertise in the field of defence. The fact that most Western support in training and retraining was offered to military professionals also contributed to a slow development of civilian expertise.... Military professionals retained significant influence on decision making inside the Ministry of Defense. At the same time, the weakened civilian leadership of the military could not credibly represent military interests at the political (governmental and parliamentary) level. However, these difficulties did not just result from the fact that civilian expertise in defence matters was insufficient. To a significant degree they also reflected a lack of military competence in these areas as well, particularly in relation to strategic defence planning.... After the system change, these deficiencies meant that the Hungarian military itself was significantly lacking in expertise in these areas, and was ill-equipped to shape the country's new defence policy. As a consequence, for much of the 1990s, Hungarian civil-military relations were characterised by two largely incompetent groups facing each other: the new civilians in the defence sector and the old military "professionals."[61]

A direct result, or perhaps causation, of weak ministries of defense and policy frameworks has been the practice of "security councils" (the nomenclature is hardly uniform) usurping the responsibilities of ministries of defense. While this practice is not unique to communist legacy governments, what is often little appreciated is the rather expansive writ that these councils exercise. These bodies sit above ministries, often working directly for the president or council of ministers, for example, the National Security and Defense Council in Ukraine or the Supreme Security Council in Moldova. Albeit in intent these are advisory bodies and not officially decision-making bodies, they are highly influential in matters of defense.[62] They are so influential that the Western assumption that a ministry of defense is the senior civil ministry with oversight of the armed forces is not necessarily the case in the context of legacy governance practices. Not a small number of new NATO allies have similar bodies: for example, the National Security Bureau in Poland (which under the leadership of Stanisław Koziej has produced arguably the best reform policies in the region)[63] and the Security Council of the Slovak Republic. Betz describes them very well:

> National security councils have been important and controversial institutions in all the states under review. Important, because where they exist they have tended to become the locus of decision-making in the sphere of defence. Controversial, because they were often vaguely defined in constitutional legislative terms and because of a perceived linkage to the powerful defence councils of the old system which were thought to have had too strong an ideological content.[64]

As these ministries of defense have yet to adopt, let alone fully implement, broad policy frameworks that oversee the management of the entire defense institution, these organizations, in effect, *act en lieu* of them, but are not responsible for their actions. It is not unusual that defense laws and regulations are drafted by officials in these bodies, *vice* ministries of defense; and on review of some of these laws, it is clear that ministries and defense officials have obviously not been consulted.[65] Regarding Ukraine, for example, "In effect, the NSDC [National Security and Defense Council] controls all major military decisions (including reform issues), as well as the armed security forces in Ukraine, including the regular armed forces, the Special Forces, the National Guard, and the Border Guards."[66] What makes these institutions problematic is that as so many ministries of defense are simply incapable of framing properly defense policy issues, it is left to these councils both to *frame* and to *develop* policy solutions. Thus, in effect, these bodies can *act* as ministries of defense in their purist form (generating policy), but are not recognized as such by all Western governments and officials due to their nomenclature.

Whereas institutionally weak ministries of defense have these national security councils to provide policy and priorities, no such bureaucratic backup exists for underperforming general staffs. The quality of the output and effectiveness of general staffs across all three typologies vary, but within the defense institutions which have had intensive operational experience (e.g., Poland, Romania, Slovenia), one finds a greater willingness to accept the Western requirement for these bodies largely to support their ministries of defense, as opposed to involve themselves solely in tactical- and operational-level responsibilities and functions. Yet, traditions are hard to overcome when legacy practices hold that all decision-making, even the most mundane, could only be addressed at the general staff. This leads to the maddening situation where colonels on a general staff dictate the direction of individual and collective training of the forces, yet without having any responsibility for providing the resources to execute these tasks, let alone recognizing that at that level guidance should be in the form of policy, vice detailed tactical training directives. Like their counterparts in ministries of defense, officers in all too many general staffs do not see their responsibilities to be largely supporting the execution of national-level policy and advising the most effective means of achieving defense outcomes.

A final element of division that has inhibited a better mutual understanding between Western and legacy minds has been the challenge posed by language. Whereas differentiation in concepts and principles are, at times, obvious, less understood is the impediment presented by language to achieving greater intellectual interoperability. Given that lexica conveys conceptual meaning, it can be vexatious to be able to convey the true meaning of a basic Western military concept when partners' languages either have no direct equivalent word (or, even more complicated, there exists *false cognates*) or the concept is simply unknown. Soukupova illustrates well the challenges of understanding Czech translations of English documents:

> Czech-written documents are full of English military phraseology, which when consulted against attached dictionaries of used terms do not correlate with the intended Czech meaning. Moreover, English phrases are adopted from American, British and NATO official military dictionaries at the same time and are very often mixed up throughout one document. As many Czechs from the security sector speak very little English and come from a very different educational background compared to their West counterparts, semantic interoperability becomes a problem when analysing any text. Perhaps the most striking evidence of this is a Czech term "schopnosti NEC," which literarily translates as "capabilities of network enabled capabilities."[67]

False cognates are essentially omnipresent in discussions and communications between West and legacy defense institutions. Even basic definitions (i.e., battalions, warships, and combat aircraft) present challenges. For instance, in most legacy defense institutions, these terms have different meanings from their Western usage. By this, in the Western context, a generic infantry battalion consists of 400 to 700 soldiers and officers who have been through a full regime of individual, collective, and leadership training, with sufficient fuel, practice ammunition, a formal annual training cycle, and an exercise program, all of which builds habitual relationships with combat support, and combat service support, formations. Anything less than all of these elements degrade its ability to be operable and suitable for deployments. In the mind of still too many legacy armed forces, a bona fide infantry battalion can consist of only 20 percent of the authorized manpower, conduct little, or *no*, collective training and exercises can be episodic, and with only minor interactions with combat support and service support formations.[68] To the Western mind, an infantry battalion needs these enabling components in order to qualify as a "capability," whereas in a legacy environment, whatever has been determined by senior officials constitutes a universal truth.

Concerning language itself, Sherr observes that in Russian and Ukrainian (and one should add Estonian for that matter), *kontrol* is translated normally as meaning "checking" or "verifying." In political-administrative terms, this can mean "oversight." But this is hardly satisfying. Only after speakers of these languages have been exposed to actual Western practice and concepts underlying a word like "control" are they fully made aware of the nuances of the term: it also means in a constructive sense, "direction, management, administration, and supervision."[69] Taking the issue of command and control (C2), one step further into mutually assured confusion, is that concepts are interpreted differently in same language. For instance, in Czech, an air force officer will understand C2 as one system (albeit it might be a stretch to assume that it will be understood as a socio-technical system), whereas land forces will distinguish C2 as two *separate and independent* processes.[70]

Other examples abound, however, and one of the most egregious linguistic impediments to common understanding is that Slavic languages (and interestingly also in Romanian, not a Slavic language) do not have direct translations of the nuanced term: capability(ies). In the context of modern Western defense planning and management, the term "capability" has become the key conceptual building block used to denote a generic military effort to achieve an envisage effect. The mere *translation* of the word itself is insufficient (it is typically translated, erroneously, even by skilled interpreters as meaning "potential"), as an understanding of its conceptual meaning (with all of its nuances) is a *sine qua non* for any meaningful discussion of something as basic as defense planning, force development, force management, and how best to plan and conduct joint operations.

Equally challenging, in Slavic languages there is no distinction between "policy" and "political" with the latter normally conflated with a strong partisan overtone. Glanz writes, "The word 'POLITIKA' [politics] in Hungary is a generic term meaning everything."[71] Thus, the suggestion that senior defense officials should concern themselves with policy/partisan politics presents linguistic as well as conceptual and cultural challenges that need first to be overcome. It should be recalled that the armed forces of these countries in the communist period were highly controlled by their respective communist parties and is a legacy from which most, if not all, have been striven to disassociate themselves, that is, any appearance of engaging in domestic political issues. Unfortunately, the semantic solution used in the communist period, which continues to find its way into the contemporary lexica of the region, has merely solved one problem by introducing another.[72]

Finally, Slavic languages use the noun "doctrine" to mean, in a legacy context, "policy," whereas conversely in the West, it is used to denote a body of knowledge that is useful in conducting military operations.[73] Thus, one finds the terminology "military doctrine," *vojna doktrina* (using Serbian as a representative example) in place of the Western concept of "defense policy." Yet, conceptually the two terms are antithetical as the former is prescriptive, while the latter is interpretative. (This particular conceptual false cognate is addressed at length throughout this work.) A further complication to effective cross-communication is that there are cases where even the term "concept," a cognate in Slavic languages, can be misleading. By this, concepts are not always interpreted in the legacy mind as a general idea which requires further thinking and interpretation, but rather are perceived through legacy lenses as *daktrina* for which there can be only one, official, meaning. Finally, maddeningly, many languages in the region do not distinguish between "effective" and "efficient." Thus, these few examples of linguistic differentiation of terms, and their underlying concepts that are essential to modern defense planning and military operations, have all too often gone unaddressed in a consistent and effective manner. One often hears complaints from officials in the region that the translation of even official NATO documents is not of consistent quality and lacks appreciation of the subtleties and linguistic nuances as mentioned above.

Civilian control of armed forces

Clearly, the challenges confronting governments in Central and Eastern Europe transitioning from communist to democratically based defense institutions are not inconsequential. Chapters 7 and 8 will address specifically these issues in greater detail and propose content and management solutions to guide advice and assistance policy. However, it is appropriate at this stage in this work to address the issue of the general state of civilian control of armed forces in these new democracies. As in the case of strategic culture, this is a significant issue and it should not be assumed that as these countries are functioning democracies, they do not continue to be faced with challenges to civil-military relations. Three of the most respected scholars of this issue in Central and Eastern Europe, Edmunds, Cottey, and Forster, contend that as a result of the systematic democratic reforms of the 1990s, these countries have made substantial progress in defense reform and "now mostly have reasonably functioning systems for democratic civilian control of defence policy."[74] They propose a very useful, and widely used, thesis that recognizes these countries as having transitioned to "second generation" democratic development challenges in civil-military relations whereby the armed forces do not interfere in domestic politics.[75] Perhaps from a legal and organizational perspective, one can make a strong case that these countries have, from all appearances, the basic elements of what would constitute modern defense institutions in accordance with Western democratic defense governance concepts.[76] That said, Edmunds and Bellamy note an important caveat that the all but universal regional practice of constitutionally investing presidents with ambiguous command authorities has resulted in parliaments possessing very little *constructive* influence over particularly the assignment of officers to senior posts (and troubling CHODs), which thereby significantly undermines their ability to effect control of armed forces.[77] While making a definitive judgment on the status of the maturity of institutions is problematic, the following chapters will suggest a more nuanced condition than the one argued by these three scholars. Watts is closer to the mark when he argues that the effects on civil-military relations from the transition from communism to democracy are much more nuanced than many assume and there are many more cases of where the armed forces have been actively manipulated by politicians (e.g., in Hungary and Romania).[78] In all areas of basic defense management, the vast majority of these countries studied are exceedingly underdeveloped, and therefore, it is argued that they are not capable of fully executing effective control (critically, in a *positive*, not just *negative*, sense) of armed forces by a civilian ministry of defense. Indeed, as Sherr perceptively observes,

Therefore, the measure of progress in civil-military relations is not the number of civilians in "control." It is the extent to which the armed forces feel themselves to constitute an integral part of the democratic order, the extent to which civil-military *collaboration* becomes the norm, the extent to which civilians can bring an informed perspective to military discussion, and the extent to which national defense policy becomes the business of the country as a whole.[79]

One is pressed hard to identify a ministry of defense in Central and Eastern Europe that has reached this state of development. What the evidence suggests is that fundamental Western democratic defense governance concepts are only slowly and unevenly being adopted across the region.

Conclusion

The allied decision, or simply its passive acceptance, of legacy armed forces as equals to their Western counterparts has produced a negative externality that continues to hinder the reform of these defense institutions. Worst of all, the unwillingness to acknowledge that many of the defense institutions of newly independent European states are unreformed, NATO and its members have provided them with more than a patina of legitimacy well out of proportion to reality. In truth, by not stating the truth, the West collectively has allowed, as argued by Clemmesen, the rot to spread throughout the entirety of many of these defense institutions, thereby inhibiting reform and reducing their ability to perform even the most basic defense tasks. The result has been the ability of individuals and organizations passively to stifle the adoption of Western democratic defense governance concepts; all the while, their military capacity continues to atrophy. In consequence, it is difficult not to conclude that the lack of progress in reforms throughout the region, particularly given the expenditure of resources and efforts, has been unsuccessful for the parties involved. As argued by Dunay, "Perhaps the greatest disservice Hungary has done to the defence reform process is to highlight the powerlessness of NATO allies to promote defence reform once a state has become a member."[80] What the evidence will demonstrate in subsequent chapters is to update Brigadier Clemmesen's pessimistic assessment published in 2000 that Western policies and programs have lost ten years. Bringing his thesis forward fifteen years, one can argue that the West has lost twenty-five-plus years.

However, what has been missing to date that would inform discussion and encourage debate has been a sufficiently large data set based on a common methodology that is necessary to support such a discussion. The many commendable works that have been written on these countries in the region almost exclusively have been compendia of country-specific studies, and few comprehensive surveys have been undertaken, let alone assessing the data using a common methodology. The next three chapters set out to provide such an understanding by examining in detail the actual state of development these defense institutions using the typology of former Soviet republics, former Warsaw Pact republics, and former Yugoslav republics.

Former Soviet Republics' Defense Institutions

When examining post-Soviet armed forces, it is critical to keep well in mind the ever-presence of the legacies of the Soviet Red Army, as their residual influences are never difficult to find. Although the intensity of legacy influence varies according to the country in question, the shadow of the Red Army remains. Sherr captures well the depth of its persistent legacy:

> The Soviet Armed Forces was not only a military machine, but a social institution, which has left behind deeply entrenched attitudes about authority, society, national security and the role of the military in defending it. Its legacy is by no means entirely bad, but it is profoundly influential, and it both shapes and hinders progress.[1]

The dissolution of the Soviet Union produced armed forces of newly independent republics which are smaller, but still mirror in many ways their newly constituted Russian counterparts. After all, in their early years they were trained and manned by, and equipped with, remnants of the Red Army, with some interesting nuances. Yet, at the same time, each has its own unique characteristics. For example, the Azerbaijani armed forces initially consisted of a disproportionate number of officers from particularly combat service support branches, vice combat arms, given the historical Russian suspicion of arming Muslim minorities. Conversely, the creation of the Armenian armed forces benefited from the long and close historical ties between Armenia and its co-religionists and protectors in Moscow. To wit, four ethnic Armenians reached the rank of marshal in the Soviet Red Army.[2]

As a general observation, the Soviet legacy can be thought of being still very much present throughout the former Soviet Union region, the only variable being the degree of intensity, as opposed to whether it remains. Obviously, these traditions and norms are at their weakest in the Baltic States (yet even among them, some Red Army influences can be found), and the further eastward one looks, one can sometimes identify the stronger influence. Or, as so wonderfully and accurately observed by General Sir Garry Johnson,

> The farther east the traveler goes the more it is noticeable that problems are more readily acknowledged than addressed, more often borne than solved and,

when solved, more often done so by consensus and the pressure of events than by confrontation and design.[3]

However, this general observation is with some notable exceptions. If it is indeed the case that the Armenian defense institution is largely inspired by the Russian model,[4] its Georgian counterpart, despite shortcomings, is arguably one of the most profoundly influenced by Western democratic defense governance concepts in many key areas (but, disappointingly, not entirely so).[5] This observation can only be assessed as nothing short of admirable considering the defense institution's completely shambolic and unpromising beginnings in the early years of independence.[6]

There is one country, however, that by its own geographic size needs to be placed in a category by itself. The Ukrainian armed forces[7] were formed from the Red Army remnants of four tank divisions, fourteen motor-rifle divisions, and three artillery divisions,[8] accompanied with immense infrastructure, and substantial defense industry. Any country that can deploy to a war zone (i.e., Iraq), and largely sustain a brigade-size force for three brigade rotations and recover the force (despite its inability to perform to Coalition expectations), notwithstanding logistics failures, is an achievement very few other countries in the world could succeed in executing.[9] But, that all said, Ukraine did not inherit an army; rather, as Sherr describes, it found itself with force groupings, comprising three Soviet military districts, without any of the requisite national administrative and bureaucratic infrastructure, thereby constituting a coherent national force. A challenge that current events in eastern Ukraine would imply it has yet to have successfully completed.[10]

The Baltic exception

The unquestionable exception to the close connection to Soviet institutional legacy is, of course, the Baltic States due to their unique status and evolution since independence, and as such, require separate treatment. Given that their historical experience of Soviet occupation was shorter than all the other Soviet republics (save Moldova), and were independent during the interwar period, regaining independence resulted in an immediate rejection of the Soviet model in Estonia and Latvia, and perhaps more slowly in Lithuania. The advantage that they did enjoy was a highly motivated diaspora and friendly neighboring Nordic states that quickly mobilized to provide advice and assistance. Moreover, Western nations provided considerable advice and assistance in the form of PME, equipment, and training. In this respect, their defense institutional experience is different from other former Soviet republics. They chose to create civil defense institutions and armed forces *ab ovo*; but interestingly, not all necessarily along conventional NATO nations' lines.[11] For example, Estonia initially received assistance principally from retired Finnish officers whose approach was based on uniquely national defense concepts stemming from the requirements of Finland's peace treaty with the Soviet Union.[12] With time, however, it became increasingly obvious to many in the Estonian defense institution that the Finnish approach was not in conformance with Estonian policy that was oriented toward admission into NATO.[13]

In adopting Nordic defense models, each with their own unique nuances, at the same time, the Baltic States shared to varying degrees one common concept: territorial defense, based on the concepts of mobilization and conscription and organizational and operational concepts that eschewed any assumption of Western/neutral states' military assistance in a confrontation with Russia.[14] In contemplating the defense of their countries, Baltic defense officials and especially many military officers almost instinctively seized on their common historical experience of guerrilla warfare (e.g., the Forest Brothers in Estonia) used against the postwar Soviet occupation.[15] This focus on territorial defense and guerrilla warfare, while arguably applicable immediately after independence, becomes less so with NATO membership.[16] To be sure, territorial defense, or in the case of Nordic countries, Total Defense, is not necessarily inimical to the overriding NATO basic concept of collective defense.[17] Indeed, Norway and Denmark long followed such an orientation, and given their size and resources, some have argued that territorial defense is an eminently well-suited concept in the case of the Baltic States.[18] While another argument has been proffered that questions the application of this concept given such stark differences between the highly economically developed and homogeneous former and the smaller, less developed and more heterogeneous latter.[19] As such, it should not, and cannot, be framed as a mutually exclusive proposition. Yet Lithuania claimed in 2006 that it would eliminate existing capabilities that did not contribute to collective defense.[20] What is of relevance and which will be addressed in this work is the need to distinguish between territorial defense as a general operational focus and *fixed* territorial defense, whereby the armed forces are based on conscription/mobilization, are tied to operationally geographic regions, and lack the ability to maneuver, so necessary for survival on the modern battlefield.

Thus, the Baltic States' experience of creating civil defense institutions and armed forces, while disconnected from Soviet models and practices, was hardly without their own unique struggles and organizational pathologies. In the end, perhaps as a reflection of their seriousness to adopt a defense model based on Western democratic principles from all possible sources of expertise, the Baltic States adopted many Western approaches to defense, which have not always been complementary. As a result, incompatibilities have developed which they have not been always willing to change and have, at times, been vexing both for them and their NATO allies.[21]

Overview of defense institutions

The judgments of this author of the state of adoption of Western democratic defense governance concepts by post-Soviet republics can be found in Table 4.1. The data of the state of defense reform and the record of success of adopting Western defense and military norms has been far from successful in former Soviet space. Even at the national level, embryonic ministries of defense (save the Baltic States and Georgia) largely resemble one another and continue to share common dysfunctionalities. For, with the exception of the Baltic States and Georgia, they were basically founded on existing military

Table 4.1 Baseline of Defense Governance Concepts: Post-Soviet Republics

	Baltic States	Armenia	Azerbaijan	Georgia	Moldova	Ukraine
Policy framework	In transition	In transition	Legacy/in transition	In transition	Legacy/in transition	Legacy
National-level command	In transition (but progressing)	Legacy	Legacy	Legacy/in transition	Legacy	Legacy
Military decision-making process	Extant on operations/constrained by *fixed* territorial defense	Legacy	Legacy/in transition (via extensive PME and training from Turkey)	In transition	Legacy	Legacy
Concept of operations	NATO/in transition	Legacy	Hybrid of legacy and NATO	In transition	Legacy	Legacy
Logistics	Legacy/in transition	Legacy	Legacy	Legacy/in transition	Legacy	Legacy
Professionalism	Extant	Legacy	In transition (via extensive PME and training from Turkey)	Legacy/in transition	Legacy	Legacy

headquarters, that is, based on a military organizational template, and have yet to escape from their military antecedents. It is difficult to differentiate these pseudo-ministries of defense and their respective general staffs, particularly given the fact that oftentimes they claim responsibilities over the same institutional responsibilities and functions. If one uses the generic definition developed by Taylor that a ministry of defense in a democracy should concern itself with policy generation and press the armed forces to achieve efficiencies, these organizations are far from reaching this objective.[22] Indeed, it is not unusual to find directorates within these organizations that would be relegated to service-level headquarters and not be located even within the defense/joint staffs of their Western counterparts. With the exception of the Baltic States and Georgia, cadres of competent civilian defense officials are still the exception; and indeed, it is not unusual to see what should be civilian ministries of defense staffed almost exclusively by active or retired field-grade officers and general officers.

In Figure 4.1, a generic former Soviet republic ministry of defense is represented. The nation in question is unimportant as its organizational structure is representative of the ministries of defense one can expect to find in most, if not all, countries (the Baltic States and Georgia's Ministry of Defense excluded). What is remarkable from a Western perspective is the fact that the ministry is essentially integrated; but unlike the Western practice of ministry of defense/defense staff integration, this legacy model is based on a pre-existing land-centric Soviet *military* organizational template. Moreover, note that there is no policy or planning directorates which only underscores the fact that such ministries are essentially incapable of functioning as policy-generating organizations. The Soviet/Russian historical proclivity to stress the importance of artillery is found less and less in some of these organizations, but in the case of this organization, it still enjoys its own directorate in the ministry, and is, bureaucratically speaking, a co-equal to the air force and army. A final important point to acknowledge is that intelligence

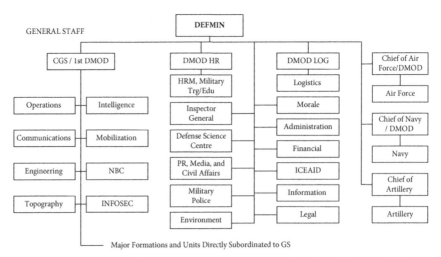

Figure 4.1 Organizational Chart of an Unnamed post-Soviet Republic's Ministry of Defense.

does not have the same meaning in a legacy context as it does in the West. Defense and military intelligence existed under communism, but these functions were often not directed outward to support commanders, but rather were oriented inwards to carry out counter intelligence.

What should be their military counterparts, the general staffs[23] of these countries, are organizationally and conceptually ill-equipped to execute policy generated from a functional ministry of defense. In general, it is an accurate statement that they do not have the organizational and procedural tools, let alone the basic knowledge and experience, to support their civilian leadership in national-level tasks. These organizations largely are oriented to focus "downward" and execute not only operational-level tasks but even tactical-level ones. The essential concept that a general staff exists to provide civilian leadership with professional advice to enable ministers to make informed decisions remains foreign. There are many explanations for the inability of these staff to adopt Western defense and military concepts. Foremost is that these institutions were created from operationally focused Soviet headquarters. In the intervening twenty-five-plus years, these systems have perpetuated themselves largely in alignment with their Soviet legacies and there has been little meaningful reform. Mundane management issues like training to centrally determined time, vice standards, continue to be promulgated from these organizations often absent of information on the true state of tactical formations, at the expense of addressing national-level and, to a lesser degree, operational-level tasks. What is surprising is that this model of training, which arguably is appropriate for a conscript force, has continued with little change to adopt modern methods. The Sovietize model of the unique role played by the professional officer corps with its own degree of institutional autonomy in the implementation of the Communist Party's *diktats* remains intact.[24]

What might strike most readers as surprising is the relatively low scores assigned to the Baltic States. To be sure, they are far and away further ahead in adopting Western democratic defense governance concepts than their post-Soviet counterparts. However, a careful review of their performance demonstrates that in a number of key areas the Baltic States, as a whole, have yet fully to embrace prevailing Western norms. This can be explained in part by the fact that many of the original personnel who took early leadership positions in the fledgling armed forces came from Soviet backgrounds and the Soviet model was all that they knew. Notwithstanding extensive Western advice and assistance (for example, sending officers, cadets, and NCOs to Western military training and educational establishments), some ingrained practices like centralizing decision-making remain. One can find misapplications of some Western, principally Nordic, models all too often adopted by copying, rather than developing solutions applicable to their situation.[25]

A unique challenge faced by each of the Baltic States was to develop a civil ministry of defense and armed forces based on *many* different Western models, assumptions, educational programs, and equipment. Thus, whereas the Baltic armed forces did not suffer from attempting to reform extant legacy institutions and process, they did have the unenviable task of having to reconcile not inconsequential organizational and conceptual differences in various Western approaches to defense governance.

Indeed, the wide array of available external military educational courses and training programs presented to them could arguably have been counter productive, in view of the fact that there *is* no single Western model by which a reforming country can emulate in the hopes of adopting the nonexistent NATO model. In effect, the West may have been too clever by half, and unintentionally availed Baltic officials to too many *different* Western approaches and models. Thus Western donors failed them by not assisting them to recognize the all too numerous subtle nuances and the need to develop some means of synthesizing solutions through a process of scaling these structures and procedures to meet their modest requirements. As a result, these interpretations of Western concepts, assumptions, and logic were translated through the lens of either former Soviet officers or civilian defense officials with little expertise and background to understand fully the implications of decisions with which they were addressing. Nor should these legacy attitudes be dismissed as having been easily rejected by officials in these countries. As a former Latvian minister of defense writes, "Soviet rule had left a culture that demanded conformity not initiative, control not delegation, compartmentalisation not cooperation, and secrecy not transparency."[26] An additional complication was faced by Estonia where its ministry of defense and armed forces were created *subsequent* to the creation of a rather effective paramilitary border guard force (*Eesti Piirivalve*) that had been developed with extensive assistance from Finland. Thus, the ministry of defense and armed forces early on had to compete for finite resources and political attention from the border guards, as well as from a private (and politically powerful) voluntary defense association organized around localized territorial defense (*Keits Elit*).[27]

Finally, in comparison with other former Soviet republics, the Baltic States saw a number of émigrés, with Western military experience, return to provide defense expertise in what was trying and austere conditions. The problem of such leaders was multifold. First, let there be no mistake that in a general sense, the diaspora is not always appreciated on their return or advent, which thereby limited their credibility, let alone their social acceptance and professional advice. Second, most, if not all, of these individuals had been serving officers, or NCOs, in their adopted Western countries. In consequence, oftentimes their military expertise was within much larger and highly sophisticated defense institutions (but largely at the tactical level) and was rarely complemented by experience of how a civilian ministry of defense should be run, let alone how to create a small one from whole cloth.

To be sure, when observing the record of operational effectiveness of Baltic States' soldiers in Iraq and Afghanistan, it is quite impressive;[28] however, the state of development of civil defense institutions remains a work in progress. All three shared a somewhat common challenging birth, yet interestingly, Lithuania made the early decision in 1996 to integrate fully its ministry of defense and general staff, as has Latvia, a move their Estonian counterparts have yet to undertake. Civilian defense authorities were at an early disadvantage in these ministries of defense, lacking expertise vis-à-vis their respective defense staffs which had been established first with many legacy-trained and experienced staff officers. This has been described in the case of Estonia as a period of a quiet civil war between these two institutions, which finally devolved into a peaceful coexistence.[29]

While large, if not indeed too large, the Ukrainian Ministry of Defense remains highly underdeveloped and its general staff largely remains profoundly dominated by its Main Operations Directorate with occasional forays in attempts at adopting Western concepts and assumptions, only to reject them thereafter.[30] Indeed, a major difficulty that has haunted the armed forces, particularly in fighting separatists in its eastern *oblasts*, is that successive governments have only reorganized the defense institution structurally, but not with a mind to make it more operationally *capable*. In the early years of the existence of the ministry of defense and general staff, the latter claimed to be in the lead for the development of policy, while leaving its implementation to the ministry—an anomalous relationship from a Western perspective, which was only partially solved by a presidential decree in 1997. Equally unusual was that as late as 2000, within the ministry of defense, a *civil* ministry, civilians represented only 30 percent of the staff.[31] Despite the introduction of additional civilians in the Ukrainian Ministry of Defense, that organization still remains dominated by a large number of retired officers and the bureaucratically powerful, yet operationally ineffectual, general staff.[32] An example of its organizational rigidity is that as late as 2010, the minister of defense was supported by *seven* deputy ministers, all of which reported directly to minister, absent a permanent secretary to coordinate policy and staff work flow.[33] The disorganized response in 2014 by the ministry of defense and general staff to the Russian seizure of Crimea and its support of separatists in Eastern Ukraine speaks legions to the underdeveloped nature of both organizations. Their inability to respond effectively, despite the large size of the armed forces (on paper, to be sure), resulted in President Petro Poroshenko organizing "volunteers" (private citizens) essentially to take over elements of the ministry of defense (e.g., medical, logistics/supply, and infrastructure) to introduce needed reforms.[34]

The Moldovan Ministry of Defense and Main Staff sit almost forlornly on the outskirts of Chisinau in the huge and much too large complex of what had constituted the former Soviet 14th Guards Army headquarters. Despite being one of the furthest west, geographically speaking, it conversely remains highly Sovietized in terms of its institutional organization and culture and retains a strictly hierarchical organizational structure, notwithstanding years of support provided by the US Department of Defense.[35] Inexplicably, despite the modest size of the defense institution, the ministry of defense and Main Staff remain unintegrated.

The relative success of Georgia creating a defense institution presents a uniquely positive case, particularly when compared to its two Caucasian neighbors. In many ways, the provenance of the Georgian Ministry of Defense and armed forces is akin to the Baltic States, to include even basing its defense planning on the concept of Total Defense.[36] As Larrson writes, "Georgia has never been a keen disciple of Russian military traditions."[37] Indeed, at the end of the Cold War, it was estimated that ethnic Georgian representation in the Red Army was seventy-second of Soviet nationalities (measured as a percentage of officers per 1,000 citizens). Due to the continued and contentious stationing of Soviet and thence Russian Federation armed forces in the country, which only left in November 2007 (from Batumi), the Georgian armed forces were created largely anew. There is, therefore, little direct lineage to the Georgian armed forces from the Red Army/Russian Federation armed forces, unlike in the case of Ukraine or

Belarus. Yet, in 1992, the bulk of conventional weapons and arms in Soviet caches was transferred to the new Georgian Ministry of Defense, thereby maintaining matériel linkages.[38] From the early days of the Rose Revolution in November 2003, there has been a strong move to institutionalize the ministry in accordance with Western democratic defense governance concepts: by 2007, 85 percent of the organization's employees were civilians.[39] But there is an almost uniquely Georgian practice of the regular and wholesale dismissal of senior leadership (to include directorate heads) in the ministry of defense and general staff following a change in government that has greatly impeded the creation of policy and bureaucratic continuity.

Georgia's two neighbors took different courses of institutional development from what has been a dynamic process of change in Tbilisi. Given that both were largely created in the midst of conflict, their ministries of defense have remained militarized for years, but more recently have begun to add civilian defense experts. In Armenia, a law was passed in November 2007 to introduce the concept of civilian civil servants to the ministry of defense in 2010, where most officials in that organization are now civilians, albeit most have military pedigrees.[40] It has been argued that the Azerbaijani defense institution has begun a policy of civilianizing the ministry of defense, but those civilian officials are largely in low-level support, vice policy-level positions.

Policy framework and conceptual coherence

The concept that all actions of a civil defense institution and armed force need to be tied directly to supporting the achievement of defense policy priorities and objectives, as developed and articulated by an elected government, remains at best underdeveloped and entirely nonexistent in some of these countries.[41] The only example of where there are more than merely embryonic elements of a policy framework that directs all the actions of the defense institution is within the Baltic States, albeit weakly,[42] and if public documents are to be believed, in Armenia as well.[43] A policy framework is essential if a legacy defense institution is to harbor any hope of achieving conceptual coherence. As suggested, even in the case of the Baltic States, however, one finds suggestions of some Soviet legacies, or perhaps they are just simple organizational weaknesses, due to their immaturity, to make achieving both a policy framework and conceptual coherence problematic. For instance, notwithstanding the fact that Estonia became a member of the alliance in 2004, its most basic defense principles remain strongly founded on conscription/mobilization and oriented toward *fixed* territorial defense, at the expense of rapid response, maneuver, and the ability for its land forces to integrate better into NATO formations. Paulauskas's comment that "Squabbles between the Estonian Ministry of Defence and the Headquarters of the Estonian Defence Forces are the stuff of legend in the circles of Baltic defence planners" implies a troubling degree of policy incoherence. To their credit, and not without their own challenges, Lithuania and Latvia have made some progress moving away from *fixed* territorial defense and conscription (albeit the former reintroduced it in 2015) to adopting professionalization and mobile operations.[44] As will be seen in the following chapters, Estonia is not the only NATO member whose defense policy remains premised on pre-accession concepts. In other post-Soviet defense institutions, policy frameworks are largely unknown and governance concepts remain firmly based on Soviet principles. The explanation for this state of affairs is that these ministries of defense are largely fictitious from a Western perspective. In essence, they do not function as civil ministries effecting policy oversight of the activities of the armed forces.

To their credit, all of the Baltic States' ministries of defense have the posts of permanent secretaries and the armed forces have implemented the concept of a chief of staff, thereby dividing leadership/command from management.[45] Conversely, this practice has not been adopted in other post-Soviet defense institutions. This has inhibited the development of a policy framework by the failure of separating leadership/command from management, that is, neither a permanent secretary nor a director of the staff will be found in any of these ministries of defense or general staff; to include surprisingly, even Georgia.[46] It is little wonder, therefore, that these organizations are almost incapable of conducting effective staff work as judged by Western standards since, *inter alia*, there are no designated officials whose sole purpose is focused on the optimization of the daily functioning of the organization. Due to legacy norms and high power distance, these organizations do not distinguish between leading/command and management. By placing all power of decision-making in the minister and/or the CHOD, modern command and management concepts and principles are eschewed. Even the widespread practice of designating deputy ministers[47] and deputy CHODs to run the organization breaks this principle (in the case of Armenia, there being two deputy ministers, but not a permanent secretary, but rather a secretariat).

What does exist in a unique fashion shared by essentially all post-communist legacy national defense institutions are military *collegia*, as in the case of the ministries of defense of Azerbaijan and Ukraine[48] or the *Colegiul Militar* (Military Council) in Moldova. These bodies can trace their roots to Czarist, and more recently Soviet, times where such bodies could be used to escape personal responsibilities for decision-making—ergo, leaving decisions to an amorphic collective. One sees these more frequently and predominantly in former Yugoslav republics; however, their functionality appears to be the same. While it is not asserted that these are necessarily secretive bodies, they add an unneeded degree of opacity over senior-level decision-making.

A major impediment to the development of a policy framework in the non-Baltic States republics has been, as stated earlier, a general reluctance to introduce civilian defense expertise. Where there are civilian officials, they are almost always retired officers (Georgia being a major exception), not all of whom have made that essential leap to acting and *thinking* like civilian defense officials, for example, in Ukraine.[49] Even ministers of defense often are retired or even active General Officers (e.g., as late as 2016, Colonel General Zakir Hasanov, minister of defense of Azerbaijan).[50] But this should not be a surprise given that there is no tradition for civilian defense officials in non-Yugoslav communist defense institutions. However, as the result of this lack of civilian defense expertise, there is an observable lack of knowledge within the entire defense institution of *defense* (vice military) as an essential subject. In its absence, a *military* framework continues to be applied, by default, to defining and solving institutional challenges. A manifestation of this approach is the widespread utilization of the concept of highly prescriptive *daktrina*, vice interpretative policy. Thus, the absence of an understanding of the essential role which must be played by *defense* based on policy that is felt throughout the entire institution inhibits its more creative and efficient operation. For example, as will be discussed *infra*, the armed forces of these countries continue to define requirements in terms of "systems" and "platforms," and have been largely incapable of making the conceptual leap to adopt "capabilities," let alone within a joint setting, and accepting the essential collaborative and integrative approach needed for their effective management. A key reason for this is that the concept of force development is overseen in most Western countries by defense civilians whose task it is to act as honest brokers to balance effectiveness with efficiency remains to be adopted. That said, Georgia is an exception to these general observations, for despite some weaknesses, its ministry of defense has many of the basic attributes of their Western counterparts (i.e., defense civilians and copious public policy documents).

If the most basic concepts needed to enable a policy framework of governance remain unadopted, it should come as no surprise that basic Western nations' force planning, management, and oversight concepts are all but nonexistent. One generally finds rigid organizational hierarchies whereby even where there are civilian defense officials in a ministry, they are more generally than not limited to administrative functions and excluded from effectively *leading* national defense (for example, in Ukraine). As such, it is not unusual to find civilian officials resorting to acts of negative control through the centralization of decision-making since there are so few effective and collaborative management tools that they control. This is often expressed in legislation or formally published in ministerial or even presidential decrees. In the extreme case of Ukraine, a very useful effort led by John Colston, Philipp Fluri, and Sergei Piroshkov produced an index of security- and defense-related constitutional provisions, laws, and regulations that is over *900* printed pages.[51] This is clearly a recipe for dysfunctionality as so vividly manifested in the response by the ministry of defense and Ukrainian armed forces following the 2014 Russian invasion of Crimea and in its ongoing conflict in the east of the country.

Defense planning techniques

It is not an exaggeration to posit that these defense institutions were established without any notion of the need to create basic defense planning tools. Table 4.2 represents this author's assessment of the state of the development of basic defense planning tools in former Soviet republics. What this table shows, as will be replicated in similar analyses of the other two sets of countries studied in this work, is twofold. First, the general observation stated early that the further east in the former Soviet Union, defense institutions and practices are less reformed is highly nuanced. But how Betz can claim that the descendants of the Red Army benefited from possessing a large cadre of officers schooled in strategic planning (in comparison with their Warsaw Pact counterparts) simply does not ring true. All one has to do is examine the long record of failed attempts at drafting defense plans in this grouping of countries, or better

Table 4.2 State of Development and Utilization of Defense Planning Tools: Former Soviet Republics

	Baltic States	Armenia	Azerbaijan	Georgia	Moldova	Ukraine
Contingency planning guidance	NATO	Extant*	Extant*	Extant*	Extant*	Extant*
Cost models	Extant	In transition	In transition	Extant (but weakly linked to policy)	Extant (but weakly linked to policy)	Extant (but weakly linked to policy)
Operational planning analysis	In transition	Unknown	Legacy/in transition	In transition	In transition	Legacy
Force management	In transition/extant	Legacy	Legacy	In transition	Legacy	Legacy
Capability trade-off analysis	Extant	Unknown	In transition	In transition	Extant (but weakly linked to policy)	Legacy
Roles/missions	Extant	Unknown	In transition	In transition	In transition	In transition
Budget execution system	Extant (but weakly linked to policy)	In transition	"Opaque"	Extant (but weakly linked to policy)	Extant (but weakly linked to policy)	Extant (but weakly linked to policy)

*These countries have recently been at war, or remain in a state of conflict, or feel sufficiently threatened, thereby making it safe to assume that their defense institutions have generated war plans. In the case of Georgia, the existence of its contingency plans is publicly acknowledged.

yet, point to a plan that was *both* viable and implemented.[52] In fact, it is arguable that the country with the "best" record in drafting defense plans, outside of the Baltics, is Georgia which has the fewest Soviet legacy traces in its defense institution. In fact, notwithstanding its inability to achieve a coherent policy framework, Georgia is not far behind the Baltic States when assessed in terms of adopting and using effectively Western-sourced defense planning tools. It also has the "advantage" in that after its 2008 war with Russia, it has officially transitioned to a threat-based planning methodology, which is easier to implement and assess, vice using nuanced capabilities-based planning methods.[53] Yet notwithstanding the publication of every possible existing Western type of defense policy and planning document, as well as using PPBS, weaknesses remain. A recent essay argued that the ministry of defense was still experiencing difficulty developing and executing long-term planning and resource management.[54] Second, an observation which will be discussed to a much greater extent in Chapter 7, a close review of the seven basic defense planning tools reveals that they must be highly integrated to produce planning coherence. Thus, one cannot conduct policy relevant capability trade-off analysis absent access to an accurate costing database, as well as using the results of operational planning analysis, in order to produce accurate, data-based, and costed capability gaps.

The fact that a number of these countries have some of the basic tools but are incapable of producing the necessary analysis to support informed defense planning should be seen, in part, as a failure on the part of Western advice and assistance programs. Generally speaking, they have tended to address these subjects *individually* and have not recognized the need for advice to integrate these disparate processes and analytical outputs to produce viable processes. An example of this is the policy disconnect with finances that existed in Ukraine under the reformist government of Viktor Yushchenko undertaken by the Western-leaning Minister of Defense Anatoliy Grytsenko. The government produced a number of ambitious policy documents that envisaged structural redirection and new investments to create new capabilities,[55] to wit the decision to professionalize the armed forces, but this was obviously not costed as it was later admitted by the government that the costs of this reform over a period of two-and-a-half years constituted the equivalent of the entire defense budget allocated for 2006.[56] This initiative, as is the case with other reforms, was never fully realized due to such impediments to reform as the lack of costing the current force, let alone ascertaining the costs of needed reforms, a problem replicated in the development of the State Program on the Armed Forces Development, which until 2005 was not even coordinated with the ministry of finance, let alone fully costed.[57] The results of this underdeveloped defense planning and analytical processes range from a complete inability to implement approved defense plans to weak management systems where resource decision-making is arbitrary, disaggregated, and ineffectual.[58]

All of the countries in this typology, to varying degrees, have introduced, adapted, or simply taken on in name-only a programming method (i.e., the PPBS); Azerbaijan is the sole exception. Although its defense budget is pubic information, how it allocates spending within the budget is a mystery, both externally and likely internally to many defense officials.[59] Or, as one study described with ironic understatement, "given the long history of corruption within the Defence Ministry, where and how the money is spent gains more significance than the increase in total military spending."[60] Even a Member of Parliament who sits on the defense committee complained that legislators have no visibility over the defense budget.[61] Notwithstanding this general opacity in resource management, to the defense institution's credit, brigade and corps commanders possess budgets to cover operations and maintenance costs. But the degree to which defense policy remains underdeveloped can be observed in its efforts to conduct a strategic defense review (SDR). Albeit initiated in 2008, and there are reports that it is in draft, it has yet to be approved and its recommendations implemented.

The Baltic States have largely embraced programming,[62] but have yet to link effectively policy to execution and as a result, suffer from the centralization of financial decision-making, vice delegating budgetary authority to capability providers (i.e., service chiefs). In the case of Lithuania, making chances to established plans must filter up through various boards for final approval by the minister: the only individual designated within its Ministry of National Defense who can change spending priorities and plans. An important major exception to this observation is found in the case of Latvia where commanders *do* have operating budgets to cover consumables which come under their control. Nonetheless, NATO officials have observed that none of three states has been able to establish jointly derived sustainable planning priorities.[63] As regards Lithuania,

> A senior Lithuanian defence official described the current state of defence reform in Lithuania as "tragic." According to him, the problem is that Lithuania has always based defence plans on a pipedream of 2% defence spending. As a result, spending on personnel is approaching 70% of the defence budget.[64]

It is an indication of the weakness of the Lithuanian defense planning system that in 2007 the minister of national defense established the policy that no more than 50 percent of the budget should be spent on personnel costs.[65] The issue of the challenges that have long faced the Baltic States to be able to develop costed defense plans has become more pressing following the 2007 financial crisis and ensuing global recession, both of which hit the economies of these countries particularly hard. In the case of Estonia, the defense budget was cut by 38 percent in the 2010–2011 financial year. As a result of diminished defense budgets, countries have adopted ten-year long-term development plans, as opposed the previous norm of five-year plans. For instance, the Estonian Ministry of Defense developed the National Defence Development Plan, 2013–2022.[66] The National Audit Office assessed the plan; and while lengthy, the key negative findings of its report need to be cited in full as they represent a revealing view of the state of underdevelopment in defense planning and budgeting, which must be balanced by the perception among some Western officials that Estonia is managing its defense institution rather well:

- Acting for the purpose of attaining the desired defence capacity has not been systematically managed.
- There were no realistic long-term goals, agreed priorities, or approved long-term procurement plans for planning and procuring material resources.

- The Minister of Defence and the Commander of the Defence Forces did not have an up-to-date overview of the situation of wartime units for a long period of time.
- The Defence Forces are unaware of the extent of the civil resources they can count on.[67]

That such basic policy and planning issues could go unaddressed or assumed away in such an important plan that is envisaged to direct the development of the armed forces for *ten years*, in a frontline NATO state no less, is disturbing. That the ministry of defense, in large part, agreed and accepted the report's recommendations is reassuring. But from a wider Western perspective, the report should have raised eyebrows in old NATO nations' capitals and caused no small degree of consternation and reassessment of their expectations of Estonia. It should also open questions within NATO as to the utility of developing plans that reach so far into the future. Even Soviet planners were sufficiently modest to limit their unrealizable plans to only five years.

The Ukrainian Ministry of Defense introduced planning and budget reforms in 2000 to initiate program-budgeting in order to transition from simple budget-execution to producing planned outcomes. In turn, the general staff developed its own planning management software (*Resource*) in 2005[68] to calculate costings and guide program budgeting. Be that as it may, there is no evidence that this data has ever been systematically used to inform decision-making. In reality, *Resource* is more akin to force management software, vice being capable of supporting national-level defense planning.[69] The repetitive failure to produce a viable five-year State Program on the Development of the Armed Forces that survives its first year is a clear manifestation of the inability of the defense institution to tie priorities to planning execution. For example, for the 2006–2010 version of this plan, the financial shortfall between what was anticipated, as opposed to what was allocated by the Ukrainian Parliament, was a startling 25 percent. With a small amount of understatement, a Ukrainian officer wrote, "We can say that until now in Ukraine we have not had a clear solution on how to optimize the cost of defense, how to allocate resources via rational planning, and finally, how to improve overall efficiency."[70] This observation can only be underscored by the fact that in 2010, some 87 percent of the defense budget was allocated to personnel costs.[71]

The Ukrainian case can be further explained by understanding how "money" is conceptualized by most legacy defense institutions and officials. In essence, money as a concept is not perceived by the military, or even by many civilian defense officials, as constituting a key management tool. Money, rather, is just "there": to pay salaries and more is always needed in order to *create* military forces. As a result of this misunderstanding, spending never changes to adapt to new policy or priorities, and so plans are never developed with the view to create options. They are all based on the assumption that more money will be provided to realize the plan. In consequence, plans are never realized because they are not linked to money and because there is never enough money, no one is responsible for planning failures. Proper defense governance is further inhibited by the long-standing and rarely challenged assumption that State Program Laws will be fully funded in future years. The fact that they never have been leads officials to conclude that defense is underfunded (after all as the

State Program *is* established in law) and not that there is a need to reassess planning priorities and assumptions.

Proper financial management is challenged by the fact that there are a number of software systems (e.g., *Resource, Parus,* and *Ruslo*), which have never been fully integrated, and thus are incapable of supporting dynamic planning and management. A further complication is that the financial program structure is changed almost annually, likely due to the inability, to date, of the ministry of defense to align defense's forty-six planning tasks with its seven budgetary programs. Most critically, armed service commanders are not designated as program managers and therefore have no authority to change where money is spent within their commands in order to create military capability. Finally, cash flow is unpredictable. The Special Fund (from the sale of defense assets) supports activities that have become autonomous of the direction and requirements of the armed forces, for example, education and medical, and frankly enables corrupt practices. Toward the end of the year, the United Treasury Account is perennially depleted and there is barely enough money to pay even personnel costs. Any mal-alignment of budget and defense programs cannot be quickly adjusted as the law precludes a transfer of funds among budget programs. Approval for transfers among budget programs must have the approval from the Cabinet of Ministers, which can take from two to three months. And, experience has demonstrated that it is almost impossible to shift funds between operations/maintenance and capital expenditures. Although the above describes the Ukrainian defense institution, its weaknesses and rigidities can be found in most, if not all, of legacy defense institutions.[72]

For instance, in 1998 Georgia introduced PPBS and its experiences provides an excellent case of how modern methods were simply grafted onto Soviet legacy financial procedures to produce added layers of unwanted opacity.[73] Even after the initial Georgian PPBS was "reformed" with Dutch assistance in 2006–2007,[74] which included creating a financial management system that was based on a four-year planning and budgeting cycle, it has been consistently ignored when Georgian defense officials have prepared budgets, *a full fifteen years* after it was originally introduced.[75] As late as 2013, the defense planning and resource management system was officially acknowledged as *still* underdeveloped due to the immaturity of the defense system.[76] On a lighter note, David Darchiashvili claims that while the first time the Georgian Ministry of Defense produced a defense budget using PPBS, it was disaster; however, it was an improvement over the previous year's budgetary submission which consisted of a two-page document![77] That all said, the optimistic view of one American expert that the introduction of PPBS in Georgia would lead to great transparency and efficiency has proven to be nonsense.[78]

Finally, the Moldovan Ministry of Defense claims to use programming, but on investigation, the system's budget barely keeps the organization on financial life-support. The 2002 "Concept of the Military Reform" was envisaged to span a twelve-year period, yet it was obviously not costed as little in the way of its planned reforms have been implemented due to the lack of funds.[79] But to the defense institution's credit, it has been able to create some basic cost models and employed both elementary operational planning and capability trade-off analyses in a defense review it completed in 2012, but which has never been published. Interestingly, prior to claiming to introduce programming in the reformed Armenian Ministry of Defense, defense officials claimed to follow a form of this method and prioritized requirements within mid-term program sets. This is an interesting and uncompelling assertion given that when this claim was made, the ministry of defense was still in the early stages of creating a defense planning cell, as agreed in its 2006 IPAP.[80]

In sum, in these countries, to varying degrees, it would be incorrect to state that their planning process is budget-driven, but rather they are simply passively resource-directed. Whatever resources made available by the state or foreign donors are used not to meet policy objectives, but rather to maintain legacy structures, even if only to keep them on life support. If policy is underdeveloped in most of these countries, then civilian oversight of defense institutions can only be weak. The prevailing Soviet norm that defense expertise is solely within the professional responsibilities of the officer corps remains in place in Ukraine, Moldova, Azerbaijan, and Armenia (albeit the latter has been developing civilian defense experts). Moreover, political oversight of the defense institution suffers from a lack of properly balanced power-sharing arrangements among the elected government, parliament, and the president. In the case of Georgia, Darchiashvili relates,

> Article 98 of the Georgian Constitution mandated that the structure of the armed forces be defined by the president, but that its size be set by the Parliament. As a result, if the president and the Parliament disagreed over the composition of the army, there was no easy resolution. Nor did it make sense that the president was supposed to structure the forces, but with no assurance that the Parliament would supply the men and arms that would be needed.[81]

National-level command

Typically, if not exclusively, presidents in these states enjoy enormous semi-powers, vis-à-vis their parliaments. Given both the enhanced status of presidencies (i.e., semi-presidentialism) in these countries and generally weak ministers of defense (not to mention prime ministers, Azerbaijan being an example where ministers are only accountable to the president),[82] it should not be surprising that exercising effective command of the armed forces, as defined by Western concepts, is challenging at best. It is a prevailing norm in all of these countries that the president (as head of state) is the commander-in-chief of the armed forces, and which also envisages a differentiated command structure in peace and war. As to the former point, the rationale for this universal model being adopted in post-Soviet republics (Baltic States excepted) in the immediate aftermath of the end of the Soviet Union there was a widespread (and perhaps justifiable) fear that elected governments could not be trusted and would use the armed forces as instruments of political repression. In many countries, it is the president who either appoints or must approve senior officer promotions and appointments, to include in some cases, the CHOD. For instance, while in Ukraine the *Verkhovna Rada* (parliament) appoints the minister of defense, in reality, that official has very little visibility over the expenditures of the ministry of defense. Indeed, the

Verkhovna Rada's laws have little real influence over how defense money is spent in the ministry. As a result, the roles of the prime minister (as head of government) and the minister of defense suffer from ambiguous authorities over the management, as well as command, of the armed forces. In fact the Cabinet of Ministers is not accountable to parliament, but rather to the president, as commander-in-chief, and the presidential administration is only accountable to the president. Moreover, the president, with or without the agreement of the minister of defense, appoints senior officers, to include the CHOD.[83] As seen in fighting with separatists in Eastern Ukraine, the president gives orders directly to the CHOD bypassing the minister of defense. Effective oversight of the defense institution by the *Verkhovna Rada* is further impeded by the lack of experts supporting members who sit on its Standing Commission on Security and Defense.[84] In Armenia, with the exception of declaring war, the National Assembly has *no* constitution role in defense, nor does the prime minister, while the minister of defense plays a dominant role in defense decision-making.[85] In Moldova, the prime minister is not even a member of the *Supreme Commandment*, which includes the president, minister of defense, chief of the general staff, and the commanders of the border guards and carabineer troops.[86]

Thus it is not unusual to see, twenty-five-plus years after the fall of communism, defense acts that outlined command arrangements are still based on Soviet concepts with a preference for the establishment of command structures only in crisis and based on the premise of mobilization. These laws lack conceptual understanding of the Western approach to command that stresses unity of command, *one* command structure in peace, tension, crisis and war, and clearly defined command authorities assigned to commanders. Not only were these legacy arrangements unworkable in wartime (a review of the dysfunctional Georgian command structure as seen in its 2008 war with Russia makes this case rather conclusively),[87] they have led to unending domestic political conflicts. Typically, one can characterize such arrangements as investing general and undefined "command" in the president, while enabling him to bypass the prime minister and even the minister of defense and issue orders directly to the CHOD.

It is important to note that all former Soviet republics analyzed in this section suffer from these dangerous arrangements and ineffectual structures, except the Baltic States. The drafters of the Estonian constitution after independence opted for the pre-1940 practice of assigning the president as commander-in-chief who appoints the wartime commander. Left out of this legal calculus was the fact that the elected government had no explicitly stated role in the command of the Estonian Defense Force. To their credit, Estonian politicians and officials came to realize that this was an untenable situation and changed the legislation in 2008 in the Defense Forces Organization Act,[88] whereby there is now no ambiguity that the armed forces fall under the minister of defense and ending a period of unbalanced civil-military relations.[89] At the same time, Estonia adheres to a troubling practice of possessing two distinct national command systems: one for crisis management under the ministry of internal affairs and a wartime system other under the ministry of defense, thereby obviating against the objective of maintaining unity of command during escalation and war.[90] Similarly in Latvia, the Constitution of 1922 was reinstituted following independence, which established the president as commander-in-chief, who would appoint a wartime commander when circumstances so dictated; yet perplexingly, said commander-in-chief and his authorities were left undefined.[91] The 1993 Law on Defense Forces wisely placed the commander of the armed forces under the authority of the Supreme Council *and* the minister of defense. Presciently, Latvian officials recognized early on the need for there to be only one command structure in peace, tension, crisis, and war. In order to ensure that there was continuity of parliamentary control of the armed forces, a politically appointed parliamentary secretary was created in 2000. This law also defines the authorities of the commander of the National Armed Forces and subordinates him to the minister of defense. Subsequent struggles have continued in the political realm to diminish the power of the president in favor of the prime minister in the area of defense.[92]

Lithuanian practice mimics other legacy practices with a twist, where the president is still designated as commander-in-chief and appoints the commander of the armed forces, but this decision must be approved by the parliament. The administration of the armed forces is left to the government, but its precise role in directing the commander is not stated. The 1996 Law on the Basics of National Security subordinated the commander of the armed forces to the minister of defense in peacetime. The commander is also a full member of the State Defense Council which perforce includes him in foreign and *domestic* policy matters. At least there is no ambiguity in law that the government would conceivably appoint another individual to this post in wartime.[93] Yet, although the commander is under the president and the minister of defense, the role of the prime minister is left undefined. As the president and the minister of defense are designated with the unique American nomenclature "national command authority," one can see the ill-informed hand of US-inspired advice, which has been improperly applied because the prime minister has been left *out* of the national chain of command.[94]

Military decision-making process

The Baltic States constituting an exception, MDMP remains very much based on legacy practices and norms. In the case of the Baltic States, delegated command has been supported by adopting various Western training concepts, creating territorial defense forces, and by their heavy involvement in overseas deployments within larger Western armies. In the case of Lithuania, for instance, between 1994 and 2014, approximately 5,000 soldiers had been on operations with allied armed forces.[95] As for other armed forces, there is no MDMP as one in a Western armed force would recognize, which is logical given the continued wide spread use of conscription. There is, however, one general exception. One can observe MDMP being used in a number of countries that have dedicated peacekeeping units which have been heavily trained by Western armies to ensure that they adhere to UN peacekeeping standards, as well as general NATO concepts whence they are deployed on such operations. The perhaps maddening practice on the part of these armed forces is that they will maintain such formations in all but complete conceptual isolation from the rest of the services, to include limiting personnel transfers to other units.[96] One interesting exception to this observation has been the training that the United States has financed and managed at the Ukrainian Army's Officer School in Yavoriv where, as an element of peacekeeping training, all young officers have been exposed to the principles of Western MDMP. However, in the short term, without an integrated approach to introducing MDMP, that is, providing sufficient numbers of educated, trained, and experienced junior and field-grade officers to tactical formations, it is unrealistic to assume that the formations of these armed forces can, with legacy tables of organization and equipment, produce consistently accurate and complete Estimates to inform course-of-action development. For example, one Azerbaijan defense expert claims that the Azerbaijan Army has implemented NATO standards for command and control within army units up to the Corps level. To be more precise, what has slowly been introduced is the concept of MDMP through an intensive training program undertaken by the Turkish armed forces which has had no small effect on the operational orientation of the army.[97] In short, one can be quite sure that an armed force has adopted MDMP when the human resource management, PME, and training systems have been transformed and re-structured to support the ensuing need to change personnel requirements to fit this model. For without a significant change in HRM policies, PME content, and training methods, there simply are not sufficient numbers of properly trained officers in tactical- and operational-level formations to undertake delegated command and proper staff roles.

Conversely, even if tactical formations were capable of undertaking MDMP it is unlikely that leaders at the operational- and strategic-levels would have any idea of what their role should be. In effect, legacy defense institutions see all tactical- and some operational-level military formations as solely executing, and not as thinking, organizations, still based on the overarching Soviet concept of iron discipline. Thus, there is little demand in general staffs for objectively determined operational planning analytical data that establishes what the force is capable, and incapable, of accomplishing. (One exception to this rule is that Moldova did produce such an analysis in its unpublished 2012 defense review.) In consequence, the atavistic concept of training to time, and not to standards, remains the prevailing training management philosophy.

Concept of operation

There is little written on how operations are conceived to take place by these armed forces, nor surprisingly are discussions with defense and military officials very informative. As none of these states enjoy secure, unchallenged borders among themselves or are in conflict or in fear of conflict, one can assume that a threat-based approach directs most training and operation plans. Indeed, in one of its policy declarations, in 2010, Azerbaijan flatly declared that any state's recognition of the Armenian occupation of Nagorno-Karabakh would be considered as an act directed at Azerbaijan. Yet in keeping with its tradition of being one of the least transparent institutions in the government,[98] the actual policy document which purportedly made this pronouncement was apparently never made public.[99] What is also clear is that force structure, systems, and training philosophy will greatly influence how an armed force will conduct operations. Of the countries assessed in this section, with the exception of the Baltic States, all of the others largely continue to possess overwhelmingly Soviet-sourced platforms and weapon systems; and as such, one can assume that legacy operational concepts will strongly influence operations, as the recent record of Ukraine demonstrates.[100] The sole exception to this observation is training for peacekeeping and peace-enforcement operations. One can speculate that the dominant influence on the development of concepts of operations will change only when there is full institutionalization of a Western style of MDMP whereby tactical-level formations are organized to act as thinking organizations. At that point, the utility of the concept of a directed and centralized operational planning process could become problematic.

Logistic support

In the Soviet system of "push" logistics, all key elements of communist ideology were merged into one system that produced a perfection of symbiosis and coherence. The ideology of industrial manufacturing and its emphasis on quantity, at the expense of quality, obsession with inputs and ignorance of outputs (let alone outcomes), and centralized control and the assumption of omnipotence at the top, all combined to provide the Soviet Red Army with a massive logistics structure. Not surprisingly, conceptual *elements* of this system remain present in legacy systems in these countries, including the Baltic States. As such, they are highly inefficient and incapable of supplying a force efficiently, particularly outside of their prescribed operational plans. The centralized development of such a plan would create supply tables to be automatically executed in support of the operational plan, that is, a "push" logistics system. Indeed, logistics is possibly the wrong term to be used in this context as in keeping with their Soviet legacy this is seen largely as supply and purchasing needed items (e.g., Armenia).[101]

Incomprehensible to the Western military mind is how support is envisaged to be distributed, and whether it is what commanders need is not part of this legacy concept. In other words, all elements of national support to the armed forces would be managed within the Soviet concept of Military Economic Science, where logistics requirements are centrally planned and administered, as opposed to being crafted at the tactical level. Perhaps it is due to the fact that logistics consists of property, processes, laws, regulations, and finances that it has been extremely resistant to reform. This observation is made notwithstanding expert claims (in the case of Azerbaijan) that "logistics are now on par to the standards promoted by NATO in various action plans that Azerbaijan has implemented."[102] This is clearly a problematic assertion as if these complex Western concepts could be so quickly implemented.

In the Baltic States, the adoption of Western logistics concepts has proceeded, particularly in light of alliance membership;[103] however, there apparently remain vestiges of legacy "push" concepts in the context of some national defense thinking. In a positive light, while on operations, the concept of "pull" logistics has become *de rigueur* when these forces are integrated into NATO nations' formations, and as a result, tactical formations possess the requisite S-4 section to plan supply and support requirements. These must be judged as constituting no small achievements. Yet, notwithstanding being members of NATO, there remains strong support for a *fixed* territorial defense orientation. In this particular model, units' mission sets perforce can be severely limited and tied to a fixed territorial location. Therefore, an element of "push" logistics can make sense given the restricted envisaged geographic area of operation and limited tasks to be performed. However, what is lost in the larger context of other post-Soviet republics is the inherent inefficiencies of continuing to use legacy supply assumptions and tables in an era when it is very unlikely that any of these countries will employ mass operational concepts on the modern battlefield. In light of such a change in operational orientation, it only makes sense to move toward adopting the "pull" concept which would also create efficiencies.

A detailed and illuminating case of the challenges facing these defense institutions when addressing the reform of logistics is provided by Ukraine. Prior to the 2010 change in government, reforming logistics was a priority in the State Program on the Development of the Ukrainian Armed Forces during 2006–2011 which envisaged the establishment of a single, *coherent* support system to improve flexibility of providing support to operational units.[104] This was to be achieved through the reform of the "Rear Area Services," making it more responsive to the needs of commanders. The government of Viktor Yanukovych quickly ended these initiatives upon taking power and directed there would be a centralized depot in each of the countries' *oblasts* (regions) of which regional government had financial obligations for, as well as claims on assets, all as part of a move to adopt a territorial defense orientation, but one facing *Westward*.[105] Yet, the crucial missing factor has long been the lack of any central military organization to manage the supply and distribution of supplies to units. In consequence, the conflict in Eastern Ukraine has demonstrated the inability of the defense institution to organize the effective supply of needed stores to deployed units. The supply system remains based on requisitions, made in writing, which are reviewed by the general staff and distributed to various depots located throughout the country, which are not linked by a common software management system.[106] Unity of effort was obviously not facilitated by the introduction of some Western reform concepts while still keeping key legacy organizations. For instance, the Directorates of the Armament of the Armed Forces and the Logistics of the Armed Forces are under the ministry of defense. Conversely, the Main Directorate of Operational Support of the Armed Forces resides in the General Staff.[107] It is little wonder, then, that Volunteers and NGOs have been critical in providing needed supplies to Ukrainian forces fighting in Eastern Ukraine.[108]

The Ukrainian case should constitute sober reading for officials in the region attempting to reform their own logistics structures of the dangers of mixing concepts and producing "conceptual spaghetti," not to mention overcoming prevailing institutional cultural norms. If one accepts the rationale for adopting a "pull" logistics system is compelling from the perspective of operational effectiveness and financial efficiencies, the decentralization of authority needed to enable such a transformation of logistics' concepts to those brought up in a legacy environment is intimidating. This may well explain why this has not been achieved to date. The presence of high power distance will struggle with the ambition to enable tactical formations and junior officers and NCOs to determine requirements. Fundamentally, for a "pull" logistics system to work, commanders need to be empowered to undertake tactical and operational planning. As an element of operational planning as practiced by Western armed forces, there must be an organic tactical capability to support the operational planning process by producing a logistics Estimate. This requires educated and trained logisticians commanding logistics' units and on the staff at all levels. This is a huge challenge for these countries. Given the fact that tactical formations in post-Soviet armed forces largely do not have "staffs," as they are expected solely to execute and not to think, there are insufficient numbers of officers or NCOs trained to develop Estimates. Equally challenging is the fact that many defense institutions conflate logistics and acquisition and these directorates are located in ministries of defense. Therefore, they do not have logistical responsibilities addressed via integrated planning even in the general staff. In other words, there is no tradition of a G-4 directorate. It is probably safe to assume that the reform of logistics structures will be one of the last elements of the defense institution to reform in these republics.

Professionalism

The record of success of achieving professionalism in these countries is mixed. Only in one of the Baltic States (i.e., Latvia) does one find professional armed forces, whereas conscription has remained the model in the region, albeit with Azerbaijan moving to a combined manning model. In light of Russia's muscular foreign policy, Lithuania in 2015 reintroduced conscription after having introduced a professional force model in 2008.[109] Reasons for keeping conscription vary, but in the context of Azerbaijan, the head of an NGO suggested that a professional force could be a threat to the regime as professional soldiers would demand better treatment, insist on enjoying all of their legal rights, and constitute a threat to corruption.[110] Even a country as Western-oriented and reform-minded as Georgia has been plagued with accusations of corruption due to a lack of institutional transparency regarding HRM policy, compensating personnel, and adhering to the principle of equality.[111] The definition and management of "professionalism" is essentially still largely within the purview of commissioned officers; ergo, legacy norms remain dominant in these armed forces. To be sure, there have been efforts, on paper, to redefine the status and obligations of the officer corps, and in some instances, stalled efforts to move away from conscription, for example, Ukraine and Georgia.[112] However, these efforts have remained on paper with the explanation that the lack of resources has impeded implementation (Moldova providing an example of this).[113] That said, one has seen in the twenty-five years since independence efforts made to introduce the Western concept of professional NCOs with the expectation that they will lower costs and improve operational performance. Where this has occurred, for example, in Ukraine, there has been a general lack of appreciation of the difficulties of adopting this concept. Probably most troubling has been the practice by Western governments to encourage these defense institutions to introduce the concept of professional NCOs into their structures (often supported with ambitious external technical assistance programs), with little or no thought given to the *policy* implications of such reforms. Surely, if an armed force introduces an initiative as ambitious as the creation of a professional NCO corps, there will be a need for fewer officers in future; and those remaining need to be retrained to distinguish between newly defined officer and NCOs' tasks, supported by delegation of authorities. Moreover, one would expect that the ministry of defense would require clear HRM policy and procedures to ensure the effective utilization of these highly trained and professional individuals. It is not clear that the introduction of NCO training in the Ukrainian armed forces included such important considerations, or whether they were made conditional. In consequence, it is difficult to be optimistic that these reforms will achieve their intended objectives.[114]

In one key area in which one can accurately state a universal truth, absent the Baltic States, the record of the reform of PME has been abysmal. There are numerous reasons for these poor outcomes. First and most obviously, legacy (e.g., Ukraine) and newly created institutions (e.g., Moldova) have been populated with those officers trained in the Soviet system. A visit to any of the educational institutions in these countries simply fails to convince that they are educating and training cadets with convincing intent, or competence, using Western concepts, although Turkish PME and training assistance in Azerbaijan arguably could be an exception. In lieu of critical thinking, leadership, and problem-solving, classrooms are largely set up to provide what in the West one would regard as NCO training. Moreover, what appears to have been missed, or ignored, by many Western officials is that military faculty members in these institutions are not cycled through so as to bring to the classroom the latest experiences from operations. Rather, instructors almost exclusively are assigned to these posts as a life time assignment; and in consequence, like any educational institution, the faculty claim academic privileges and are resistant to change. And, notwithstanding years of curriculum exchanges with their Western counterparts, they still are incapable or unwilling to teach such basic techniques as the Western style of military decision-making with any credibility since they had never had to do this in their professional careers. Given the lack of a functioning HRM system, as well as job protection laws, these faculty members continue to turn out young officers essentially weak in critical thinking, ignorant of the Western concepts that many of these countries are implementing piecemeal at the national level and leaving them ill-suited to be able to implement and execute them.

Conclusion

Post-Soviet republic armed forces, in the end, present an admixture of elements of remarkable reform and many legacy concepts indifferent to change. Yet the one common characteristic that they do share is that since their inception, all have been born into a process of *creation*, vice *reform*. Moreover, as they have endeavored to create themselves from the ashes of the Red Army, many remain mired in its inheritance of anti-democratic defense governance concepts. There is no question that the Baltic States' defense institutions, at one extreme, have been created whole cloth with a deliberate effort to exclude, *in extremis*, Red Army legacies. As such, they have unquestionably achieved the greatest progress in adopting Western democratic defense governance concepts. However, a troubling aspect is the persistence of the concept of *fixed* territorial defense concepts and assumptions (focusing on the sub-tactical) that were adopted after independence that now should be subject to review. The result of which is dedicating limited resources in assets that are unmovable targets, and as one respected think tank observed, runs the risk of procuring too many stand-alone capabilities and undermining cohesion with allies in crises.[115]

Ukraine presents a unique case given its size, and in the recent conflict with separatists in its east and the Russian Federation demonstrates a defense institution that has been starved of financial resources, remains unmodernized, and largely denuded of equipment and facilities often by corrupt means, but has still been able to engage in protracted combat operations. Yet, there is no better assessment of the dismal state of the Ukrainian armed forces than provided by Denisentsev:

> When Ukraine gained independence, it had the second most powerful armed forces in Europe after Russia, and the fourth most powerful in the world after the United States, Russia, and China. The degradation of the Ukrainian Armed Forces in the 22 years since the country's independence has been completely unprecedented in terms of its speed and scale. It is hard to find any other example in human history of such a strong and capable army of a large state deteriorating so rapidly—and during peacetime no less—and to the extent that it now hardly qualifies as a cohesive armed forces.[116]

The Moldovan defense institution has somehow managed to remain afloat in one of the poorest country in Europe. Although possessing a large percentage of personnel trained and educated in the West, it continues to struggle to implement the collective lessons from their individual experiences. In fact, Moldova is a sobering and important example of the limits of the use of piecemeal training and education in Western countries. As one US official observed to this author, legacy thinking has its own force of intellectual gravitational pull when Western influence is not constantly present. By this, officials' minds are pulled unconsciously back into a comfortably coherent world of communist thinking ruled by legacy concepts. Two Caucasus defense institutions, Armenia and Azerbaijan, are difficult to assess properly as they are remarkably opaque and each remain on a war-footing. For instance, a rather detailed public information paper of Armenia's defense review, which lasted from 2008 to 2011, did not release any information as to financial priorities, which one might have expected in such a document.[117] As both countries remain essentially in a state of war, this is not unusual. However, with what little public information is available concerning Armenia, it is clear that it is selective in reforming itself in accordance with some Western norms and practices. Georgia is in a class by itself. Due to the remarkable transparency in the country's defense governance, it is possible to gauge with a degree of confidence the extent and depth of reforms. As this chapter has demonstrated, the Georgian defense institution has undertaken a large number of reforms in many critical areas. That said, legacy gravity, or simply Georgian cultural norms of centralization, is still observable, which in itself should be troubling to its leadership. As it continues to employ legacy, as well as introducing Western democratic defense governance concepts, antithetical as they may be, officials risk not being able to produce envisaged defense outcomes as the basis of the organization's operating system struggles with these contradictory approaches. At a time of crisis, it could well create, as it did in 2008, unwanted "conceptual spaghetti" instead of coherent and lethal military force.

Former Warsaw Pact Republics' Defense Institutions

Unlike their former Soviet and JNA counterparts, the significant cultural, linguistic, historical, and geographic differences that exist among former Warsaw Pact countries make generalizations of their characteristics challenging. That said, Szemerkenyi succeeds in capturing their essence:

> The Warsaw Pact system inhibited pure military professionalism and pride as well as the military's political neutrality, and loyalty to the communist Party was a fundamental part of the military professional. Initially, the structure consisted of a web of incentives and disincentives, including material benefits, the possibility of social upward mobility, and promotions which largely depended on political loyalty. This system became less dominant by the mid-1980s as the military began to adopt characteristics of political neutrality and professionalism. While the officer corps remained nominally servile to Moscow, it gradually became more and more politically disinterested as military professionalism increased.[1]

There are a number of areas in which they share similar conceptual and organizational characteristics; however, their disparate national characteristics ensure that their defense institutions produced uniquely national armed forces. To be sure, they all experienced domination by Moscow and the Soviet General Staff, which endeavored to produce mirror images of the Red Army. However, their manifestations of subsequent weaknesses need to be controlled as they are reflected through these different national and institutional prisms. In one area, they do share one important characteristic: after 1991, their early strong support *ostensibly* to adopt Western democratic defense governance concepts. And, in this respect, it can be stated that all of them achieved the objectives identified by Cottey, Edmunds, and Forster of effecting successfully the first generational change in civil-military relations, that is, the subordination of the armed forces to constitutionally defined civilian control.[2] That said, they did have two distinctly different experiences of Western assistance to reform prior to accession to NATO. It was only *after* Poland, Hungary, and the Czech Republic were invited to join the alliance in July 1997 that it initiated a formal process to conduct detailed reviews "of the prospective new members' military needs, and agree military reforms and related timescales with them," that is, PARP.[3] Given that these three states were admitted to the alliance on March 12, 1999, there was, comparatively speaking, precious little time to make all the reforms necessary to adopt and implement Western democratic defense governance concepts. By contrast, those nations that joined the alliance on March 29, 2004 (i.e., the Slovak Republic, Romania, and Bulgaria[4]) had a longer experience with the involvement of the NATO International Staff, as well as receiving reform advice and assistance from allied nations. Thus, for over six years this second tranche of nations were exposed to a more mature review method established by the MAP process, whereby they were subjected to regular assessments. What must be assessed as vexing is that this additional time and scrutiny did not appear to have had any notable success in effecting deeper institutional reforms, albeit Romania constitutes a conditional exception. By any objective measure, the individual and collective experience of NATO nations providing advice to these desperately politically, if not bureaucratically, willing nations to join the West should have been more systematic and effective. In addition, experiences gained from assisting these defense institutions should have been collected and used to inform similar efforts in more challenging countries. Unfortunately, there is no evidence to suggest that any such bureaucratic and intellectual effort was ever undertaken.

Overview of defense institutions

Table 5.1 provides the author's judgment of the state of adoption of Western democratic defense governance concepts by of post-Warsaw Pact countries. It might come to be a surprise to many that, in general, despite being members of the alliance since 1999, Poland, the Czech Republic, and Hungary score rather modestly. For instance, Soukupova writes that the reform of the Czech armed forces has lagged behind other sectors of society and she claims it a truism that anything related to security is inevitably political.[5] Ostensibly, the most advanced would be Poland. The reason for Polish progress is multifold, but no small credit is due to the massive amount of external technical assistance given to the Polish armed forces from the United States, Germany, and Norway and a strong financial commitment by successive governments to spend money on national defense.[6] That all said, Corum is perhaps making an overstatement when he claims that the Polish Army is one of the largest and *best* trained.[7] But, the Polish armed forces has been exposed to extensive change. Critically, the Polish Army commanded Multinational Division Central-South in Iraq from September 2003 to October 2008, as well as deployed a brigade headquarters and forces to Afghanistan from 2010 to 2013. As a result of this, tens of thousands of officers, NCOs, and soldiers gained invaluable operational experience.[8] The United States transferred 2 FFGs frigates to the Polish Navy in 2000 and 2002, and the Polish Air Force has procured 48 F-16C/D Block 52 multi-role fighter aircraft. Germany has donated modernized former NVA MiG-29s, an entire brigade set of main battle tanks (Leopard 2A4) and supporting training packages, while Norway transferred 5 Kobben-class (Type 207) submarines. This constitutes the most extensive introduction of Western *capabilities* into a former communist armed force. The Polish case posits a critical question that is central to this work. It remains an open question: how best an armed force can transition from one

Table 5.1 Baseline of Defense Governance Concepts: Post-Warsaw Pact Republics

	Bulgaria	Czech Republic	Hungary	Poland	Romania	Slovakia
Policy framework	In transition	In transition	In transition	Extant (albeit via National Security Bureau)	In transition	In transition
National-level command	Legacy/in transition	In transition	Extant	In transition (but progressing)	In transition	In transition
Military decision-making process	Legacy/in transition	In transition	Extant on operations	Extant on operations/legacy in territorial defense	Extant on operations/legacy in territorial defense	Extant on operations/legacy in territorial defense
Concept of operations	NATO	NATO	NATO	NATO	NATO	NATO
Logistics	Legacy/in transition	Legacy/in transition	Legacy/in transition	In transition (albeit with strong territorial defense focus)	Legacy/in transition	Legacy/in transition
Professionalism	Legacy/in transition	In transition	In transition (advanced)	In transition (advanced)	In transition (advanced)	In transition

based on the concept of highly centralized command, where platforms and systems are tied to mass and surprise and do not allow tactical thinking, to one that is based on decentralized execution and employing the nuanced concept of *capabilities*. As will be shown, the Polish case *could* provide a compelling argument that the adoption of both new capabilities and ensuing requisite new training concepts (e.g., based on the concept of tasks, conditions, and standards, vice training to time) is likely to be one solution to making this hugely difficult transition. Clearly, given that the engineering of legacy platforms and systems ensures that individuals are allowed only to execute, attempting to employ new training and operational concepts using legacy equipment, perforce provides limited space for the adoption of basic Western operational approaches. Support for this position can only be surmised from the experience of the Bundeswehr following their experience of inheriting Soviet-designed and supplied equipment to the NVA following unification in 1990.[9]

However, this chapter will argue that the Polish case provides only ambivalent evidence that a technological shock alone can spur the rapid adoption of Western concepts given a weak policy framework in a defense institution. Evidence to support this assertion is found in the limited employment on operations of the FFG-7 frigates and the notorious challenges faced by the Polish Air Force in integrating F-16C/D Block 52 multi-role fighter aircraft into its existing fleet of aircraft. To the point, although introduced in 2006, these aircraft only became operational in 2012.[10] Moreover, the Polish Air Force, and evidently the defense institution, is obviously still struggling to understand how best to use this capability as witnessed by the fact that of the five deployments[11] by the Polish Air Force in support of the NATO Baltic Air Policing operation (as of 2016), not one of these has yet to be comprised of F-16s, but rather have been undertaken by its MiG-29s. Yet, both the Hungarian and Czech air forces have supported these missions with their JAS 39C Gripen multi-role fighter aircraft. Albeit a task force of Polish Air Force F-16s were deployed to Iraq in summer 2016, it is still troubling that it took ten years after their introduction before they undertook an operational deployment.[12] Polbielski makes the strong argument that Poland missed an important opportunity to address these key weaknesses in the armed forces when the country's 2006 Strategic Defense Review introduced a major modernization program acquiring Western platforms and systems. Missing from this policy decision was the inclusion of an overarching strategic plan of making them a catalyst for transformation. In addition to a long list of challenges (e.g., integrated military intelligence, HRM systems, integrated logistics, C4ISR systems), he notes that no financial resources were identified to address them.[13]

Perhaps another surprise is the relatively high marks for the Romanian defense institution. One respected academic writing in 2002 opined that "The armed forces are impoverished and demoralized; they are unlikely to be able to make a contribution to NATO in the foreseeable future."[14] This view, commonly shared at that time, was to be countered by consistently strong Romanian government support to NATO and US operations in Afghanistan and Iraq in the form of continuous deployments of infantry battalions and Special Operations Forces, and to include the deployment of a Mountain Brigade Headquarters to Afghanistan in 2010.[15] Another important factor is the fact that unlike some allies and partners, the Romanian Army (like the

Polish Army) systematically analyzed and *internalized* the lessons learned from their deployments, and such analyses were published and debated in professional military journals.[16] The nature and size of the deployed forces of these two countries led to much greater attention to, and assessment of, their operational performance. Both armies, in fact, deployed standing units, vice ad hoc task-organized formations, and subjected them collectively to the full four phases of deployment (i.e., activation, deployment, operations, and recovery). Adopting this principle of deploying formed-units has gone far to create a forcing mechanism to press for change in the way they are organized, equipped, trained, and indeed, *think*. Conversely, those armies that have deployed ad hoc task-organized units have lagged behind in systematic reform. For instance, Bulgaria deployed ad hoc units to Iraq and suffered losses,[17] but from 2011, its contributions to the International Security Force in Afghanistan (ISAF) were taken from standing formations.[18] Yet, as late as 2010, the Bulgarian Army still had not adopted a decentralized concept of training; and in consequence, its field exercises had strong legacy appearances. Finally, Slovakia is judged as underdeveloped in its defense institution, the causation of which, in part, can be traced to its creation out of the rump Czechoslovak armed forces. The lack of strong institutional management to drive the armed forces was documented in a US government report in 2000 that found that the army's combat readiness was virtually nil and that the army had conducted no combined arms training.[19] As will be discussed *infra*, these weaknesses have continued to persist, which have inhibited the creation of predictable defense outcomes.

Taken as a general grouping of defense institutions, none of them had any modern historical experience of being led by a cadre of civilian defense officials with unique expertise in "defense," vice military affairs. Ministries of defense, such as they existed, were largely responsible for acquisition and managing defense industry and had few, if any, similarities with their Western counterparts. Since independence, these institutions have been progressively staffed with civilians with expertise based on Western democratic defense governance concepts,[20] but many remain dominated by active or retired officers with little or no education, training, or experience in inherently civilian responsibilities and functions. A unique case in this grouping has been the creation of the Slovak Ministry of Defense from scratch, which has remained dominated for many years by retired officers.[21] These institutions, as a general observation, are still weak in effectively using civilian defense experts, as they lack the bureaucratic clout of their Western counterparts vis-à-vis the armed forces. One sees an overcentralization of the management of finances in ministries, thereby reinforcing the use of negative instruments of control, vice enabling actions to encourage the armed forces to develop and operate in accordance with policy-endorsed priorities. As a result, those ministries are still dominated by active and/or retired officers who struggle to understand, let alone accept the creation of a strong policy framework which enables and *expects* the interpretation of policy and guidance from the entire defense institution.

If one accepts this general assessment, then it is essential that reforming defense institutions emerging from communism needed to place a high priority on establishing a civilian-dominated ministry of defense run by defense experts: clearly a short-, medium- and long-term challenge given that these countries simply had neither such expertise, nor the educational institutions capable of training them. Indeed, effective personnel policies for civilian defense experts should be seen as constituting an essential element of civilian control of armed forces. As observed by a former defense minister, parliaments can pass the best and most far-reaching defense reform legislation, but absent a cadre of civilian defense officials with power of the purse, such reforms are unlikely to be realized.[22] Szemerkenyi makes the further insightful point that "Good personnel policy is critical for effective civilian control of the military.... However, without the necessary financial control this legal right remains purely theoretical." Moreover, without sufficient authorities and funds to pay near-market labor rates, these newly democratically elected governments will not be able to attract and keep quality personnel. It should be self-evident that given this unique expertise, concerted efforts need to be taken to recruit and retain these individuals.[23] Such a deliberate and carefully planned effort has not been widely followed in the region.

Poland presents an excellent documented case study of how such a process was poorly planned and executed. Gogolewska writes that in lieu of a carefully planned process of bringing civilian oversight to the ministry of defense, an unsystematic development program was instituted in which personnel postings were filled via a random process that took little consideration of individuals' expertise. This was further exacerbated by the centralization of decision-making by the minister of defense (the bureaucratic norm throughout the region) and the adoption of universal civil service regulations made applicable to the ministry of defense. Yet the Polish government made no provision for the unique expertise needed to function effectively within a civil-military environment within a ministry of defense. It also created a separate administration that had the effect of detaching civilian personnel policy from the structures in which these individuals were expected to function. These errors, according to Gogolewska, were compounded by creating qualification requirements which exceeded those of their military counterparts, but accorded these civilian officials with *lower* salaries and benefits. These conditions, to her mind, contributed to the slow development of an effective civilian defense cadre within the ministry of defense:

> Instead of a carefully planned civilianisation of the MoD there took place an unsystematic development of the non-military component of ministerial personnel. Recruitment did not follow any carefully devised plan with target figures of civilian employment; rather, it was a random pattern of openings (and sometimes closings) of civilian posts in various departments and officers of the MoD. In that process of tentative civilianization, apart from the general lack of political will, two other factors had an additional negative influence over the development of democratic civilian control of the military. There were the adoption of the "Minister Administers It All" model of the management and control of the MoD, and the introduction of universal civil service regulations for the ministry.[24]

Gogolewska further makes a strong argument that initial and subsequent legislation compounded this situation and created an unhealthy imbalance of power within the ministry of defense. A separate personnel administration was established for civilian defense officials; however, this was done with ambiguous sectors of responsibility that had the effect of detaching personnel policy from managerial oversight and individual performance.

The absence of a strong cadre of civilian defense officials, in consequence, has allowed many counterproductive legacy pathologies to continue to go unaddressed. Legacy concepts and assumptions were equally hard to replace, and many key debilitating practices and organizational templates remained in many of these defense institutions well after their entry into the alliance. One trait that all these defense institutions share is a continuation of the bureaucratic practice of overly centralizing decision-making, particularly apropos financial management. This practice, in itself, can normally be dismissed as producing ineffectual managerial oversight in any organization; however, in the case of these countries, the practice of budgetary micromanagement has continued within a framework that ensures that even the most routine and mundane decisions still require ministerial/CHOD approval. As an example, in the Bulgarian Ministry of Defense, every invoice, and even travel voucher, is now approved by the CHOD or the permanent under-secretary, whereas until recently, it was approved by either the minister of defense or a deputy minister: progress of sorts.

Given that these ministries of defense were essentially created from existing military headquarters, and often in some haste, many responsibilities and functions were left unresolved, and some of them are simply inappropriate in a democracy.[25] This is not to imply that these ministries will remain deterministically weak. Rather, the lack of clear institutional responsibilities and functions, on both the civilian and military side, has left both operating in a suboptimal fashion. This was an issue with which the Slovak Ministry of Defense and General Staff struggled following their formation in 1993 in two different geographic locations.[26] This situation was somewhat improved with their integration in Bratislava in the fall of 1999, but interministerial coordination remains a challenge.[27] As Maria Vlachova perceptively observed as regards the Czech Republic, organizational tasks delegated from the ministry of defense were not always supported both with the necessary legal authorities to enable their execution and with the necessary financial resources. It is little wonder that due to the lack of clarity in this critical area of basic organizational management that effective communication to facilitate, for example, consensus building has been impeded.[28]

Policy framework and conceptual coherence

As a result of these traditions and personnel conditions, it is little wonder that the development of a strong and overarching policy framework has been slow to emerge. After all, with only the slow introduction of civilian defense expertise, these ministries of defense have been dominated by field-grade and general officers for at least the first decade and a half after the end of the Warsaw Pact. A younger generation of civilian defense officials with expertise in defense policy is emerging; however, they remain at a disadvantage of trying to change existing concepts, assumptions, and logic in order to create a coherent policy framework. An example of the lack of a policy framework that creates policy *coherence* is vividly provided by the Czech Republic.[29] Albeit highly Westernized in many other facets of its society and economy, the Czech defense institution has struggled to develop a policy framework, and its record of producing a prodigious number of policy documents bespeaks a long-standing inability to develop any semblance of a consistent policy framework. This could be simply a manifestation of a larger problem perceptively identified by Betz that although formal structures have been changed to reflect Western democratic defense governance concepts, in reality, reforms have been largely cosmetic and rhetorical[30]—suggesting conceptual false cognates. Moreover, while some might assess the Czech case to be extreme by regional standards, upon a review of other defense institutions in the region, the Czech example is very much representative of the challenge of developing a policy framework in order to achieve policy coherence. Table 5.2 presents a list of no less than *24 policy pronouncements* produced by the Czech defense institution since 1995, a clear indictment of the inability of successive governments to create an effective policy framework and see policy priorities and objectives through to implementation. The inevitable result is policy *incoherence*. For example, as late as 2010, that year's Defense White Book continued to argue the need to deploy forces while maintaining the ability to defend national territory, without acknowledging that, since 1999, the latter is a collective defense task of NATO.[31]

What is all too often missing from assessments of policies and plans in all these legacy defense institutions is an obvious connection between policy and its central role in producing defense outcomes. Again, the Czech Republic provides a most damning example of how policy priorities are simply not executed in reality. A simple review of personnel data from 2013 (i.e., all ranks distributed across the armed forces) demonstrates the inability of this defense institution to organize the armed forces in the most basic, coherent manner. It is nothing short of scandalous that defense officials have countenanced a personnel structure that has almost three times as many officers as there are enlisted soldiers, not to mention the warrant and noncommissioned officer corps are equally bloated (see Table 5.3). Clearly there is no relationship between the quantity of policy documents and the ability of the defense institution to organize a properly balanced and sustainable force structure, a challenge that was identified for reform as far back as 1994 by the Czech minister of defense Vilem Holan.[32] That such a basic policy connection has failed in the particular case of the Czech Republic, one can only speculate as to the degree to which other policy disconnects remain to be discovered, let alone addressed both within this country and in others.

Indeed, if the mere concept of a policy framework is not well understood (or, perhaps, accepted) among these defense institutions, it is little wonder then that in many countries the concept of a policy hierarchy is enigmatic, reflecting the practice of conflating policy (which must be interpreted) with *daktrina* (that answers all questions of defense and is to be followed blindly). As such, it is not unusual to see policy documents which do not recognize, let alone complement, other, seemingly superior, documents. For instance, the widely encouraged, but highly ineffectual Western advice that countries should draft "national military strategies" documents are oftentimes developed completely devoid of higher policy guidance and priorities, let

Table 5.2 Czech Security and Defense Policy Incoherence[*]

Year	Strategic documents
1995	White Book on Defense
1997	National Defense Strategy
1997	Intended Concept of Development of Armed Forces of the Czech Republic till 2000, with foresight till 2005
1999	Military Strategy
1999	Security Strategy
2001	Security Strategy
2001	Doctrine of the Armed Forces of the Czech Republic
2002	Concept of Development of Professional Armed Forces of the Czech Republic and Mobilization of the Armed Forces of the Czech Republic
2002	Military Strategy
2003	Security Strategy
2003	New Concept of Development of Professional Armed Forces of the Czech Republic and Mobilization of the Armed Forces Reconfigured to New Resource Framework
2004	Doctrine of Armed Forces of the Czech Republic
2004	National Armaments Strategy
2004	Military Strategy
2006	Report on Defense Provision in the Czech Republic
2007	Defense Plan for the Czech Republic
2007	Transformation of the Defense Resort of the Czech Republic
2008	Long-Term Vision of the Resort of Ministry of Defense
2008	Principles of Defense of the Czech Republic 2030
2008	Military Strategy
2009	Defense Policy of Czechoslovakia and the Czech Republic between 1989 and 2009
2011	Security Strategy of the Czech Republic
2011	Defense White Book
2012	Defense Strategy of the Czech Republic (replaces Military Strategy of 2008)

[*]I am grateful to Dr Kristina Soukupova for documenting this series of policy statements and planning documents.

Table 5.3 Personnel Figures for the Armed Forces of the Czech Republic

Generals	Field grade officers	Junior officers	WOs	NCOs	Enlisted	Recruits	Unassigned	Total no. of soldiers
18	2,091	3,376	6,052	7,375	1,078	1,067	676	21,733

Source: "Personnel Size of the Defence Department in 1993–2013, Real numbers of persons in accordance with Czech Laws valid as of January 1, 2011 (observing the Czech Law No. 221/1999 Col., following updates made by the Czech Law No. 272/2009 Col.)," http://www.army.cz/scripts/detail.php?id=51638 (accessed May 22, 2016).

alone even addressing priorities. It is the rare case that any of these exogenous models address critically important issues (e.g., identify critical decision points in the policy and planning process and who decides where money is spent and personnel are distributed), thereby making their value meaningless.

An important managerial reform that has been slowly embraced in its entirety is the principle that leadership/command and management need to be separated if they are both to be accomplished effectively. This implies the creation and empowerment of civilian permanent secretaries/military directors of staff to run and *drive* the daily operations of their respective organizations. In the West these officials ensure staff coordination and that only the most critical and relevant policy issues are raised to the level of a minister, or the CHOD. Given that those early civilians brought into these newly civilianized ministries were almost exclusively retired military officers, these new civilian ministries quickly became overly centralized and strictly hierarchical, producing unnecessary delays in decision-making. And, whereas centralized decision-making may provide the illusion of control, in reality, it results in preventing ministers and CHODs from thinking of how best the defense institution should be oriented in future and pursue policy coherence.[33] In recent years some permanent secretaries have been appointed to ministries of defense, but not all of these officials have come from within the system organically (admittedly largely because the system has not been organized to grow them), and therefore are political nominees, or have been drawn from other ministries. At best, these individuals can only function as deputy, or assistant, ministers, which thereby makes them de facto members of the political team, and the practice then does not lend itself to solving the problem of dividing management from policy leadership.

On the military side of the house, some CHODs are still referred to as the first soldier (e.g., *Pierwszy Zolnierz* RP, in Poland) and all decisions, ostensibly, are made by him. Given that such a breadth of responsibilities would be all but impossible, particularly in large armed forces, the legacy practice of the appointment of numerous deputy CHODs remains a widespread weakness and impedes the proper management of these armed forces. For example, as late as 2012 the Polish CHOD was supported by three deputy CHODs, who conveniently were in effect representatives of the three services. The fact that the Polish armed forces have been unable to divide command from administration is remarkable in that this was one of the key reform objectives identified as early as 1992 by the Zabinski Commission.[34] Finally, confusingly the Czech Armed Forces has both a first deputy CHOD and a deputy CHOD/chief of staff.[35]

Defense planning techniques

The lack of extant, let alone strong, policy hierarchies has had widespread destructive implications in the development of planning processes of these defense institutions (*vide* Table 5.4.) Unique among all the typologies, as members of the alliance, all six of these countries should profit from being capable of largely relying on alliance contingency planning guidance as constituting clear inputs into their respective

Table 5.4 State of Development and Utilization of Defense Planning Tools: Post-Warsaw Pact Republics

	Bulgaria	Czech Republic	Hungary	Poland	Romania	Slovakia
Contingency planning guidance	NATO	NATO	NATO	NATO	NATO	NATO
Cost models	Extant (but weakly linked to policy)	Extant (but weakly connected to policy)	Extant (but weakly connected to planning)	Extant (but weakly connected to planning)	Extant (but weakly connected to policy)	Extant (but weakly connected to policy)
Operational planning analysis	In transition	In transition/extant	In transition/extant	In transition/extant	In transition/extant	In transition
Force management	Legacy	Legacy/in transition	In transition	In transition	In transition	Legacy
Capability trade-off analysis	In transition	In transition	In transition (but weakly linked to policy)	Extant (but weakly linked to policy)	Extant (but weakly linked to policy)	Extant (but weakly linked to policy)
Roles/missions	In transition	In transition	In transition	In transition/extant	In transition	In transition
Budget execution system	Extant (but not connected to policy)	Extant (but weakly connected to policy)	Extant (but weakly connected to policy)	Extant (but weakly connected to policy)	Extant (but weakly connected to policy)	Extant (but not connected to policy)

defense planning processes. There is also evidence that at least one country, Romania, prior to joining NATO (c. 2002) developed its own operations plans, according to a senior defense official.[36] Whether this has continued since gaining membership or if the practice is widespread is unknown. If used by defense officials as constituting planning inputs, this should be judged as constituting an important step in developing a disciplined and policy-supporting practice. That said, if one examines the performance of published defense plans, this linkage appears to be weak at best.

Moreover, one can detect cases where weak policy frameworks inhibit effective (and costed) defense planning. Most egregiously, a number of general staffs have mischievously developed their own development (transformational) planning documents. In some key cases, these have been created without any civilian policy oversight, let alone effective policy approval. One such case of civil-military policy discord was in Romania. In 2004, the ministry of national defense conducted a SDR to determine requirements and defense. The general staff, on its own authority in 2007, developed a "transformation strategy"[37] of the armed forces which essentially ignored the policy guidance in the 2004 review. In 2008, facing the prospect of diminished financial resources, the ministry of national defense proposed conducting another SDR, which the general staff opposed since it had its own transformation strategy. However, the transformation strategy was not a standard (routine) planning document. This document was drafted by the general staff in isolation and presented to the National Defense Council, chaired by the president, and bypassing the ministry of national defense. Disturbingly, it ignored the process and procedures established in the 2004 Law on Defense Planning.[38] Although the minister of national defense, as a member of the National Defense Council, agreed the strategy, the ministry had only two weeks to analyze it before the strategy was endorsed. Critically, the ministry of national defense never accepted all of the document's conclusions, a major point of contention being that the general staff did not *cost* the plan. Finally, in Bulgaria, a plan to restructure the armed forces (Plan 2004) contained a classified section which was not released during public debate, but elements of it were changed without the knowledge of the government as a result of bargaining between the ministry of defense and general staff.[39]

Due to the slow and uneven adoption of modern planning and execution concepts, defense planning can be considered to be one of the least developed competencies in these defense institutions. The causation for this lack of reform is largely twofold. First, the government of reforming countries simply had no idea of the magnitude of the reform necessary that their respective institutions had to undertake. While there were purges of communist party–aligned officers in many countries, the fact remains that the only cadre of experts in military affairs (as distinct from "defense") were the officer class and their conceptual foundation was, and in many ways very much remains, based on legacy concepts and, importantly, values.[40] Second, as one will see, the West's generous response for requests for advice and assistance is admirable; however, it was plagued by a general disaggregated approach focused largely on the armed forces and the officer corps, thereby strengthening the bureaucratic positions of these individuals in areas which are inherently civilian in nature.[41] The problems associated with how the West chose to assist these countries will be addressed in detail in Chapter 8; however, it is important to state in this context that with minor exception, efforts at assisting these countries to adopt effective defense planning tools were largely ineffectual. Wedded still, as most of them are, even as late as 2016, to Soviet-sourced, or designed, "platforms" and "systems," in some ways the introduction of highly complex and nuanced Western planning methods and techniques based on objective operational planning analysis data and financial costings of capabilities was simply bound to fail. Clearly, an enormous undertaking would be required before such exogenous methods could be successfully introduced in a legacy defense institution. If nothing else, given these circumstances, then a very carefully planned and integrated application of relevant assistance was needed.

Perhaps the best example of where such a Western defense planning concept did *not* take hold, and whose introduction has set back overall reform efforts, has been the introduction of the US-inspired system of budgetary programming. The literature on the introduction of this methodology in former Warsaw Pact countries is quite extensive, and as the *Planning*, Programming, Budgetary Systems method purports to contain the key elements of defense planning tools, it serves as an excellent case to provide an accurate assessment of the status of the actual reform of these key functions within these defense institutions. Of the defense institutions in this typology, five implemented the US Department of Defense's exportable version of PPBS (Bulgaria, Czech Republic, Hungary, Slovakia, and Romania).[42]

Conversely, Poland developed a hybrid PPBS that has all the characteristics of being a budget-driven method. As such, it has suffered a long record of disunity between the ministry of defense and the general staff in planning and budgetary execution. Financial decision-making remains highly centralized in the ministry of defense, and general staff J-5 planners must plan absence accurate costing data. The results of such an arrangement are predictable. The general staff created the "Army 2006" modernization plan, which in the end proved to be neither politically nor financially supportable.[43] More recently, Polish planning methods again failed in the case of the ten-year technical modernization program launched in 2012. By the end of 2015, it was reported that this plan had not met its acquisition objectives due to the fact that the plan had not been properly costed.[44]

When addressing the general issue of defense planning, it must be recalled that not only did these countries lacked educated and experienced civilian defense officials, but they also did not have institution memory in national-level defense planning. As noted by Pal Dunay, Hungarian forces, like their Warsaw Pact counterparts (Romania excepted), were highly integrated into larger Soviet formations. "Strategic planning" (such as it was) was conducted in the Soviet General Staff into which Warsaw Pact members had very little institutional insights.[45] Following the end of the Cold War, democratic governments came to learn quickly that the financial management of their defense institutions was, almost uniformly, a mess. Coming from a political culture where financial costs were not a major factor in what little defense planning and budgeting that took place, and bereft of any institutional understanding of costs based on market-determined prices, there was little that new governments and inexperienced defense ministers could salvage. To provide perhaps the proper context of the degree to which these organizations were financially data-bereft, Czech minister of defense

Vilem Holan launched a major reform of the armed forces in 1996 by forcing the introduction of *double-entry bookkeeping* management.[46] Indeed, defense budgetary data during the communist era were not easily available as resources for defense were extracted from other ministries and defense funding was allocated to secret services.[47] For instance, in the case of the Czech Republic, the defense budget circa 1993 was almost incomprehensible to Czech government officials and it was challenging at best to ascertain on what funds were actually spent. In the relative same time period apropos Hungary, Barany writes,

> MPs [members of parliament] may be told that the annual defense budget earmarks 21 billion forints (Ft) for the salaries and benefits of personnel, but they receive no figures broken down by individual units. In government budgets "defense" makes up merely 4 pages, supplemented by 120 pages of footnotes and explanations.[48]

To be sure, categories of defense expenditure were known, but there was not an analytical body of information that could articulate the costs of, for example, units, infrastructure, and so on.[49] In general, Warsaw Pact countries' defense budgets were designed to be impenetrable, not only to their citizens and the outside world but even to those officials with oversight responsibilities.

Clearly, it was not hard to make the case to officials for the immediate reform of this key responsibility of any ministry of defense. In an abstract sense, the model being offered to these countries by the United States had many attractions. As a concept, PPBS was envisaged to help a defense institution focus over the mid- to long-term (one to five years) on developing and assessing the inherent value of proposed new capabilities. To its advocates' credit, it was proper to emphasize shifting the debate from the micromanagement of inputs to a conceptual framework where the focus, *en principe*, was to be on *outcomes* that were to be joint and not merely service-specific. Given that the existing financial systems were legacy based, the need for civilian dominance of this critical field of defense management is without question. The methodology of having the defense institution develop programs was also seen as advantageous to defense management and parliamentary oversight as this would create greater transparency into the component factors that make up what until then was a largely opaque Defense Vote and would enable legislators to address specific problems, vice simply cutting overall expenditures. In sum, the introduction of the PPBS methodology was perceived by many as constituting a magic bullet to provide civilian control of the defense budget. It was envisaged to give commanders financial management responsibilities, that is, aligning resources and defense policy priorities and connecting them to defense outcomes, creating a common defense planning lexicon, and all via a methodology that would facilitate healthy civil-military relations.[50] In fact, PPBS in new and aspiring NATO members can be said to have reached its apotheosis when the alliance's International Staff, in their regular assessment of progress of aspirants and partners alike, assessed the degree to which reforming countries were adopting PPBS, simply assuming that this method constituted, in effect, the gold standard for defense planning and resource management.

Introducing transparency, and critically, civilian control of *defense planning*, and the translation of these plans into budgets, was a critically important objective for these defense institutions. However, introducing programming, *before* the creation of an effective staff to develop and manage a policy framework with authority to *enforce* policy-determined objectives and priorities, had the unforeseen effect of creating a cadre of defense officials (almost exclusively active or retired officers) who immediately seized control of the emerging programming progress. For instance, in 1994, Slovakia decided to reform its defense budgeting and finance system, but it did not include defense planning into the new department, which only caused greater confusion when in 1996 it decided to introduce PPBS.[51] Yet, when it was implemented, the ministry of finance rejected the methodology and insisted that the ministry of defense use the same methods as other ministries.[52] The ensuing result was to reinforce centralized control, ensuring that both policy and its supporting plans were bureaucratically isolated from *financial* execution. A telling example of the disconnect between policy and financial execution was provided in 2013, when the Slovak Ministry of Defense publically acknowledged in its defense white paper that the armed forces personnel structure was seriously unbalanced: 70 percent of its ground equipment was past its life cycle, and it could reach only 54 percent of NATO standards to achieve interoperability. The ministry went on to acknowledge that this poor state of affairs placed in serious doubt the armed forces' ability to defend the country, let alone meet its international commitments.[53] This is a remarkable document for its complete candor of the poor state of the development of the Slovak defense institution, and the ministry of defense even acknowledges what it perceives to be its causation, which includes, *inter alia*, poorly functioning *defense planning*.[54] The paper acknowledged that planning has been so underperforming that since 1993, it has yet to complete a single major project to reequip the armed forces, which may be due to the fact that the CHOD and armaments director have lost sufficient financial responsibilities taken for granted in other NATO countries.[55] What makes this policy statement different from so many other similar documents is the acknowledgment that greater attention needs to be directed to improving internal management and linking finances to outcomes, that is, via planning.[56] While surely unintended, the PPBS methodology has reinforced many legacy norms, in large part because many of these newly trained budget officers saw programs not as management tools to be "owned" by those entrusted with producing outcomes (e.g., a chief of air force to provide 24/7 air policing capability), but rather as budgetary instruments over which the defense institution was to be centrally and tightly controlled.

Moreover, the mere framework of the American-inspired PPBS did not integrate well with the emerging structures and procedures being developed by young parliamentary democratic governments. For instance, the Czech Ministry of Defense, with US assistance, introduced the PPBS methodology and perforce adopted long-term planning horizons out to five to ten years. However, there was little effort made to explain this to the Czech government, which has, like most other democracies, a one-year budgetary system. In consequence, within a short time, it simply "crumbled."[57] Soukupova cites a Czech-language publication that claims that it was a disaster as not only was the methodology too complicated and complex, but it led to planning failures due to the lack of checks and balances.[58] The government admitted officially in 2011 that although formally implemented in 2002, it truly never did adopt the system.[59] As Szemerkenyi noted, "It is somewhat pointless to commit the government to allocate a specific share of the national budget to defence without an approved outline for the overall budget."[60] Perhaps worst of all, the method did not achieve one of its key objectives of increasing transparency with parliamentarians as the latter have not accepted multiyear programs, and so have largely ignored the ministry of defense's inputs and only assign a "blunt number" for defense.[61] As could be expected in a reforming organization, new procedures were introduced, either without the full knowledge of existing complementary processes or in spite of such procedures.

As regards Hungary's experience with PPBS, programming was introduced in 1998 with the assistance of Western advisers, yet a detailed examination of the description of the process reveals what appears to be the introduction of a needlessly complex set of discrete subprocesses.[62] Evidence of its weaknesses was demonstrated when the ministry of defense conducted two defense reviews (1999 and 2003). These reviews had the objective of merging policy objectives with envisaged defense outcomes, yet recommendations for modernization were subsequently ignored by governments. The 2007 global financial crisis resulted in the government publishing two national-level policy and military strategy documents,[63] but they lacked proposals for how these recommendations could be implemented, particularly as regards modernization.[64] When PPBS was first introduced, the Hungarian defense planning system was comprised of a bottom-up method of planning and programming, yet the legacy-bound general staff and armed forces continued to operate on the basis of a top-down system.[65] Despite being "implemented," as late as 2010 a Hungarian official acknowledged that they did not have a "real complex programme based approach, areas of resource planning have been isolated from each other, and the program budgets do not contain costs of manpower and running costs of military infrastructures." As a result, programming, it is claimed, is isolated from budgeting as there are different time frames and is governed by different regulations. Notwithstanding the fact Hungary's PPBS is based on capabilities, planners have found that using this method is complex and complicated.[66] Thus, by the early 2000s, Hungary was seen by many analysts as having one of the worst managed armed forces, and one academic even argued that means needed to be investigated to ascertain how Hungary could be evicted from the alliance.[67]

Finally, in the case of Bulgaria, the alleged successful adoption of PPBS needs to be reconciled with the fact that this new system conceptually and bureaucratically coexists with five legacy plans that are still mandated by legislation and *are* tied to money:

(1) Armed Forces Development Plan
(2) Long-Term Investment Plan
(3) Annual Unified Financial Plan
(4) Annual Unified Procurement Plan
(5) Annual Unified Construction Plan

In reality, the Bulgarian Ministry of Defense continues to have two operating systems, but where legacy documents preclude using programs as management tools. As a result, resource decisions are being made within a legacy conceptual and legal framework of rigid quasi five-year plans, instead of a flow of programming decisions responding to changing performance and resource levels. Moreover, existing programs are not linked to anything beyond one year, thereby causing additional confusion to decision-making based beyond the near-term. The state of underdevelopment of defense planning can be observed as late as 2015 when a Council of Ministers' endorsed modernization plan was not based on finances, but rather the plan acknowledged the need to develop *another* plan based on finances.[68] Rather presciently, Dimitrov argued in 2001 that the Bulgarian defense institution did not have the requisite bureaucratic and financial management conditions to enable its proper functionality, although his conclusion that the existing hybrid defense budgeting process matched that of developed democracies is unconvincing in light of the above analysis.[69]

PPBS, in effect, was perceived by political officials as a Western solution to their immediate problems, while many officers involved in national-level defense likely saw it as the answers to their prayers. After being criticized repeatedly by their own political leadership and NATO officials for their inability to articulate even the most basic rationale for defense expenditures, PPBS was seen as constituting a magic algorithm, that is, a scientifically based system: if information were fed into it, a correct answer would come out of the other end. The answer would be "scientifically" sound, and critically in line with legacy norms. The operators of this system could not be held responsible when the result failed to answer the posed question. After all, it was "scientifically-based," and so it was impossible to hold defense officials responsible, let alone accountable, for any of its failures.

In the end, what is likely the largest contributing factor for the inability of PPBS to deliver what these countries needed was that such a convoluted methodology is simply too complex and inappropriate for these countries. In the case of Romania it is troubling that the providers of this method can claim that from working "on PPBES in over forty states, they ranked Romania as the leading example of success, benefiting from the conditions necessary for its functioning and the political will for its implementation."[70] If this were the case, then this declamation needs to be tempered with a revealing comment made in 2010 by a Romanian defense official who acknowledged that while embraced and implemented in 2002, it still could not be fully utilized due to its intensive personnel requirements.[71] This has been a common complaint about the methodology. Notwithstanding individual, and collective, training programs in Western resource management principles and methods after its implementation, the Czech, Hungarian, and Slovak defense institutions did not possess the organized capability to conduct regular analyses of value for money, let alone develop costed alternative capability options. Moreover, in long-standing Western democracies, this institutional discussion is part of a civil-military process, with both sides weighing in with their own unique expertise. In the case of former Warsaw Pact defense institutions, there were and largely remain few defense civilians with sufficient *gravitas* to argue with what remains largely a single data set developed by military officials. As Szemerkenyi writes,

The dominant presence of the military in the MoDs combined with their monopoly of insight into the fiscal aspects of defence renders civilian impact on the defence budget minimal within the executive as well. Budgetary item figures are proposed by members of the military, and are not seriously challenged by civilian policy-makers or budgeteers. Civilian influence at the first, planning stage of defence policy-making is superficial, non-effective, even non-existent. ... Parliament's fiscal powers are restricted by and large to delimiting the size of the defence budget.[72]

Combined with a very weak capacity in the form of developing, let alone enforcing, a policy framework, PPBS actually has produced a pernicious outcome by lending an air of Western legitimacy to what remains nonfunctioning planning and analytical systems in these countries. It obviously appealed initially to officials as it was from the West, and it allowed officials to advertise its scientific and objective nature, while enabling programming branches to control the defense budget. In an almost surreal fashion, defense officials in the region would appear not yet to have grasped that their defense institutions do not have key Western management concepts (e.g., force management) and objective data to enable them to make informed decisions. It is nothing short of comical, then, that a senior Slovak defense official could make the statement that the ten-year defense plan (i.e., Force 2010) would secure policy objectives since the "process is directly linked to capabilities" in a system that had yet to internalize the conceptual meaning of capabilities, and in an armed force that had yet fully to embrace key Western democratic defense governance concepts.[73]

National-level command

Post-Warsaw Pact republics have universally struggled to develop national command arrangements and authorities that are in keeping with those found in long-standing NATO nations. What is remarkable is not that some states in the other typologies share precisely the *same* systematic weakness in this critically important aspect of civil control of the armed forces, but rather years of NATO membership have yet to exert a meaningful influence across these countries to reform what are clearly problematic command arrangements. As for background, notwithstanding the privileged position in society of the armed forces under the communist party, there was no question that they were firmly under the control of the civilian party leadership. A positive result of this legacy tradition is the fact that the armed forces of the Warsaw Pact (the Polish military's response to the Solidarity movement in 1981 being a notable exception) were conditioned not to interfere in national affairs, a norm not practiced by their respective ministries of internal affairs.[74] This is an important distinction to make, given that drafting new democratic constitutions explicitly ensured that the control of the armed forces was placed under the authority of the head of state (i.e., president) and some even included provisions that the president confirms promotions and appointments of general officers (to include the CHOD), or even more disconcerting, the appointment of wartime commander in the case of war (who may not even be the CHOD). These countries created arrangements to disaggregate command and responsibility with the intention that the armed forces could not be used as an instrument of repression. In the case of Hungary, this norm went to the extreme case of embracing the unusual solution of placing the ministry of defense under the prime minister, while the general staff and armed forces fell under the authority of the president to ensure that the armed forces did not fall under the elected government.[75]

Poland likely reached the apotheosis of confusion in national command in its 1991 defense law by making the president the commander-in-chief, while stating that the minister of defense "commands the armed forces of the Republic of Poland. Whether or not senior officers, for example, were subordinate to the president or the defence minister in a chain of command was unclear and open to interpretation." This patently unworkable arrangement required a change in the constitution to clarify these critically important distinctions.[76] Poland presents an example, in fact, of how such clarification in the command of the armed forces is unlikely to be a simple, or a single act of legislation and/or constitutional redrafting. In the constitution of 1997, a compromise was agreed whereby the president remained as supreme commander-in-chief of the armed forces, but in peacetime he would discharge his duties through the minister of defense. In the case of war, it was envisaged that the highest commander of the armed forces would be nominated by the prime minister. Yet, at the same time, parliamentarians left powerful authorities with the president: for example, the authority to nominate the CHOD and general officers. The peacetime oversight of the armed forces fell under the authority of the Council of Ministers, but the critical issue of what precisely was the role of the president in wartime remained undefined.[77] As late as 2013, a key policy document lamented the weak state of command at the national level and cited that the minister of defense possessed ambiguous authorities to control the armed forces, particularly as it related to accountability, implementation, and *decision-making*. To the credit of the National Security Bureau, it recognized that existing national-level command arrangements were insufficient and that greater clarification was needed to include providing the minister of defense with more specific and expanded command authorities.[78] Moreover, the government transformed its Operational Command to a Joint Operational Command and invested its commander with command authorities previously exercised by service commands (which were closed) and the general staff.[79] Although incremental progress was made, additional needed reforms remain undone, i.e., to clarify wartime command appointments before the outbreak of conflict and develop of command authorities to enable commanders effectively to exercise command.

In practical terms, the continued inability of these governments to come to terms with precisely defining command authorities of senior *elected* officials continues to bedevil governments. Command authorities, in general, have yet to be explicitly defined, in defense acts. No more accurate description of the vexatious nature of this situation can be found than in the prescient 1998 observation by Szemerkenyi: "Establishing the intricate web of relations and authority between legislative and executive, Prime Minster and President, and Minister of Defence and General Staff in post-Warsaw Pact central Europe was bound to cause frictions."[80] The current state of ambiguous authorities, unclearly assigned among senior political officials, all but guarantees institutional disorder and discord in national defense as the responsibilities and functions of the head of government (i.e., prime minister), and very often the minister of defense, are still not explicitly stated in either the constitution or enabling laws.[81] Indeed, by empowering the president to approve military commanders (or, for instance, in the case of Bulgaria, to appoint and dismiss all general officers and bestow ranks, and where even the CHOD acts under the president's authority),[82] unless both the president and government are of the same party, acrimonious discord is guaranteed.

Nor should it be assumed that these incongruencies were quickly and effectively reformed by subsequent legislation, particularly after these nations became members of the alliance. As late as 2009, that year's revision to the Bulgarian Defense Act continued the legacy of reinforcing the role of the president as commander-in-chief, approving the appointment of general officers, as well as reinforcing the odd practice of, in emergency or wartime, establishing a strategic command through merging the ministry of defense and general staff. Precisely how such an arrangement could ever possibly function in crisis and war is not known, given that it was never subjected to rigorous assessments, simulations, or exercises to validate either the structure or its operating procedures.[83] That all said, the 2009 Defense Act did mark a major improvement in starting the process of aligning responsibilities with accountability in the area of national-level command. But as is so often the case, key issues of command authority in Sofia still remain to be resolved as regards the concept of escalation. "The [2009] Act, however, did little to resolve the existing conflict between the President and the Government with regard to who has the authority to declare martial law and a state of emergency, or how differences would be settled in case of conflict between them."[84]

In sum, twenty-five years after independence, national command arrangements and relationships in former Warsaw Pact countries remain mired in legacy concepts, assumptions, and logic. Zipfel, writing in 2001, is sanguine that the Czech command system of the president as commander-in-chief is functional as all the president's decisions must be countersigned by the prime minister and minister of defense. But this is unlikely to be proven until there is an actual national-level crisis and this countersigning system is put to the stress of political crisis.[85] Moreover, how can a system be countenanced as supportive of democratic norms and principles when, as in the case of Bulgaria, two former CHODs (General Miho Mihov and General Nikola Kolev) who clashed with ministers of defense during their respective terms in office, were later appointed to the president's cabinet?[86]

Military decision-making process

While it is acknowledged that the Warsaw Pact armed forces had their own distinct and unique manners in which they internalized and manifested the Soviet-imposed model, in one area they essentially shared all but universal commonality, that being how formations were expected to be commanded. And, by this, it is very clear that all of them used the practice of centralized command and control, vice delegating authority.[87] In consequence, the entire system was bereft of any educational or training institutions that emphasized the systematic development of leadership skills.

While correct, Peterson Ulrich perhaps understates the depth of the problem in observing: "The Soviet-era military and education systems did not focus on leadership development and the cultivation of professional competencies related to leadership skills."[88] More to the point, training was directed explicitly to ensure that the antithesis *was* the case. Complicating the strict top-down approach were ad hoc, if not at times capricious, personnel management practices that did not promote individuals on their abilities, let alone leadership qualities.[89] The combined result of this command philosophy and supporting procedures gravely ill-suited the armed forces following their entry into PfP, let alone when they gained membership in NATO. The philosophy of command, and its operationalization, is not a practice that is easily changed in the short term, particularly when there is no determined and consistent pressure to change from senior political leadership. The practice of command is simply too firmly founded in history, societal norms, and culture to expect radical changes over the short, or even medium, term. However, it is difficult to identify any of these countries' governments which perceived the *need* for such a consistent effort. After all, one cannot expect many senior military leadership, brought up in the centralized command school, and by definition not just a product but a beneficiary of that philosophy, to advocate its wholesale reform.

To be sure, it became obvious to many defense officials that membership in NATO would entail significant internal reforms, to include the adoption of a form of the Western MDMP. This became very clear particularly to the Polish and Romanian armies following their repeated deployments to Iraq and later Afghanistan. While keeping in mind that every old NATO ally interprets and implements MDMP in their own nuanced fashion, it is clear from interviews and research that legacy armed forces have initiated reforms to implement MDMP (particularly as a function of adopting NATO's newly issued *Comprehensive Operations Planning Directive*).[90] But progress has been uneven. Due to their significantly large and consistent deployments of ground forces to Iraq and Afghanistan, the Polish and Romanian armies in particular have made strides in adopting a form of MDMP which is used on NATO operations, but not necessarily when back at home station. For instance, notwithstanding the long record of Polish deployments, Polish Army sociological studies have uncovered that soldiers do not feel that they are fully part of decision-making.[91] Perry and Keridis make the point that Romanian officers in particular struggled to implement reforms that would enable the delegation of authority downward, as well as allowing for a freer flow of information.[92]

Other countries have also struggled to embrace MDMP as they have insufficient numbers of trained young officers and NCOs who are *empowered* to undertake these tasks. One might expect progress to be slow in many countries given that Warsaw Pact kit, being largely Soviet in origin, would inhibit such reforms. As regards PME, Dunay observed that the Hungarian national military education and training system was simply too modest and bereft of qualified personnel to be able teach Western concepts and, by necessity, had to develop a parallel approach using Soviet and Warsaw Pact legacy procedures, as well as Western concepts and processes.[93] Note that this situation is not limited to Hungary. In a number of other countries, this author has spoken with young officers and NCOs who complained bitterly of their inability to operate in accordance with NATO's doctrine and concepts when in-country as they had on operations in Afghanistan and Iraq. A common norm, therefore, holds that NATO's mission command concept is suitable for deployments, while legacy concepts (e.g., territorial defense and detailed command) remain the prevailing case in home station.

In the final analysis, the implications of the slow and uneven adoption of such a fundamentally important concept as MDMP extend far beyond whether battalions are employed in the most agile and effective manner as their Western counterparts. Simply stated, without the ability to undertake the full MDMP or Estimates process, effective interoperability with long-standing NATO nations is essentially compromised as to undermine their ability to contribute effectively to operations. Furthermore, as argued earlier in this work, MDMP is more than merely representative of the Western approach to organizing for training and operations. Rather, MDMP also serves as that critical initiating point whereby tactical formations have the ability to respond to guidance and thereby, *inter alia*, establish requirements and determine capability gaps expressed in objective data. Thus, it is little wonder that armed forces in this region have been so weak in the area of force management (and, by extension, force development) given that they are not data-driven from the bottom up. It is simply not self-evident to these defense institutions that there is a need to meet these responsibilities as there is no systematic process by which such objective requirements data are formally generated, let alone sent forward and assessed. Indeed, in some countries, it is the prevailing norm for a subordinate commander, even a general officer, *not* to initiate formal communication on the issue of requirements and capability deficiencies (i.e., issuance of a Statement of Requirements). Thus, coupled with the systematic lack of using costings in decision-making, the slow introduction of MDMP has had negative effects that are felt throughout these defense institutions and have impeded the creation and implementation of effective defense planning.

Concept of operation

If one area of defense management and organization reform has been readily adopted, officially at least, it has been that of changing these nations' concept of operation. That said, not all nations have been capable or willing to adopt these new concepts either quickly or effectively. As to the latter point, the end of the Cold War altered substantively NATO war-planning efforts for obvious reasons; that is, the Soviet Union and Warsaw Pact disintegrated. The end of the Cold War and the domination of the Soviet General Staff of these nations ended the overwhelming influence of concepts of operation being premised on the concentration of mass and surprise. Since the end of the Cold War, the retirement of the alliance's strategy of flexible response (MC 14/3), and its supporting family of General Defense Plans,[94] NATO, over time, encouraged its members to undertake expeditionary operations. This has become a key operational focus of the alliance, for which former Warsaw Pact countries were unprepared and equipped to support. With little capital for reinvestment, these armed forces have struggled to meet these new alliance commitments. Moreover, it should not be overlooked (as will be addressed *infra*) that not only are these legacy formations ill-prepared for deployment operations with their old equipment, but their logistical support structures and procedures are not responsive to supporting a distant and demanding operation where tasks and even missions can change rapidly. Finally, one should not underestimate the continuing influence of legacy thinking which manifests itself in the operational sphere. While the Hungarian defense institution never embraced, for instance, the concept of territorial defense after independence, others did so and they continue to suffer no small degree of operational incoherence.

One can discern very clearly this undercurrent of territorial defense orientation in Poland (i.e., the Komorowski doctrine)[95] and the Czech Republic, where territorial defense is cited (using the authority of the constitution no less) as the primary mission of the armed forces.[96] There remains in Poland two schools of thought that have yet to be reconciled: one for a large peacetime army and another that envisages a large reserve component of local defense units. Yet, neither model has actually been fully implemented as both the president and government have differed on the details of a shift to focus more on territorial defense.[97] Paszewski argues persuasively that currently the armed forces are incapable of conducting effective territorial defense due to the lack of a long-term territorial defense strategy fully supported with needed modernization.[98] What does appear to plague the armed forces is operational incoherence due to the lack of clarity in policy and *priorities*. In effect, Polish operational thinking remains betwixt and between deployability abroad in support of allies[99] and legacy infrastructure that is more suitable to supporting a *fixed* territorial defense orientation. What else could explain why the defense institution continues to possess fifty-three logistics depots across the country along with supporting force structure?[100]

To be sure, it is no sin for an alliance member to take their territorial defense seriously. However, in the case of some of these countries, this is often interpreted as constituting *fixed* operations based on legacy infrastructure which limits the ability of members to deploy forces. In the age of microprocessors, GPS, and Google Maps, unmovable sites and formations are little more than fixed *targets*. One can only wonder if senior political officials in these countries (and frankly NATO commanders and officials) understand and appreciate the fact that these countries are maintaining two conceptually *different* armed forces with all of the ensuing inefficiencies and contradictions, all fraught to impede interoperability.

Logistic support

In probably no other field has the disparity between Western basic concepts and their application in reforming alliance countries been manifested as it has in logistics. Reform has been slow in coming for likely a variety of reasons. Fundamentally, the key challenge to reforming logistics in these countries has been stymied by a variety of strong influences; any single one likely was sufficient to impede reform, but combined, they have produced only modest successes.[101] As previously argued, Warsaw Pact armed forces premised their logistics organizations and planning on supporting a Soviet centrally planned operational war plan. Legacy logistics concepts, therefore, were based on supporting an established operations plan and exploiting internal lines of communication. Support to forces was dominated by the "push" concept, organized on a depot system of supply and support, all of which was based on logistics tables to support the mass operational concept. This premise allowed these armies to keep the organic support planning and execution structures small and concentrated at operational- and even national-levels. The supporting system that was built around army, corps, and divisional structures was controlled at the top of these structures. Finally, modern management software has only been slowly introduced into these defense institutions, thereby perpetuating the use of paper and approval stamps and slowing progress of delegating downward of decision-making authority.

Thus, these defense institutions have faced the challenge of needing to adapt to new and variable operational concepts (which has not always been clearly communicated throughout the armed forces) to conduct expeditionary operations, but at the same time saddled with predominantly legacy concepts, platforms, and systems. Under normal circumstances, one might have expected an organization requiring such a fundamentally different orientation in its most basic activities and operations to adopt an incremental and/or phased reform program. After all, to alter the manner in which legacy platforms and systems could be supported is likely to prove difficult, given that their operational employment was likely left unchanged in most cases. Critically, a phased approach also would require the likelihood of a dual structure and separate procedures, and expensive capacities in a time when defense budgets had not been growing. Consequently, these armed forces have been moving forward, albeit at different speeds to be sure, to reform their logistics organizations. For instance, the Hungarian Strategic Defense Review of 1998 envisaged reforming the defense institution's logistics structures by adopting, *inter alia*, Western principles of privatization, outsourcing, civilianization, and integrated supply structures, all with the view of cost savings.[102]

It should be stressed that Western logistics systems operate on a number of key concepts, such as transparency and accountability, which are inimitable to legacy logic. In the case of Romania, Watts documents how officials associated with the acquisitions and property management element of the defense institution were none too keen to see the introduction of the liberal democratic concept of transparency. Accountability was also stymied by the practice of a parallel budgeting process which existed until 2001 whereby funds for acquisitions and property management fell under the authority of the general staff, as opposed to the ministry of defense. The delay to remove these responsibilities from the armed forces postponed needlessly civilian oversight of this important civil function.[103] Lastly, of significant importance, all of these countries have suffered from unclear institutional responsibilities and functions in almost all areas of national support to the armed forces. Nowhere is dysfunctional decision-making made so embarrassingly public than in the case of a major procurement process, when mishandled. An excellent example of this is the untidy procurement by Poland of multi-role fighter aircraft. According to Gogolewska, the Polish defense institution suffered from the predictable legacy pathologies: unclear division of functions among departments, overlapping responsibilities, poor coordination of work among various cells, and as a result, disjointed decision-making processes.[104]

Professionalism

A discussion of how the armed forces of former Warsaw Pact countries have instituted professionalization must be seen within the context of its legacy manifestations. First, more than in the Soviet Red Army, by the late 1980s, the earlier model of a politically neutral institution subservient to the Communist Party was giving way to a new generation of officers who were generally politically disinterested. Moreover, as Dunay has argued strongly, the Hungarian officer corps equally suffered from low levels of professional competence which was to impede subsequent attempts to adopt Western norms.[105] Be this as it may, the changed nature of the officer corps in the majority of these countries was the direct result of the increasing technological sophistication required by the armed forces. In consequence, the leaders who emerged as these countries were integrating into Western security structures were not exclusively communist *apparatchiks*, but nor were they universally competent. Second, admittedly it is difficult to generalize about professionalism, post-independence, due to the fact that these countries adopted different policies toward the retention of their legacy officer corps. For instance, the Czechoslovak Republic carried out the most sweeping depoliticization (lustration) of the officer corps of all Warsaw Pact countries,[106] whereas the Polish, Hungarian, Romanian, and Bulgarian governments did not.[107] The Czech Republic, following the Velvet Divorce, continued what was one of the most comprehensive investigative processes of personnel.[108] Conversely, the Slovak Republic ended their review at independence, but had to address the issues again in 2002 given the presence of some 5,000 individuals in the defense system who had not been properly vetted when the country was being considered for alliance membership.[109] Further concerning Hungary, one source cites that the political decision not to undertake lustration resulted in a very graduated change in its officer corps, which by extension also occurred throughout many of the region's armed forces.[110] Dunay argues that one of the reasons for the lack of reform in the Hungarian officer corps was simply a symptom of the lack of interest on the part of senior leadership in the ministry of defense and among the main political parties. The ensuing negative effect of this decision was the adoption of the practice by senior military leadership of developing reform plans that they had every confidence would not be approved and funded.[111]

As a critical element of the reform of these armed forces, all have moved from conscription to a professional force, with the introduction of the concept of a professional NCO corps. Fortunately, the concept of a trained and empowered professional NCO corps has historical antecedents in these armies prior to 1945. For example, in some countries, NCO corps were a long-standing institution. The Bulgarian armed forces, for instance, established its first NCO training institution (mechanical school in Ruse) in 1881, some three years after it attained its de facto independence from the Ottoman Empire. Peterson Ulrich makes an observation (c. 2002) that still holds throughout the region that whereas NCOs in Slovakia were vested with some authority in technical areas, "instilling leadership responsibility and delegating authority have to date proven difficult to accomplish."[112]

In the move toward professionalism and the correspondingly important priority to undertake expeditionary operations, two key institutional capabilities remain underdeveloped: the adoption of modern HRM and force management concepts. In effect, the move from conscription to a professional force was not accompanied with the epiphany of the corresponding realization of the need for the development of an enhanced management function that is required to provide extant HRM structures with needed inputs establishing, *inter alia*, current and future personnel requirements. Indeed, in the absence of such inputs, it could be argued that this lack of objective data derived from operational requirements has allowed HRM structures to continue legacy personnel management practices which have inhibited furthering professionalization.

Vlachova cites the experience of Czech participation in expeditionary operations as an example of the inability of a legacy HRM system to address the needs of the armed forces within the context of NATO membership. She argues that despite efforts at reform, HRM remained at the time of her writing (c. 2001) far from being reformed; it remained disaggregated, and was still struggling to address recruitment, training, and retention. The lack of an effective and centralized HRM structure has obviated against efforts to develop management practices based on merit and, critically, performance.[113] At the time of her writing, rank was tied to the post itself; that is, upon assuming the post, the officer was automatically promoted irrespective of other factors, let alone if the position could have been filled by a better candidate. Moreover, the management system had yet to ensure that positions possessed the commensurate authorities, as well as financial means, to function properly. Little wonder that she concludes that the HRM system in the Czech Republic is far from being reformed and well-functioning.[114]

Romania initiated a sweeping reform of its HRM system essentially by implementing many key elements of the US military personnel management system through the development of an HRM handbook in 2001–2002.[115] This has included the introduction of promotion boards made up with, and managed by, the military (Slovakia also adopted a similar board system) and are claimed to introduce greater fairness and transparency in the HRM system.[116] Watts argues (c. 2001) that the reformed Romanian system was the most successful in adopting Western concepts and was more advanced than that of Poland or the Czech Republic.[117]

Conclusion

If there is one common theme to be taken from this assessment of the former Warsaw Pact defense institutions, it is how remarkably *unreformed* they are. They have all gone through the NATO accession process and are members of NATO. Yet they still continue to possess, in different intensities, legacy concepts which are antithetical to Western democratic defense governance concepts. This should be a salutary lesson of the limits of effectiveness of external advice and assistance when not carefully designed. Due to its national political commitment to defense, and with considerable US and German assistance, the Polish armed forces are unquestionably the most reformed and advanced. However, Polish and NATO officials should be concerned by the continued application of legacy assumptions (e.g., *fixed* territorial defense) that bleeds resources from developing more effective and lethal capabilities and its lingering combination of legacy command and MDMP concepts. Poland also provides a salutary lesson on the difficulty of introducing Western kit into a legacy defense institution. As there has been so little acquisition of any defense equipment in new NATO nations, let alone from Western industries, one can only speculate that if the Polish Air Force has difficulty employing properly its fleet of F-16s, how can NATO expect legacy armed forces still equipped with Soviet-designed equipment to be capable of adopting modern Western training techniques, let alone integrating themselves effectively on the modern conventional battlefield. That within NATO nations in Europe, the T-72 main battle tank (and its variants) is one of the most numerous in the allied inventory should give NATO officials and its commanders pause.

Romania needs to be recognized as being serious about reforming its defense institution, notwithstanding continuing charges of corruption. Without doubt both Poland and Romania have benefited from engaging in extensive operations in Afghanistan and Iraq. Some US government support has been put to good effect in both, for example, the development of SOF. An important indicator of the functionality of the Romanian defense institution will be whether the Romanian Air Force is given sufficient delegated authorities (and budgets) to enable it to ensure the smooth introduction into service of 12 F-16 Block 15 mid-life upgrade multi-role fighter aircraft.[118] The salient question is whether reforms will continue with the end of combat operations in Afghanistan and will governments find national resources to maintain these hard-won capabilities, such as SOF. Hungary, the Czech Republic, and Slovakia, albeit different in detail, can be summarized as being resource-starved and still struggling to overcome fully persistent legacy concepts. Although recipients of considerable Western advice and some equipment, one can conclude that this has not been sufficient to shock their systems so profoundly as to force painful political decisions to adopt Western concepts in place of their communist counterparts. Bulgaria is arguably the least reformed of the new NATO members and has progressed modestly from a 1999 analysis which concluded that the armed forces were capable of conducting only limited defensive operations within the country.[119] The defense system is dangerously unbalanced with too much money going to personnel and needless infrastructure (e.g., a bloated PME structure, a complex of spas, and even a *ski resort*), while operations and maintenance and acquisitions budgets are starved—a point openly and honestly addressed in its 2010 White Paper.[120] In the aggregate, what should be assessed as most troubling is the consistent decline in the ability to produce defense outcomes, using legacy platforms and systems, or even with Western capabilities. These are political failures, to be sure, but no small amount of blame needs to be assigned to the continued under performance of defense institutions.

Accountability should also be leveled toward Western governments and the NATO International Staff. All too often, Western support for reforms has been superficial and structural, which has had the effect of not removing the conceptual roots of pernicious legacy concepts. The improper management of advice and assistance programs has allowed the introduction of new Western processes without successfully addressing the need to dismantle existing legacy concepts, and therefore has often produced yet more "conceptual spaghetti." More systemic efforts need to be directed to creating effective polices to require personnel, and indeed the institution, to forget more effectively their communist legacies. Failure to address all of these shortcomings will only result in a continued mismanagement of many of their armed forces. Arguably, the alliance has a bigger problem than many officials are either aware of or willing to acknowledge.

Former Yugoslav Republics' Defense Institutions

Like the Soviet Army's orphans, the former Socialist Federal Republic of Yugoslavia's republics' defense institutions continue to manifest in many key ways their heritage from the JNA.[1] Such legacies can be assessed as constituting both strengths and debilitating weaknesses. Prior to the atomization of Yugoslavia in 1991, the JNA, by any measure, was one of the most technologically sophisticated communist armed forces. It was also the preeminent federal institution in Yugoslavia and enjoyed a healthy defense budget and strong sense of autonomy and professional identity:[2]

> the Yugoslav system differed very significantly from the Soviet model of maintaining strong civilian (and authoritarian) control over the military. Thus, behind the façade of civilian control the Yugoslav military obtained de facto far-reaching institutional and corporate autonomy ... the federal army as an institution controlled the state borders and air space, and monitored the key civilian institutions, all electronic communications, the mass media and the pockets of mostly silent opposition. The JNA directly controlled large chunks of federal real estate and managed or supervised a very extensive military-economic complex. The federal army also served as the ultimate ideological and security watchdog for the communist regime.[3]

Further distinguishing it from its other communist counterparts, many of the JNA's platforms and systems were indigenously designed or built under license from the Soviet Union. But it also purchased components and systems from the West and even selectively sent officers to attend Western PME courses. Finally, it was uniquely supportive of providing forces to UN peacekeeping missions, starting with the Sinai in 1956, thereby exposing the force to multinational operations. Indeed, this national commitment to supporting UN peacekeeping continued until the armed forces' dissolution.[4]

Notwithstanding the technical sophistication of the JNA, it would be a mistake not to recognize that the predominant organizational culture in which the JNA's officer corps existed was profoundly communist.[5] Bebler writes that there were party cells down to the platoon level, and some 95 percent of the officer corps belonged to the League of Communists.[6] As Hadzic notes, notwithstanding the many conceptual volte-faces experienced during the life of the JNA, there was never any move to abolish political commissars or security officers.[7] The League of Communists of

Yugoslavia may have been comparatively more enlightened and less nasty than its counterparts to the east (e.g., Romania),[8] but *communist* it was and so highly entwined was it with the League of Communists that after the purges of liberals in the early 1970s, it was referred to as the 9th Republic in the Federal Party Presidency.[9] The JNA held representation in all three branches of government, directly controlled a sizable percentage of the country's GDP, possessed its own legal system and its own extensive social support sector, and, via the direct transfer of authorities from the presidency to the Federal Secretary of National Defense (always a general officer), largely controlled itself.[10] As such, many of the current organizational weaknesses and procedural pathologies that confront successor defense institutions have their provenance in JNA concepts.

Clearly the most important and indeed unique characteristic of the Yugoslavia defense institution among communist countries was its bifurcated defense system. In addition to the large conscript-based JNA, Belgrade after 1968 created extensive Territorial Defense Forces, organized around and under the command of its individual republic governments' ministries of defense (Republic Secretariats for People's Defense). As the political crisis in the Yugoslav Federation was reaching its final climax in the early 1990s, Belgrade and the JNA's actions in 1988 of placing Territorial Defense Forces firmly under the centralized command of the JNA under a three-phase plan called *Jedinstvo* ("unity")[11] were a contributing factor to precipitating the federation's ultimate demise.[12] All of the subsequent armed forces of these newly independent republics were based on, or included, descendants of these Territorial Defense Forces. Although the JNA as a model was delegitimated, its legacy influences can still be seen and it has served as the basis in many areas for the development of defense institutions in newly independent republics. Many serving personnel in former Yugoslav republics were former JNA officers, NCOs, or members of their republic's Territorial Defense Force. Thus, these individuals have the experience of having been proud members of a large and sophisticated armed force. Unfortunately, as will be shown, this background has ill-prepared them for developing and operating much smaller, significantly less sophisticated, and largely cash-strapped armed forces. Given the violent dissolution of the federation, legacy JNA personnel have not always been accepted in the defense institutions of the successor states and there remains a noticeable split in these defense institutions between those officers with a JNA pedigree and those who came up through Territorial Defense Forces. One also hears from a younger generation of officers a resentment of the legacy JNA officer corps given that their upbringing and education were communist, that is, rigid and structural. These very different backgrounds have not infrequently produced policy, conceptual, and capability incoherence.[13]

Overview of defense institutions

A number of important distinctions can be made among these six defense institutions as to the degree of progress made in adopting Western democratic defense governance concepts (Table 6.1). Slovenia is clearly the most developed, thanks to its early break from the federation in 1991 during its ten-day war of independence,[14] as well as a concerted effort to place the armed forces under a very strict regime of civilian and parliamentary control.[15]

> Several other factors have contributed to this very high degree of civilian domination over the Slovenian military. These include the widespread rejection of the previous Yugoslav model of civil-military relations (which contained both militaristic and praetorian proclivities); the small size of the Slovenian armed forces; the paucity of Slovenian military traditions; the underdeveloped corporate identity of the Slovenian military officers; and the army leadership's extremely low political profile. The parliamentary system of government gave this domination its constitutional and legal foundation and form.[16]

As a result of the UN arms embargo against all republics of the former Yugoslavia from 1991 to 1995,[17] Slovenia focused its resources on education and institutional development. These efforts, balanced with the continued positive legacy of former JNA personnel (whose expertise is not always acknowledged by the bureaucratic and political leadership that emerged from Territorial Defense Forces), show in its technical sophistication. Indeed, Slovenia continues to harbor a tension between those leaders who are supportive of embracing deployability and those who are keener to maintain territorial defense concept as a key planning assumption.[18] But, this tension must be balanced by the large number of officers and soldiers who have been on operations. Thus, like Poland, one can draw a correlation, if not indeed clearly establish causation, that having a large number of personnel on missions abroad has the beneficial effect of enabling a deeper understanding and adoption of Western defense and military norms.[19]

The JNA was more successful in disarming Croatia (as many of the JNA officer corps and police posted to Croatia were ethnic Serbs), and its defense institution was born out of its war of independence.[20] Its wartime legacy created structures that have been judged, over time, to be unsupportable and unnecessary. Given the nature of its early political birth in war and under authoritarian rule, a number of its institutional characteristics have been slow in developing, but continued progress in reform is discernible. The JNA was successful also of stripping Macedonia of defense assets (and vandalizing that which could not be carried off), but it was the only state (save Montenegro) to leave the defunct federation peacefully.[21] It proceeded to develop a defense institution from a compromised Territorial Defense Force while as a de facto NATO protectorate. But, within ten years, it had to fight an insurgency against elements of its own ethnic Albanian population.[22] Yet, it has made discernible progression in developing a functional defense institution, despite a bloated ministry of defense. Montenegro's Territorial Defense Forces were abolished in 1992, thereby leaving it at its independence from the rump federation in 2006 with essentially legacy armed forces, but with only rudimentary organizational structures upon which to build a viable national defense institution. It has struggled to create a coherent defense institution from the elements of forces left in the country by the Serbian-Montenegrin armed forces on independence in 2006. Bosnia and Herzegovina, after

Table 6.1 Baseline of Defense Governance Concepts: Post-Yugoslav Republics

	Bosnia	Croatia	Macedonia	Montenegro	Serbia	Slovenia
Policy framework	Legacy/in transition	In transition	In transition/extant	In transition/extant	Legacy/in transition	Extant (but weak, e.g., in planning and HRM)
National-level command	Legacy/in transition	In transition	In transition	Legacy	Legacy	Extant
Military decision-making process	In transition/extant	In transition/extant	In transition/extant	Legacy	Legacy/in transition	Extant
Concept of operations	Legacy/in transition	NATO	In transition	Unknown (likely basic)	Unknown	NATO
Logistics	In transition	Legacy/in transition	In transition	Legacy	Legacy	Extant
Professionalism	In transition	Extant	In transition	Legacy/in transition	Legacy/in transition	Extant

its bloody civil war, continues to face the challenge of creating an effective federated ministry of defense from the three previous warring factions and a limited defense budget.[23] It is also unique in that the international community played a dominant role in supporting the governance of the entire state. The Office of the High Representative in Bosnia-Herzegovina created the Defence Reform Commission, with the task of assisting in the reform of defense structures.[24] And, finally, Serbia received the better part of what remained of the rump of the JNA in its transformation from the morbid federation to the Serbian Republic.[25] Yet of all Balkan states, it is the only one that has not seen the destruction of the ancien régime as a rationale for fundamental military reform.[26]

Thus, notwithstanding their common heritage, and dare one say, traditions of technical expertise, blended with communist ideals (e.g., centralization), this remains a disparate grouping of defense institutions. It is fortunate that to a higher degree than has been the case in the other typologies, academics and analysts have had access to a remarkable amount of information on the state of the development of these defense institutions that provides an informative basis for a deep comparative understanding and cross-country analysis. It should not be forgotten that these former Yugoslav defense institutions, in general, while they are not by any measure fully Westernized (Slovenia being arguably the sole exception to this observation), their unique status places them almost in a nether world. The data show that most of them are not as profoundly affected by deep communist legacy pathologies as are many post-Soviet republics, and therefore, have been better prepared to make the difficult transition to adopting Western democratic defense governance concepts. What has held them back in many ways has been the late arrival of Western assistance (Croatia being a notable exception) in comparison with former Soviet and former Warsaw Pact armed forces due to the UN arms embargo, as well as the fact that in many of them, there exists a general lack of national political will to *drive* deeper reform to adopt Western democratic defense governance concepts.

What distinguishes these defense institutions from the others assessed in this study (the South Caucasus and Moldova excepted, to be sure) is the important fact that all of them experienced birth either in the midst of wars of independence or certainly in the direct shadow of nearby highly violent wars. Or, in the tragic case of Bosnia and Herzegovina, under the Dayton Accords, the defense institution was the product of first creating a unified army of Bosnians and Croatians, later to be merged with the army of the Republika Srpska.[27] All of them had a legacy of possessing republic Territorial Defense Forces, which included extensive trained personnel, logistics depots, and infrastructure. Of critical importance is to understand that these armed forces have been, since their inception, optimally designed for territorial defense. Thus, they emerged from well-developed organizations, designed to conduct decentralized territorial defense. As such, the concept of civilian control of territorial defense has not been a contentious issue in these countries as they had long been closely governed by civilian political authorities, albeit Yugoslav communists. Moreover, they had, to varying degrees, the unique advantage of possessing a cadre of civilian defense officials schooled in republic university faculties in the Yugoslav theory and practice of territorial defense. The exceptions to this observation (that is still quite visible) are Serbia and Montenegro, where there remains a contemporary manifestation of JNA autonomy witnessed by the very stark lack of civilian defense officials in either ministry of defense.

Policy framework and conceptual coherence

Albeit this typology has cases where countries have adopted Western democratic defense governance concepts, there remain areas where "success" is nuanced and key differences with their Western counterparts remain. The inability to free themselves completely of legacy concepts, assumptions, and logic has inhibited the adoption more rapidly of a policy framework and the achievement of greater conceptual coherence. If one accepts the fact that there is a tradition from the JNA of operational decentralization, conversely since independence, all of these defense institutions have been subjected to a high degree of centralization of command and financial management. This is often manifested in the opacity of group decision-making (namely *collegia, vide infra*) that has obviated against individual accountability. Equally, critical thinking has yet to become the norm, as can be seen in much of the staff work is ineffectual, predictable, and inefficiently managed: yet another symptom and cost of centralized decision-making. Notwithstanding its technological sophistication, the concept of life-cycle costs does not appear to have been widely or deeply embedded within the JNA as this concept has not been easily or broadly accepted in these successor armed forces. Critically, the communist concept of the state of perpetual war between communism and its democratic/fascist enemies has largely been inherited, intentionally or not, by these six defense institutions as there is only a smattering of institutional understanding of the concept of graduated escalation, let alone its criticality in crisis management. What must be the most surprising common characteristic that should have been passed down from the JNA is the fact that it had possessed a task-based, medium-term, resource-allocation defense planning methodology that remained in operation until the end of the federation. Surprisingly, this method of defense planning was evidently not adopted by republic Territorial Defense Forces in its entirety as basic planning concepts are difficult to discern in almost all of these successor ministries of defense, to include Slovenia (*vide, infra*).

When one considers the seeming sophistication of the JNA, it is all the more surprising to find that such a basic concept as the preeminence of a policy framework in successor defense institutions has not yet taken root throughout the region. Generally speaking, if post-communist defense institutions from the three legacy typologies were to possess a strong sense of a policy framework, one might have thought that the obvious place to find them would be in former Yugoslavia. To be sure, Slovenia with many caveats passes this test[28] and Macedonia is quite far advanced, notwithstanding the comment made by Yusufi that defense policy documents issued since independence have not been created within a strict policy hierarchy and many of the papers produced by the ministry of defense did not produce new decisions or changes in policy.[29] This, therefore, raises the question: why were these needless documents even drafted? It is equally curious that the small Slovenian defense institution can continue the practice of separating the ministry of defense and general staff. This has arguably impeded greater integrated policy formulation, and it has apparently encouraged instances of convoluting civilian and military responsibilities.[30] To be sure, since independence all of these countries have produced a plethora of documents; and not all of these are exogenous to their respective planning and management systems. However, it would appear that the tendency toward centralization of information and decision-making, added with ambiguity in clearly defined institutional responsibilities, compounded by weak cadres of civilian defense experts and political authorities unknowledgeable of defense have all contributed to impeding the adoption of the concept of policy *driving* the operation of these defense institutions.

More specifically, manifestations of the prevailing weakness of policy frameworks easily can be observed, for example, in the absence of policy in these defense institutions for HRM, and particularly the effective adoption of modern defense planning practices and techniques. There are planning and management processes, but there are weak points in their policy frameworks that are inhibiting policy from *driving* the defense institution's personnel requirements. As a result of this lack of a policy framework one finds the partial implementation of Western democratic defense governance concepts. For instance, all of these armed forces have transitioned from conscription to professional forces, but most continue to struggle with developing an adequate policy framework to implement fully this concept to where defense institutions understand the value of their human resources. The mere observable fact that soldiers in these armed forces are often referred to as contract soldiers (vice professionals) and NCOs are often seen conducting menial tasks (e.g., shoveling snow, mowing grass, standing guard duty) demonstrates that these concepts and supporting assumptions are struggling for dominance, and producing "conceptual spaghetti." Another factor that explains this lack of policy framework and conceptual coherence in these defense institutions is in the legacy of a highly centralized JNA command and management system where all policy decisions were made in Belgrade. Slovenia is arguably an exception, but again with caveats. In this weak policy environment, it is often the case that policy is not accepted as needed by the defense institution to frame how to execute key activities, such as HRM or force management. Support for this observation is found in Kotnik's critique that the Slovenian armed forces "[lack] sufficient combat orientation as a military organization" as witnessed by its weak career structure.[31]

An illustrative and highly documented example of why a policy framework has been so difficult to take hold in these countries is provided by the case of Serbia.[32] It is surprising in that as the successor republic that was the home of the JNA, one might have predicted that critical elements of the central brain of that defense institution would have provided a solid foundation from which to provide a policy, planning, and management foundation of the successor defense institution. However, due to Milosevic's policy of centralizing power throughout the government, but particularly as regards the armed forces and police, a policy framework based on Western democratic defense governance concepts has been very slow in taking hold in Belgrade following the emergence of democratic governments. For instance, shortly after the dissolution of the State Union of Serbia and Montenegro in 2006, reforming governments in Belgrade quickly published a plethora of policy and planning documents related to defense while also developing the necessary laws on defense in the Republic of Serbia.[33] In effect, these policy statements and objectives did not appear to be reinforced by broad guidance and priorities in order to enable officials to achieve concrete reforms in critical areas of defense management. A further complication was that while the number of documents was impressive, they did not appear to have been issued in any context of a hierarchy. To wit: "It is interesting that the new [Serbian] Constitution does not mention a National Security Strategy, but only that a defence strategy should be passed by the National Assembly."[34] A document developed by the ministry of defense and circulated at the December 2006 South East Europe Clearinghouse meeting stated that the National Defense Strategy document, after the Constitution, "represents the highest starting document and which is sort of base [*sic*] for all other strategic documents." However, the juridical basis for this assertion was not made clear, nor did it clarify this document's relationship with, for example, results from defense reviews and other policy documents.[35]

A presentation prepared by the ministry of defense established a hierarchy: the National Security Strategy informs Defense Strategy, which in turn informs any defense white papers, as well as Military Doctrine, and finally all of which directs/ informs defense reviews and subsequent ministerial guidance. One can question the utility of possessing within such a modest defense institution a policy hierarchy (note that none of these planning documents, per se, appear to be tied to money) that comprises five discrete and separate steps.[36] Moreover, it is not known if this hierarchy is based upon policy, regulation, or law; nor is it clear that these documents are tied to specific policy/resource decision points in the defense planning cycle, assuming they exist. Fundamentally, it is not evident that all of these documents (which would appear to comprise every possible generic defense policy document) are necessarily important.[37] To add confusion to Serbian defense planning, it has included an unusual practice of drafting, *inter alia*, a long-term defense plan, 2010–2020, in June 2011, and conducting an SDR (April 2015); while both were approved by the government, neither of them were ever released to the public. In the end, it is difficult to accept an optimistic observation of the early state of policy development in the Serbian defense institution in light of the subsequent lack of an effective policy framework since in the years following independence, critical areas of basic defense management continued to remain unaddressed.[38]

Another former Yugoslav republic that experienced difficulty developing a strong policy framework is Croatia, but for completely different reasons.[39] During the Yugoslav Federation, Croatian representation in the JNA's officer corps was disproportionately low,[40] and indeed the Tudjman government did not trust these officers and so they were quickly marginalized, thereby removing needed national-level military experience while also promoting politically compliant officers.[41] Tudjman thought both the JNA and the republic's Territorial Defense Forces were unreliable, and therefore used the ministry of interior's forces as the foundation of the independent republic's army. Unlike in Slovenia, Tudjman considered the Territorial Defense Force concept to be of marginal use should he opt to fight an offensive war with Serbia to create Greater Croatia in Bosnia.[42] Therefore, the simple lack of an officer corps experienced in national-level policy, within the context of a state born in conflict, contributed in restricting the development of a policy framework. The prevailing argument against its subsequent slow development was simply that the state was able to secure its independence absent such documents, and therefore their utility was suspect.[43] This lasted until the death of Franjo Tudjman in 1999 and the election of the reformist Social Democratic Party, which replaced the Croatian Democratic Union.[44] A review of these early policy documents reveals, however, some expected challenges. First, these early documents addressed policy only in a general sense, but did not delve into critical areas necessary to provide sufficient guidance for the management of the defense institution, such as HRM, logistics, and finances. In hindsight, defense officials would have been better advised to have *drilled down* in these specific areas, vice spending time drafting yet more public documents. Second, the panoply of policy documents developed by the ministry of defense shared (not surprisingly) precise titles as do their American counterparts, which leads one to question precisely how useful they were in establishing a policy framework. Evidently the US model that was adopted precluded further development in this area. For example, the 2003 National Military Strategy, which complements the National Security Strategy and the Defense Strategy, was adopted by the president in March 2003. It is an indicative manifestation of the state of transition to full democratic management norms that this version of the National Military Strategy document "was prepared by the military with no involvement of civilian experts, was accepted, providing more or less general proclamations while neglecting concrete details and activities."[45] Yet, in a short period of time, the ministry of defense was able to create in 2006 its ten-year Long-Term Development Plan that was evidently developed with little, if any, input from the general staff.[46] Its subsequent unaffordability suggests very weak costing models and/ or their lack of use in the review.

Yet another influence for the slow pace by which a policy framework has yet to take hold in Croatia is due in no small part to the lack of clearly defined institutional responsibilities and functions. This has complicated the adoption of the concept of clearly ascertaining institutionally how policy should be developed and implemented. For instance, its 2003 Annual National Programme announced that Croatia would undertake an SDR, "despite the fact that no legal, procedural, strategic or doctrinal foundations existed for the adoption of this document."[47] With young democracies creating new or transitioning legacy ministries of defense and general staffs, one should not be surprised that institutional responsibilities and functions were confused and contradictory in those early years of independence and peace.[48]

Related directly to the issue of clarifying civil-military responsibilities and functions is that in some of these six countries, officials have adopted the Western concept of separating leadership/command from management responsibilities, such as Slovenia, Croatia, and Macedonia, whereas Serbia has yet to adopt this principle.[49] To be sure, one finds throughout the region the posts of state secretaries. But this post is almost exclusively limited to providing administrative oversight of certain sectors, as opposed to providing overall management of the organization.[50] Yet no small degree of conceptual incoherence is observable in that all these defense institutions (save Slovenia in formalistic sense)[51] continue the JNA tradition of collective decision-making in both ministries of defense and general staffs in the form of the use of *collegia*. While it is difficult to assess the degree to which these bodies control the operation and function of these defense institutions, it is clear that they continue to dominate the internal decision-making process (particularly as related to HRM). For instance, in Serbia, matériel requirements proposals are reviewed by the minister of defence's *collegium*. They probably are best assessed by ascertaining the degree to which they support, or undermine, leadership/command and management.

Within general staffs, these bodies coordinate the activities of the armed forces and serve as a decision-making forum of senior field-grade and general officers. One hears the argument that they provided value as they obviate against subjectivity in important decision-making, such as personnel promotions, and play an important role in improving critical decision-making. In the case of Macedonia, its *collegium* is comprised of the chief of the general staff his deputy, the director of the staff (still a somewhat unique post in this region), and heads of all staff directorates, and its membership can be expanded to include representatives from units and, at one point, even members of the NATO Training Team. Given these defense institutions do not have the tradition of chiefs/directors of staff, *collegia* act as a collective body for coordination, yet this comes at the expense of unempowering commanders and removing individual accountability and responsibility. It has also inhibited separating leadership from management.[52] Moreover, in many of these countries there is the practice of either joint meetings of the two *collegia*, or where the CHOD attends regularly, or on an invited basis to the minister's *collegium*. A final and disturbing problem with the continued existence of these bodies is that they are largely unknown to most Western officials and observers, leading to a misunderstanding as to how decisions are made.

In terms of their institutional conceptual assumptions, post-JNA defense institutions run the gamut of a ministry of defense: from that of Serbia, that is still largely staffed by uniformed officers, to that of Slovenia where the ministry of defense has long been civilian-led.[53] As to the former, an indication of how far it has come since the Milosevic reign is that it was only in 2001 that the defense budget was transferred from the general staff to the ministry of defense, and in May 2003, by decree of the Supreme Defense Council, the general staff was finally subordinated to, and became an organizational unit of, the ministry. In 2006, it was reorganized along J-directorates.[54]

An exceptional case even by former Yugoslav republics standards is the small and still developing defense institution in Montenegro, located in the old JNA II Corps Headquarters building in Podgorica. It was established in 2006 following independence and was based on State Union reforms that were part of policy initiatives that defined institutional responsibilities within the context of democratic and civilian control of armed forces.[55] The general staff is embedded in the ministry of defense as one of the directorates, and the status of the CHOD is that of an assistant minister dealing with military issues. An effort to reduce the oversized ministry of defense (currently some 335 personnel) resulted in the 2010 Strategic Defense Review recommendation to merge the functions of the J-1 and J-4 with their ministerial counterparts.[56] Due to the lack of developing supporting legislation and regulations, these sectors stagnated and were reestablished in 2013.[57] The responsibilities and functions of the armed forces, although defined in policy documents, in actuality, are still being clarified, refined, and implemented.[58]

Croatia had early US support in the form of a private defense contractor providing advice on the organization, operation, and training of the armed forces. This was subsequently also the case in Macedonia and Bosnia and Herzegovina. In the case of Croatia, according to Bellamy and Edmunds, the company's advice turned out to be inappropriate, as it was based on American-centric concepts:

> MPRI was contracted to provide military training and education, which included a programme of reshaping the democratic control of armed forces formed part of the Long Range Management programme. As a result of this influence, the General Staff and Defence Ministry were organised into huge structures of eight departments each. These were modeled on the Pentagon and bore little relation to Croatia's needs. Indeed, one of the most important steps taken by the Croatian Ministry of Defence in 2003 was an internal reorganisation which rationalised this structure down to a more manageable four departments.[59]

In spite of this reform, the ministry of defense for years has retained an oversized administration, often with divided and not clearly articulated and agreed responsibilities and functions.[60] It was only in 2013, as a result of its Strategic Defense Review, that the government announced the appointment of a director of the general staff who will possess managerial responsibilities and there will be only one deputy CHOD. Moreover, on the civilian side, the ministry of defense gained a permanent civilian secretary with responsibilities in the areas of legal and administrative issues, and the general staff is now fully integrated within the ministry of defense.[61]

Vestiges of Bosnia and Herzegovina's tragic modern history can also be found in its efforts to establish the federation's ministry of defense and the struggle to adopt Western democratic defense governance concepts. Vetschera and Damian presciently capture the early challenges which can explain, in part, why the creation of the federated defense institution has been so slow and painful:

> While necessary to concentrate on overcoming the legacies of the war and to establish state control over defence functions, the reform did not address the persistence of old, pre-democratic thinking in the entities' defence laws, which were left substantially the same. These laws were basically carbon copies of the old communist Yugoslav laws on defence and armed forces and were frequently incompatible with basic human rights, fundamental freedoms and international humanitarian law.[62]

This point is supported by another observation apropos early federation defense legislation that manifests conceptual incoherence. "The Defense Law of the Federation of Bosnia and Herzegovina was adopted in July 2002. The Law makes reference neither to civil-military relations, nor to the democratic control of the armed forces."[63] Thus, defense reform in Bosnia and Herzegovina is unique to all other efforts of defense reform in Europe, in large part due to its highly decentralized state. NATO and Bosnian officials have been confronted with the challenge of building a unified armed force from two distinct armies and three previous warring factions, all within the context of a weak and financially challenged central government.[64] The Defense Reform Commission was created in 2003 by the Office of the High Representative of Bosnia and Herzegovina,[65] followed by a second iteration in 2005,[66] which was created with the objective of driving reform of the entities' armed forces. The reports argued the need to establish a new structure for the ministry of defense, which included a joint staff, two commands, and a number of brigades. On July 18, 2005, the Republika Srpska and the Yugoslav Federation formally signed the Defense Reform Agreement, which was ratified by the Entity and central parliaments and became effective on January 1, 2006.

This agreement was a major step toward PfP membership and it effectively abolished the two entities' ministries of defense and transferred all their functions to the state-level ministry of defense. Significantly, the new structure contained two chains of command: one operational under the new state-level structure, the other administrative under the entities. Additionally, it eliminated conscription, created a single state-level defense budget, and established a professional and multi-ethnic military. An accompanying revised force structure was approved in July 2006.[67] Concurrently, in January 2006, a second commission of experts was formed to determine in detail the envisaged force structure of the unified armed forces in accordance with the Law on Defense and recommendations from NATO HQ and an MPRI contractor team funded by the US government. The Defense Reform Commission that dealt with the amalgamation of the two ministries of defense of the entities into one Bosnia and Herzegovina ministry of defense tried to fill the gap that arose.[68] In effect, Bosnia and Herzegovina adopted a force structure, absent the identification of operational requirements, roles, and missions of the armed forces. Once appropriate policies and priorities are drafted, vetted, and approved, one would conclude it logical to revisit the force structure issue. Further evidence of a weak policy framework to drive the operation of the ministry of defense and armed forces is found in the confused manner in which policy documents have been drafted and adopted.[69] That said, Aybet makes a strong case that the two defense reform commissions, and pressure from NATO in the form of conditionality prior to being invited to join PfP, had the beneficial effect of creating a state entity, whereas efforts in other sectors have not been as successful.[70]

Defense planning techniques

Upon review of the status of defense planning techniques in this typology (Table 6.2), defense planning systems in these countries are quite weak. Clearly, the JNA defense planning system did not even survive its predominant successor state, nor did the planning processes in republic Territorial Defense Forces translate well into providing a basis for national defense planning after independence. Slovenia, Macedonia, and Croatia have been able to produce formations, and in some cases, excellent tactical capabilities (e.g., SOF) that have been the product of policy directives. To the credit

Table 6.2 State of Development and Utilization of Defense Planning Tools: Post-Yugoslav Republics

	Bosnia	Croatia	Macedonia	Montenegro	Serbia	Slovenia
Contingency planning guidance	Extant	NATO	Extant*	Unknown (but likely basic)	Unknown	NATO
Cost models	Extant (but weakly linked to policy	Extant (but weakly linked to policy)	Extant (but weakly linked to policy)	Extant, but basic (per 2013 SDR)	Extant (but not connected to policy)	Extant (yet not closely used in force planning)
Operational planning analysis	In transition	In transition	In transition	Legacy	Legacy	Extant (but weakly linked to policy, per 2009 SDR)
Force management	In transition	In transition	In transition	Legacy	Legacy	Developed
Capability trade-off analysis	In transition	Extant (to be tested, per 2013 SDR)	Extant (but not linked to policy)	In transition (per 2013 SDR)	Extant (but not linked to policy)	Extant (but weakly linked to policy)
Roles/missions	In transition	Extant	Extant	In transition	In transition	Extant (but incomplete)
Budget execution system	Extant (but weakly linked to policy)	Extant (but weakly linked to policy)	Extant (but weakly linked to policy)	Extant (but weakly linked to policy)	Extant (but weakly linked to policy)	Extant (but weakly linked to policy)

*Military support to civilian authorities, that is, counterterrorism missions.

of Croatian defense planners, they acknowledged in their 2013 Strategic Defense Review that financial challenges facing the country would necessitate a hard review of existing structures and activities, and those not directly supporting essential tasks would be abandoned.[71] This stating of the obvious (i.e., defense cuts) is remarkable as it is hard to find this candor in other legacy defense institutions just as it is difficult to document defense plans that have produced envisaged defense outputs. A qualified exception to this observation is Slovenia, which has been able to accomplish this objective by raising and maintaining its army units, creating its air-sovereignty radar system, and successfully procuring the *Triglav II* corvette from the Russian Almaz Shipbuilding Company (adapted export version of the Russian *Svetlyak*-class patrol boat) as an element of reparation payment to the former Yugoslavia.[72] Yet, equally, there are reports that such successes are tempered by excessive micromanagement of finances. The CHOD controls no more than 5 percent of his *own* budget, and the Mid-Term Defense Program is so restrictive as to limit the ability of battalion commanders to manage their units' finances to meet their assigned missions and tasks.[73] Alas, the positive JNA legacy of delegating budgets to commanders would appear to be limited solely to the Slovenian armed forces. Moreover, important conceptual gaps in methods remain. The ministry of defense has acknowledged that it has not succeeded in tying more closely national defense planning with operational planning undertaken by the armed forces.[74] Moreover, its policy and strategy documents have yet to adopt the practice of placing threats in priority.[75]

What the nuanced Slovene case demonstrates is that this defense institution has been able to develop some key defense planning capabilities, albeit there is clearly room for improvement. This is no small achievement for such a modest defense force, and it validates the foresight of Slovenian defense officials in the early years after independence during the UN arms embargo to concentrate national funds and foreign grants on the training and education of personnel and the creation of modest, but sufficient, national training and educational institutions. But the Slovene case is unique in that the other successor states of the former Yugoslavia did not have the benefit of a short and sharp war of independence that left the country with secure borders in a state of peace. All other states remained in conflict or were under the shadow of potential conflict (or in the case of Macedonia, a civil war in 2001) that did not allow them the luxury of adopting early on Western defense planning techniques. Causation for subsequent weaknesses in defense planning capabilities can be attributed to two sources: the imperative to conduct operations in the early years of independence and the form in which much Western advice was subsequently provided.

Following the breakup of the federation, there was an immediacy in most countries to raise and maintain forces on a wartime footing. The defense institutions of Croatia, Serbia/Montenegro, Bosnia and Herzegovina, and Macedonia were simply preoccupied with either fighting wars of independence, civil wars, or simply trying to stay out of regional conflicts. This required their armed forces to conduct operations absent establishing the proper structure and size of the defense institution, let alone ascertaining the requirements of modernizing their armed forces. In consequence of these realities, such basic responsibilities, such as force management, remain largely unknown. Likewise, formal operational planning analysis based on Western concepts has retained solely a tactical focus and application. However, with peace and regional political settlements, these countries soon became beneficiaries of NATO nations', and particularly US, security assistance programs. In the case of Bosnia and Herzegovina, Croatia, Macedonia, and Serbia, the United States provided either in-country resident private contractors or extensive temporary assistance programs to support the development of their respective defense institutions. In the case of addressing nonexistent to weak national defense planning capabilities, in all cases (save Montenegro and Slovenia) the default methodology of the United States has been the PPBS model.

Notwithstanding arguments one hears that the assistance provided was not based on the US Department of Defense's methodology, this fact remains that US methods were implicitly employed given that it was taught by US personnel and is based on American experiences and models. For instance, a review of a key policy document from Bosnia and Herzegovina presented a schematic of its Planning, Programming, and Budgeting System which looks suspiciously similar to the US programming model.[76] And lest this author be accused of single-mindedness criticism of US-inspired methods, an analysis of the defense planning methodology that has been generously exported by the Norwegian Ministry of Defense has been equally unsuccessful in at least one country that received it (Serbia). It is claimed that the methodology and cost models are based on that used by the Norwegian Ministry of Defense which can be characterized as being, *inter alia, heavily* resource-constrained in orientation. Oddly, risk and threat analysis does not appear to be an essential element of the planning methods, but rather the approach stresses a fine-tuning of resource allocations, vice forcing the entire system to undertake a rigorous process of the identification of capability requirements that address national policy priorities and that fill validated gaps. Finally, this author has yet to discern if the costing models, despite enormous implementation efforts, are providing costing data in a way that supports decision-making. As an example, the 2006 Serbian Strategic Defense Review received positive reactions from Western governments and NATO, but they ignored the fact that the review process was flawed as it did not include costings.[77] This same critique holds for the 2010 Strategic Defense Review.

The provenance of the programming methods and assistance aside, the salient question is why did these methods not produce their envisaged objectives? A review of the challenges faced by these countries to implement PPBS demonstrates the following explanations. It needs to be recognized that following peace settlements and political opening to the West, NATO and developed PfP nations embarked on providing assistance and advice with only a superficial understanding of the nature of these defense institutions. In short, underlying institutional legacy concepts and critical assumptions (e.g., conscription and overcentralization of decision-making) were not challenged, but allowed to remain in effect. An excellent example of how these assumptions were allowed to stand unquestioned, which has impeded the adoption of Western planning and budgeting techniques, is the basic fact that most Western planning systems are based on the norm of delegated authority, which in these countries is exceedingly rare. In consequence, what is observable in the countries that have adopted PPBS has been they produce "conceptual spaghetti" where a budgetary programming structure was essentially "bolted" on top of existing legal concepts and financial management structures, which continue either to work in blissful ignorance of the other or engage in various forms of bureaucratic conflict as they struggle against each other. For instance, notwithstanding the introduction of PPBS, the Macedonian defense planning system as late as 2007 was not required "to develop planning assumptions, recommendations or alternatives."[78]

In the case of Serbia, the program structure introduced essentially replicated the legacy budgetary structure and provides an excellent case in point of this pernicious problem. A detailed analysis published in 2009 of the implementation of PPBS in Serbia found three major shortcomings. First, the introduction of these methods produced institutional confusion. Second, a central coordinating authority either was weakly empowered or was not designated. One could speculate that this was the predictable result of the managerial norm to centralize all decision-making. Third, and likely as a product of these aforementioned shortcomings, there was an observable lack of communication within the defense institution concerning programming. McNab observes that a key implication of the above conditions in Serbia (which is found in essentially every other legacy defense institution) demonstrates the discernible lack of linkage between strategic planning and financial decision-making.[79]

One defense official from the region described his own defense institution's underdeveloped PPBS methodology as not being capable of executing defense plans, but essentially being a *financial* planning system, inefficiently combining a bottom-up and top-down allocation system. In effect, the PPBS mind-set has encouraged, for example, in Bosnia and Herzegovina, a resource-constrained approach to defense planning, vice one that stresses creating priorities based on policy.[80] A closer examination of the actual bureaucratic and legal conditions of the financial management systems, the weak policy framework, and underdeveloped planning capabilities in this typology reveals that a highly complex methodology such as PPBS, which is based on, *inter alia*, the principle of delegated authority, simply would not be allowed to function. The evidence that supports this conclusion can be easily found in the fact that these defense institutions, at best, are still struggling to connect operational planning analysis and costings to plans. In the case of Serbia, the armed forces remain organizationally unbalanced and financially- and manpower-deprived, and are consequently too large for the defense budget. After years of effort and assistance from US contractors, in 2012 the Macedonian Ministry of Defense formed a working group to simplify its existing programming structure, which suggests the obvious question: why was a less complex approach not developed from first principles?[81]

In addition to, or perhaps because of, the introduction of the PPBS and Norwegian costing methodologies throughout the region, a weakness that appears to be essentially common is the lack of a full institutional appreciation of the importance of using costings in defense planning. This is most ironic given that these PPBS methods are based on the assumption that planning is to be initiated with the assumption of being resource-constraint. JNA planning legacies, such as they were inherited in these defense institutions, do not appear to have included the essential need for accurate costings of armed forces. It is not surprising given its post-Yugoslav federation history that the Serbian defense institution emerged from the fifteen-year Milosevic regime with a budgetary system that did not possess the ability to track costs.[82] This has had a debilitating effect on the ability of these young defense institutions to plan properly as they lack accurate costing data that captures important factors such as the full life-cycle cost of a capability. For example, when developing the "Croatian Armed Forces Long-Term Development Plan, 2006–2015", life-cycle costs were not factored into financial projections, and costs were based on 2004 prices, with the further dubious assumptions that both GDP and the defense budget would rise by 2 percent per annum.[83] To be sure, there is no small element of friction in civil-military relations due to these assumptions. However, to be fair, it was only in 1998 that the Croatian State Auditing Office began to validate the general staff's annual report to parliament.[84]

It can be inferred that some of these defense institutions conduct a form of contingency planning as they come from a strong and lingering tradition of organizing themselves to undertake territorial defense operations. Such planning continued into the era of independence given the then prevailing security environment in which they found themselves; and in many cases, these plans were actualized in war. What is less clear is whether these methods have evolved to where plans are now developed in accordance with senior national political guidance to ensure that they conform to national-level policy, let alone whether they are subject to rigorous and systematic review by both civilian defense officials and political leadership. Ostensibly, most of these countries declare in their diplomatic and defense policy pronouncements that they do not perceive external threats or risks to their security (e.g., Croatia),[85] which would obviate against the formal need for contingency plans based on territorial defense concepts. It would also argue against the need for threat-based planning methods. Moreover, it would be instructive to know, in greater detail, if the methods employed to develop operation plans have perforce evolved to where they are reflective of the fact that all of these countries have moved from a tradition of conscription to a professional force. Planning for these professional forces, even for territorial defense operations, is qualitatively different as to require a fundamental reexamination of key planning assumptions. Finally, while NATO's *Comprehensive Operations Planning Directive* is widely adopted by these countries, it is largely perceived by defense and military officials as being an operational-level tool, which is, of course, very much the case. That said, if developed further, these analytical tools could provide the basis for the development of an operational planning analysis logic that could be used to develop capability profiles to inform national defense planning. This is a missing critical planning data linkage lamented by, for example, Slovenian and Croatian defense officials.

National-level command

This chapter has argued consistently that post-Yugoslav republics are distinct from their other communist legacy counterparts. This universal generalization fails the test in many countries as regards the structure and procedures supporting the national-level command of the armed forces. Like the other typologies, most former Yugoslav republics initially adopted the principle of assigning command of the armed forces not to the head of government, but rather to the elected head of state. Conversely, Slovenia very early on defined the president as commander-in-chief, but one who has no defined legal responsibility over the armed forces.[86] More importantly, as the prime minister has no explicit powers of national defense, by default the minister of defense is the key decision maker, at least in peacetime, thereby critically aligning responsibility with authority.[87] Yet one needs to temper a too positive view of the Slovenian experience in adopting Western command concepts and authorities when examining the restricted powers of the CHOD:

> the CHOD has no power over the authorities which are inherently a part of and inseparable from the military. The CHOD has no authority to issue tactical and technical manuals and training programs. Critical for the professional development and the military career system is the fact that the defense legislation enables untrained personnel to reach command assignments or other positions in military staffs; this practice directly affects military effectiveness and calls into question the professionalism of the military.[88]

While restrictions on CHODs are not unheard of in other Western defense institutions, if these are but a representative sample, then the ability of the Slovenian CHOD, both to provide professional military advice and to be effective in leading the armed forces, is seriously compromised.

Indeed, Edmunds is perhaps too optimistic in his assessment of Croatia: "While this division of responsibilities is not inherently unworkable or undemocratic, it is unwieldy and unclear as to where institutional responsibilities lie."[89] But, as he argues in another of his works, it simply makes no practical sense to designate the president as commander-in-chief, but then deny him or her any authority over how the armed forces are financed or developed.[90] In one specific and critically important aspect of civilian control of armed forces, this arrangement, which essentially empowers the head of state to bypass the elected head of government, is especially problematic in parliamentary democracies. To be sure, parliaments are charged with the responsibility of providing oversight of armed forces. But, due to the strong role of presidents as commanders-in-chief, they have very little institutional and constructive means to carry out this mandate. This provides an opportunity to make considerable mischief when the president approves the appointment of senior field grade and general officers, to include the CHOD. This is the case in Macedonia, for example, but with the added complication that the CHOD is accountable both to the president and to the minister of defense,[91] as well as charged with approving documents used by the army.[92] To complicate matters this situation could be exacerbated when the president and the government are led by two different parties: cohabitation.[93]

This issue rarely elicits interest in a country, except when the process fails. We are fortunate that the record of Croatia is well documented and widely assessed by experts, which therefore provides a representative example. Following the end of the Tudjman era, and the election of the Social Democratic Party, an effort was made to reduce the powers of the president in defense matters and particularly as related to his influence over personnel decision-making.[94] Croatia had the unique situation where the general staff reported to the president, thereby removing the minister, the ministry, and indeed the parliament from providing direct oversight of the armed forces.[95] Croatia's Defense Law, to its credit, made an effort to clarify this imbalance by stipulating that the president of the Republic of Croatia exercises command authority through the minister of defense.[96] Precisely how well this process works is questionable, particularly if there is cohabitation, let alone in a period of crisis with potentially rapid escalation. Indeed, Vesel rightfully argues notwithstanding even the constitutional reforms of 2000 that addressed this situation, the president retained too much authority over operational issues that should be within the purview of the minister of defense.[97] It is only speculation, but one might conclude that some of the contentious operational authorities retained by the president could well include that the president, as supreme commander, has opaque command authorities over the CHOD in wartime.[98] Any such arrangement violates the long-standing Western principle that there must be consistency and continuity in the chain of command throughout all the stages of escalation.

The fact remains that Croatia's imperfect command arrangement is replicated among former Yugoslav republics, for example, in the respective constitutions and laws on defense in Serbia, Macedonia, and Montenegro. Indeed, in the case of Macedonia, in the original wording on the Law of Defense, the minister of defense was acknowledged as part of the national command structure; however, a 2002 ruling by the Constitutional Course clarified matters in the spirit of ensuring unity of command, thereby limiting the chain of command from the president (supreme commander) to the CHOD. Equally, in response to the overall centralization of authority under the Milosevic regime, the Serbian president is the constitutional head of the armed forces, but does not possess any authority over operational issues. The authority to issue orders rests with the CHOD, but only *after* being authorized by the president. What relationship the CHOD has with the minister of defense in such circumstances is not stated.[99] Moreover, within the context of command authorities at the political level, the precise definition of authorities among the president, prime minister, and minister of defense apparently remains sufficiently unclear as to enable a degree of subjective control of the armed forces, which, it has been argued, undermines professional autonomy.[100]

Due to its tragic recent history and torturous creation as a reconstituted republic, Bosnia and Herzegovina possesses a national command structure that was designed largely by the international community to ensure decision-making by consensus of the two entities. Article 12 of the Defense Law outlines the operational and administrative chains of command assigning command and control of the armed forces to the presidency.[101] More specifically, "by the Constitution of BiH, all members of the BiH Presidency, by virtue of their official duty, perform the function of the civilian commander." But like in other legacy defense institutions, the Bosnian constitution and laws that address command are imprecise and can only lead to confusion in time of crisis. For instance, the white paper identifies that operational "command" and "control" can be two distinct command authorities, as opposed to one, but as these terms are not defined at all, it is not known which precise authorities are contained in either term.[102]

Military decision-making process

Given the legacy of a professional JNA NCO corps that exercised leadership and lower-level tactical command,[103] the implementation of decentralized territorial defense, and the early provision of Western military assistance to the JNA, of all legacy armed forces, one would have expected to find the exercise of MDMP almost second nature in these former Yugoslav republics. Yet the data from the literature and interviews with officials and analysts reveal a more nuanced and uneven practice of this critically important Western concept. To be sure, the Slovene and Croatian armed forces, for different historical reasons, came to employ MDMP to a greater extent than other successor JNA armed forces. In Slovenia, the strict control of armed forces by elected civilian authorities precluded the practice of centralizing authority within the general staff (the ministry of defense being another matter) as seen in other defense institutions (e.g., Serbia). Croatia, due to the immediate need to fight against the rump of JNA, and the subsequent presence of advisers provided by the US government after its war of independence, has progressed in adopting this Western concept.[104] Other countries, such as Macedonia, have implemented MDMP, but this may be only as a function of, and manifested in, its expeditionary deployments. This is arguably the case in the armed forces of Bosnia and Herzegovina due to the presence of many Western advisers at a critical point in its creation. Yet, one could conclude that MDMP is not fully implemented in large part due to the lack of institutional operational planning analysis as the command climate exhibits the least enlightened aspects of JNA legacy: centralization. All too often mundane operational- and tactical-level issues are pulled up to, and addressed by, CHODs and ministers. It is not possible to express a generalized value of the degree to which this is exhibited in the armed forces of the former JNA, but one can establish a range. If Slovenia and Croatia are at the higher end, Serbia and Montenegro still have progress to be made. The latter's small size and highly unbalanced force structure could obviate against it adopting this concept for some time.[105] Conversely, the Montenegrin government's adoption of 2013 SDR includes identifying the need to consolidate empty brigades and battalions into one viable infantry battalion and a composite battalion.[106] Such a necessary reorganization could facilitate introducing MDMP in short order, if the reform were implemented. The Serbian CHOD in the mid- to late-2000s had ambitious objectives to adopt NATO, and British, training philosophy and standards,[107] and official sources even claimed that they were in the process of adopting NATO staff procedures.[108] It is also claimed that training management has been delegated to commanders to decide specific and general training tasks.[109] Yet centralizing forces in the defense institution would appear to have overruled these efforts. It was only in 2013 that legislation was drafted to amend the Law on National Defense and the Law of Serbian Forces to delegate approval of operational doctrine of the armed forces from the president of the republic to the CHOD.[110] But, in the end, what will hamper the development of this capability in any armed force is the lack of skilled staff and properly trained officers and NCOs in sufficient numbers that will enable a battalion or brigade to conduct 24/7 operations. Moreover, until such a time that collective training (based on assigned missions and tasks) is recognized as essential to the creation and maintenance of a modern army, and therefore funded as a matter of due course and directed by empowered commanders, the institutionalization of MDMP in these armed forces will be problematic.

Logistic support

The JNA, along with its Romanian counterpart, was doctrinally based on the principle of Total National Defense. There is no evidence that there were ambitious deliberate plans to invade neighboring countries, let alone launch Soviet-inspired Operational Maneuver Groups to range far behind enemy lines. As such, the JNA logistics concept was based on supporting the conscript JNA maneuver force in the field and the individual republic Territorial Defense Forces which would be engaged in circumscribed defensive and resistance operations. These concepts envisaged interior lines of communications and a large network of logistics depots, supported by an extensive and geographically dispersed defense industrial base, the latter being an essential element of the logistic support system (i.e., providing maintenance). The economic coherence of the former Yugoslavia's defense industrial base has largely dissipated with the implosion of Yugoslavia and subsequent civil wars. The communist managerial practice of overriding market forces to spread defense industry throughout the country (and particularly to exploit the defensive nature of Bosnia and Herzegovina's terrain)[111] could not survive independence; however, industries continue to exist throughout these countries.

As a general observation, logistic support of a territorial defense concept was not a terribly problematic policy option for these armed forces as their mission focus was initially modest and largely limited to securing their new borders and developing basic capabilities to support sovereignty protection.[112] With joining PfP and contributing forces to UN peacekeeping operations, legacy fixed territorial-based logistics concepts and principles needed to be reviewed with the objective of revising them. Croatia acknowledged the need to change its existing territorial-based force structure in 2005: "the armed forces are more likely expected to take part in operations abroad rather than at home."[113] Yet, the challenge to achieve this objective has remained elusive. Its 2013 Strategic Defence Review acknowledged this objective has yet to be achieved.[114] As stability spread throughout the region and the requirement for effecting territorial defense operations dissipated, the logistics concept supporting this operational focus should correspondingly have changed. Certainly, one would have thought that the adoption of NATO nations' concepts such as expeditionary logistics and increasingly relying on the civilian sector's global logistics backbone via HNS arrangements, would have become a *sine qua non*. To be generous, one can assess progress in this area to have been modest. Legacy concepts, assumptions, and principles remain entrenched in law, regulation, norms, and, most challenging, within training and education institutions in these countries. Thus, one finds "push" logistics present within the individual and collective mentality of these defense institutions and armed forces.

Perhaps given the limited expertise regarding defense outside of the armed forces in these countries (Slovenia being a major exception), there has been poor understanding among the political classes of these countries about the potential efficiencies that could be found by adopting modern logistics concepts. And, to be fair, the particularly JNA legacy that relates to infrastructure was not terribly conducive to enabling civil officials to frame the problem they face. Legacy assumptions remain unchallenged/un-assessed as they relate to managing the sprawling post-JNA defense estate in these republics. For instance, in the JNA, utilities and consumable expenses at bases were not managed and financed locally, but rather were centralized, thereby removing *incentives* by which local commanders and base managers could optimally and efficiently manage resources.[115] Likewise, smaller, residual Serbian industries continue to exist, albeit with the stated proviso that they must be increasingly self-sufficient. That said, their existence needs to be carefully considered as they perpetuate the legacy practice of intellectually focusing the defense institution to the procurement of products of these industries, and their subsequent heavy involvement in routine maintenance. This is as opposed to turning the question around to ask: what do the armed forces need to enable them to execute their new missions, that is, expeditionary operations, or a more mobile and operationally maneuverable forces required by a smaller and professional force? This requires a completely different approach as it concentrates responsibility for the development of support requirements at the tactical level under the direction of service chiefs and joint operations commanders, and not from ministries of defense.

There has been only modest progress in most countries. Macedonia was able to develop and publish a basic national logistics concept in 2004, which has provided the basis for the development of procedural manuals. Yet, for the full implementation of a "pull" logistics concept to take hold, the entire armed forces need to change. Montenegrin logistic capabilities remain very modest and are largely based on depots and the armed services providing for their own requirements, as needed. Related to all armed forces, to adopt fully Western concepts tactical units will require trained and experienced NCOs and officers to draft accurate logistics Estimates, and concomitantly, existing organizations throughout the entire defense institution need to be reviewed to determine if their continued existence is required. Delegation of financial authority to lower-level commanders and staff is needed to enable the full implementation of HNS agreements in order to obtain cost-effective support from commercial suppliers, either nationally or on deployments. Moreover, in order to move toward adopting a modern supply system, a dedicated IT structure and appropriate software is needed and it has been slow in coming to most of these countries. In one case, operational logistics planning was side-tracked by the terribly mistaken belief that this could take place within an imported US model of PPBS. In short, this is one area of defense management and planning where legacy assumptions and principles persist, and are often ignored and go unaddressed; all the while they continue to bleed defense budgets, while not providing the armed forces with the support they will need to meet currently declared, let alone future, missions.

Professionalism

Albeit founded to protect the communist party, the JNA nevertheless possessed a strong tradition of a sense of its own professionalism, as well as institutional autonomy that even isolated it for a while from political manipulation by the Milosevic regime. But, by spring 1991, the JNA was actively fighting in the service of that regime.[116] Thus, any discussion of professionalism in post-Yugoslav armed forces needs to begin with this common base point. By extension, all six of these countries have subsequently struggled to overcome their common JNA HRM concept that was based on conscription, and to introduce the professional force model. What appears to be lacking is a firm understanding that HRM can never be functional if the armed forces are not properly structured and organized around viable operational units (battalions, brigades, ship's companies, etc.). An armed force based on empty units will never be able to create a pyramidal personnel structure, thereby introducing needed discipline into the system, and effective management can be further enhanced if a cohort concept were also introduced. Even a defense institution as sophisticated and advanced as that of Slovenia declared in its 2009 SDR the need to restructure its tactical formations, but literally within pages discussed the continued challenges posed by HRM, thereby failing to make this important conceptual connection between HRM and the organization of tactical formations.[117] Furthermore, the Slovenian Ministry of Defense's claimed objective of gradually reaching a rank structure based on 1:2:5 ratio (officers, NCOs, soldiers) can only be interpreted as constituting a lack of political commitment to develop more quickly an effective and *cost-effective* pyramidal rank structure,[118] because as of 2013, these ratios stood at 1:1.8:2.8.[119] The Slovenian Ministry of Defense also has its own unique HRM challenges in that the defense institution and armed forces must engage in collective bargaining with *five* separate labor unions.[120]

But, as armed forces created from the remnants of the JNA, most of these defense institutions inherited a large number of officers and NCOs whose numbers bear no direct correlation to national requirements, let alone what is affordable. Again, it is instructive that all of these defense institutions have struggled to make this transition. Indeed, Edmunds writes that the JNA possessed a well-developed and partial merit-based personnel system, although how this squares with the critical role played by the party and *collegia* is not explained.[121] The creation of successor armed forces, often in the midst of conflict, obviously obviated against the creation of effective HRM policy. Moreover, with the dissolution of Yugoslavia, there was a consistent move on the part of newly-created independent governments to consolidate power to include the armed forces. Following the end of hostilities in the region, all countries at different times transitioned to professional forces. However, all have struggled to implement fully the concept of a professional force. Abandoning conscription by any armed force has never been an easy transition;[122] however, this has been particularly problematic in these six countries. It has been compounded by the reality that whereas the JNA was an extremely large armed force, its successor armed forces were also large at birth and remained so well after the end of open hostilities. Peace, however welcome, necessitated demobilization. Serbia and Montenegro were especially hard hit financially and served as the federal successor of the JNA as late as 2007. Thus, the Yugoslav Federal defense budget had the additional strain of needing to provide support for over 16,000 military refugees from other former Yugoslav republics.

Following the succession of hostilities, differences in the character of armed forces have been reflected in methods and success rates of demobilization. For instance, in Bosnia-Herzegovina and Croatia, these armed forces were largely made up of reservists who had taken arms and who had civilian professions and education. The armed forces in Serbia-Montenegro, on the other hand, were mainly made up of long-term professionals from the JNA who lacked sufficient expertise and training to make them marketable in the private sector.[123] However, poor economic conditions have contributed to keeping oversized forces, the reduction of which has been sporadic and politically painful. Where designed with forethought, resettlement programs to decrease the size of armed forces have been developed. For example, in Macedonia from 2005 to 2007, this was done in tandem with the creation of personnel policies and the professionalization of the armed forces in 2006.[124]

Clearly, one of the key weaknesses one finds within these defense institutions related to HRM has been the simple lack of coherent personnel policies, let alone supporting strategies and implementing procedures. To remain on the topic of transitioning from a conscript to a professional force, this is a highly complex process, and all concepts and assumptions governing the planning and management of the armed forces must be carefully reviewed, and policy must be revised and changes implemented. On a more broad level, even the most basic HRM policies have had to be developed *ab ovo*, some of which may not have seemed so obvious in the early years of independence, but have become problematic over time. For example, in Croatia, "the lack of a developed human resource management system within the military or Ministry of Defence means that even when an officer has received military training abroad there is no systematic way of recognising these qualifications or linking them to job assignments or promotions."[125] Further, as late as 2007, Croatian HRM lacked explicit policy and implementing strategy that were supportive of existing defense policy priorities. To the credit of Croatian defense officials, this critical policy lacuna was recognized in the 2005 SDR and the subsequent Long-Term Development Plan (2006–2015), which identified HRM development in the form of the "Concept of Unified Personnel Management" as a priority effort and argued its successful development being essential to completing the transition to a professional force.[126] Such a policy takes on immediacy when one considers that Croatian defense officials realized that they were suffering from maintaining an aging force, with the average age of the force being a shocking thirty-eight years old.[127] But there were other disturbing trends due to the lack of adequate HRM policy. On review, it was found that there were imbalances throughout the force. For instance, the structure suffered from an excess number of management officials, but there was still a lack of qualified personnel,[128] and individuals were not being assigned to postings in accordance with their expertise and career path requirements. The lack of a consistent HRM policy was the principal reason that human resource potential of the armed forces was not being fully utilized. It is little wonder that the government admitted that the force was experiencing difficulties in meeting the demands of its tasks.[129] The politicization of the armed forces under the Tudjman regime resulted in a bureaucratic structure that obviated against developing and maintaining performance record-keeping. Subsequent governments and their ministers have had to address how to encourage and endorse promotions based on merit, absent such performance data.[130]

Whereas the Croatian case is well documented in the literature, the case of other countries is not so well represented. However, after spending time with all of these other armed forces in-country, it is clear that Croatia is representative of the lack of development in HRM in these professionalized armed forces. Croatia and Slovenia arguably have made the most progress simply in coming to terms with the depth of the challenges that they face, which remain considerable. For example, the Slovenian process of approving promotions undermines the CHOD's authority. Specifically, recommendations for all officers' promotions are approved by the minister of defense, but these lists are then vetted by the HRM directorate, thereby diminishing the CHOD's vote to one-eighth of the total recommendation. His authority is arguably further diluted since his list of recommendations is first vetted by the intelligence and security service before being forwarded to the board. On these issues Furlan writes: "These control mechanisms and an ignorance of military advice (when for example the Minister strengthens the defense administration by utilizing military human resources or decorate [sic] military personnel without the CHOD's knowledge and consent) undermines the CHOD's legal authority and reduces the credibility of the office."[131] As late as 2001, the HRM directorate of the Slovenian Ministry of Defense not only established HRM policy but also managed personnel postings, thereby breaking the principle against mixing policy and execution in one organization.[132] This is yet another example of a weak policy framework.

Due to history, tradition, societal norms, and the persistence of legacy concepts, it is difficult to find a case where there is integrated evaluation of performance, objective selection, cohort management, and a competitive assignment process. What one does find are embryonic elements of all of these processes, but often without any direct linkages and are therefore incoherent. For instance, selection (in some cases based on the Western board system) is not always linked to follow-on assignments. There are personnel performance evaluations, but they are not necessarily conducted on an annual basis. In Montenegro, initially after independence these were conducted only once every four years, except for personnel in new assignments where there is a performance review after the first year. Subsequent legal and administrative reforms have changed this practice to annual evaluations, both for military and for civilians. It should come as no surprise that in the absence of centralized and integrated HRM structures and processes, some of these armed forces have continued the JNA legacy of using *collegia* for coordination and decision-making from individual units up to the general staff and the ministry of defense.

Officials in these countries argue that these are effective bodies since if a nominee meets all established criteria (professional skills, length of service, health standards, and language requirements), the decision-making authority cannot refuse selecting a person for promotion. Actual promotion, however, can take place only if there is a vacant position of corresponding rank. In the case of appointments of senior officers, then, the procedure is as follows: the *collegium* at the general staff reviews personal files of lieutenant-colonels eligible for promotion to the rank of substantive colonel and submits its recommendations through the country's CHOD to the minister of defense. The *collegium* at the ministry of defense reviews the CHOD's submissions and gives its recommendations to the country's minister of defense. Similar procedures hold for general officer ranks, with the difference that instead of appointing an officer, the country's minister of defense submits his recommendations to the country's president, who then grants General Office rank and/or appoints an officer to a flag position. The continued use of such collectivist bodies directly undermines the authority of commanders to provide their professional advice as to individuals' performance and prospects for future promotions. These are key inherent responsibilities of commanders in Western armed forces. Indeed, it is arguable that the continued existence of *collegia* and the introduction of modern HRM practices are simply incompatible.

If Slovenia and Croatia are at one extreme in the recognition of the need for adopting modern Western approaches to HRM, on the other side has been the unfortunate Bosnia and Herzegovina armed forces. Due to the merger of the two factions' defense institutions in 2005, personnel assignments at all levels have had to be balanced by political and ethnic considerations to create a single defense force.[133] As such, some of the weaknesses in the effective utilization of personnel are more profound and deep-seated in this armed force. The decision to transition to a professional force has been hampered by the lack of a functional, integrated career management system, supported by, for instance, formal expertise and an assignment process to positions based on central selection.[134]

In short, in terms of professionalization of these forces, even where there does exist elements of a modern military personnel management system to support professionalization (i.e., attraction, recruiting, selection, job assignment, postings, career management, training, education, quality of life, retention, and release/retirement), these components are often lacking integration into a coherent whole. Where there is adequate HRM policy (e.g., Macedonia), the lack of the aforementioned elements of a modern system inhibits the implementation of policy objectives and priorities. It is clear that additional reforms in all of these countries will be required in order to adopt the critical characteristics of transparency, clarity, and the empowerment of commanders. Thus, in essence, the challenge remains to create coherent tactical formations and comprehensive policy frameworks that can be translated into functioning HRM systems and procedures.

Conclusion

It should be evident from the foregoing analysis that the successor former Yugoslav republics have both benefited from and had the challenge of overcoming JNA legacies. What is interesting is that these JNA legacies are observable, palpable actually, in all six of these defense institutions. The only variable is the degree to which these legacy concepts are manifested. To be sure, Slovenia is the showcase former communist republic that has been able to overcome most of its legacy past and seemingly adopt Western democratic defense governance concepts. However, a closer look reveals no small degree of conceptual incoherence in the form of centralization of decision-making in the ministry of defense, a proclivity among some officials for the return of territorial defense model, an inability to produce implementable defense plans, and modest operational combat capabilities in relation to the size of the force.[135] Indeed, in both Slovenia and Croatia, one can discern a continued divide between those officers and NCOs with JNA pedigrees and those from Territorial Defense Forces, or without either lineage.[136] In Serbia, domestic economic stagnation continues to press on a defense budget that forces the use of legacy equipment, reinforced by the need to support its sizable domestic arms industry. Its defense institution has moved in fits and starts toward reform, but JNA-sourced legacies remain strongly engrained in the institution's soul. Empty battalions and brigades and excess infrastructure continue to bleed money and attention, all to support an atavistic concept of territorial defense. Montenegro faces enormous challenges due to its small size, modest resource base, and disaggregated force structure left at independence in 2006. It is no small prediction that without significant political decisions to implement the reforms outlined in its 2013 Strategic Defense Review, and introducing greater policy and capability coherence, the armed forces will atrophy and essential basic sovereignty protection tasks will go unmet. Despite continued and unresolved lingering ethnic tension, the Macedonian defense institution has made commendable progress despite limited resources and a civil war in 2001. Implementing and better linking funding to policy priorities continues to present challenges, but this is hardly a unique problem in the region as all defense institutions struggle to link policy priorities to money. Finally, Bosnia-Herzegovina can hardly be thought to have a unified defense institution in fact due to the continued stalemate at the national political level.

It is perhaps surprising that with the exception of Slovenia, the successors of the JNA have been unable to capitalize on its strengths and sophistication. For instance, the positive legacies of decentralized command, delegation of budgets to commanders, and a professional NCO corps (with leadership responsibilities) should be a more prominent feature of these armed forces. Slovenia and Croatia provide exceptions to this observation. Clearly the trauma of the breakup of Yugoslavia, where all of the successor republics, to varying degrees, were exposed to crises, open warfare, and, in some cases, domestic political repression, combined to have the effect in many of these defense institutions of obviating against decentralization. Thus, for a proper understanding of these defense institutions today, it is essential to recognize the varying degree of influence of recent warfare and JNA legacies continue to have on them.

Building Defense Institutions:
Sharpening the Western Mind

If an objective observer were both to examine the scale of the task set before the Western Alliance in 1991 and compare the results of the democratic transformation of these legacy defense institutions, it is clear that in view of the meager results (as documented in the previous three chapters), one is challenged to find many systemic successes. To be sure, Cottey, Edmunds, and Forster have accurately argued that democratic norms are secure and there is little evidence of the armed forces challenging elected civilian authorities.[1] And, in this respect, the West and newly independent states are due a fairly high degree of credit for this not inconsequential achievement. The common desire on the part of every defense institution to adopt "NATO standards" was essentially embraced by most officials throughout the region (to be sure, with varying degrees of sincerity), and indeed, continues to be heard to this day, even in partner countries where public support for NATO membership remains ambivalent.

That said, there is no excusing Western officials for their collective failure to exercise better judgment to gather appropriate expertise the better to define this complex challenge. This point is eloquently argued by Bellamy and Edmunds:

> the international community has shown little sensitivity to the structural impediments to reform described earlier. This has resulted in unrealistic expectations, and in the past, at least, the articulation of inappropriate and ineffective policies.[2]

Clearly, the West in general, with few exceptions, has continued to underestimate the realities *in situ* and the deep-seated impediments and resistance to reform. Even the highly respected analyst Jeffrey Simon was perhaps too optimistic when writing thus in 2004: "Though Central European militaries have evidenced significant reforms and been restructured to accommodate NATO, force modernization continues to be greatly restrained by scarce resources."[3] Yet it is not just limited resources that have hampered modernization. As observed by Abrahamsson, changing the military requirements of a nation inevitably and profoundly affects the attitudes, behaviors, expectations, and values of an armed force.[4] As already seen in previous chapters, vast sums of money, incalculable man-years of labor, and significant equipment transfers have taken place, but with meager results, both in terms of deeper institutional reform and in terms of producing consistent and predictable defense outcomes.

If there had been a concerted effort by NATO and its principal members systematically to gain an appreciation of the scale of the task confronting these defense institutions to reform, surely these institutions would be further ahead in adopting Western democratic defense governance concepts than one has seen to date. As will be argued in this chapter, many of the Western-sourced concepts, assumptions, approaches, models, and techniques that have been exported to the East have been often been misunderstood or misapplied; in the worst cases, they have actually been counterproductive to achieving their intended goals. In many cases, these suggested solutions have overlaid existing legacy concepts and, in some egregious cases, have been used to *reinforce* them, often with a thinly applied patina of legitimizing Western modernity. The reason for this lack of success can be traced to Western officials that either did not undertake a proper mission analysis of the challenges or simply ignored given analysis and/or advice. Rather, all too often, Western officials responded to requests for assistance with existing national methods, models, and, critically, *concepts and assumptions*, which have not produced envisaged change. In short, much of this well-meaning work must be regarded as having been marginal to the greater goal of enabling these defense institutions to adopt Western democratic defense governance concepts. The Western approach to building ministerial capacity has generally been to take defense planning and management concepts, which are unique to their own national processes and conditions, and all but export them with little consideration given to two key points. First, the reality is that legacy concepts continue to dominate these organizations and are antithetical to their Western counterparts. Second, Western assistance is almost entirely and exclusively delivered without any understanding, or appreciation, of the conceptual context in which the information is being conveyed. A proper mission analysis of these defense institutions would reveal that most are *still* largely using, to varying degrees, legacy concepts. Even one of the countries that has ostensibly adopted many Western democratic defense governance concepts, Poland, as seen in Chapter 5, remains plagued with "conceptual spaghetti." It is little wonder then that other countries struggle amidst such conceptual and organizational confusion.

In the end, that which will enable the adoption of Western democratic defense governance concepts by these defense institutions is when there is sufficient collective critical mass of officials, who have an understanding of these basic Western concepts and principles, but who can also make the necessary changes in legacy institutions to enable the full adoption of them by *retiring* their legacy counterparts. This author does not imply there is solely the need to achieve *operational* interoperability within NATO; this is a given. Rather the more challenging objective is to create greater *intellectual* interoperability with their Western counterparts. While not enjoying any official definition, it is defined in this context as constituting a deep understanding and sharing of common key Western democratic defense governance concepts, as well as their key assumptions and *logic*. But, as these basic institutional tenants are highly contextualized and are indeed contemporaneous reflections of these nations and their defense institution's core values, it is clear that such a metamorphosis can only occur over time with strong political pressure. But, disturbingly, all too many officers, NCOs, and soldiers in these countries are *still* being trained and educated in unreformed educational and training organizations. Yet this is not to imply that the ideal solution is to rely solely on sending personnel to PME and formal individual, leader, and collective training programs made available in old NATO nations. Such an approach has already been adopted, intentionally or not, thereby condemning the reform of these defense institutions to a time line that can only be measured in multiples of decades. There are other solutions and practices, if properly applied, that can speed up this process. After twenty-five-plus years of efforts, if one cares to look for it, there *is* a bulging database of failed practices that should be mined for a better understanding of these challenges. Thus, it is useful to examine a select number of some of the more egregiously failed advice and assistance methods that have been employed by NATO and NATO nations to discern, by extension, potentially better approaches to exporting Western advice to reform non-Western defense institutions.

This chapter is organized in five sections. The first section will provide a brief synthesis of the common pathologies that continue to persist in the three legacy typologies. While the three previous chapters endeavored to document the actual state of the adoption of Western democratic governance concepts by these defense institutions, this section will identify those key challenges common to all three the better to enable a wider understanding of the choices facing decision makers on both sides of the conceptual divide. The second section will present another synthesis of a general representation of common Western concepts, models, and *assumptions* that have been used in the design and programming of their assistance programs with the objective to identify where and why they have not been successful. The third section will argue that the West needs to reassess its own basic assumptions regarding how it organizes its advice and assistance programs offered to post-communist European defense institutions. What is required is nothing less than a change in Western logic that contains lessons from the disciplines of change management, anthropology, and a better appreciation of the systematic challenges posed by the persistence of legacy concepts. The fourth section, using the common challenges to adopting Western democratic defense governance concepts, will identify the concepts and assumptions by which Western officials should redirect their efforts to provide advice in clear programmatic language. The fifth and final section will apply these suggested methods to the three typologies and recommend approaches to avoid reinforcing legacy concepts, and will identify where there are country-specific opportunities to effect reform.

Synthesis of legacy institutional pathologies

Chapters 4 through 6 went to pains to tease out, where possible, discernible differences among these defense institutions of their challenges to adopt Western democratic defense governance concepts. A careful reading shows that there is no small degree of legacy pathologies unique to each of these three typologies. Yet the universal pernicious character of communism did tend to produce common characteristics that have impeded the nuanced understanding, as well as adoption, of Western democratic defense governance concepts. To be sure, these common characteristics vary in how they are manifested, as well as in their intensity. That said, their representation in this section will serve to support a contextual analysis that provides a basis against which the following section can critique the West's approach to providing reform assistance, and particularly the assumptions upon which they have been based. As will be argued, the delta between Western assumptions and Central and Eastern European institutional and cultural realities is quite wide and deep, and it begins from first principles.

Arguably, the single most important impediment to adopt Western democratic defense governance concepts by legacy defense institutions is the active discouragement of all personnel, except the most senior leaders, from being *allowed* to engage in critical thinking as an essential element of their professional responsibilities. The concept that strength and military success can *only* flow from iron and blind discipline has yet to be discredited and retired. David Glanz's observations made in 1998 are as true now as they were then:

> In fact, in addition to the other military legacies of communist rule, because of its pervasiveness, persistence, and intangible nature, *the intellectual legacy of Soviet rule may prove to be the most difficult problem in the military to overcome.* In fact, this reality poses the greatest barrier to military reform in the three countries and, at the same time, the greatest challenge to foreign military assistance that seeks to foster military reform.[5]

If one becomes a senior leader of an armed force but has never been allowed to engage in critical thinking during one's entire professional career, its advent late in one's professional life is unlikely to be very successful. As critical thinking is all but avoided in unreformed PME institutions (where rote and passive learning remains the norm), it is little wonder that most staff work in these countries is highly underdeveloped and lacks such basic key characteristics as problem definition, objectivity, trade-off analysis based on data, and the development of actionable options. With some exceptions, one can find this weakness at all levels in all legacy defense institutions. What is maddening is that many Central and Eastern European officers have been trained and educated in Western PME institutions, and critically, many more have been on demanding international operations (e.g., Iraq, Afghanistan, and UN peacekeeping operations). On operations and international exercises, these individuals will demonstrate remarkable fluency in their ability to engage in critically analyzing the operational environment. However, when these individuals return to their national environment, they quietly file away these concepts and legacy procedures are once again followed.

As a corollary of the systematic discouragement of being allowed to engage in critical thinking, the primacy of employing the algorithmic approach to solving *all* problems continues. In essence, this holds that there is *one* scientifically based solution (expressed mathematically) to all defense planning and management problems. This fallacious concept has its roots in legacy norms that officials (unless they are senior party officials) were never to be trusted to make any decisions. As so vividly and bloodily demonstrated by the Soviet Red Army in the Second World War, operational planning analysis consists of the accurate application of the correct correlation of forces algorithm to produce the *one*, scientifically determined correct solution to an operational move.[6] After the Cold War, this approach to operational planning by these armed forces has been elevated to providing a conceptual basis for national-level defense planning. This legacy concept is closely related to, and feeds into, another inheritance, that being escaping from the responsibility and accountability of one's own professional actions. Soviet ideology was based on the premise that as it was scientifically derived, it was, *ipso facto*, perfect. Ergo, a scientifically developed algorithm was perfect, by definition, and therefore any sub-performance could be blamed on an individual who did not understand fully the algorithm, science, or underlying communist ideology. Evidence of this legacy can be found in defense planning that is defined as constituting a series of algorithms. Of course, such nirvana for planners does not exist. Western problem-solving processes are only capable of *framing* questions, which then can only be solved using human factors, such as argument, civil-military collaboration, and consensus-building, all to produce a range of possible solutions.

As a direct result of these legacy attitudes, all these institutions, to varying degrees of intensity, are simply all but incapable of consistently conducting rudimentary defense planning. Notwithstanding early optimistic and highly well-informed assessments that a number of legacy defense institutions were capable of conducting effective defense planning,[7] the subsequent record has demonstrated that conducting effective *planning* (vice producing unrealizable plans) remains elusive at best. To be sure, all of these ministries of defense have directorates of defense planning, and they all draft defense plans, but as demonstrated in Chapters 4 through 6, it is difficult to identify where any of these plans actually have systematically changed the allocation of money, personnel distributions, or adjusted structures. Too often, Western officials see what they recognize as comparable structures (and documents) by their titles and simply assume that their activities and outputs are comparable to their Western counterparts.[8] Plans are produced, but they are almost always denuded of priorities, nor are they defined in their financial costs, let alone sufficiently informed by operational planning analysis (e.g., even in Slovenia). As such, they are almost always simply aspirations, always assuming defense spending will increase, and, therefore, are *not* plans.[9] As a reflection of their legacy heritage and positive law systems, legacy defense officials perceive plans as *contracts*, with little understanding of the need for flexibility to enable the basic tenets of plans to stay current in light of expected shifts in policies and financial realities. Plans are seen as inadaptable after their approval, and indeed, they very often become enshrined in law, for example, the Ukrainian Five Year State Program on the Development of the Armed Forces. In short, defense plans resemble Soviet-inspired rigid operational plans which are often translated into uncosted, or inaccurately costed, development plans. That such a pernicious legacy persists more than twenty-five years since the end of the Cold War clearly manifests a debilitating incapability to undertake such a critically essential national-level task. That so many Western officials are remotely unaware of this fundamental weakness is nothing short of amazing. The evidence demonstrates that the fact that unrealizable national defense plans are still being produced throughout the region must be judged as one of the most serious challenges to these institutions and constitutes a major failure in Western provided advice and assistance.

Post-communist positive law (i.e., civil code) has had a highly negative effect on the ability, or perhaps willingness, of officials to engage in critical thinking. Activities are allowed *only* insofar as they are explicitly sanctioned in law. As such, all activities and authorities are narrowly defined and the delegation of authority is highly restricted and the practice of interpreting law is not common. This approach only encourages the further centralization of decision-making and produces an environment that forbids any activity unless it is explicitly permitted. Not surprisingly, this becomes a very convenient excuse by many not to lead, let alone take calculated risks, to press for change. In consequence, the inability of ministries of defense to take an active and dynamic role in interpreting basic legal foundations (i.e., the constitution and Defense Acts) tends to result in policy needing to be *expressed* as legislation, as opposed to being articulated in policy memoranda or regulations. Thus, policy is conflated as law which has the detrimental effect of impeding, as opposed to facilitating, needed change. After all, parliaments have finite time to assess and draft and redraft legislation. Worse yet, if it is assumed that policy must be expressed in detailed legislation, even something as basic as defense planning can result in a stand-alone piece of legislation (of twenty-plus pages in length) written by nondefense planning experts in a very restrictive manner.[10] In short, the conflation of law and policy has been a major impediment to enabling governments and ministers of defense to make even the most basic of organizational and procedural reforms.

As a result of this combination of factors, policy frameworks, even where they exist, are weak. In effect, "policy" is conflated with partisan political life (i.e., *politika*).[11] Consequently, existing policy direction and priorities remain a function of relationships and decision-making processes are often built on personal power, as opposed to specified and defined authorities, balanced by individual accountability. Thus, it is common to find published policy documents which are completely and utterly ignored by the bureaucracy. In fact, it is equally not uncommon that such documents are hopelessly out-of-date, thereby providing a visual appreciation of the state of underdeveloped policy frameworks, disconnected from resource decision-making. The inability of a ministry of defense either to promulgate policy that directs every action of the organization or to ensure that its policies and priorities are executed simply means that the ministry is not fully functioning as defined by Western democratic defense governance concepts. For without such a capability, legacy practices and even basic military missions continue unhindered. For instance, absent ministerial-sanctioned contingency planning guidance, it should come to be no surprise that these armed forces continue to be oriented to, and trained in accordance with, legacy concepts, assumptions, and standards. To illustrate the state of underdevelopment, it is difficult to identify countries that have been able to formulate even the most rudimentary and coherent HRM policies—the lifeblood of any armed force.

Directly related to the issue of the lack of policy frameworks is the absence of clarity in institutional responsibilities, which is often due to contradictory legislation. As roles and missions remain regularly contested, essential subsidiary concepts, such as command authorities, remain unknown, let alone defined. For instance, Darchiashvili documents the contradictory nature of Georgian defense and security-related policy documents and legislation in such critical areas as who can declare a state of emergency (with or without parliamentary approval), what are the basic roles and missions of the armed forces, and what is the relationship between the ministry of defense and the general staff.[12] As remarkable as it may seem, notwithstanding their respective positive law traditions, there remains great confusion and opacity of the roles and missions of all security ministries, let alone *within* defense institutions themselves. The practice, or perhaps one should say the culture, of staff coordination and consensus-building is also underdeveloped, which only compounds the need to establish institutional clarity in responsibilities. Such an endeavor, without doubt, takes on added meaning when one considers that most countries in the region possess paramilitary forces with both law enforcement and national defense responsibilities in *wartime*. It is not always clear in most of these countries how these organizations would function in an international crisis. The confusion surrounding Georgian government actions in the Georgian-Russia War of 2008,[13] Russian officials' response to the Beslan hostage crisis in September 2004,[14] and the lack of a coherent Ukrainian response to the Russian invasion of Crimea and its support of armed separatists in eastern Ukraine in 2014 provide chillingly representative examples. From a traditional Western perspective, the concept of each discrete role can be led by only *one* organization and all others are in support, as well as a basic understanding of the concept of escalation, are only slowly being accepted. Finally, the concept of Transfer of Authority, whereby formal and validated procedures allow for the transfer of specific responsibilities to other organization (particularly in a state of escalation), is equally unknown as an essential concept, both for national defense but also for the effective response to national disasters.

The basic Western conceptual building blocks of force development and force management also remain foreign in the Central and Eastern European region, and they are either simply not formally conducted or only exist in their most basic embryonic state. With the possible exceptions of Poland and Slovenia, ministries of defense and general staffs appear blindly unaware of the essential need for the daily management of the force in its *entirety*. Since the requirement for force *management* has gone largely ignored, it is little wonder that force *development*, which logically should build on the continuous examination of the capabilities of the current force in relation to government guidance, is even more underdeveloped.

Directly related to the lack of force management and force development concepts is the fact that conceptual defense thinking in the region remains largely tied tightly to "systems" and "platforms," vice capabilities. Platforms and systems are seen as discrete items, conceptually detached from integrative training and logistics, all to create synergies with other systems to produce measurable effects, that is, capabilities. Capabilities, as a conceptual building block, remain all but unknown in most legacy defense institutions, mainly because many Slavic languages do not possess a distinct word for "capability." Moreover, as there has been very little defense procurement of sizable Western kit, due to limited finances, many of these defense institutions have yet to procure and then maintain a major Western capability. Those that have procured a critical mass of Western equipment (e.g., Poland with F-16s, FFG-7 frigates, Type 207 submarines, and Leopard main battle tanks) have experienced a profound shock to their entire defense institutions, whose implications are still being absorbed.

With one notable exception (Yugoslavia), communist armed forces simply did not have civilian defense experts or officials. They were thoroughly militarized as there was no perceived need for a cadre of civilian defense, vice military, experts to provide a necessary policy continuity and act as a conduit between senior political officials and the armed forces. The introduction of democratic governments in these countries changed the civil-military relationship, and this gap was quickly filled either by former military officers or by inexperienced civilians who often perceived their tasks as administrative, as opposed to being experts in defense.[15] This dearth in the quality and quantity of civilian expertise has resulted in the continuation of a military orientation of defense institutions that has only begun to diminish, but not in all countries. In fact, it is arguably the case that the lack of experienced civilian defense officials has, *inter alia*, impeded the development of a policy framework.

Finally, the last key difference between old and new NATO nations and partners relates to the continuation of, and in some cases increases in, institutional incentives that have encouraged individuals to engage in rent-seeking. The end of the Cold War and the Balkan wars removed the raison d'être of many of these armed forces, that is, regime survival. Absent a clear policy framework and firm management, the previous Cold War operational focus was lost and, by default, has been replaced with norms that encourage officials to promote their own personal interests. New pernicious incentives that were introduced had the effect of discouraging individuals from service to nation first, no matter how patriotic and committed an individual officer may be. Grants of housing, higher pay for serving in a ministry of defense and general staff, as opposed to serving at the tactical level, and significant allowances to volunteer for deployments have all combined to produce a uniquely different military culture from general liberal democratic norms.

To be sure, the degree to which these common challenges are present in legacy defense institutions, as well as their intensity, is all very much country-dependent. However, it would be imprudent to assume that elements of them do not exist in all of the countries being studied. Notwithstanding the three typologies developed for this work, it needs to be repeated that all of these armed forces were subjected to the domination and total control by communist governments over many years. As examined in Chapters 4 through 6, these institutional cultural norms have proven to be deep-seated and are highly resistant to change. It should be little wonder in light of this continuing *conceptual divide* that the suggestion of adopting Western democratic defense governance concepts has been so poorly and unevenly accepted and implemented essentially by all of these countries. It is to some of the unsuccessful approaches that the work will now turn.

Incoherence of Western gifts

In the twenty-five years since the end of the Cold War, former communist defense institutions have been exposed to what must be all possible aspects of what constitutes

Western democratic defense governance concepts. Yet, as a general critique, both Western donor and Eastern recipient countries have generally failed to appreciate that reform of these defense institutions, absent the wholesale dismissal of the entire officer corps presented, optimistically, a long-term challenge that requires constant high-level political management. From an Eastern perspective, the way forward was equally unclear. General Henryk Szumski, the then-Polish CHOD, pointed out that reform was an ongoing process, but lacked coherence. In short, he argued that reforms "were superficial, partial, and not based on a final vision." No one had a firm picture of what the final result would look like.[16] This lack of coherence was abetted by Western advice and assistance projects which tend to be largely designed and managed as one-off training events, PME courses for individuals, seminars, or workshops. A former Latvian minister of defense observed that this plethora of advice was "often uncoordinated and short-term in nature" and had the result of producing confusion, vice providing solutions.[17] Thus, it was left to severely underdeveloped defense institutions the responsibility of discerning which of the countless models, organizational templates, procedures, and techniques were even generally, let alone optimally, well suited for their requirements. And, fundamentally, one can pose this important question: how many of those Western officials providing assistance had any inclination of what they were proposing was antithetical to the conceptual basis of the recipient country's defense institution? The fact that one sees repetition of assistance programs, projects, and subjects, uninformed by experience, speaks legions to the failure of Western policies and the assumptions upon which these programs are based. In the following section, the most egregious examples of patterns of advice and assistance that have been particularly ineffectual, are discussed.

National models

In a general sense, what must be considered to be one of the most well-meaning practice but, in the end, one that has had a pernicious lasting negative effect, has been to encourage a defense institution to adopt a donor country's own national models and methods.[18] While the United States is not the only country to have used this approach to providing advice and assistance, given the size of its efforts in the region, the results of this approach can be seen throughout the region. Truth be told, it has had negative effects on a number of levels. First, this practice encouraged the perception among legacy officials and officers that solutions to their challenges were in the form of Western templates, as opposed to using critical thinking to develop indigenous options to meet their unique conditions and requirements. Second, the immense size and budget of the US Department of Defense defies emulation in most of its activities and structures. Too often, recommendations for modernization and/or change are offered, absent any thought given to the scale of these countries and, importantly, the long-term financial liabilities of this advice.[19] Third, nations which were NATO aspirants faced the political problem of not wanting to appear to be ungrateful, or openly rejecting the recommendations of adopting national models being proffered by donor nations. Finally, as these young or reforming defense institutions were based, to varying degrees, on legacy concepts, it made them singularly ill-prepared to be able to discern, as observed by Sava, between what they *wanted* in terms of reform and what they *needed* to achieve their national reform objectives.[20]

One might have thought that Western programs would have been better equipped to provide this type of advice. With some exceptions, this has not been the case. In what must be considered a highly egregious example of inappropriate advice aligned to realities, a private US-based defense consultancy recommended reshaping the Croatian Ministry of Defense and General Staff with a model *based* on the US Department of Defense. Little wonder that in 2003, Croatian defense leadership realized how inappropriate this structure was and restructured both organizations into a more manageable and *affordable* structure.[21] In short, Edmunds judges that the practice of importing models is problematic and counterproductive in the case of defense reform,[22] and is also generally discredited in the field of economic development (known as the "visiting economist syndrome").[23]

Documents

If the US Department of Defense is deemed inappropriate as a model for emulation by countries in Central and Eastern Europe, one must equally question why US policy and strategy documents have been deemed to constitute the gold standard of defense policy and planning. Indeed, this case provides a multilayered example of conceptual false cognates and contextual confusion that warrants deeper examination: the difference between the legacy understanding of *daktrina* and the understanding of Western democratic concept of policy. As to the former, this was promulgated during communism in the most exacting scientific setting to produce the one document that addressed coherently *all* aspects of military affairs. There was never a question of any officer having the authority to interpret *daktrina* or it containing shortcomings. It may surprise some Western officials and analysts that this understanding of *daktrina* is very much alive in many legacy defense institutions, and the conflation of *daktrina* with policy serves only to confuse legacy-educated officials. Conversely, policy in the West is the outcome of a collaborative and consensus-building process based on objective data *to inform decision-making*. This is another excellent example of how nuanced seemingly basic discussions can cause confusion and/or reinforce misinterpretations of language and concepts. Moreover, it should be clear that both concepts, that is, one directive and the other interpretative, are clearly antithetical, and the introduction of the modern concept clearly necessitates the retirement of the legacy one, in all of its manifestations, for the modern version to function. A failure to do so has resulted inevitably in "conceptual spaghetti."

With this background understanding, precisely what role can Western security and defense policy documents play in such settings? Too much time has been wasted encouraging reforming countries to adopt National Security Strategies, National Military Strategies, and other such documents.[24] Early US defense assessments of Central and Eastern European defense institutions and armed forces from the late 1990s onward habitually argued the need for all of these institutions to draft and implement these documents.[25] Even the NATO International Staff took up this advocacy and made the adoption of such documents key partnership objectives which countries should achieve as a means of bringing their defense planning processes into conformance with Western democratic governance concepts. While *en principe* the documentation of policy developed in a consensus-driven fashion can be beneficial to clarifying defense planning objectives and priorities, two key nuances must be recognized. First, the value of these documents within the US policy process must be taken *addito salis grano*. These documents were only adopted by the United States on the cusp of winning the Cold War and, ergo, can hardly be claimed that their value has been *validated*. Second, if anything, the record of these documents ignores the normal, nonlinear nature of political decision-making—a point almost always ignored in their advocacy by Western officials. To wit, the administration of George W. Bush released only two National Security Strategy documents during its eight years in office, despite the requirement in law that this is an annual requirement.[26] That these documents are not always created in their intended sequence, let alone necessarily used by defense planners in the three US military departments as they create their respective program objective memoranda (i.e., budget proposals), is likely not taught to these recipient officials. No less an authority than Robert Gates, former US secretary of defense, wrote, "Personally, I don't recall ever reading the president's NSS [National Security Strategy] when preparing to become secretary of defense. Nor did I read any of the previous National Defense Strategy documents when I became secretary. I never felt disadvantaged by not having read these scriptures."[27]

In the end, such documents are entertaining in theory, but are lacking in political reality regarding policy and planning nuances. Moreover, their possible utility begs the important question how their introduction avoids their conceptual conflation with *daktrina*. Arguably, the drafting of yet more *documents* has precluded defense institutions from gaining the critical understanding that policy is *money* and the two need to be connected. In effect, these exogenous documents trumped the institutional development process by shortcutting the necessary vigorous policy development process. Betz's wonderful description of the all but comical development of such documents in the late 1990s in the Czech Republic, which, in the end, proved to be meaningless, should put paid to any future avocation of this wasteful and distracting practice.[28]

Defense reviews

Related to Western policy documents has been the advocacy by Western officials that reforming defense institutions should conduct SDRs. Note that while acknowledging that defense reviews are inherently a process that may, or may not, result in a final published product, SDRs are almost always perceived by legacy defense institutions as *documents*, and not a disciplined process to align and balance policy with the defense budget and existing force structure. Generally speaking, all defense reviews should contain the same analytical methodology, but can be delimited in their scope; that is, an SDR is a whole of government endeavor, while a force structure review is limited to the defense institution itself. Reviews should use existing defense planning tools, such as organizational responsibilities and functions matrixes, operational planning analysis of the current force, and costing models, but its logic needs to be driven by a systematic and rigorous questioning of all institutional concepts and assumptions. An example of this could be that the air force has sole responsibility for air surveillance, air policing, and air defense. During a review, current assumptions related to these missions need to be intensively examined to ascertain whether a service alone, jointly, and/or with new/different combinations of capabilities, but at lower costs, could be introduced to achieve the same desired outcome. In essence, defense reviews should encourage a vigorous internal debate based on data and costs, resulting in new and innovative courses of action.

Thus, if executed properly, defense reviews potentially can be extremely useful management tools to any defense institution. Not surprisingly, the NATO International Staff and many Western countries (e.g., the United Kingdom) have been keen to encourage reforming defense institutions to undertake these reviews. But reviewing assumptions is problematic in legacy defense institutions where the value of clear organizational responsibilities and functions is simply not clearly understood. For instance, imagine a post-Soviet republic's defense institution where the ministry of defense is a civil institution in name only and where many of its responsibilities and functions are duplicated by the general staff. The most serious challenge faced by all legacy defense institutions is the simple fact of the matter that very few of them have basic (let alone sophisticated) *defense planning tools,* and lack officials who know how to *use* them, or senior leaders who could understand the recommendations produced by them. For example, costing models, even where they exist and are accurate, are not habitually used to support trade-off analysis and inform decision-making. Given the general lack or full utilization of planning tools, force management is all but in its infancy and so there is missing objective databases to support the review of a defense institution's activities. That Western officials, well meaning to be sure, could advocate undertaking a rigorous review of an organization's basic and fundamental activities absent it possessing the basic tools to *conduct* such analyses hardly seems prudent. Conversely, conducting defense reviews is precisely what these countries require. However, to ignore the fact that they do not have the basic tools and institutional logic to carry out such a complex process cannot be seen as constituting constructive advice.

In the end, what is lacking in importing these Western models has been an understanding of the conceptual realities of legacy defense institutions, as well as the highly contextual nature of Western concepts. By ignoring their proper *context* and disregarding the persistence of legacy concepts, these documents have been widely accepted as new a *daktrina,* and have contributed to continuing the practice of isolating money from supporting policy priorities. As such, these documents and highly nuanced PARP reports are nothing short of being dangerous. They raise expectations in the West that these legacy defense institutions have reformed and possess competence and capabilities which are not based on hard evidence. For instance, an analysis of the conduct of the Georgian armed forces in its war with Russia in 2008 observed that the country's 2005 National Military Strategy, drafted with Western advice, contained an entry that introduced the concept of decentralizing decision-making, but which was clearly not employed by the Georgians in that conflict.[29] Without any doubt, adopting this concept in its entirety is essential if legacy armed forces are to become like their Western counterparts; but as a concept, it is extremely difficult to effect. As the Georgian defense institution and armed forces discovered,

> decentralization of military operations quite expectedly appeared hard to implement in practice, since it requires extensive and lengthy training of armed units and high professionalism of the military servicemen. Today there is no governmental institution in Georgia, including the MoD, with such knowledge and experience (the ability to make independent decisions when orders are inadequate and/or when unforeseen emergency situations arise).[30]

Programming alchemy

With the establishment of East-West defense dialogue after the end of the Cold War, there were actually no existing programs specifically designed to assist reforming communist defense institutions. But in one key area, the US Department of Defense, in particular, had an established tool with which it could assist reforming defense institutions. The Office of the Secretary of Defense offered a program to introduce the concept of, and assist in, and the application of, defense economics. It was envisaged to export the American concept of programming, based on long-standing US DoD PPBS training programs to spread the knowledge of "modern" methods. Indeed, there was a program sponsored by that organization that was even self-funded. These multiyear assistance programs were launched in a number of countries in the early to mid-1990s, and later prospective NATO members were evaluated in 2001–2002 to ascertain the state of sophistication of their planning and programming capabilities.[31] Indeed, PPBS became a catchall concept and term, and even the NATO International Staff came to use this term as a benchmark in their evaluations of the state of defense planning of aspirants and partners.

If PPBS is the gold standard for planning and resource management as some may think, then those same advocates have a challenging argument to make since not one other US federal department uses the methodology.[32] The point of argument is not directly to delegitimize the Department of Defense's programming methodology (albeit, previous secretaries of defense, such as Robert Gates, are on record strongly critiquing it and calling for its fundamental reform),[33] but rather to make the case for how highly *unique* and *nuanced* the methodology is, even among old NATO nations. Accepting this point to be the case, one can then ponder the wisdom of advocating such a conceptually complex and contextually unique methodology to *any* reforming young democracy emerging from rigid, opaque, and highly centralized control systems.[34]

Leaving aside a consensus among influential academic writers on strategic planning and public finance that PPBS does *not* constitute the state of the art for effective planning and budgeting,[35] any sophisticated planning and budget system based on Western democratic governance concepts, and one that did not concurrently reform the entire defense institution, surely would be destined to fail. But, for the sake of argument, even if one assumes that PPBS is apposite for the US Department of Defense, one has a challenging argument to make that the unique bureaucratic politics, scale and immense complexity of the US system makes the use of programming appropriate for small reforming legacy defense institutions with parliaments and cabinet governments.[36] For instance, a key assumption of the US PPBS methodology is multiyear funding: a concept that is largely an anathema to ministries of finance in Central and Eastern Europe, many of which do not use, let alone understand conceptually, "programs."[37] Moreover, multiyear programming has the pernicious effect of insulating budgeting from policy decisions as programs are locked into envisaged future defense budgets. Because the methodology was sold as a complete package of *planning*, programming, and budgeting, it was assumed that PPBS would provide all that was necessary to assist a ministry make the transition to an efficient, transparent, and accountable system.

The reality that one finds years after its introduction is not encouraging. What the relevant analyses of the performance of PPBS presented in Chapters 4 to 6 demonstrate is that its adoption succeeded in ensuring that *policy* frameworks have remained weak in these ministries. The introduction of PPBS created a cadre of autonomous programming officials with financial control of budgeting who have generally ignored both policy and planning guidance and continue to isolate money from funding policy priorities. As assistance to these countries was in the form of technical education, vice management consulting to effect holistic organizational change, all too frequently one finds a PPBS method laid on top of antithetical legacy financial management systems and planning documents (e.g., annual matériel and/or acquisition plans), thereby resulting in both bureaucratic and "conceptual spaghetti."

What was apparently not considered when introducing these methods was how they could be misunderstood, or even potentially twisted by officials. For instance, Serbia defined its programming structure based on existing organizations,[38] vice activities and envisaged outcomes. This practice is found throughout the region and simply highlights how change management, vice solely technical assistance lacking proper context, must lead in the introduction of Western concepts. It is little wonder then that PPBS continues to be seen by defense officials in the region as something mysterious, shrouded in opacity and practiced only by a chosen-few high priests, cloistered within the programmers' bureaucratic inner sanctum. Given that PPBS is perceived as scientific, and is often supported by its own "secret" software, only underscores the perception that it is a highly complex *algorithm*. Thus, PPBS has been internalized by defense institutions as a scientific method to provide operational answers via scientifically determined algorithms: untouched by any critical human brain. In essence, in legacy defense institutions there remains an ingrained proclivity to find scientific/technical, vice managerial, means to provide answers to all planning and management issues. Indeed, one continues to hear all too frequent pleas from ministries of defense and general staffs for copies of Western defense planning "algorithms" to assist them in the operation of their PPB systems.

Disturbingly, since very few defense officials have any idea how it actually works, PPBS in its worst manifestations has isolated those who are responsible for producing defense outcomes (e.g., service commanders) from any predictable planning assumption of the resources available to them.[39] The adoption of a "NATO compatible" PPBS methodology[40] (whatever that could possibly mean since planning and budgeting are *national* responsibilities) has added legitimacy to an opaque process which relieves officials from responsibility for producing outcomes. As the system is scientific and therefore perfect, any shortcomings in the operational effectives of the armed forces are simply dismissed by programmers as manifestations of an inadequate defense budget, that is, more money will produce desired outcomes. That the adoption of PPBS has inhibited the creation of a clear line of responsibility from policy to planning to execution appears to be missed by too many both within and outside of these defense institutions.[41] Finally, it is an interesting observation that despite all of the training and software provided to these defense institutions in support of the PPBS method, very few have been able to develop accurate costing models that are habitually used to inform decision-making.[42] What is clearly the case is that the adoption of PPBS has not solved the challenge facing *all* of these countries, namely their inability to develop and implement *costed* defense plans.

At some point, one should think that a repeated failed effort to produce functionality would result in a search for a simpler and less complex method. What is perplexing is that this particular method was introduced in the region at all. The fact of the matter is that PPBS is not widely used by other old NATO nations and those that adopted it in the 1960s subsequently rejected it in short order.[43] In fact, older NATO nations use other and less complex budgeting methods. For example, the United Kingdom has successfully used Resource Accounting and Budgeting since 2001–2002, as well as Balanced Scorecards, which are less complex methods. Equally, since early 2002, Australia, Canada, the Netherlands, and New Zealand have employed Outcome Based Budgeting. The point being argued is that there are other, and *less complex*, methods that should be explored for possible adoption to assist young democracies improve defense governance.

What is clear in hindsight is that Western officials misdiagnosed the root cause of dysfunctionalities in legacy defense institutions, that is, a lack of policy framework tied to money. Clearly the recommended solution, PPBS, has not helped these defense institutions produce viable defense plans, which was its original objective. PPBS has not brought defense officials, outside of programming departments, into institutional settings to discuss how defense budget allocations need to change in order to produce defense outcomes. Unfortunately, Western officials and the International Staff have not provided sufficient practical advice to assist these ministers of defense to understand that they need to make "defense" fit the existing defense budget. In lieu of delivering such a hard and accurate message, Partnership Goal General (PG) 0022 is defined as stable budget planning and has been adopted (alas) by too many defense institutions.[44] The problem with encouraging ministries of finance to develop stable medium-term expenditure plans (three years) is that it has given ministries of defense false expectations for stable budgets. Leaving aside that it is highly problematic that any parliament would agree such a commitment, simply on the grounds of national sovereignty, the fact of the matter is that such assumptions have acted to encourage defense officials to accept the planning assumption of multiyear funding without any assurances that the funds will ever come to hand. This has enabled defense officials to avoid facing the all-too-often truth that their current budget is too small in relation to the existing legacy-derived defense institution, and thus avoid making hard resource decisions. As Chapters 4 through 6 have amply demonstrated, none of these countries have been able to develop defense plans that have corresponded with actual budgets. There is no shortage of examples of ambitious development plans (which sometimes are even endorsed by government and parliament) which were subsequently underfunded, at which point they are simply declared unimplementable (e.g., Slovenia),[45] resulting in planning stasis.

As a result of this prevailing conceptual miasma, programming, financial management, and budgeting in all of these defense institutions, to varying degrees, remains isolated, and even in some cases impervious to the realities facing the rest of the organization. Consequently, it is rare to read a policy document or hear an official discuss money as constituting a critical management tool that needs to change as directed by policy to create and maintain endorsed capabilities. Instead, money remains conceptually defined in legacy terms as a given, and all existing problems would be solved if only there were more (often articulated in the context of an aspired certain percentage of GDP). This line of argument can be found in the 2010 Serbian Defense White Paper, which states authoritatively (and nonsensically) that to implement the methods provided by the International Monetary Fund (left undefined), defense requires *at least* 2 percent of GDP.[46] The use of this example is not intended unduly to criticize Serbia, as one can find almost the precise verbiage in other policy documents from all of these countries. Rather, it illustrates that these defense institutions struggle to adopt the basic concept that in a democracy existing finances must be optimized and ministries have no authority to dictate to parliaments their financial aspirations.

Logistics: The dog that has yet to bark

Logistical structures in all three typologies have been some of the most resistant elements of defense institutions to reform: a state of affairs that has a number of explanations. As functional organizations (no matter how inefficient), they have largely gone unnoticed by reformers. Western assistance in this area has been largely subsumed by supporting troop contributions in Iraq and Afghanistan, but this has been almost exclusively within the realm of expeditionary logistics. Such support, therefore, had little corresponding effect on changing national-level logistics legacy concepts. Notwithstanding some efforts to conduct bilateral logistics exchanges, such as NATO's LOGEX command post exercise series (which addresses multinational logistical support of operations),[47] effective support to reform these legacy organizations has been hampered by continuing intensive conceptual dissonance. In legacy defense institutions, logistics, to varying degrees to be sure, is conceptually not understood as defined in the West. In communist times, the driving logistic concept was based on Military Economic Science, where society essentially exists to support the armed forces. Thus, legacy logistics remain highly centralized, based on the concept of depots, and an all but comprehensive role played by defense industry in both producing kit and its essential role in providing maintenance. Operational concepts dictated that supplies were provided centrally as ordered by the general staff or senior commanders to exploit battlefield opportunities. What one can observe is that since the end of the Cold War within legacy defense institutions, logistics became the accepted new name of procurement, supply, and storage, but Western concepts have not taken hold. The reason for this is that very few armies have fundamentally changed their tactical unit structures. In legacy times, battalion command posts were expected only to execute orders (e.g., in some cases, the command group consisting only of a commander, driver, and signals NCO). Note that even today many units still do not have a second command post and redundant communications that can enable the predictable delivery of logistic support as is the case in the West. These reorganized and expanded tactical formations have yet to be created, let alone understood, even in some new NATO countries.

The subsequent adoption by many countries of territorial defense concepts has resulted in stores being based near units. As a result, transport/supply units were not deemed necessary and have been either cut or reduced to the nonactive reserve. To save money, defense institutions have cut exercises severely, so exercising support during demanding training and exercises has become an unnecessary activity and this essential military capability has been widely lost. This has been compounded by the move to save even more money that has resulted in repair units becoming localized (and even civilianized), and therefore unable to deploy into the field. Military medical services have also become territorially localized and have become completely hospital based. Field medical facilities have all but disappeared from many of these defense institutions. As a result, ministries of defense have had active control over a key part of the logistics system, that is, procurement, and this has become the dominating concept in these organizations. The net result of the devolution in support to the armed forces is that now there are few legacy defense institutions that can deploy forces on their own. They simply do not have the necessary doctrine, deployable combat service support units, or requisite training.

This explanation of the general state of logistics in legacy defense institutions is essential to appreciate the challenge of providing effective advice and assistance. There can be fewer instances whereby Western and communist concepts are so different as to be profoundly antithetical as in this case (see Table 7.1). For instance, in the West, logistics is a concept based on enabling commanders to plan and carry out their missions. In the communist and legacy mind, *society* and the *economy* exist to provide the necessities to the armed forces to protect the country, party, and revolution. Hence, legacy logistics practices such as supporting a vast hospital system, which is larger than the military needs, are seen as assets despite bleeding defense money and not supporting commanders to improve their units for operations.

Clearly, bridging this deep conceptual divide will not be easily accomplished, nor will this be accomplished quickly. An indication of the difficulty of Western defense and military officials to understand the profoundly antithetical nature of communist-inspired logistics and its resistance to change can be discerned from a press report that assessed the challenges facing the Iraqi Army. After the United States spent over ten years providing training and equipment to the Iraqi Army, in spring 2016 its operational effectiveness was assessed as problematic, due in part to its continued practice of sending equipment for repair back to factories and depots in Baghdad, as opposed to undertaking repairs in the field.[48] Clearly, a concerted effort by Western donors will be necessary to effect fundamental change in logistics. What is required is a new and strong policy framework that requires the wholesale review and revision of

Table 7.1 Antithetical Logistics Concepts

Principles	Logistics	Rear area (security)
Guidance	Government policy	Военная доктрина (*Vayennaya daktrina*) *Military Doctrine*
Concepts	Supply, procurement, maintenance, private industry	*Military Economic Science*, design bureaux, government-owned defense industry
Determining demand	Government determines how much to spend	Armed forces determine what society *must* provide
Key assumption	Decentralized	Centralized
Customers	Lower-level operational commanders	General Staffs, higher-level operational commanders
Ownership	Ministry of defense/defense staff/ agencies	Ministry of defense, defense industry
Requirements determination	Operational commanders via the Estimates process	General Staff via centralized operational planning
Execution	"Pull" by commanders	"Push" by General Staff
Characteristics:	• Flexibility, with the inherent ability to supply all units	• Rigidity and predictability, allows battlefield exploitation, but abandons some units
	• Maintenance is operationally focused	• Maintenance is largely provided by defense industry and locked to it
	• Software based	• Paper based

all associated concepts and assumptions that relate to logistics. Some key issues that require attention and revision include the following:

(1) New national logistics concepts that reorganize the roles/missions between ministers of defense and general staffs: Ministerial acquisition directorates must be realigned to be responsible only for *how* to buy what is needed and not *what*.

(2) Logistics must be defined in policy as constituting more than procurement, and outputs from existing defense industry (which are depot based and centrally determined), but rather focuses on meeting the requirements of tactical and operational commanders.

(3) Ministries of defense need to collate and validate material requirements, but allow defense agencies to manage acquisition. Tactical formations must be able to determine their logistics requirements, via the Estimates process, vice determined centrally by general staffs. Defense-owned defense industry needs to be privatized. They bleed defense budgets, rarely provide what commanders need, and offer opportunities for corruption.

(4) Decision-making authority for particularly consumable purchases must be decentralized to create efficiencies. Commanders must be enabled to determine how to use infrastructure and resources, vice being directed centrally. Budgets for consumables need to be selectively delegated to commanders and formations. Greater policy emphasis must be placed on outsourcing where it achieves

efficiencies, except where the forces require an organic support capability for operations and deployments. Depots still try to provide all supply requirements and ignore opportunities at outsourcing and using lower cost commercial logistics opportunities.

When formulating policies to assist legacy defense institutions to reform their logistics concepts and organizations, Western planning assumptions equally need to review and revise their existing advice and assistance programs.

(1) Understand that logistics, as an operational enabler, is all but not understood in legacy defense institutions.
(2) There is an immediate need for defense institutions to create military logistics supply organizations in many armed forces, which are led by commanders, and include headquarters, dedicated communications, and transportation assets.
(3) As communist and Western defense concepts are antithetical, it must be understood that they cannot coexist in the same institution. Western officials must insist as a precondition to assisting the reform of legacy "logistics" organizations that the recipient country must accept the concept of mutual exclusivity. Thus, new concepts can only be introduced if their legacy counterparts are retired, that is, organizations must change and staff retrained. Failure to retire legacy concepts will result in a mish-mash of concepts that will struggle among themselves and produce dissonance and waste.
(4) Only within the context of a new logistic policy framework, Western support should concentrate on supporting commanders and staff to show how operational logistics work in a Western operation. Legacy armed forces must be introduced to, and supported in, the development of the Estimates process (e.g., S-4s at all battalions/squadrons and above, with intensive Western education and training modules).

Noncommissioned officer (NCO) corps

A common recommendation from Western countries to reforming armed forces is the adoption of the concept of a professional NCO corps. Like the other reforms addressed in this chapter, the creation of a professional NCO corps has been expressed in many reforming countries' PGs and IPAP Goals. Many NATO allies, particularly the United States, United Kingdom, and Germany, have provided training programs to assist in the adoption of this concept. Indeed, the United States went so far as to help establish NCO academies in a number of countries (e.g., Ukraine) to provide formal training to produce Western-trained NCOs. The problem with this particular reform is that it has yet to be conducted fully within the context of the need to reform the entire character, let alone the personnel management system, of an armed force. In the case of Ukraine, an NCO academy was created in Kharkiv in 2006, but the effort did not successfully introduce this "model." This was due to the fact there were unsuccessful attempts made at reforming the Ukrainian officer cadet and officer corps, which should have been reduced in size and their responsibilities realigned.[49]

While one can make a very strong argument that there is great utility in an armed force possessing well-trained and professional NCOs, it is essential to recognize that this concept has to be considered in the highly contextualized environment of Central and Eastern Europe. There is an historical legacy of NCOs in some of these armies, including the JNA and even the Czarist Army, but this institution was never as strong as it has become in the West. Moreover, a strong case can be made that these armies (conscript and profession) already *have* NCOs, in the form of junior officers, who are trained and are expected to function *as* NCOs. The suggestion that the weakness in these armed forces is due to the existence of an underdeveloped NCO corps[50] is a reflection on a peculiar Western proclivity that requires conformity to Western concepts in order for Western units to be able to operate with them. In fact, it would appear that in many cases, the wrong problem was identified and the ensuing solution was misguided. What has been lacking in this push for NCO development (supported by extensive bilateral training programs) has been a failure on the part of Western officials to grasp the simple reality that these armed forces do not encourage the employment of what is considered to be the "heretical" practice of delegated command and control. For example, high power distance, and the lack of policies enabling this practice will combine to obviate against an armed force using this model. In short, the mere training of a cadre of NCOs in leadership has simply not been sufficient to the need.

In fact, a more systemic impediment to the challenge of introducing a professional NCO corps would be the lack of professional knowledge, experience, and abilities on the part of legacy officer corps to know how to *use* NCOs and the need to change their own and the institution's behavior. After all, with the exception of possibly only Russia,[51] PME institutions in the region have hardly seen any reform and one continues to find in them many legacy practices, instructors, and even curricula. Clearly, notwithstanding some progress, the wider issue of HRM, let alone how to introduce the concept of delegated command, has yet to be fully addressed from first principles.

Professional military education

Within the context of HRM, Western assistance has been active in encouraging PME reform. Yet, these efforts have proven it difficult to achieve meaningful results.[52] These institutions remain mired in teaching legacy-based concepts that have short- and long-term consequences. As to the former, the lack of reform is clearly inhibiting the effective management and command of the armed forces in something as mundane, but critically important, as staff work.

> [A]s in other post-communist states, few and far between are those who *ask themselves* how policies, programmes and directives should be implemented. The vastly safer and almost universal practice is to await orders about how orders should be implemented. If directives are not to become conversation pieces, their authors must walk them through the system themselves. Not surprisingly, the result is a system overmanned, overworked and largely inert.[53]

By not reforming legacy PME organizations from first principles, the officer corps continue to approach problem-solving by vainly searching for scientifically derived answers. It is little wonder that most staff officers in post-communist defense institutions are incapable of doing effective staff work, expressed in clear and brief writing. This is in contrast to Western methods that teach cadets, junior officers, and NCOs first to *frame* problems, supported by critical thinking, argument, collaboration, cooperation, and consensus-building to develop courses of action.

In lieu of reforming to meet changed requirements, in many cases, faculties of defense academies have been successful in getting their respective institutions and curricula certified by ministries of education, making them eligible for civilian academic credit. It is a tribute to the creativity of some military faculty who have been able to convince their civilian counterparts of their academic expertise and legitimacy when many enjoy the dubious distinction of possessing terminal degrees conferred upon them by their own institutions. While it is an overstatement to claim that all defense educational organizations are mired in legacy (Poland, Romania, and Slovakia are good examples of defense institutions that have worked assiduously to reform their respective PME systems and curricula),[54] most need to adopt fully Western concepts. In fact, many have all but become hybrid civilian universities. For instance, only 5 percent of the Polish Military Technical University's student body consists of military cadets. Polish government officials now acknowledge that Polish PME responds to the civil market rather than that of the armed forces, placing a needless drain on the defense budget and impeding deeper professionalization.[55] Fortunately, recent Polish pronouncements acknowledge that PME has been slow to reform, and it is envisaged that rationalization and improvement of this oversized sector of the defense institution is finally at hand.[56]

This problem has not been limited solely to Poland. Reform has yet to arrive in Hungary where the civilian student body of the Zrinyi Miklos National Defense University was over 80 percent in 2012.[57] Moreover, most of these academies have maintained their previous legacy curricula. For instance, as late as 2011 the curriculum of R. S. Rakovski Defense College in Bulgaria was still largely based on Warsaw Pact doctrine[58] despite a claim by Bulgarian academics that it had adopted educational modules based on NATO standards (again, whatever that could possibly mean).[59] In addition, some have adopted the ingenious conflation of science with PME, thereby producing officers who are trained in science and technology but lacking exposure to management and leadership skills inherent to the profession.[60] Indeed, throughout the region, one finds PME curricula to be highly scientific and technically oriented (reflecting the credentials of their faculty), as opposed to emphasizing management, critical thinking, and leadership, which are key subjects in Western PME institutions. Keynes's cynical definition of education can have no better application: "The inculcation of the incomprehensible into the indifferent by the incompetent." That fundamental reform of PME institutions has been so long in coming can be identified as having been one of the key impediments to reforming defense institutions.

The obvious and most difficult solution to this mismatch of legacy capacity and contemporary requirements would be to remove legacy military faculty from their posts and staff these institutions with officers and NCOs who have Western PME and have recent operational experience. This is likely to be much more effective and efficient than retraining existing legacy teaching faculty: a practice that is difficult to find *anywhere* else in academe.[61] Indeed, one can question whether Western officials have fully come to understand and appreciate the depth of this challenge. In a cultural sense, cadets and students in unreformed PME institutions still have the legacy luxury of selecting the traditional non-thinking approach. One just follows orders, gets paid, and will never be held responsible as he or she will never be entrusted to initiate anything; ergo, one never has to make, let alone defend, a decision. In this tradition, one is, by definition, a passive listener in legacy PME curricula. In fact, listener becomes one's label, vice thinker or initiator. In it is not an inconsequential observation that in the Bulgarian language "listener" and "obedient" share a common root. Added to this cultural "pull" is that most faculty throughout the region have been brought up *in* the legacy system, spending their formative years within it during the waning years of communism. How such a "retrained" professor (with Western advice) could hope to possess any credibility before reform-minded "coursants" by attempting to teach Western concepts, principles, and logic imbued in modern warfare and defense management, without ever having been formally educated and *experienced* in these highly contextualized environments, beggars logical explanation. Finally, PME needs to be seen as only a piece of the challenge. Knowledge in itself cannot alone produce changes in behavior. Change can only be accomplished by practice, that is, appropriate (and demanding) follow-on assignments,[62] or as so presciently observed by John Keats, "Nothing ever becomes real 'til it is experienced." In short, the lack of reform in this area is scandalous as it has allowed a small cadre of pseudo-academics, many without possessing requisite operational experience and authentic academic credentials, to carve out comfortable niches for themselves and continue to teach legacy methods.[63]

Changing Western logic

Notwithstanding the dedicated and persistent efforts by Western professional military and civilian defense officials, their *logic* and approaches to facilitate the adoption of Western democratic defense governance concepts among the three legacy typologies have largely not recognized local cultural, bureaucratic, and political realities. Simply speaking, all too often the challenges have been framed to fit with existing solutions and programs, befitting a "structural" mind-set. By this, problems and challenges have all too often been addressed using Western-sourced structural and procedural tools, indeed *Western logic*, that were designed to support other Western defense institutions. This is because such experts know the internal logic common to Western defense institutions and where policies and incentives are clear, and there is an agreed understanding of what constitutes defense "outcomes," that is, defined as capabilities. In short, the West enjoys common defense and military lexica and operating grammar, all based on Western democratic defense governance concepts. Clearly some of these commonalities can be traced to old NATO nations' common Western heritage, but no small credit needs to be given to the efforts of NATO particularly during the Cold War, which sought to maximize the defense outcomes of all of its members through intensive defense planning reporting, readiness evaluations, and achieving common training objectives. What should be of concern is that when defense budgets have been, and are likely to remain, under strain, there are likely to be diminished funds available from the West to aid its new allies to reform, in addition to an onset of inevitable donor fatigue. It has to be recognized, as well, that the easy reforms have long been adopted. Thus, the challenge before members of the alliance is how to encourage legacy defense institutions to make politically difficult reforms, and where possible, assist and reward these efforts. Make no mistake about it: all of these countries will require assistance for years to rid themselves completely of legacy concepts that are inhibiting them from making greater contributions to the alliance. The following discussion aims to provide an argument to political leadership and parliamentarians to make a strong case of the need, when reviewing the advice and assistance options, to review first principles, and critically current Western *assumptions*. Only after Western officials have fully reassessed their long-standing assumptions (to be identified *infra*) can one optimize assistance *approaches* for these countries, but based on a different logic. After all, as purportedly attributed to Albert Einstein, one cannot solve problems using the same thinking which was used in creating them. Four issues related to providing advice and assistance will be discussed in this section: the inherent political nature of changing a government institution,[64] the centrality of data, framing reform as one constituting change management within its proper cultural realities, and methods to change effectively legacy concepts and prevailing institutional logic.

Primat der Politik

A central argument of this work has been to critique the West's approach to providing advice and assistance to post-communist European defense institutions by defining the challenge as constituting a military, *technical* problem, and thereby assigning responsibility for addressing it to Western armed forces. Thus, defense reform has been addressed through military-to-military contacts, training, PME, and exercises. In many cases, for example, the United States, training and educational support programs have not differed greatly from long-standing assumptions and advice and assistance programs. Lost in defining this problem is the fact that fundamentally the reform of *any* public institution is a *political* issue. In consequence, all subsequent *assumptions* and *logic* need to be acknowledged and *managed* as such. Arguably, the almost universal failure to recognize the fundamental political nature of the challenge of reform can explain, in large part, the lack of success in reforming legacy defense institutions. After all, as all Western armed forces axiomatically declaim any political involvement within their governments, it is ironic that arguably the least inclined, if not prepared, public institution to address both institutional reform and its political realities has been given the lead to accomplish this ambitious and politically sensitive objective. Equally, having Western armed forces lead and manage these efforts has misled both civilian and military leadership to manage this assistance as bottom-up and technical, vice political, in nature. This has enabled officials in the region to declaim the political pains associated with reforms. By employing this logic set, officials have been able to avoid accepting reforms as their own, let alone acknowledging that they need to change their own behavior in order to facilitate reform.

Therefore, it makes little sense to expect senior officials in the region to accept fundamental reform without them accepting that these managerial and organizational changes are political. This thereby requires the requisite political consensus within governments to buy into these efforts and to support them against the inevitable resistance to change by any bureaucracy. One of the key tenets of change management in the corporate world is to examine whether senior managers are capable of supporting and furthering change (particularly by changing their own individual *behaviors*);[65] similarly, it would make logical sense to encourage governments intent on reform to conduct a thorough review of their defense institution's leadership and replace those individuals unwilling to support change. In addition to demonstrating to allies or partners their seriousness to change, it would also provide governments with the rationale to retire unsupportive senior officials. As this has yet to take place to date in the region, it is clear that it must fall to senior Western political officials to begin this sensitive, but critical, dialogue.

Given how the problem has been framed as a technical challenge to be overcome, Western officials all too often have ignored, or consciously avoided, approaching senior political, defense civilian, and military leadership with the message that *they* need both to understand the consequences of these reforms and to be aware that inherent in these reform efforts is the need to change their own respective *behaviors*. As a consequence of not pressing senior leaders that they, of *all* people in the defense institution, need to adopt new knowledge and understanding, and dare one suggest, *logic*, has allowed them to avoid taking ownership of reforms. Oftentimes, most of these officials have no understanding of the nature of these reforms, let alone their potential implications for their own status and position in the organization. As it is all too rare that they have been educated, or often even properly briefed, on these new and radically different concepts, it is little wonder that they have not universally embraced, let alone declared *ownership*, of them.

The centrality of data

As they continue to use legacy concepts, these defense institutions have struggled to operate effectively since they do so often without a *factual* appreciation of the consequences of national-level decision-making. "Data" are defined in this context as both constituting what the armed forces are capable of undertaking (via operational planning analysis) and ascertaining the actual financial costs of all of its organizational functions.

In legacy defense institutions, it is either procedurally or culturally proscribed to communicate officially upward (e.g., commanders submitting a Statement of Requirements). Hence, it is not a great surprise that one still finds that general staffs and ministries of defense are bereft of basic objective data that should be generated organically through its normal daily operations to inform decision-making. This is a three-stage problem, in fact. First, there is the need of simply gathering the *right* data. Second, there is the challenge of managing data systems, which likely never existed under communism. Third, there is also the need for educated and trained personnel, in sufficient numbers, who are capable of *interpreting* data accurately to inform decision-making.[66]

What Western defense officials have generally assumed when engaging these defense institutions is that basic staff skills exist and that there is a regular internal dialogue based on objective data. This has been a fallacious assumption, as with minor exceptions, such discussion and debate are weak in legacy defense institutions. Serbia presents a representative case of where performance of units is measured "with resource usage and inputs rather than activities, outputs, or outcomes."[67] To be sure, individuals educated in Western PME institutions, with NATO staff experience, or have deployed on operations, have been exposed to these processes and can appreciate their value. However, the concept of debating the outcomes of operational planning analysis has yet to be fully embraced, since many in leadership would see such communication as a challenge to their authority.

The obvious question is: how to reform this debilitating practice? In many cases, the cultural norm of not communicating upward is reinforced by regulations which proscribe such acts, the reform of which should constitute a basic first step forward. But, as these are norms and behaviors, they are not easily changed. It will take enlightened political leadership to empower lower-level officials, officers, and NCOs to break from their own self-imposed culture of self-constraint (e.g., high power distance and uncertainty avoidance) to express their professional views and opinions. Clearly, bureaucratic action alone cannot remedy this pathology as only initiatives by senior leadership can help change such deep-seated practices.[68] Thus, a critical priority for the adoption of Western democratic defense governance concepts must be the introduction of these planning and reporting concepts that create an ongoing internal dialogue and debate within the defense institution using objective data to determine solutions to problems in defense management and military operations.

The implications of the introduction of such data would be widespread. The underperforming HRM systems in legacy defense institutions have been slow to adopt modern methods and means due to, *inter alia*, the lack of data expressing current and projected personnel requirements of the armed forces. Similarly, all but absent force management concepts would have a basis for their creation and would be supported by the systematic stream of operational data from units and forces sent upward in the organization. Finally, another area that has all but defied improvement and reform, that is, legacy logistics structures, can only transition from the "push" to "pull" logistics concept through the introduction of a tactically derived Estimates process based on commanders' requirements.

Contemporaneous with the issue of the lack of operational data used within these defense institutions is the continued lack of appreciation of the need to be able to *cost* outcomes. In past, without the benefit of a market economy (i.e., with price discovery provided by markets), it was impossible for communist economists to ascertain the true resource cost to the nation of defense. As such, to say that these institutions at their transition/creation at independence were uninformed of the financial costs of *anything* is an understatement. A pernicious narrative that continues to be heard in these defense institutions is that it is the duty of society to provide the resources necessary to defend the country as determined by the officer corps. Thus, with minor exception at independence, these defense institutions started without objective financial baselines, or worse, recognition of the need to be cost-conscious. To be sure, all of these institutions have, to varying degrees, a growing expertise in financial management. What still needs to be adopted is the concept that priorities must be *costed*. To be sure, with external assistance, almost all of these countries have created, or have adopted, imported (and which are often unsuitable) cost models. Yet, notwithstanding the introduction of these models, the creation of a costing culture accepted by the organization has yet to be realized. The problem with achieving this important goal has been due less to technical impediments as it has to the management of this critical defense planning tool. There are numerous explanations for this slow development.

The introduction of models to cost defense plans must be seen as constituting truly a Sisyphean task. In a strictly bureaucratic sense, the basic concept of having to take into account financial considerations when planning "defense" remains to be fully embraced. For instance, many general staffs are expected to produce defense plans, absent using cost databases. Costings are often the responsibility of ministries of defense, thereby removing any incentive or needed sense of financial reality in the development of defense plans. It is little wonder that so few defense plans are affordable, let alone accepted and adopted. Worse yet, the data from models (where it is shared) are simply not seen as constituting legitimate planning factors or are conveniently ignored. This has made for a perfect storm given that defense plans remain as foreign to most of these armed forces as is their costing. As pedestrian as it may seem, a serious challenge to developing costed plans has been to determine *where* to place these models within the organization and *how* and *when* to use the data in the planning process. All too often the technical advice from the Western donors providing the methods/models did not factor in a proper understanding of the existing bureaucratic realities and institutional incentives. Thus, Western cost methods, models, and management concepts all too often have not supported rational defense planning, as placing them where they would have the greatest effect would threaten existing bureaucratic interests and personal incentives. The reason for this is that the seemingly scientific/technical nature of these systems has reinforced an atavistic mind-set that holds policy and planning should be subject to scientific, algorithmic solutions. While Locksley addresses this phenomenon in the context of Russian defense reform, it is valid for all legacy defense institutions:

> This argument is best reflected in the Russian employment of an algorithm to solve the problem of military reform. This is an attempt to find the universal unity of truth. Yet, an algorithm may be appropriate for a topdown, status-oriented, hierarchically structured polity which responds to Stalinist inputs—it is utterly useless when applied to a network of interests where military reform is a living process governed by external events, people and political problems. The algorithm is unable to embrace the complexity of social totality; it is diagrammatic proof that the Russian approach to thinking about problems is more about the imposition of abstract schémas than the quest to comprehend thoroughly complex social and political questions.

The intellectual technology of the algorithm (with its phased steps of problem-solving) asserts that intuitive judgements and educated guesses are inferior to problem-solving rules, it does not explain how military reform moves from one stage to another and it ignores multiple levels of decision and interacting networks.[69]

It is with this misunderstanding of defense management that defense officials all too often placed these new models and expertise in newly created programming directorates of ministries of defense. This has had the added negative effect of concentrating *all* financial matters (to include *contracting* in some ministries) within *one* directorate, enabling it arbitrarily to make opaque de facto financial decisions that should have been made during the planning stage. Placing cost models outside of planning directorates further weakened their ability to formulate financially viable defense plans closely linked to policy and even encouraged planners to ignore the financial realities and responsibilities of their defense plans. In short, defense planning directorates need to possess the responsibility and capability to cost *everything* in formulating defense plans. The principle that all defense plans must be costed prior to their review by the policy directorate, and their implementation by officials responsible for delivering defense outcomes, is equally needed. Sadly, this reform is only taking hold in a most painfully slow process. For instance, following the all but collapse of the Latvian economy in 2008 and with the defense budget slashed by a third, its ministry of defense was forced to reexamine its planning procedures and assumptions. After this review, the institution's cost models were moved from the responsibility of programming to the defense planning directorate.

Finally, the concept of costings has been misunderstood by officials in these defense institutions. There is a prevailing perception that cost models exist as scientifically accurate instruments. All too often, officials perceive them as essentially algorithms that are *correct* in that they must be accurate. Missing from this thought process is the consideration that costings, while based on quantitative principles, must be seen as management tools, and as such, inherently contain acceptable degrees of inexactitude. This does not in any way depreciate their value as they are essentially simple in principle. The reality, then, of these tools is that there is a degree of subjectivity in their data, but this can be greatly mitigated over time if the data and the methodology are open to all for use, review, and revision. This is the case with the Canadian armed forces, where Cost Factors manuals are updated annually and are made available throughout the defense institution. What this implies, therefore, is if cost models are to be utilized effectively to inform decision-making, they must be developed and managed in an *open* process within the institution. It has been counterproductive to assign their development, let alone management, to officials who are largely trained as engineers and mathematicians (i.e., products of the scientific approach of officer education) and to allow them to define these projects as *technical*, vice *managerial* in intent. In the end, it is ironic that one of the most basic and seemingly straightforward tools for modern defense management has been improperly introduced into so many of these defense institutions. Western nations thus simply got it wrong when they did not properly define the degree to which these legacy defense institutions were oblivious to the value of cost models and that so many would be improperly employed. Indeed, the introduction of American-styled programming and placing all financial management (including cost models) in PPBS directorates has reinforced cultural proclivities to centralize financial decision-making. One can only imagine the mischief such practices offer to those who can control the costings, programming, and, in some cases, even their financial execution.

The challenge, therefore, is to encourage defense ministers that in many cases they already possess many of the key tools needed to make more informed decisions. But the management and utilization of these tools must be changed in order to produce costed defense planning options. Clearly, effecting this change is not a technical challenge to be left solely to experts working at the staff level. Rather, it points once again to the inherently political nature of the challenges that must be addressed in order to adopt Western democratic defense governance concepts.

Change management and culture

If one accepts the proposition that the principal challenge facing these defense institutions is political in nature, then another definitional starting point is needed. It is posited that defining and addressing this challenge in line with the tenets of change management could provide a suitable foundation from which to determine a coherent approach to base reform. This does not refer to change management as defined in a sterile or business context, but rather to an approach that is interpreted through the lenses of an understanding of national and institutional cultural norms and incentives. This assertion in no way is implied to diminish the importance of existing technical assistance comprising education and training programs. But, as important as these tools are, they should be used *only* as a complement to efforts led by recipient countries' senior officials themselves to deliver change. Such an endeavor must be politically driven, and consequently, it is clear that the entire foreign policy apparatus of Western governments, not merely their armed forces, must be involved when necessary to deliver sharp messages to encourage reluctant political leaders. This encouragement is likely necessary in order to convince some of these governments to effect institutional reform in a systematic fashion, and to be prepared to apply pressure when the inevitable slacking occurs. A distillation of Kotter and Cohen's eight steps of change management (i.e., sense of urgency, establishing a guiding team, vision and strategies, communication, empowerment, short-term wins, consistency of effort, and creating a new culture)[70] might well be implemented through the following actions:

(1) Leadership-led should be defined as the will and urgency to maintain continuous political pressure/support from national officials during the entire duration of the reform effort. Governments with legacy defense institutions would be prudent to ignore pleas for additional funds prior to making hard policy decisions. As sagely observed by Christopher Donnelly, when funding was made available to these defense institutions prior to making reforms, it was largely spent on keeping the old system on life support, and critical changes

(such as reductions and, most importantly, appropriate restructuring and functional reorganization) were delayed ad infinitum. In fact, providing more money prior to making reforms can actually impede needed changes.[71]

(2)   The full commitment from the political team in the ministry of defense to press for envisaged reforms.

(3)   The minister of defense and the CHOD's vision of reform and implementing strategies and priorities through both civilian and military bureaucracies with a clear explanation of what needs to change and when the change must be implemented. The vision needs to include clearly stated consequences for those who try to obstruct or impede its realization.

(4)   To obtain quick wins, begin with a systematic audit to determine and document the defense institution's prevailing cultural attributes, its shortcomings, and, fundamentally, where money is actually being spent. The results of these analyses need to be used to ascertain where legacy concepts remain, and which need to be delegitimated, and those Western ones that need to be reinforced or introduced. A plan must be developed that will seek to change the defense institution's *incentives* to support those new concepts and create disincentives for their legacy counterparts.

(5)   Senior leadership has to articulate a policy of incentives that covers individuals who demonstrate their willingness to embrace change and further its implementation in the institution.

(6)   Decentralize decision-making and delegation of financial responsibilities to those officials who are responsible for producing defense outcomes and thereby introduce a new policy that executing operations successfully is the institution's most important priority.

In the end, a defense minister, CHOD, the entire political team in the ministry of defense, and the government itself will be able to judge if this approach is effective by observing whether individuals, alone and collectively, have been able to change their *behavior*. Therefore, the outcome should not be in the form of *yet more* new documents, or foreign-sourced procedures, but rather presented as a cold judgment of the degree to which the institution functions differently. Externally provided technical assistance perforce will be needed to provide a factual baseline of proficiency and equally needs to be carefully designed and executed to support the senior leadership's change management objectives.

A final set of assumptions has to be changed, and these relate to how Western donors need to perceive their own efforts in supporting reform efforts in legacy defense institutions. Donor officials simply need to insist on new levels of conditionality when supplying such assistance, therefore firmly tying advice and assistance to its proper political nature. If both sides are to move beyond the fallacious assumption that the challenges faced by these defense institutions are technical in nature, three principles need to be accepted by ministers of defense and CHODs in recipient defense institutions. First, external experts should have access to examine agreed areas requiring advice and assistance (and, by extension, to recommend other areas which may produce causation). In these bureaucracies, oftentimes data are classified and not even releasable within alliance channels. Whereas certain data may be sensitive, how the data are derived and the management of that process is not, and they must be open for review and analysis. Second, the defense institution and armed forces have to recognize and accept the *authority* of the experts and their proffered advice. This is a sensitive issue, to be sure, but perhaps not for the reasons one might expect. NATO International Staff and Western donors need to acknowledge that previous advice has not always been prescient and they will have to make strong efforts to demonstrate that the proffered advice indeed will *address* causation and not simply symptoms.[72] Conversely, new NATO members and partners need to become more demanding of the performance of advice and assistance and end the silly practice of simply accepting donors' gifts without question, notwithstanding any perception of being admonished by the "stern schoolmaster" from Brussels.[73] Third, and possibly the most difficult, is the need for a defense institution's *acceptance* of the advice being recommended. This is not to suggest the blind acceptance of truth so familiar in the communist period. Rather, defense officials need to change their behavior by being prepared to accept the logic and facts being recommended. To be sure, changes to an institution are to be considered within the proper political and bureaucratic context of the recipient organization. But it is facts and the logic of arguments that institutions need to learn to accept and end the practice of offering excuses that such methods and concepts are unacceptable due to a legacy defense institution's unique culture, history, and existing law. Acknowledging and agreeing these principles as a conditionality of advice and assistance represented by these three principles will be no easy task. It is a regrettable fact that only the most pernicious and politically protected concepts, organizations, and ways of conducting business remain to be isolated and changed. But they must be addressed if these defense institutions are to be capable of meeting their basic Article 5 commitments, let alone making useful (i.e., self-supporting) contributions to expeditionary and peacekeeping operations.

Methods

One initiates discussion of how Western donors can best refocus their advice and assistance efforts in light of the aforementioned conceptual divide. The persistence of legacy concepts in essentially all of these defense institutions explains why so many of these defense institutions continue to struggle to adopt fully Western democratic defense governance concepts. Therefore, agreeing advice and assistance program needs to be conditioned on addressing the following issues before advice and assistance should be contemplated. In effect, the following analytical points should produce an objective diagnosis of the problem.

(1) **Political sponsorship.** As a *sine qua non*, Western donors should insist on the political leadership from legacy countries to agree the principle that the adoption of Western democratic defense governance concepts is of a primarily political nature, and therefore requires continuous political oversight and

involvement in transforming the conceptual and normative bases of their respective defense institutions.

(2) **Operational focus of armed forces.** Directly related to the first point of the political nature of institutional reform is the need for political leadership to commit themselves to supporting initiatives that require the armed forces to adopt an operational focus and to shift attention and finances to supporting the creation of defense *outcomes*. In all too many of these defense institutions, low priority is given to the creation of predictable and measureable defense outcomes, and thus other priorities, such as social welfare, claim an ever-growing share of the defense budget. Enlightened senior military leadership that focuses on producing defense outcomes has to be empowered to shift personnel and change finances to achieve these results.

(3) **Identification of the organization's dominant concepts.** Arguably one of the key debilitating legacy concepts that hinder progression toward the adoption of Western democratic defense governance concepts is the all but immutable concentration of *centralized* power at the very top of the organization that discourages at best, and prohibits at worst, initiative and responsibility. The immediate consequence of this practice has been the inability of armed forces to function as their Western counterparts, which has resulted in bloated institutions, empty tactical units that exist only on paper, and a lack of focus on delivering real defense outcomes. One tool to achieve this objective is to encourage legacy defense institutions, led by their respective policy directorates, to conduct formal audits to ascertain and document their organization's prevailing concepts and assumptions. These can be defined as constituting any sanctioned activity and/or the expenditure of funds on an activity. Albeit tedious, such endeavors can produce surprising results for senior leadership and can help explain to the organization how it actually functions, and critically, where the *money* is actually being *spent*.

(4) **Determination of causation.** Using this understanding of dominant concepts, discern the *causation* of existing areas of institutional weaknesses. Oftentimes, the manifestation of operational and bureaucratic underperformance has no discernible linkage to causation. For instance, HRM is almost universally acknowledged to be underdeveloped in these defense institutions. Yet very little practical progress has been made by HRM advice and assistance projects. An explanation for both this institutional weakness and the inability of Western donors to provide the correct expertise, again, relates back to basic assumptions. In the West, HRM is a key element of armed forces' *capabilities*, and hence, it needs to be understood and explained as such. For instance, the training and certification of joint terminal attack controller personnel essentially requires the active involvement of almost all elements of the defense institution to create and keep this highly valuable and effective capability. The point is the performance of HRM directorates, in and of themselves, can neither exist nor be judged in a vacuum, but it is in their realm of responsibility that symptoms of weaknesses are reflected and do not necessarily express causation (i.e., the need to understand the role played by *collegia*). Thus, absent data and context focusing

on symptoms, vice discerning causation, will only perpetuate ineffectual advice and assistance efforts.

(5) **Mutual exclusivity of concepts.** If one accepts one of the basic tenets of this work that Western democratic defense governance and legacy defense concepts are antithetical, then it follows that any attempt to provide assistance to a legacy defense institution must address *replacing* existing legacy concepts with their Western counterparts. The change of any public institution's basic conceptual basis is, by definition, a political act. As such, it must be seen by Western nations as constituting such a reality. Starting with a concept audit, the existence of legacy concepts will have to be acknowledged and new ones openly debated and adopted; at the same time all of the laws, regulations, and procedures that supported legacy concepts must be carefully and comprehensively identified and a schedule set for their retirement. An important contribution to reform would be if senior officials adopted proper incentives to encourage a strong dose of amnesia of their institutions' legacy heritage to clear out, as argues Koter, "historical artifacts".[74]

(6) **Empower policy.** Organizationally, a high priority must be the need to empower policy directorates in order to enable them to develop and manage "policy frameworks" to guide the operation of the entire defense institution, including, importantly, the management of donor assistance.[75] This step implies immediately shifting responsibility for planning and managing the budget to the policy director. These moves are imperative in order to initiate polices to drive the implementation of new concepts to create a new operating logic. Such tasks imply the existence of a powerful directorate organic to the defense institution and seen as the minister of defense's key implementation body. Absent this capability, these defense institutions will continue to struggle to exercise policy control over the entire institution. Many impediments to creating such a management capability abound, namely, deeply engrained vested interests in maintaining the status quo, prevailing legacy concepts, and unwieldy positive law. However, case-specific and innovative solutions need to be tested, and successful approaches institutionalized and shared among allies and partners. In the end, what is absolutely essential is to infuse the entire defense institution with an understanding that no activity should be undertaken or money spent that is not endorsed by the policy directorate. Not only does this directorate have to be supported by the strongest team in the ministry of defense with deep experience and knowledge of the entire institution, but it must have a stranglehold over the planning directorate. All policy options have to be assessed by the planning directorate for feasibility, to include financial cost. It is only logical, therefore, that the ministry's costing team must reside within the planning branch and respond to the chief of plans. This will ensure that all plans developed by the branch and approved by the policy directorate will have been *costed* before being endorsed as constituting a *plan* and its execution to be overseen by policy and plans.

(7) **Anchoring policy to reality.** It is clear that the traditional Western approach of starting to reform legacy defense institutions with drafting documents to

produce policy is unlikely to produce effective results as the entire Western democratic defense governance concept of policy still remains exogenous in too many countries. Rather, focus should be placed on developing policy context from existing realities. For instance, every government organization has some semblance of an annual "planning" cycle, if for no other reason than to develop a plan to spend public funds on its assigned responsibilities. In consequence, there are extant decision points that require staff work and estimates to enable leadership to make informed decisions. In a bottom-up fashion, these key decision points should be the initial focus of attention as these dates in an organization's planning calendar should serve as the basis for the timing and definition of information requirements. In short, by conducting an audit of a defense institution's extant planning/budget cycle, decision points can be discerned, and when policy and priority requirements need to be expressed and endorsed. The mere act of determining these dates and making them known throughout the defense institution could be a revelation and constitutes a key reform in itself. But, taking this further, a better appreciation of the necessary data needed to make informed decisions can be discerned, and the embryonic elements of a policy framework can at least be sketched out to demonstrate what is currently missing in policy and what is needed to tie it to financial decision-making. Whether the nomenclature of these policy planning documents is recognized by title by Western officials should be irrelevant. What is important is that defense officials can gain an initial understanding of what a policy framework should contain through the heavy contextualization of using the extant planning and budgeting system, no matter how imperfect it may well be.

(8) **Human factor.** Of equal importance is the need to recognize the human factor in these reform efforts. Any reform program which ignores, or simply assumes away, the human factor in changing a defense institution will not succeed. This must be seen as a common issue that both recipient and donor countries need to address collectively. Critically, it is imperative that both sides need to document the organization's prevailing norms, incentives, and, conversely, disincentives to carry out reform policy directives. This task must be seen as constituting more than just an issue for HRM, but rather should be addressed as what it is: a policy issue. Further, incentives supporting newly adopted Western democratic defense governance concepts need to be introduced. For example, the most demanding assignment in any armed force is to deploy on operations and ideally *to command* a deployable unit. In many legacy armed forces, such assignments are considered contemptible as the best assignments are staff postings, or best of all, coveted (and tenured) academic chairs at defense colleges. If the policy directorate of a reforming ministry of defense has the objective of being taken seriously in NATO, then there is a need to create incentives for such assignments to ensure that the organization becomes operationally oriented. Fortunately, in all of these defense institutions, one can find individuals with the requisite intelligence and drive to become leaders. But, to make such a seismic shift, legacy personnel incentives must be reviewed

comprehensively and systematically and in turn replaced by those which will produce a more effective and professional cadre.[76]

(9) **Separating leadership/command from management.** The communist military organization was based, *inter alia*, on the principle that to command was to enjoy all but unlimited power over subordinates (mirroring the total power of the communist party over society). Elements of this norm remain. An element of this concept of power is the continued practice by many to conflate management with leadership/command. Namely, a number of these defense institutions has yet to adopt the practice of separating management from leadership/command. By eschewing the adoption of this concept, decision-making is inexorably pulled upward. Such centralization forces leadership to concentrate on mundane, day-to-day decision-making at the expense of thinking of the future, let alone commanding and managing. To be sure, there is no shortage of other elements of these organizations that need to be addressed to make such a system functional. But the lack of dividing management from leadership/command also manifests itself in underperforming heads of directorates since they lack empowerment and which does not let juniors grow. The introduction of the post of chief/director of staff and diffusion of decision-making among the staff will initially cause significant stress on the system and individuals unaccustomed to making decisions. However, this reform must be seen as constituting a critically important first step, *conditio sine qua non*, toward developing a more functional and efficiently run organization.

Typological-specific approaches

It is appropriate to bring the discussion of applying the suggested methods addressed *supra* to the three legacy typologies. As will be noted, while most of these methods are applicable to all three, the precise application, sequencing, and intensity vary. Moreover, their cultural inclinations and political aspirations have to be controlled in order to provide more specific recommendations and suggestions for the most effective implementation of reform actions. This analysis is informed, therefore, by a review of, where available, the findings of Hofstede's cultural tools (see Appendix 3). Note, as well, that addressing these countries within their specific typologies enables general observations which are applicable to all, with exceptions identified.

Post-Soviet republics

One needs to acknowledge that at the outset of any discussion related to post-Soviet defense institutions, save the Baltic States (*vide infra*), it makes little sense to propose or assume that any of these nations can, or will, adopt fully Western democratic defense governance concepts since none of them either have the aspirations or enjoy the likelihood of NATO membership for the foreseeable future. Thus, it would only distract Western officials and planners to assume that they should, or could, adopt the Western "model," let alone all NATO "standards." Rather, as members of PfP, they should be encouraged to adopt as many basic reforms as possible so they can meet their partnership commitments to NATO (e.g., achieving interoperability). What one finds in an analysis of these defense institutions is that they remain profoundly underdeveloped because, *inter alia*, they struggle to relieve themselves of their communist heritage. There remains a high concentration, or "non-division," of powers within them, i.e., management from command, training from execution, and execution from evaluation/analysis. This general observation, it must be acknowledged, is conditioned by the fact that these nations are a disparate grouping, and the efforts to create systemic reforms by various governments and officials, in particularly Ukraine and Georgia, will demand particular political attention as they will express greater willingness to change.

All of these states have received considerable attention, advice, and technical assistance programs from Western nations. As many reforms have been largely laid atop underlying Soviet concepts, the result can be seen in many courses of "conceptual spaghetti"; for example, an inability to adopt Western planning methods, or raise a professional NCO corps. Thus, these reforms have not produced the operational effectiveness and financial efficiencies officials would have anticipated. And, as most of these armed forces are still largely based on the organizational remnants of where Red Army forces were stationed in 1991, they remain burdened with unused and unneeded infrastructure. Moreover, most formations are empty and arguably ill-organized for their envisaged employment; the armed forces of Armenia and Azerbaijan are arguably exceptions due to their long war. As a result of these characteristics, they are not fit for purpose and are bleeding money due to their inability to plan effectively and comprehend money as constituting a critical planning tool.

In consequence of these realities, the following approaches should be tested when examining how they might be able to effect reform in light of the lessons from past experience. The campaign to adopt policy frameworks within these defense institutions must begin as soon as possible, but it must be recognized that this can only be a long-term objective. If nothing else, they must be encouraged to renounce the pernicious concept of *daktrina* as a legitimate concept in a democracy and initiate an institutional debate of how best to replace the philosophical foundations of this concept. This author would argue that due to the residual strength of legacy concepts, reform efforts should be almost exclusively focused on conducting a conceptual audit, supported by a deep review of the implications of these findings. One can only imagine the degree of resistance that will meet such an endeavor, but until reform-minded governments and Western-oriented senior military leadership accept the need to review their institution's conceptual "soul"—that is, where the defense budget is *actually* being spent, how promotions are actually being conducted, and so on—it is difficult to envisage how they could begin adopting basic Western democratic defense governance concepts. No one should underestimate the degree of resistance these institutions will form against such an endeavor; and as such, this should be designed with the assumption that the effort will be an evolutionary process depending on continuing political pressure on the leadership of the defense institution. Some possible early wins in the review efforts could be to free costing data and distributing it throughout the entire institution to enable, and indeed force, an informed discussion apropos the costs of producing defense outcomes. With this data freed and distributed, one can imagine that some insightful individuals and organizations will see how better to cost platforms and systems, and just possibly, make the conceptual leap to *capabilities*. Once this has transpired, and if only imperfectly understood within the existing planning system, it should not be too terribly challenging to make the jump to costing capabilities. If Ukraine is representative of this group (absent, to be sure, the Baltic States), Hofstede's findings of high degrees of power distance and uncertainty avoidance will have to be overcome by leadership in order to empower all individuals in the organization to support this endeavor.

In light of the above discussion and prognosis, retiring the conceptual soul of the communist Scientific Man in these defense institutions is clearly a mid- to long-term challenge. Given that many key, if not fundamentally basic, conceptual challenges remain to be overcome, the approach of instituting a change management campaign within the defense institution should be delayed. For, without basic operational planning data and financial costings, it is difficult to envisage how an early change management approach could find the necessary institutional purchase. And, to be sure, without this data, defense planning *qua* planning is simply meaningless— producing voluminous, time-consuming, and irrelevant "science projects." In light of this assessment, Western donors should be extremely judicious in offering collective training and broad military-technical advice. The record to date is clear that such efforts are unlikely to find the necessary conceptual understanding and acceptance to enable these resources to be effectively adopted by these defense institutions. It is perhaps a pessimistic, if not deterministic, assessment, but one can be forgiven to assume that such well-meaning efforts, like so many before them, will likely result in yet more confusion and producing yet more "conceptual spaghetti." It will take time before it is widely accepted that the conceptually coherent Soviet defense model no longer is applicable, let alone affordable.

The Baltic States, as generally recognized, are very much an exception to the prevailing post-Soviet republics' norms. Importantly, as members of NATO, they can also be held *accountable*, in a political sense, to their alliance commitments *and* allied expectations. As regards their respective defense institutions, most of the challenges that they still face could be overcome by a clearer statement of government policy and priorities, supported by a disciplined change management campaign to develop *coherent* defense policy. Notwithstanding high levels of uncertainty avoidance, there is a need for greater honesty and internal debate based on data to determine where money should be spent to achieve more predictable and lethal defense outcomes and acknowledging the need to empower commanders. Alas, too many Baltic defense efforts are more akin to aspirations that do not always take into consideration second- and third-order effects, an appreciation of which could only help them better meet their commitments to the alliance. Thus, while these three states have unquestionably succeeded in learning and adopting basic Western democratic defense governance concepts, there remains a serious problem in their inability to express a more coherent logic behind their individual defense policies and expected outcomes. To the point, in at least Estonia, and the others to a lesser extent, too much institutional focus is on maintaining *fixed* territorial defense because of its skepticism of the alliance's collective defense commitments.[77] Yet, in an era when sensor technology and computational abilities are growing quickly, it makes no sense to divert limited resources to any efforts that focus on *fixed* territorial defense capabilities (e.g., logistics depots and land-based communications).[78] Thus, it is not so much communist legacy concepts, as it is their history, geography, and fear of the behavior of an unpredictable neighbor that impedes these countries from adopting greater defense coherence and frankly confidence. That all said, peculiar national defense obsessions and a lack of sufficient institutional self-critical thinking have not helped.

According to Paulauskas, notwithstanding the Baltic States' efforts to date, they were incapable as late as 2012 of meeting their alliance objective of each deploying, let alone sustaining, *one battalion* on operations. Perhaps more distressing is that since accession to the alliance, all three have lost interest in effecting reform.[79] It should be an alliance *policy* priority to provide, therefore, these former Soviet republics with additional reassurances and more effective cooperative support programs to enable them to implement fully Western democratic defense governance concepts. Finally, the implications for the Baltic States is that they, too, need to press forward on their own accord to reset their defense logic by encouraging a more open debate and accepting new ideas and approaches to produce more predictable defense outcomes.

Post-Warsaw Pact republics

Western defense officials need to place former Warsaw Pact republics at a high priority for political attention and financial support to complete the reform of their defense institutions. Simply stated, they are members of the alliance; and all of them, to varying degrees, remain unsatisfactorily unreformed. To be frank, the continued presence of conceptual legacies makes them effectively a *liability* to the alliance. As they are in the alliance, old members of the alliance must simply hold their defense institutions to a high level of competence. In all of these six countries, the conceptual divide remains to be fully addressed. Notwithstanding some great strides and achievements, as argued in Chapter 5, "conceptual spaghetti" is not difficult to find. As members of the alliance, old NATO members need to send to their senior leadership the message that they are liabilities to Western collective defense as long as they retain their conceptual legacies. One can think of no more an appropriate set of countries that should undertake deep audits to identify those concepts that continue to hold them back from becoming more Westernized. For example, Poland, the Czech Republic, and Bulgaria state de facto policies that embrace if not physical then arguably a mental *fixed* territorial defense orientation. In all of these countries, decision-making remains highly centralized and (with the exception of Hungary) power distance is relatively high on the Hofstede scale. The authority to spend money is held at the highest levels within ministries of defense, thereby denying commanders freedom for operational creativity and experimentation. Arguably, by adhering to legacy concepts, they are unwittingly undermining the alliance's Article 5 commitments and the deterrence it inherently brings to all members. But, one should not place the onus solely on these countries for their inability to adopt fully and comprehensively Western democratic defense governance concepts. For instance, this author recalls vividly a conversation with a senior Slovak military official in 2011 in which he stated that their armed forces had completely "implemented" all of NATO's planning documents, but the armed forces were still seriously under-preforming. This reality speaks to the need for these countries to conduct deep conceptual audits that includes a *ruthless* review of already adopted Western concepts to ensure that they are clearly appropriate for their envisaged tasks and national requirements. Care is needed when assessing these Western concepts to establish whether they have indeed been adopted or are only a façade, that is, adopted in name only, or are the product of cherry-picking attractive elements that underscore existing legacy norms. The results of these conceptual audits need to be translated into formal and ministerial-approved change management campaigns to replace, in the short- to medium term, legacy concepts. All of these efforts will need to be focused on the regular creation *and validation* of defense outcomes that are in alignment with government policy.

The development of strong policy frameworks and the creation of effective defense planning tools tied to budgeting need to be addressed as none of these countries have yet to develop capability coherence. Policy and planning all too often continue to be seen as the *drafting* of documents, vice the continuous hard review of *costed* options to meet validated priority capability gaps. This implies the need for a planning and budget process responsive to policy to replace current sclerotic planning and execution methods widely used in these countries. Without these conceptual and institutional reforms, it is difficult to envisage how these defense institutions can break the legacy practice of defining money as a given, and all problems can be solved simply with more, ignoring the need to ensure that they are not wasting the current budget with oversized staff structures and empty tactical units.

Western donors should continue providing individual, collective, and leadership training. But all assistance needs to be balanced with greater conditionality that such efforts are provided only where legacy concepts are actively under review to obviate against layering Western concepts on top of legacy ones. As a priority, old NATO members need to agree a common message that legacy PME must be reformed in the immediate term, no matter how bureaucratically and politically unpalatable it may be. While the Russian reform practice of closing down their entire PME system for two years has its attractions, such an approach is likely to be difficult in many of these countries. But this is not an issue: if it is not possible to sack legacy instructors, then they should be put on gardening leave, and a program of short courses and modules that address building staff skills and critical thinking using Western military and defense experts must be introduced. These programs can be augmented with indigenous personnel who have the necessary training, education, experience from deployments and, dare one say, the *gravitas* to teach nuanced Western defense concepts and their ensuing logic, thereby building modern PME institutions.

Post-Yugoslav republics

These defense institutions present the alliance with a rather complex problem set as they are quite politically heterogeneous. Slovenia and Croatia are in NATO, while Macedonia and Montenegro have expressed their desire to join; Bosnia and Herzegovina and (dare one even consider) Kosovo are in no position to join for the foreseeable future, and all the while the Serbian public continues to harbor great ambivalence over the prospects of membership. This heterogeneity is also reflected in their respective levels of the adoption of Western democratic defense governance concepts. They all still enjoy, or suffer from, common JNA institutional legacies. In fact, with some exceptions, the challenges to the adoption of Western concepts are in many ways common and reflective of their history and only vary in intensity. To varying degrees, all will require continued Western advice, ranging from Slovenia needing the very least and Serbia likely the longest and deepest engagement in large part due to its long political and military isolation, from which it is still only emerging. While establishing a conceptual audit as a priority has its attractions (and could very well be appropriate for even an advanced defense institution such as Slovenia's), it is recommended that such an effort be preceded by a *cultural* audit. The rationale for such a recommendation is that notwithstanding that the JNA was a communist defense institution, it also contained some positive attributes, many of which are similar to Western concepts. Notwithstanding the nostalgia for the large and technologically advanced JNA one can find in some countries, as a model it is simply no longer applicable for small armed forces in a democracy now based on, *inter alia*, professionalism, as opposed to conscription. Yet the wrong JNA concepts and legacies remain intact. Even in the rather reformed Slovenian defense institution, following the implementation of its relatively sophisticated professionalization program (PROVOJ launched in 2003), the existing ratio of individual specializations remains premised on the concept of conscription.[80] That said, ministers of defense and CHODs should still see some of their JNA legacies as an opportunity by formally identifying those concepts that are still applicable to their contemporary national security realities and requirements, and, by extension, *delegitimizing* those legacy practices that are not. In other words, they should formally *refine* the historical narrative and give it open and official sanction. For example, the JNA had a professional NCO corps, delegated budgets to commanders, a high level of scientific and technological sophistication, the existence of data being used to inform decisions, and elements of decentralized command.

Interestingly, these concepts existed in the JNA notwithstanding a relatively high score of power distance and uncertainty avoidance in them based on Hofstede analyses, which can only mean that culture is not necessarily deterministic. The salient point is that there is a record of adopting these practices in these cultures and, therefore, some investigation of resurrecting some useful JNA legacies could prove fruitful. Yet, not all of these practices survived intact within the JNA's successor armed forces, let alone fledging defense institutions, but their memory is not so far in the past and could be used to embrace new missions and realities. Building from the results of a cultural audit could serve as a basis to undertake a conceptual audit to identify those legacy concepts that continue to block these defense institutions from adopting Western democratic defense governance concepts. The results of this analysis should serve as the basis for a change management campaign. In addition to forcing the system to produce quantifiable defense outcomes, it could facilitate the development of a new institutional *logic* that is in accord with the new international security environment where armed forces are mobile, regional, and multinational focused.

Like their communist legacy counterparts, former JNA defense institutions must address their continued lack of an effective policy framework, as well as weak planning and budgeting concepts and practices. They have all been exposed, to formal programming methods and almost all of them have tried to adopt programming. These concepts should be systematically replaced by less complex planning and budgeting methods that closely link policy to money. The precise new method is not as important as long as it is simple, institutionally transparent, and precludes dubious assumptions such as the essentiality of multiyear budgeting. Critically, these new methods should be implemented only following a careful review of their existing financial management system to ensure that legacy concepts have been retired and new methods can be adopted.

Hard messaging from Western nations needs to be employed to press them to reform their PME structures and accept that regional and innovative solutions are needed given their modest sizes. Finally, Western nations should continue their programs of providing training support to these defense institutions, but as in the case with the Baltic States and former Warsaw Pact members, this assistance needs to be conditioned on their acceptance of changing legacy concepts.

Conclusion

If nothing else, this chapter should leave the reading audience with few, if any, illusions as to the complexity of the challenges to be faced in assisting these defense institutions to free themselves from communist legacy concepts and adopting Western ones. It is clear that both Western and Eastern political and defense officials have grossly underestimated the challenges associated with attempting to make such deep, fundamental reforms. Whereas there was a dearth of knowledge and understanding of the enormity of task at hand to effect reform in these countries following the Cold War, with twenty-five years of data, there is no possible explanation for officials to ignore the need to review fundamental concepts, assumptions, principles, and policies. This is equally applicable to Western and Eastern government officials. The summary of existing legacy pathologies has been identified, and their manifestation in each of the typologies has also been analyzed and explained. The policies and assumptions that have directed the delivery of Western assistance programs can now be seen to be wanting in many ways. Simply stated, Western and Eastern officials have underestimated the challenge and depth of the problem, and the continuation of using existing advice and assistance concepts, assumptions, methods, and programs is simply not credible. Rather, Western logic needs to be reviewed and systematically reoriented toward addressing the underlying causes of the continued inability of Eastern countries to adopt Western democratic defense governance concepts in a mutually exclusive manner with their inherited legacies. At the heart of the challenge to Western nations is the need to accept that the solution of providing technical solutions using training at the tactical level has had twenty-five years to succeed and simply has not. Rather, using principles and practices from change management and greater national and institutional cultural awareness should guide the development of new policies and methods. Finally, a one-size-fits-all approach simply has not worked and should be eschewed. As argued in the final section, Western and Eastern defense officials need to think more clearly in terms of strengths, weaknesses, and incentives, manifested by the three legacy typologies in order to refine and redirect reform efforts. Precisely how Western defense officials should rethink the current problem is the subject that will be addressed in the penultimate chapter of this work: that is, how to improve policy and management of Western assistance programs and methods.

Reforming Western Policy and Management of Defense Reform

It's more important to know what sort of person has a disease than to know what sort of disease a person has.

Hippocrates

At the ending stage in this work, it is appropriate to look at the problem of how best to encourage post-communist defense institutions to adopt Western democratic defense governance concepts differently from how the West has heretofore managed advice and assistance. To this point, the focus of the work has been on examining legacy defense institutions to ascertain the degree to which they have been able to adopt Western defense and military concepts. It is now appropriate to examine the problem differently: that is, to focus on how the West has managed its advice and assistance efforts to date. While there has been no lack of sincerity or commitment of considerable Western resources to assist these defense institutions, as this work has documented, the ensuing results have been modest. There is no shortage of explanations for the lack of greater success in reforming defense institutions. This is unfortunate, as recent history provides a prescient example of what is required:

> Integrating the German military into a democratic, functioning society was a major policy issue between 1950 and 1955. Its primary focus was civilian: a large number of civilians from different churches, labour unions, and youth organisations attended courses in America and other universities to discuss what kind of soldiers Germans wanted in their army ... nothing like this has even come close to being adopted in the Central Europe, although the tasks faced there are no less momentous.[1]

By ignoring recent history and depreciating the challenge of the task, and not matching resources to the actual requirements of reform,[2] the West mistakenly assumed that the reform of communist legacy defense institutions was a *military* problem. The default organizations charged with this task and *driving* advice and assistance programs has been Western armed forces. Thus, by seeing the task of reforming these defense institutions as either a military responsibility or at least one that should be managed by their armed forces, Western officials have unwittingly allowed them largely to default to defining the problem within their own limited institutional framework, vice examining the challenges without a technical lens, such as by using change management, sociological, or even anthropologically informed approaches. *En bref*, Western officials downplayed the lessons in the established literature which have long argued that the adoption of foreign, exogenous military reforms will fundamentally disrupt a society and its underlying social orders.[3] In consequence, the West's response has not consistently defined the challenges as inherently one of creating a new balance in civil-military relations in these young democracies. As presciently observed by a former Latvian minister of defense, even where Western officials acknowledged the need for addressing specifically civil-military relations, it has done so as an issue to be addressed superficially:

> Western experts have dealt with democratic control with attention directed primarily to its constitutional and legal aspects. According to this philosophy, once the armed forces were placed under layers of control—civilian, democratic, parliamentary—a fundamental settlement would be in place. In the real world, it is the capability of the civilians in Defence Ministries and Parliaments that weigh heavily in the balance.[4]

This point is reinforced by Cottey, Edmunds, and Forster, who argue that without an adequate degree of civilian defense expertise to scrutinize proposals from the armed forces and interpret their meaning, the ability of senior civilian leadership to understand fully the implications of proposed defense policies will be limited. In the view of these scholars, such a cadre of expertise must be accepted as a *sine qua non* for a country to graduate to an elevated status of second generation of security sector reform.[5]

There is no value in, or any intention of, this work to apportion culpability for not having foreseen the immense challenges presented to assist these defense institutions to reform. Rather, this chapter will reexamine these Western assumptions that incorrectly informed policy in order to provide insights as to how political efforts and material resources can be redirected to ensure that in future they produce a higher return on Western investment. This will be accompanied by assessing existing current Western nations and NATO's policy guidance and managerial assumptions that have been employed when developing policies to govern advice and assistance programs. Given that the US government has supplied the lion's share of assistance throughout the region, considerable attention will be directed to how it has designed and executed these programs in the region. What Western nations have created is a number of armed forces imperfectly designed and constructed, but critically lacking the necessary institutional *brains* that can *sustain* their armed forces over time. Without addressing this critically important component of the defense institution, unwittingly, the West has, by their advice and assistance programs, contributed to creating unbalanced defense institutions that has produced disjointed civil-military relations. In the end, the inability of these defense institutions to produce consistent defense outcomes is fundamentally a failure of national-level policy and management of the armed forces, all of which are perforce *civil* responsibilities in a democracy.

An interesting observation of this situation is to ponder the question: which institutions are precisely accountable for this lack of performance? The problem with such a line of enquiry is that it does not take fully into account the simple fact that governments jealously, and justifiably, guard their national prerogatives, as required by law. In consequence, it is unrealistic to expect NATO to address this issue using a fully integrated approach. Given these political realities, it is clear that the only realistic way that these challenges can be addressed is if, for example, the United States were to undertake a review of its own laws, policies, and concepts with the objective of reforming content and management of these programs. It would take a brave individual to attempt to make the argument that the current method of making the US Department of Defense the lead for reconstruction or national capacity-building has produced optimal solutions. The experience of Iraq and Afghanistan should put paid to any notion of the effectiveness of this approach.[6] These challenges will be addressed by being distilled into two basic categories: policy and management.

Policy of building defense institutions

The key impediment to the effective alignment of Western policy to meeting the ambition of reforming legacy defense institutions in Central and Eastern Europe has been the general lack of appropriate national-level policy and, in the case of the United States, clear legislative authorities[7] that recognize the complex nature of the challenge to produce organizational change. To be sure, there is a clear policy to engage these countries, but objectives and time lines regarding institutional development and modernization are left unstated. Very early on in the alliance's policy to develop its relationship with former adversaries, it determined this interaction would be managed and executed largely by their respective armed forces. At the time, this was hardly an uninformed decision given that these countries had strong armed forces and equally weak, or nonexistent, civilian ministries. Thus, by default, diplomats and the political leadership of Western nations effectively removed themselves from actively guiding and managing key elements of this process, which has allowed their armed forces subsequently to *drive* what they have perceived to be reform priorities and objectives.

An important policy decision in the United States was, in effect if not by intention, to treat these defense institutions largely as normal US Security Assistance recipients (using U.S. Code Title 22 funding program—International Military Education and Training (IMET) and Foreign Military Funds (FMF)). After 1991, this legislation was only slightly revised.[8] This was subsequently complemented by Department of Defense Security Cooperation programs (utilizing U.S. Code Title 10 authorizations and appropriations) emphasizing the improvement of tactical proficiency and deployability of these armed forces.[9] Apropos the latter point, there is no question that communist legacy armed forces were, and remain, in need of reform to improve their tactical proficiencies, which makes them quite suitable to receive this assistance as this is very much within the intent of the law.[10] But one should not conclude that improving tactical proficiencies and reforming defense institutions are mutually exclusive; on the contrary, they are inexorably linked and the relationship must produce a healthy symbiosis. As such, the reform of tactical formations and the introduction of new or modification of existing equipment can be seen as legitimately constituting a *technical* challenge. But optimizing the performance of the defense institution to know how to employ and sustain the armed forces is a *policy and managerial responsibility*, and needs to be addressed as such. Yet this remains inadequately addressed by Western policy. For instance, current US policy states that as a guideline only 10 percent of a country's IMET grant allocation should be directed to support non-armed forces assistance (under Expanded-International Military and Education Training, E-IMET), leaving the lion's share to be directed toward tactical training and PME. Note that this percentage can be adjusted upward for policy reasons, such as encouraging the improvement of human rights practices. But policy even regarding this apportionment of funding is imprecise as E-IMET is defined, *inter alia*, as constituting discrete inputs, i.e., resource management, civilian control of armed forces, and improving military judiciary systems. Nowhere is this defined in clear terms of *reforming/creating* civilian defense institutions, let alone acknowledging the challenge of overcoming the existing conceptual divide.

Since the early days of the Cold War, the Departments of State and Defense have developed a system to deliver world-class PME and training, as well as US-sourced military equipment. Arguably, the normative basis of this process and its managerial assumptions have been largely based on the notation of selling/granting education, training, and equipment to allies, which assumed (rightly or wrongly) that this assistance was going largely to non communist armed forces (Yugoslavia, for example, being a conspicuous and obvious exception). From the outset, the assumption has been what these defense institutions largely required was technical assistance, such as training, education, equipment, and exercises, as opposed to anything qualitatively different that needed to address deep political, cultural, and even sociological issues. In other words, the traditional US technical approach to Security Assistance was largely accepted after the Cold War, if only by default, and based on a complex patchwork of different legal authorities that spawned the development of assistance programs. One does not detect a unique policy-directed *approach* to determine precisely what these defense institutions needed, as opposed to simply assuming that existing policies and policy assumptions were fit to purpose.[11] There have been other innovative initiatives to offer assistance to these armed forces; for example, Warsaw Initiative Funds (now known as the Wales Initiative Fund) appropriated to the Department of Defense's budget and executed using U.S. Code Title 10 authorities to support defense institution building.[12] While not insignificant, the problem of all of these policy and resource changes is that they left all but untouched the organizational *and* management structures that were already charged with the execution of defense reform in the region.[13] Thus, notwithstanding some minor policy adjustments, a *militarized* approach to managing the support to building defense institutions has been largely allowed to occur.[14]

Although her analysis is directed to the US policy deficit regarding "building partner capacity," Dale's very perceptive (and frankly, damning) critique is very much a reflection on the West's general inattention to the need for clarity in its approach to this challenge:

> Without sufficient national-level strategic guidance, good decisions about the use of partnership tools in support of national security may still be made on a case-by-case basis. But the natural default, practitioners suggest, may be toward embracing available opportunities, building further on evident successes, and falling in on existing patterns of engagement. In effect, that approach means optimizing at the sub-systemic level—focusing on the trees rather than on the forest—which may not optimally address defense and/or national-level strategic priorities.

Likely the most critical implication of the lack of policy objectives is that without them, how can successes and failures be judged? This is an important point as Dale observes that the default mechanism has simply been to focus on programmatic outputs (i.e., events executed), as opposed to ascertaining discernible defense outcomes.[15] The lack of needed policy and priorities, with the view toward establishing objectives and expectations has essentially left these efforts adrift. Such guidance might have made evident the need for a cross-disciplined analysis to produce a proper *diagnostic* of the requirements to reform these defense institutions. It simply is not sufficient, as stated by a British defense official, that "it is important for partners to decide their own reform agendas and priorities."[16] With inadequate civilian defense expertise (which admittedly is growing slowly over time), it has been a Sisyphean task for officials in legacy defense institutions to determine what accurately constitutes their reform priorities, let alone understand the antithetical nature of the prevailing concepts that continue to *drive* their defense institutions. In short, whereas many officials in Central and Eastern Europe have been adept at expressing what they "want," Western officials have not always been capable of ascertaining, let alone persuading them, what it is that they actually need, absent close and continuous working relationships.

An inability to measure progress or performance

In this atmosphere of weak policy direction, unclear expectations, and unbalanced priorities, an ensuing implication has been an inability of Western governments and NATO to ascertain progress in effecting defense reform. As a result, there are no objective metrics of institutional reform that are being used by NATO, or leading NATO nations. To be sure, there are regular NATO assessments (e.g., PARP surveys and IPAP assessments), and disparate reports are undertaken by nations on a case-by-case basis, which are at times shared within and among governments and NATO headquarters. That said, these assessments/studies cannot be assumed to use a consistent methodology; nor have most of them been designed with the intent of providing governments with a *comparative* perspective of institutional progress toward reform.[17] All too often, what has substituted for a nuanced method of determining changes in institutional behavior are binary, linear matrices more appropriate to assessing performance of tactical formations. As Rand and Tankel argue, the lack of systematic and agreed metrics has resulted in the practice by US combatant commands reporting unconnected good news stories and antidotes of tactical success.[18] In effect, absent policy establishing clear objectives, the execution of advice and assistance activities has become conflated with achievement.

Compounding this inability to measure success in the absence of clear policy and objectives has been the lack of formal methods to assess whether the application of, and approaches to, defense reform has been *successful*. This is a twofold problem. First, in the United States, there has been little organic capability within the Department of Defense to ascertain *which* methodological approach is appropriate and optimally suited to the identified task. It is assumed, a priori, that the organization authorized and funded to execute a project knows the best methods of providing technical assistance. Different methods, customized to meet the unique conditions and *pathologies* of post-communist legacy defense institutions, are simply not seen as constituting an essential element of the planning and assessment systems. Second, the current decision-making process does not always undertake a formal diagnostic to ensure that the *correct* problem has been *identified* in order to ascertain proper *causation* of legacy behavior. As a result, all too often the selection of assistance methods is based on what *appears* to be in need of reform, followed by aligning this to an existing advice or assistance program, which is typically training. Not surprisingly, officials managing these activities focus on ensuring policy and legal inputs are strictly followed as these are the only areas where one can typically be found to have been professionally underperforming.[19]

That said, it is posited that there is an inherent challenge to policy when attempting to link programmatic inputs to measurable institutional reforms, that is, to ascertain what is relevant at the expense of that which is not. For instance, how does one assess improvements in the functioning of a ministry of defense and/or general staff? One should hope that binary judgments on the existence of meaningless policy papers and the superficial adoption of Western structures and models not only have been shown to be useless but can produce misleading conclusions of competence when not warranted. On the other hand, what might seem to be minor, or even irrelevant, actions, under full examination from a wider perspective, could be incredibly significant. For instance, the seemingly minor act of sending of an official e-mail on routine administrative business (vice using paper documents with numerous all-important approval stamps) more accurately can be interpreted as groundbreaking as it signifies overcoming high uncertainty avoidance and the implicit devolution of decision-making and open communication. This actually occurred in a new NATO defense institution in the 2011 timeframe that the author witnessed and the sender of the e-mail (which constituted the first official e-mail in that armed service's headquarters) was convinced that he ran the risk of being fired or charged for violating some unwritten security rule. But the first e-mail had been sent and thereafter the practice became routine, flattening the organization and improving its efficiency. How this achievement could be linked to discrete planning inputs is anyone's guess, let alone how such an act could have been preplanned using a technical focus. The salient point is that while advice and assistance programs perforce need assessment measures to discern if the concept, approach, and execution of the methods are effective, different measures and assessment norms are needed. This could well be best directed by experts in organizational sociology, vice solely defense specialists.

In fact, perhaps the entire question of policy regarding the measurement of reforming legacy defense institutions needs to be reframed in a completely different fashion. First, in light of the findings of various US government reports,[20] it is clear that in donor governments, management of these efforts needs to be elevated to higher-level officials in foreign and defense ministries. In effect, there is a need to eschew the long-standing use of tactical and linear planning templates and performance should be measured against policy objectives and resource inputs. Second, institution building does not lend itself to binary, or even linear, judgments. It is doubtful that many would consider the initiation of new means of internal communications in the form of the first official e-mail to be included in any institution-building checklist. Rather, it would appear that policy needs to look at the problem from a different vantage point. It is interesting to recall that within NATO councils, national business is judged as precisely that: national, and generally not appropriate for open discussion in allied councils. However, what *has* long been an acceptable topic of intense debate, particularly during the Cold War, is the question of *military outputs*. In essence, whether a nation produced the military capability and capacity that it had agreed within the context of its Force Goals (renamed Capability Targets) is judged very much a subject of enquiry and ruthless debate. It is proposed, therefore, that the question of progress in defense reform needs to return to Cold War logic: is the country capable of meeting its collective defense commitments? If this is not the case, then deeper questions need to be posed, however, with a different twist. Can one postulate a situation whereby a failure in an ally's ability to produce stated defense outcomes is not indeed one, or possibly a series of, *policy* failures within the defense institution? The point being is that when there are tactical failures, poor performance, or nonexistent capabilities, these results must be seen as being inherently *political* in nature, as they are the products of policy *failures* and need to be addressed as such. It makes no logical sense to focus on policy and programmatic inputs without sharper attention and political focus placed on *military outcomes*, which could begin as something as basic as assessing readiness levels of all units within the armed forces.[21] After all, it is more than conceivable that a review of the performance of inputs could produce a passing grade without creating policy-sanctioned outcomes. Thus, this issue needs to be addressed intensively at the national level and within the evolving NATO-integrated defense planning and reporting process.

Unbalancing civil-military relations

There is nothing inherently ineffectual with having the armed forces of NATO nations involved in the provision of technical assistance to assist in reforming these armed forces. Yet acting alone and in a political vacuum, unintended consequences can occur. Writing in 2000, Patterson Ulrich persuasively excoriates the record of the US military institution of not furthering the democratization of these armed forces.[22] There are, however, two externalities that have emerged that have become counterproductive in enabling these institutions to become self-sustaining and need to be addressed in policy. First, by adopting a military/technical approach to defense institutional reform, the West has largely ignored its fundamental political nature. Institution building (which concurrently implies in most cases institutional *deconstruction*) is inherently a *political act*; and in consequence, it creates a civil-military relations challenge of the highest order. Thus, the West has made the erroneous assumption that this type of reform can be successfully executed absent very close and continuous political pressure from the highest levels of a nation to encourage and guide change. It is almost inconceivable that a defense institution, still in many cases largely manned and dominated by legacy officers, and oftentimes promoted to key defense civilian posts, would be able to understand fully how to reform their organization, let alone become enthused advocates of reforms, the outcome of which would likely deprive them and their cadre of their positions and influence.

Second, by giving the lead to the armed forces, the solution to many requests for assistance from legacy defense institutions has been, not surprisingly, of a military nature, irrespective of causation. It should be, then, no surprise that there have been a disproportionate number of officers who have been educated in Western military professional educational establishments, as opposed to their civilian counterparts. Betz argues that in the 1990s in relation to Poland and Hungary (and surely this condition extended to other defense institutions), this emphasis on soldiers, vice defense civilian officials, only worsened the expertise balance in countries.[23] There is a partial explanation to this state of disproportionality in that with rare exception, there are few formal educational programs designed specifically for defense civilians,[24] and it is far *easier* for armed forces to bring military personnel to established Western PME institutions where they can be integrated into their student body and funded on an incremental cost basis.

Equally, civilian expertise in defense policy development, planning, budgeting, and force management is not easily or quickly developed; nor is education and training all that easy to find. Where such courses in the West do exist, they have been largely designed by armed forces for the education of their own officers and NCO corps. In consequence, these courses are nation-specific and rarely provide a *comparative* presentation and analysis of these subjects. This, therefore, leaves those aspiring to become civilian defense officials to study strategic studies in civilian universities, which rarely address such mundane, but important, subjects as effective techniques in defense management and various budgeting methods. The unintended result of this practice is that over twenty-five years the West trained and educated, in the Western approach to war, many more military officers than they did for their putative civilian superiors. Thus, the West unwittingly reinforced an already existing imbalance in civil-military relations within these countries. The obvious policy challenge, therefore, is to determine whether to continue to contribute to this imbalance or design new approaches and programs.

Partnership goals policy

To its credit, the alliance and its members tacitly acknowledged in 2004 the need for greater attention to be paid to supporting new allies and partners' efforts to reform national-level defense institutions. This was initiated with the promulgation of the Partnership Action Plan on Defence Institution Building (DIB).[25] The initiative was envisaged to augment NATO's imaginary toolbox (plans, procedures, and concepts) to bring these countries closer to NATO. Boonstra writes that this toolbox has grown and has become rather unwieldy and is therefore increasingly difficult for countries to understand how best to use it.[26] The DIB initiative gave greater emphasis to encouraging more engagement between donor and recipient nations. A key policy and planning tool has been for countries to adopt DIB-specific PGs, which are evaluated in each country's PARP. Since 2004, NATO has modified PARP to emphasize defense reform.[27] These objective goals are meant to serve as demonstrable policy declarations of the degree to which partners take to develop a closer relationship with, or possibly eventual membership in, the alliance. A unique problem that confronts PfP members is their poor record of success when it comes to their appreciation of, the role and possible advantage presented by, the adoption of PGs, and arguably, by extension, Capability Targets when they become alliance members. These agreements were created during the early development of the PfP program and were modeled on NATO Force Goals. Generally speaking, they are useful tools to enable a reforming government to gain a better understanding of the Western approach to preparing and conducting operations. The adoption of PGs can represent a major commitment on their part to demonstrate the degree to which they take their political commitment seriously to implement Western democratic defense governance concepts.

However, the policies regarding the selection of PGs and the advice provided by the International Staff and Western nations have not been effective. This has been due in no small part to the exogenous nature and content of PGs. Equally, as PGs can span the entire activities of the defense institution, the mere ability to exercise proper policy oversight of them, let alone developing the capability to aggregate their components, has been challenging for legacy defense institutions. What should have been a very disciplined and considered process of adopting commitments has not always been the case. NATO's International Staff and NATO nations' officials all too often have been keen to sell the latest priority of the alliance, or simply have been unaware of the full consequences (*particularly* financial) of the impact of a PG on defense institutions. In fact, some NATO aspirants have seen agreeing PGs as constituting "more is better," and agreed so many PGs as to make their realization all but a fantasy. Barany recounts that during 1999 to 2000, Romania accepted eighty-eight objectives, but was able to fulfill only two of them. Learning from this experience, in the following PARP cycle, Romania agreed only thirteen objectives, but achieved all of them. Slovenia and Slovakia, on the other hand, were more judicious in their early selection of PGs (fifteen and twenty-two, respectively) and enjoyed a higher rate of implementation.[28] Experience of working in the field with these defense institutions over many years suggests that NATO nations and the International Staff need to exercise more prudence when assisting new allies and partner defense officials to select goals that are supportive of current policy priorities of a defense institution and are achievable. Indeed, NATO policy needs to recognize that PGs and, on gaining membership, Capability Targets are potentially missed opportunities if they are not properly managed.

As a heuristic, policy of legacy defense institutions would benefit from addressing the following points when examining the selection of Capability Targets/PGs:

(1) As a *sine qua non*, they need to be perceived by the Policy Branch as policy *enablers*. In consequence, the bureaucratic ownership of Capability Targets/PGs needs to reside in the Policy Branch of ministries of defense. Therefore, Policy Branch needs to validate that they are selected from an existing list of national objectives which are in priority order.

(2) Conduct a detailed examination of the current Capability Targets/PGs development/selection process. Prior to the selection of any Capability Targets/PGs, there is a need for a disciplined full appreciation of all of the stated and implied tasks associated with undertaking these endeavors. One might find that a rather decentralized process exists whereby they are generally selected by narrow specialists and/or are highly technical and are not accompanied by other, broader goals, let alone possibly missing key enablers.

(3) Selection of Capability Targets/PGs should be made only after a careful cost/benefit analysis. It is often ignored in legacy defense institutions that policies have financial consequences. Capability Targets/PGs entail costs, not only defined in terms of financial resources, but also defined in terms of opportunities. In consequence, these proposals need to be carefully costed, weighed, and analyzed to determine if there is indeed a return on investment in relation to policy priorities of the defense institution.

(4) Attention is needed to ensure that Capability Targets/PGs and national goals are conceptually consistent. This issue needs particular attention by the Policy Branch so as to ensure that a deep conceptual gap does not exist between aspiration and ground reality. A collective analysis undertaken by Policy Branch and the requesting office within the ministry of defense or general staff could result in a better understanding of the precise nature and extent of the legacy concept that is to be replaced.

(5) Agreed Capability Targets/PGs need to be supported by a detailed management and oversight plan. Simply stated, Capability Targets/PGs are not self-implementing, and therefore, a well-considered management plan of action is required for them. One can observe that those Capability Targets/PGs that have been most effectively used by partner nations are those that were selected from already established nationally sanctioned priorities and managed through existing planning and management procedures to ensure that they are not exogenous to the defense institution's approved priorities and objectives.

(6) Once vetted and adopted, Policy Branch must develop a method to determine, from a *policy perspective*, how the progress of implementation is measured, how it validates progress/success, and develop an effective means to ensure that

this information is communicated to all relevant officials, and particularly to leadership.

(7)   As Capability Targets/PGs should be perceived as constituting political capital used in a country's dealings with NATO and its members, it is absolutely essential that progress in their adoption needs to be carefully documented and communicated effectively by Policy Branch to the NATO International Staff.

Finally, there is an important incentive for a partner nation to develop effective PG management procedures, since if a country becomes a member of the alliance, these same procedures can be used, with some variation, to manage its Capability Targets.[29]

Management of building defense institutions

If the policy adopted by Western countries to support the Federal Republic of Germany to rearm was a successful case of defense institution building, in comparison Western policy to assist reforming legacy defense institutions must be judged in a much more critical light. Policy and law were only slightly altered in the case of, for instance, the United States, by far the largest contributor of assistance, while largely leaving in place Cold War bureaucracy, planning concepts, programmatic assumptions, and management logic. The implications of policy not providing the necessary and appropriate authorities, aligned with resources, can be best seen in an assessment of the management of these efforts by NATO and donor defense institutions. In defense of the armed forces which were entrusted with undertaking this important responsibility, it is arguably unfair to compare rearming a defeated country from scratch with reforming a defense institution in its entirety, and in most cases using the same personnel who until 1990 had been military and ideological enemies. As NATO nations' armed forces and the military officials in the alliance itself dominated the design and execution of the preponderance of advice and assistance programs in Central and Eastern Europe, it is understandable that they would focus on the tactical- and operational-levels of war given that those at the strategic level are limited as these responsibilities predominantly fall under civilian authorities. Since every NATO nation conducts its own national business in accordance with their unique constitutional and legal traditions, there is no single NATO defense institutional *model* to serve as a comprehensive template for reforming legacy defense institutions. Thus, it is little wonder that there has been no pressure to contemplate, let alone develop, such a formal model and nor to create a lessons learned process as they specifically relate to defense institutions. All of this is entirely unfortunate. Legacy ministries of defense in Europe are at a particular disadvantage because as almost all other elements of their governance fall under the European Union's Aquis Communitaire, there are no detailed guidance specifically related to the unique competencies which fall under defense ministries and armed forces. As policy did not recognize the need to change significantly guidance to Western armed forces, NATO nations have been forced to undertake this challenging task using essentially existing assistance programs, absent adequate policy reinforcement to assist in what has been inherently a *civil-military* relations and governance challenge.

Mis-managing Western advising

At the most basic level, the United States and many other governments largely directed their respective armed forces to provide advice and assistance in reforming/creating civilian defense ministries in a legacy environment, an area of expertise singularly lacking in Western armed forces. Indeed, a variation on this mistake has been repeated in both Afghanistan and Iraq to no small negative effect.[30] What is remarkable has been the lack of attentiveness by officials of the true nature of the challenge since reforming public institutions inherently produces political challenges. There seems to have been limited memory in the United States, let alone recognition, of the challenge of reforming the US Department of Defense and the bloody bureaucratic fights which rocked the department during the debate leading up to the passage of the Goldwater-Nichols Defense Reorganization Act in 1986,[31] or in Germany over the many painful post-Cold War reforms undertaken within the Federal Ministry of Defense.[32] If such endeavors were exceedingly difficult to achieve in mature democracies such as the United States and Germany, a proper comparison with the tasks being faced by these defense institutions would have better informed officials of the complexity of the undertaking before them. Instead, an approach defining the solution to the challenge of reform consisted largely of *technical assistance* continues mainly with serving and retired officers and NCOs sent to support ministries of defense, *civil ministries*, to advise on what are inherently civilian responsibilities and prerogatives.

As regards specifically the United States, a confluence of untested assumptions and poorly structured management has resulted in what could have been a powerful reform capability, but in the end produced what can only be judged as suboptimal results. Both the Departments of Defense and State used extensively private firms under contract to embed resident advisers with the task of reforming these defense institutions. The use of such an instrument can arguably be beneficial if managed correctly so as to avoid the moral hazard wryly observed by Emma, thinking of Mr. Elton and Harriet Smith, in Jane Austen's *Emma*: "There are people, who the more you do for them, the less they will do for themselves." The execution of these projects has been overseen in principle by the Defense Security Cooperation Agency; but in reality, the vast majority of them have been managed by the US Department of the Army's US Army Security Assistance Command. By assuming the program management of these projects (and they have almost all have been managed by the US Army, vice the other two military departments), two very odd, but perhaps predictable, outcomes occurred. First, the contract on-site representative only until recent years had been based in the United States, as opposed to the country where the work has been undertaken. Thus, even if we assume the Department of Army possessed the necessary expertise to be able to provide proper management oversight of the appropriate *content* of these programs, a *very* problematic assumption in itself as the record demonstrates, such expertise was not provided continuously on-site. The default of this contractual arrangement has been to make the chiefs of the Office of Defense Cooperation (junior to mid-field grade officers) responsible for the oversight of resident reform programs that seek to transform defense institutions. Thus, almost from inception, these advice programs have been militarized as the individuals recruited for these assignments have been almost exclusively retired military officers and NCOs and the projects oftentimes have been led by a retired senior field-grade or general officer. Indeed, in one solicitation for contractor support to the Georgian Ministry of Defense, to *advise* the minister on defense reform, the qualifications for the team lead inexplicably specified a retired senior officer with brigade command experience.[33] Equally, the United Kingdom posted active duty brigadiers, field-grade officers, and civilian defense officials to a number of Central and Eastern European countries prior to their gaining admittance to NATO as embedded advisers in ministries of defense.[34] But, at least in the case of the United Kingdom, these officials reported to Policy Branch in the Ministry of Defense in London.

Second, it is not suggested that all such efforts are inappropriate. However, what needs to be accepted is that such teams of retired military personnel, led oftentimes by retired general officers, could be assessed as being appropriate in assisting armed forces, and perhaps even general staffs. However, this is caveated with the condition that these individuals need to be briefed and trained to understand the challenges presented by the persistence of legacy concepts. Otherwise, it is difficult to accept that such endeavors *can be* successful when executed in ministries of defense where the responsibilities and functions are inherently civil and not military. No better example of the inappropriateness of assigning a team of experts dominated by American retired military officers can be found than in the case of Croatia as documented by Bellamy and Edmunds, cited in Chapter 7, which advised the creation of an oversized ministry of defense and general staff modeled on the Pentagon.[35] To be sure, this initial contract between MPRI and Croatia was executed as a commercial endeavor. But the US government later supported the company's activities in the country whose revenue grew from $105,000 in 1995 to $6 million in 2003.[36]

In general, the challenge posed by employing military advisers to ministries of defense should be self-evident. Such programs were often conducted by Western military officers (many of whom have had little, or *no*, expertise in national-level defense policy or management) supporting inherently civilian functions and responsibilities. As regards the Baltic States prior to the accession to NATO, Clemmesen's views on such an approach are nothing short of scathing:

> The [foreign] advisors and support project officers arrive eager to do good during the months they work here. However, they are unfortunately only too likely to be without any prior knowledge or understanding of the defence problems of a small, poor, front-line state. ... They only know their own system that mirrors the development of their own forces and the politico-economic and geo-strategic requirements of their own state during recent years .... There are cases where a supporting state's representative has simply left the Baltic state with two choices: either it copies the supporting state's proven system (ignoring and compromising all previous developments) or loses the opportunity for support. There have been too many cases of supporting states' representatives actively undermining each other's support projects, creating serious problems and delays for the Baltic state.[37]

Nor should decisions made by the North Atlantic Council in assigning appropriate responsibilities in this area to NATO's integrated command be spared from constructive criticism. For instance, there has been the practice of establishing NATO training teams in a number of PfP nations to assist them in supporting reform (e.g., Bosnia-Herzegovina and Macedonia). Nations offer up personnel for these assignments, normally on a six-month basis. The list of shortcomings with this approach is, sadly, prodigious. Firstly, there are no formal educational or training programs to prepare these individuals to be effective advisers in these countries.[38] Secondly, nations nominate whom they wish to send and there is very little discretionary power over their acceptance, except in the most egregious cases of an individual being completely incompetent. For instance, in a visit to Skopje in November 2006, this author was briefed that within the NATO training team the SOF adviser was, in fact, an army logistician. Thirdly, these short postings obviate against the ability to gain and use experience. Fourthly, these teams are also financially starved and dependent on external funding if they are to carry out any independent projects. Fifthly, NATO does not provide a basic corpus of expert advice to which these individuals can turn, as the issues on which they are to advise are, of course, largely national business. All of which leads to the question of what their utility can possibly be? If this were not sufficiently troubling, NATO has confused the management of these endeavors by placing their management within the integrated command structure. It makes very little sense to assign efforts that are inherently civil in nature, for example, defense reform, to a military chain of command. For instance, the NATO Advisory Team in Bosnia-Herzegovina is part of the NATO Headquarters Sarajevo, both of which are under the command of Allied Joint Force Command in Naples. Thus,

> Some members of the NATO Advisory Team indicated that it would be preferable if NATO HQ Sarajevo reported directly to Brussels, which is where the Defense Policy and Planning Division, as well as the Political Affairs and Policy Division, sit, and where there is more knowledge on defense reform processes.[39]

There is a report of a similar situation in Kosovo where efforts to ensure that the alliance's training mission for the Kosovo Protection Corps (now the Kosovo Security Force) includes making it accountable to the International Staff, thereby leaving it less dependent on the varying degree to which Kosovo Force commanders define this aspect of the force's mission as important.[40]

Scientific management of art

The manner by which donor countries have planned and managed their engagements with legacy defense institutions has been based on the assumption that advice and assistance follow a predictable and linear path, and can be executed over time on precise dates, all of which produce a clearly definable outcome. In other words, it is an approach based on proven procedures and logic that has long been used successfully for the planning and execution of exercises and collective training events. Thus, Western armed forces have largely addressed reforming national-level civil responsibilities of a legacy defense institution using planning assumptions and methods optimized for tactical conditions and realities. In consequence, these programs have been based on, and subsequently managed by, the employment of these assumptions and methods. This approach is most clearly found in the methods employed by the United States.

The lead agency with responsibility for planning, management, and execution of US Security Assistance and Security Cooperation efforts in Europe is European Command (EUCOM), a geographic combatant command.[41] One former senior official of EUCOM, writing of the challenge of building partnership capacity, asserts that these commands are optimal to their given tasks:

> The logical place for such organizations is at the Geographic Combatant Command (GCC) level. These organizations will need to tie into capability- and capacity-building activities within other agencies and coordinate their activities to ensure they are harmonized and synchronized. The GCC also is the natural integrator for all country plans since the U.S. Office of Defense Cooperation in each country in a theater reports to the GCC.[42]

This argument is circular as it ignores the civil and national-level component of the essential need to engage defense institutions at equal levels if capacity-building is to succeed. For example, none of the current arrangements cited by the author are immutable, and they can be changed either by revising U.S. Code Title 10 or, even more easily, by revising the *Unified Command Plan*. As to the civil component, it is unfortunate that all too often this critical element of Western democratic defense governance concepts has long been a lowest priority in the planning and programs of many combatant commands. The problem with this practice is at least fourfold.

First, attention to civil issues is generally given lower priority in the allocation of resources than tactical programs which are within the areas of competence of these commands and their service components. This approach has been allowed to remain in effect despite, for example, the inability on the part of the Departments of Defense or State to demonstrate how the monetary value of results of, for example, the IMET program, managed by component commands and executed by the Services, compares to its related costs. Both departments reported that they do not collect data at this level in order to conduct evaluation of the program's effectiveness.[43] Disappointingly, reliance on this program of spreading Western democratic defense governance concepts is undermined by the observation that it is not designed to change behavior.[44] Policy has also failed to ensure that individuals sent on IMET courses are not subject to the all-too-frequent practice that when they return from Western PME courses they are fired, sent to their old posting, or simply sidelined.[45] In short, that there has been no small degree of policy incoherence in the execution of these education and training programs is an understatement.

Second, there appears to be a lack of Western understanding that the causation of tactical-level shortcomings in allied or partner nations is to be found in weaknesses or failures in national-level *policy* which these commands are not optimally staffed to address. If after twenty-five years of exposure to Western tactical military concepts, there are tactical-level lacunae in expertise in legacy armed forces, these must be judged as manifestations of failures in legacy defense institutions' defense policy and/or management processes. More troubling is that not all tactical-level advice and assistance furthers the adoption of Western democratic defense governance concepts. Patterson Ulrich all but excoriates the disconnection between policy intent and program performance regarding US assistance she witnessed in the Czech Republic in the 1990s. By her analysis, some 80 percent of defense and military contacts did not contribute to US objectives to further the democratization of the armed forces as intended by policy.[46] Clearly, there is a strong need for allied and partner defense and military shortcomings to be addressed in a complementary fashion in order to ensure that improving tactical proficiency is supported by changes in existing national-level policy.[47]

Third, due to the extensive tactical-level expertise in these commands, it should be expected, therefore, that their recommended approaches are invariably in line with using traditional methods and existing programs of providing Security Assistance and Security Cooperation. Indeed, the planning methods employed by EUCOM at least do not generally distinguish between tactical-level activities and those associated with improving the functioning of the defense institution. A RAND report found that planners are confronted with having to select among *123* different legal authorities under to use just U.S. Code Title 10 funding.[48] To all appearances, the planning system is set up ideally to plan, manage, and execute military-to-military *tactical* projects (e.g., exercises).[49] As the planning system requires that tactical events and exercises be planned and coordinated at least twelve to eighteen months in advance, any activities related to civil issues are forced into a planning straightjacket that misses untold opportunities as national political realities change (which normally have a short window of opportunity), thereby making the utilization of such a rigid, linear, and predictive approach inappropriate.

Fourth, as almost all of these programs and projects are planned and executed by the US armed forces as discrete events, long missing from this management practice has been an appreciation of the need for overarching continuity in messaging and content. Speaking generally, one former Eastern European defense official observed, "One further negative aspect of international assistance relates to confusion brought about 'by the plethora of [Western] advice and assistance, often unco-ordinated and short-term in nature, offered by supporting nations and organizations.'"[50] In effect, such a decentralized and, dare one suggest, *disaggregated* approach simply assumes the existence of conducive national- and operational-level policies, concepts, and collective critical thinking that can accept the Western approach of modern warfare.

While perhaps an unpopular observation with some officials, institution building should be seen as being more akin to art, manifested more as a form of edgy Expressionism, vice the tactical level's preference for more symmetrical and ostensibly visually pleasing Classicism. In essence, institutional development is not necessarily a linear, objective process, and management processes that treat it as such are bound to produce suboptimal results.

Structural disparity

The long-standing nexus between US geographic combatant commands and allied/partner defense institutions also points to the vexatious issue of disproportionality.

Despite recent efforts by the Department of Defense to shift greater "military diplomacy" responsibilities to these commands,[51] it is problematic that a joint operational-level command has organic expertise and capabilities to interface and interact effectively on civil issues with ally/partner's defense institutions. Geographic combatant commands are not habitually manned with senior-level field-grade and flag/general officers, let alone a strong cadre of senior civilian officials, with such backgrounds and who are properly prepared to understand cultural and political nuances. As a result, all too often the grade and level of experience of the staff managing, or providing oversight over, these projects is too junior for the tasks at hand. Marshall's unconvincing argument that these commands are ideally suited to manage resources in capacity-building is undermined by the systematic lack of expertise habitually assigned to these headquarters.[52] Addressing this clear shortcoming, a working group led by former EUCOM commander General James Jones has strongly advocated the need for a whole of government approach in better engaging allies and partners with particularly the Department of State playing a stronger managerial role.[53]

Almost always coming from tactical formations, staff and flag/general officers assigned to these commands are confronted with understanding the complexities of legacy defense institutions with the view of helping them, *inter alia*, pursue defense reform.[54] Military personnel posted to these headquarters can come from virtually any career field, but are immediately faced with planning and executing of Security Assistance and Security Cooperation programs based on a patchwork of complex legislative authorities.[55] This problem is not restricted to these commands. Officials from the Department of State have gone on record expressing their concerns with the uneven training being provided to military personnel assigned to work in embassies to manage these programs;[56] yet admittedly, this needs to be balanced by the reality that the Department of State does not make this training a priority for its own foreign service officers.[57] To be sure, there is substantial service variation of professional requirements to be eligible to serve in these positions. The Department of Defense has recognized these issues as it attempts to expand, standardize, and improve the development of foreign area officers, but progress remains to be achieved.[58] Additionally, as related to the qualifications of military personnel responsible for planning and managing "Title 1206" equipping programs (now titled "Title 2282"), it is noteworthy that they use the same systems and procedures used for traditional Security Assistance programs. A Department of State Inspector General's report identified numerous shortcomings in acquisition experience within the Department of Defense's workforce, to include those assigned to embassies.[59] Not surprisingly, then, officials responsible for these activities tend to focus on aligning policy and legal inputs in their decisions as these are the only areas where one can typically be found to have been professionally underperforming, as no one in the bureaucracy is *accountable* for failure to reform a ministry of defense.[60] Compounding these efforts (seen so vividly also in Iraq and Afghanistan) is the assumption that almost all problems can be addressed through individual, collective, and leadership training. Hence, if an effort does not succeed, then the response is all too often to conduct the identical training event, *ad infinitum*.

In sum, the inherent orientation of these endeavors managed by geographic combatant commands is overwhelmingly to stress a tactical focus, at the expense of addressing civil shortcomings in defense institutions. Given these commands' focus, tactical- and operational-level training, as well as activities that can be ascribed to improving readiness and interoperability, receive priority over projects whose outcomes are more nebulous and long-term by their very nature. In fact, Patterson Ulrich makes a damning argument that the pursuit of interoperability has been made at the expense of achieving greater democratization in these post-communist armed forces.[61] In their defense, these commands face the dilemma of determining the allocation of resources to address immediate-term issues, but are executed at the expense of longer-term investments. As there is no one *responsible* for the success or failure of enabling an allied or partner defense institution to modernize by adopting Western democratic defense governance concepts, the value of long-term investments is surrendered to meeting *understandable* and short-term results from these tactical- and operation-level activities. This critique is not to disparage in any way the importance of these programs and their military objectives. However, what needs to be recognized is that these activities and their supporting funding are being executed absent a necessary complementary structure that is needed to support developing greater Western democratic defense governance objectives. In fact, by not addressing these national-level governance shortcomings, tactical- and operational-level objectives that these commands support are not being sufficiently addressed in national-level policy, and therefore are often not sustained.

Given the demonstrated complexities of attempting to build new, or reform existing, defense institutions, as well as the challenge of managing these efforts from at least the perspective of the US government, serious consideration is needed to review current relevant policy and legislation. As these efforts almost invariably involve the Department of State, the Department of Defense, and its contingent organizations (e.g., DSCA, the Military Departments, geographic combatant commands, and their service component commands), oversight and coordination of these reform efforts would be better achieved if managed from the National Security Council. The need for consistent policy messaging from the highest national political level particularly to new allies implies the need for greater oversight of the performance of advice and assistance efforts and thereby introducing long overdue authority to apportion responsibility and accountability of executing agencies and officials.

Conclusion

Western policy and management practices have unwittingly underwritten a de facto approach to supporting defense reform that has provided considerable assistance and expertise, but has not been properly designed and executed. Therefore, these efforts have often been incomprehensible within recipient defense institutions. What has been lacking has been appropriate management structures and procedures that can identify the success of advice and assistance methods, or provide for a proper review of programming assumptions and content. One can only conclude that the causation of the lack of progress in desired reform rests firmly at the policy level and in how laws have been drafted that are not influenced by the actual challenges facing reformers in these new democracies, let alone how advice and assistance programs need to be managed if they are to have their desired effect. What is remarkable is that given the scrutiny that foreign assistance and economic development programs have come under for many years, political attention has only recently been directed to these defense advice and assistance programs.[62] Perhaps, unlike economic development, improvements in military effectiveness are less easy to discern and unrelated rationales can easily be claimed as justifying the success of these programs; for example, improving, by assertion, tactical interoperability. The fact remains that the current focus on inputs and the accountability for the proper use of funding alone remains an enormous weakness in the West's management of military integration of these new allies and partners.

It is likely that the most daunting challenge that will face Western officials is not so much to change policy, but rather how best to incentivize reform and change within their own defense institutions and introduce better methods to plan, execute, and evaluate performance of advice and assistance programs. What is remarkable about the Western approach to providing assistance to legacy defense institutions has been the lack of application of what is the hallmark of their armed forces. As services that not only allow but require critical thinking on the part of all of its members, it is surprising that there has been little consistent institutional reflection on the performance of these advice and assistance programs. One possible explanation is that where there has been progress in achieving reform is at the tactical level in certain units of these armed forces. Without question, Western armed forces are exceedingly competent at training foreign tactical formations. As much of the activities and emphasis has been focused at this level, particularly in light of the imperative to encourage these countries to provide forces for operations in Afghanistan and later Iraq, civil issues of governance have simply not been a priority item for Western officials. Where there were imperatives for defense reform and acceptance on the part of the ally or partner, technical assistance has been generously provided, to include the use of resident defense advisers. In consequence, while it is clear that there have been episodic, at best, efforts at undertaking mission analysis of the requirements of these defense institutions, it is equally clear that those studies have obviously missed some key and nuanced aspects of building defense governance. Perhaps the officials that have undertaken these assessments simply have not had the necessary expertise to be able to appreciate the full magnitude of the challenge. Bridging this managerial gap and determining new methods of management and responsibility must become a priority for Western officials. Precisely how this might be accomplished is addressed in the final chapter.

Conclusion: Getting to "Honest Defense"

Seldom, very seldom, does complete truth belong to any human disclosure;
seldom can it happen that something is not a little disguised or a little mistaken
Jane Austen, *Emma*

In light of the modest reforms achieved to date by the defense institutions examined in this work, it would be a brave individual to claim optimism concerning the outlook for their continued reform. That the West could have spent twenty-five years and not inconsequential resources to help newly emerging democracies reform their respective defense institutions with such limited success should be seen as a major cause for concern among all NATO members. Through ignorance or neglect, newly democratic governments have seen their legacy defense institutions devolve into "zombie"-like organizations. They have not been killed outright, but rather have been allowed to slip into a state of nonlife due to the lack of firm policy direction, all the while being slowly starved of financial resources. Hard financial shocks to budgets, or strong political leadership over bureaucracies, that could have energized these organizations back into a conscience state have almost always been followed by governments' relenting and restoring sufficient monies to the system, creating missed opportunities and allowing many of them to slip back into an operational stupor. Even the best functioning defense institutions, while definitely not in a zombie state, are still struggling to come to conceptual terms with important management responsibilities, the most important of which is understanding that money as a critical planning tool.[1]

This is not to imply, however, that all these efforts have been in vain. It can be stated with a fair degree of objectivity that most of the nations in the region possess a collection of islands of expertise that are operating on the basis of Western concepts and principles. However, key Western democratic defense governance concepts remain to be adopted and internalized in a more effective manner (e.g., defense planning, force management, training policy). In consequence, these atolls of competence remain adrift in a sea of legacy concepts and managerial pathologies. And, in some cases, they are even drowning in them. Clearly, one can state with confidence that all of them will continue to require varying degrees of advice in order to adopt Western democratic defense governance concepts and considerable political will to implement them.

The challenge that confronts Western officials is that the low-hanging fruit of reform has long been gathered.[2] By extension, therefore, it is only those problem areas of national responsibility which are all too often, bureaucratically speaking, *sulfurous* that remain to be addressed. Alas, it is a reality that there are often very good reasons, normally political, that certain areas within legacy defense national institutions have resisted reform for so long. Unfortunately, these key areas of activity are critical to the proper functioning of any defense institution and/or potentially are multipliers of improving effectiveness if reformed. Too often, the causation for the continued use of legacy concepts is overlooked, assumed away, or has been provided with sufficient Western advice and assistance to acquire a superficiality of Western modernity while continuing to operate (blissfully) in accordance with legacy norms. A perfect illustration of this is various "perfect" PPBS models that do not produce measurable defense outcomes. Hence, Western and Eastern officials need to change policy that targets legacy concepts that tenaciously resist retirement as a priority area in the modernization of these defense institutions.

This work has had the objective of addressing five key questions which relate to the lack of reform of Central and Eastern European defense institutions. From an analysis of the data related to these five issues, the work equally posited seven theses. It is appropriate at this point to review these issues and assess the strength of the theses.

State of Central and Eastern European defense institutions

That Western and Eastern political, defense, and military officials have misjudged the severity of the challenge to adopt Western democratic defense governance concepts, there should be little doubt. Relying on a wealth of data and analysis that is available in official documents, the literature, and open press, there can be little argument that overall most of these institutions are, to varying degrees to be sure, in serious need of deep change. If nothing else, this work served the purpose of bringing attention to the slowness by which Western democratic defense governance concepts have been adopted. That governmental institutions are challenged when attempting to bring about systemic change is hardly newsworthy. Yet it should be acknowledged that it is troubling that there appears to be complacency, if not ignorance of this state of affairs, both in old NATO and in Eastern/Central European capitals. The events in Ukraine since the winter of 2014 have obviously turned a bright light to the inadequacies of the state of development in all legacy defense institutions, but it is not yet clear that this new level of awareness extends to an examination by Western governments of their individual and collective policies and approaches to providing advice and assistance. Moreover, it is equally unclear whether Eastern officials feel an immediacy to address their own national policies and priorities. One would think that recent changes in Russian policy toward the "near abroad" should have a salutary effect on politicians throughout Central and Eastern Europe, and which should focus their respective policies to determining causation of the underperformance of their defense institutions. What the data employed in this study demonstrates is that just as Western policy has been inadequate to the task at helping these young democracies reform their defense institutions to Western standards, officials in the region are equally unaware of how best to confront the challenge. Clearly, NATO policies and the national policies of major allied nations simply must be reassessed to address this state of affairs. For without a much more concerted effort to press for reforms of concepts, assumptions, and logic, the legacy rot will continue to metastasize.

Impediments to reform

Upon reflection of the data presented in this work, the reform of legacy defense institutions has been impeded by a misunderstanding the challenge. First, Eastern officials have been slow, if not at times unwilling, to acknowledge that their respective defense institutions continue to rely on employing legacy concepts than they have been prepared to admit even to themselves. More often than not, this has been due in no small part to the fact that they have not known what the Western "right" solution should look like in their own national context. Or, even when being brutally honest with the challenges that they face, the solutions often being proposed are structural and procedural Western "solutions" which simply do not address the deeper conceptual divide that continues to dominate the governance of their defense institutions.[3] Second, Western officials, civilian and military, simply have not understood the complexity of the challenge of reforming institutions that have been subjected to the malicious iniquities of communism. False linguistic cognates, antithetical concepts, and opaque institutional assumptions have simply gone unrecognized and unaddressed as being causation for the inability of these countries to adopt Western democratic defense governance concepts. There were warnings published in the literature as early as 1996,[4] but this sage counsel was ignored. To be sure, the willingness by which all of these countries, to varying degrees, have participated in peacekeeping and combat operations in Iraq and Afghanistan gave these defense institutions a political pass from Western nations and NATO. Perhaps the most problematic decision was to allow into the alliance those countries with profoundly unreformed defense institutions. As von Riekhoff observed, "new NATO members may undertake reforms without genuine conviction, in a rather superficial or purely cosmetic way, in order to satisfy NATO demands."[5] In short, NATO and its member nations got the political incentives wrong from the beginning of PfP and its first principles, and they have failed to spend the time and resources to ascertain how best to rethink how these institutions can adopt Western democratic defense governance concepts.

In light of the persistence of these communist legacy concepts, with minor exception, the key impediments to achieving reform are twofold. First, there remains a lack of institutional recognition of the need for these defense institutions to embrace the concept of policy frameworks under which all activities within the institution must conform. Instead of policy frameworks, on close examination what one widely finds is *policy incoherence*, which has led to *institutional and capability incoherence*. Developing a policy framework is no small task and realistically might well take years yet to achieve.

That said, what is troubling is that Western officials (and frankly many analysts) have failed to argue the need for the adoption of such a fundamentally important concept. Like so many other interactions with these defense institutions, many Western officials and analysts simply assume the existence of such concepts and even if there is a perception of a problem, it is seen as being a weakness of a functioning bureaucracy, vice evidence of the absence of Western concepts. Communism as manifested in bureaucracy was founded on the principle of absolute, unpredictable, and unaccountable power by the party. The liberal democratic concept of policy, in general terms, should be seen as being founded on the principles of authority, responsibility, and accountability. None of these concepts were organic to these defense institutions when the Cold War ended and it is arguable that one of the reasons why these organizations have yet to accept them is that Western officials and analysts have not recognized that they remain elusive concepts to adopt. Thus, NATO and its members' praise for the development of model policy documents (e.g., National Security Strategy, National Military Strategy, etc.) has actually been counterproductive since it has conveyed a false message: that nicely written *strategy* documents are what are graded, as opposed to producing coherent capabilities. In consequence, the drafting of "science projects" is seen as constituting Western policy, as opposed to establishing priorities and linking them tightly to defense expenditures.

Second, directly related to the first point is that Western officials and analysts have been remiss in not seeing that purported policy and planning documents have rarely been linked to *money*. To one brought up in a legacy defense institution, money is not perceived as constituting the organization's most important management tool. Rather, money is simply there to pay, as a priority, salaries, benefits, and pensions. Any leftover is then distributed to support operations and modernization in more advanced countries, or in the least reformed, to support social programs and health care for the armed forces and its retirees. When challenged as to why expenditures are aligned as they are, the standard explanation one hears from officials is that there is insufficient money to enable the armed forces to modernize. It is the rare Eastern or Western official that questions this illogic. As a general, if unstated rule, a defense budget needs to be largely balanced in more or less equal thirds: personnel, operations and maintenance, and acquisition and infrastructure. Once a defense budget breaks this balance, inevitably, capabilities suffer. Even the seemingly advanced Slovenian Ministry of Defense is complacent in assuming that it will be able to modernize the armed forces by striving to achieve a reduction in personnel costs to 50 percent, with 30 percent of the budget allocated to operations and maintenance and 20 percent to procurement and infrastructure.[6] Note that the figure for personnel costs in 2013 stood at almost 70 percent![7] In the case of Bulgaria, the ratio of expenditures is even worse: 73 percent to personnel, 21 percent to operations and maintenance, and a mere 6 percent to modernization.[8] What almost defies explanation is such imbalances have continued to reduce defense outcomes, yet it has largely gone unsanctioned politically by NATO's leading nations.

It is little wonder, therefore, that absent a policy framework (and priorities) and an institutional recognition that money is the key managerial enabler of policy, weak defense institutions have responded by even further centralizing decision-making particularly of money at the level of ministries. One sees throughout the three typologies systems that preclude defense officials and commanders and their staffs any ability, or the expectation, that they must become adept at making decisions, particularly of a financial nature. Thus, no information systematically flows upward, officials and officers are not expected to make recommendations, staff work is turgid, and briefing senior decision makers with options is all but unknown. As a result, stasis reigns.

In the final analysis, the solution to these difficult challenges will require strong political courage on the part of governments and ministers since almost by definition, addressing these long-standing imbalances implies reductions in personnel and shifts in where money is currently spent. One would think that without creating and empowering strong policy frameworks, and reconceptualizing money as the institution's key policy implementation tool, it is difficult to see how the adoption of Western democratic defense governance concepts could take place. Surely, this is not a minor issue of solely academic value. Long-standing members of the alliance need to see cracking this problem as constituting one of the most important challenges to assisting new NATO members to become providers of security, vice solely consumers. Equally, one would think that legacy defense institutions, alone or collectively, should see this as constituting a high priority and initiate projects with interdisciplinary inputs to ascertain how these challenges can be overcome. To make these reforms take hold there is a need for the wholesale reform of existing bureaucracies with the introduction of professional development training in short modules to teach critical thinking and staff skills, vice more meaningless degree programs offered by legacy PME institutions.

Best and less-effective Western defense reform practices

Western armed forces have long maintained training and educational institutions which foreign military could be attended within their home country, or in the form of traveling assistance training teams. Western officials have seen their existing world-class education and training programs as constituting their primary "toolbox" when providing international advice and assistance. This is not necessarily to imply that there was a concerted effort to define advice and assistance requirements to be based on existing assistance institutions and programs. But what is clear is that, by default, these activities were determined to be largely within the expertise of Western armed forces. Missing from consideration was serious acknowledgment of the necessity of directing long-term and concerted efforts to help allies and partners develop ministries of defense where they did not exist, or fundamentally overhaul those that existed but in name only. What was evidently underestimated is that the armed forces of these countries already *existed*, whereas a requisite civilian brain *did not*. Thus, where these programs and projects assisted these fledgling ministries of defense, often times it was in the form of military programs and personnel. But this is not necessarily a condemnation given that Western ministries of defense not infrequently have military personnel within them. However, as seen in this work, what has been missing is an abiding commitment by Western capitals to address civil issues in new or reforming ministries of defense, supported by the need to create innovative means quickly to educate defense civilian officials. By not addressing more strongly the ability of these institutions to manage effectively civil issues, all too often legacy armed forces have ignored and undermined civilian defense officials, or where the latter has responded in kind through exercising negative control of the armed forces (e.g., in Slovenia as argued by Furlan).[9]

As has been argued in the case of economic development, this author is reluctant to suggest that in such a complex environment presented by legacy defense institutions, there are likely to be any "best practices."[10] While Western advice and assistance is based on world-class standards, they can actually have a deleterious effect as they tend to lead to predesigned and overspecific plans that preclude experimental joint problem-solving thereby not achieving a best fit.[11] The positive deviance school of thought makes a strong argument that knowledge alone is not enough to effect change. It is only through practice that behavior will change and to get to this point, external experts offering advice and assistance need to rethink how they conceptualize enabling change.[12] Arguably, what the data demonstrates in all three typologies is that changing the conceptual basis of an institution is not linear, nor is it predictable. The reform of these institutions must be seen as predominantly a political challenge. As argued by Michael Oakeshott, reform cannot be addressed via technical means alone, let alone using rational, predictive planning. Here, Oakeshott's distinction between technical and practical knowledge is instructive. The former is the type of knowledge that is formulaic and what can be put in a checklist.[13] The latter relates to what an expert actually knows: "the habits, skills, intuitions and traditions of the craft. Practical knowledge exists only in use; it can be imparted, but not taught."[14]

It is within this political context that one can best understand the challenge of enabling a defense institution to change its fundamental concepts, particularly when they are antithetical to Western democratic defense governance concepts. As a possible feeble nod to the idea of best practices, the data and ensuing analysis in this work identifies that the most important reform practice is the need for officials at all levels to understand the pernicious nature of communist legacy concepts. It is only with such an understanding that advice and assistance can be proffered with the objective of avoiding the unintended creation of producing "conceptual spaghetti." Yet such practical knowledge is only going to be successfully applied within an environment with considerable and continuous political oversight, and when necessary, pressure from the highest levels of governments. To be sure, it is unlikely to assume that long-standing NATO nations' PME institutions are going to make such fundamental changes to their organizations that provide assistance. However, from tactical to the national-level curricula, it would follow that Western institutions need better education and training as to the importance of culture and not just cultural sensitivity, but more importantly, understanding allies and partners' prevailing concepts, incentives, and motivations. Moreover, a greater formal understanding of legacy defense institutions, as well as those individual national characteristics, if properly managed and executed, could improve the delivery of advice and assistance programs.

Conversely, the data should make clear that there are certain assumptions, models, and programs that need to be reviewed with a very critical eye. As a new first principle, policy needs to recognize that these programs and projects which seek to reform any defense institution are, by definition, *political* and not merely technical. Clearly, new policy oversight is needed to ensure that such programs and projects are designed, managed, and supported within a political context and understanding. Importantly, Western foreign ministries and the NATO International Staff must rethink their previous efforts and messages to the governments in Central and Eastern Europe regarding defense reform.[15] Sharp and consistent messaging, linked closely to advice and assistance projects, is long overdue.

As regards specific practices, policy needs to review the practice of advocating national models. This is not to be confused with concepts, but adopting wholescale actual models has rarely worked if for no other reason than because of the need for a recipient country essentially to change their prevailing cultural norms. Nor does this practice pass the positive deviance test, nor Oakshott's distinction between technical and practical knowledge. For example, the practice of advocating the adoption of Western-style policy documents should be simply stopped. Western officials need to recognize that there are precious few examples (and this may be generous) of where the publication of "strategy" documents has had any noticeable effect where it matters most: rearranging priorities of a defense budget. From experience and appearance, policy documents and defense budgets in legacy defense institutions live in parallel universes that rarely, if ever, connect; and when they occasionally do, one might speculate that this was more the result of coincidence than intention.

An enormous amount of Western effort and resources has gone into advocating for, and assisting in, the development of NCO corps in these armed forces. This is a logical extension of the decision to professionalize the force that has largely become the norm. The transition to a professional NCO corps makes excellent sense for a variety of reasons, not the least of which is to lower personnel costs. However, like many models applied without a proper context, this has proven to be a slow process, Slovenia and the Baltic States' armed forces being singular exceptions. Critically, these Western-sponsored advisory programs and projects have almost exclusively been initiated without changing the officer corps, that is, shrinking and reeducating those remaining in the force to learn how to *use* professional NCOs. A common complaint heard throughout the region is that the officer corps does not know how to use NCOs at best and sees them as a threat at worst. In other words, they have not been fully empowered to act as leaders. Not advocating at the political level with national leaders and defense officials the necessity of changing the officer corps, in parallel with the creation of an NCO corps, has impeded the introduction of this concept. The point being that the NCO experience in the region is an excellent example of a good idea improperly implemented by Western officials not having conducted a full analysis to determine all of the cultural, political, and sociological challenges associated with such a major change.

Finally, apropos the issue of programming, even a cursory reading of this work will suggest that this author finds the PPBS methodology to be suspect at best. The case against using programming, particularly early in the reform of a communist legacy defense institution, is already argued throughout the work. To be blunt, this author has yet to see where it has worked; the inability of these countries to produce viable defense plans proves this point. The persistent proclivity to centralize budgets has made the adoption of this methodology all but impossible, but even with decentralization, the methods are so complex and labor-intensive to argue against their utility. Added evidence for this observation is that every defense institution in the region continues to struggle to produce financially viable defense plans connected to budgets. Surely, a less complicated and more transparent budgeting method, at least to start, is needed. One simple method would be to assume no budgetary growth for five years and then begin the process of trying to make the *current* defense institution *fit* that budget, using the principle of working toward a budget divided in thirds. Complexity, particularly in the case of PPBS, has been the enemy of the practical and has greatly impeded producing predictable and measurable defense outcomes.

Performance of Western policy and management practices

The de facto, if not de jure, decision to define the reform of these defense institutions as a military problem has by extension determined that it is the West's armed forces problem to fix. Contextualizing this question from a different perspective, how well has Western policy and its *management* practices performed in assisting these allies and partners adopt Western democratic defense governance concepts? If one posits that in light of the West's unsuccessful efforts to replace legacy concepts, Western nations perforce will have to reexamine the basis of their current policies and approaches to providing advice and assistance to these nations, and new policy direction must acknowledge that the previous pillars based on the ineffectual principle of the "three Ts" (i.e., technical approach, using training as the key assistance delivery vehicle, largely at the tactical level) can remain intact in principle. However, this approach needs to be completely subsumed under, and made responsive to, a wider policy that acknowledges that the ultimate reform of these institutions is inherently political. The adoption of Western democratic defense governance concepts can occur only through continuous political dialogue, discussion, debate, and supported with expert advice. As argued in Chapter 7, said advice must be based on principles of cultural awareness and employing the approach of change management informed by each individual country's requirements and realities. It is interesting that one important recent study of methods used to encourage economic development has come to a similar conclusion:

> The conventional approach to economic development, to making poor countries rich, is based on a technological illusion: the belief that poverty is a purely technical problem amenable to such technical solutions as fertilizers, antibiotics, or nutritional supplements.[16]

Indeed, the author equally finds that solely a technocratic approach to economic development tends to depreciate the value of a country's history which in end impedes development.[17]

In sum, what has largely been missing in the West's approach in encouraging the adoption of Western democratic defense governance concepts is an institutional appreciation of the need for all managers overseeing the design of assistance programs, as well as all instructors or experts, to be educated in understanding legacy concepts and the cultural conditions of these defense institutions. Critical is the need for a better appreciation of the continued conceptual divide that exists largely unaddressed, and an understanding of the current structure of incentives and disincentives in legacy systems. Moreover, as the challenges facing these defense institutions are deeply rooted and based in an organization's most basic institutional assumptions and conceptual makeup, there are going to be very few occasions when solutions will be a simple one-time (fire and forget) project. Thinking needs to be transformed from episodic engagements to long-term commitments with the appropriate content and deep appreciation of the conditions of these organizations.

Finally, Western officials need to reinforce the message that all activities and expenditures conducted by their defense institution must be focused on producing policy-determined outcomes. Defining advice as technical assistance consisting of discrete inputs has defined performance as constituting the execution of a series of activities or events. As such, the managerial focus has been to look at assisting reform in terms of a series of inputs. There has been too little attention given to *what* all of these inputs are envisaged to produce. Oftentimes, even this is couched in managerial outcomes: improved efficiencies and effectiveness. But it should not be terribly difficult to begin, formally, to measure whether these efforts are having a positive macro-effect on producing clear military outcomes.[18] Within the alliance such assessment tools have long existed, if indeed they need to be more frequently and sharply employed (e.g., Tactical Evaluations (TACEVALs)). After all, if a defense reform effort is not conceived as enabling a defense force to deliver predictable defense outcomes in whichever defined environment, then frankly what could possibly be the point of it all? Moreover, this outcome should not be conflated with effecting interoperability, which is not the same result or output. Clearer thinking of the envisaged outcome in military terms needs to imbue all advice and assistance efforts.

New approaches to adopting Western defense concepts

From the perspective of legacy defense institutions, what surely must constitute the most important challenge to be addressed is the widespread practice of the centralization of decision-making and budgets. At best, Western efforts to address this communist legacy practice have been ineffectual, and at worst, reinforced centralizing proclivities (e.g., PPBS). As long as decision-making is centralized with ministers and CHODs, and financial decision-making is not delegated to officials responsible for producing outcomes, these defense institutions will continue to struggle to become producers of security. Arguably, at the heart of this pathology of centralization has been the unwillingness on the part of senior officials, civilian and in uniform, to enable and empower officials responsible for producing outcomes. In consequence, the ability to produce predictable defense outcomes has been undermined. And to be fair, it is difficult to hold commanders and directors responsible for producing outcomes if they are not entrusted with the necessary policy framework (e.g., training policy that assigns responsibilities to commanders and not general staffs) enabling them to make decisions, let alone the ability to make decisions to manage financial and personnel inputs. Thus, centralization needs to be seen as a communist legacy that is preventing these defense institutions from adopting Western democratic defense governance concepts. What is necessary, therefore, are strong policy frameworks to push *downward* operational and financial decision-making to the level of commanders and directors who are responsible for producing outcomes, for example, chiefs of services, logistics, HRM, and medical services. To the charge that such acts will only fuel corruption, the response should be that this issue has long been addressed effectively in the West by ensuring that officials understand that one's authority is balanced by the principles of responsibility and accountability. To be very blunt, any concept that impedes a commander or director from producing defense outcomes must be scrutinized and alternatives developed and tested. That ministries of defense and specifically PPBS directorates continue the practice of centralizing decision-making will only continue the practice of enabling legacy defense institutions to remain unfocused, bloated, and bleeding money for nondefense purposes.

Related to the issue of the need to empower commanders and directors is the concomitant need to ensure that these individuals have not only proper education and training but are also placed in stressful command and management assignments throughout their careers in order to ensure that they can grow professionally. Hence, the all too common practice in many legacy armed forces of sanctioning hollow formations, undermanned ships, and pilots starved of flying hours has had the deleterious effect of creating not only non-operational units, but also missing the critical opportunity of developing commanders. This has also precluded officials from determining those who are suitable for higher command and senior staff responsibilities.

From the perspective of Western nations, what will not produce different effects from current Western assumptions and programs is what Marshall cites as a need to "standardize capability- and capacity-building systems."[19] If anything, Western donor defense institutions have long offered standardized capability- and capacity-building programs and projects. Indeed, arguably, this has been one of their key flaws. What the record of advice and assistance in this region has demonstrated is the need for Western governments to change policy and finances to provide managers of these efforts *greater* flexibility in enabling them to diagnose proper causation of the lack of ability to implement reform measures. After all, Goldman and Eliasen write,

> The impact of diffusion on any particular military is rarely one of perfect emulation. Culture and organizational norms often have a prismatic effect, deflecting or bending the original innovation to fit the demands and widely held beliefs of the new setting.[20]

Ignoring these prismatic realities results in advice and assistance efforts that assume legacy governmental institutions are a mirror image of the donor. On this faulty assumption, donors align their policies, advice, and assistance programs accordingly. For example, until recently US policy and legal interpretations have impeded the use of certain Department of Defense funds from engaging non-ministry of defense and armed forces officials since the law only allows military-to-military interactions.[21] Albeit policy is changing, as of this writing this restriction can be waived, but on a case-by-case basis.[22] Thus, it is assumed that a ministry of defense *is* the senior civil ministry with oversight of the armed forces. The problem with this strictly Western interpretative approach is that this is not necessarily the case. In almost all of these countries, the institutions that support presidential administrations (e.g., cabinet of ministers and security councils) often times act as policy-generating institutions, either because policy is not being developed in ministries of defense or it overrides their efforts. As these bodies exist in most new NATO members, and some of them are quite powerful (e.g., National Security Bureau in Poland), they need to be better understood and *leveraged* wherever possible to further the adoption of Western democratic defense governance concepts.[23] Western nations' policy and legislation need to be reviewed to ensure that relevant nondefense institutions can be consistently and fully engaged by Western defense officials to strengthen their engagement in the reform process.

Why "Honest Defense"?

In the end, as argued in this work, fault for not having achieved deeper and faster reform of legacy defense institutions lies on both sides of the conceptual divide: The West has looked at the problems of transition to Western democratic defense governance concepts too often as being simply technical, while their Eastern counterparts have grossly underestimated the enormity of the task of reform they face. As a modest first step, it is posited that both sides need to start, *tabula rasa*, and rethink from first principles how to reform legacy defense institutions. This is needed in order to confront their common reality: the existence of too many dysfunctional defense institutions which are slowly, but assuredly, wasting away in a Europe with a Russia that could remain an unpredictable spoiler long after Vladimir Putin leaves national office. Arguably, the most logical first step in this reassessment should be the adoption of a new, common approach that is based on the principle of *honesty*. Whereas former Secretary General Anders Fogh Rasmussen in winter 2011 called for the alliance to adopt the Smart Defense initiative in order to collectivize capabilities in a time of austerity,[24] it is long past time for all member nations also to adopt a similar initiative that recognizes the need for *Honest Defense*. By this, Western nations need to abandon their policies and practices of accepting their Eastern counterparts' professionalism without testing and questioning it. Senior Western officials need to take a harder line in interactions with their Eastern allied counterparts and start demanding painful political decisions to start the process of adopting, in a mutually exclusive manner, Western democratic defense governance concepts. Equally, Eastern allies and partners should insist that Western donor nations and their defense institutions end their attitudes of false compliments and become brutally honest as to their failures and weaknesses. In essence, these officials need to demand that Western officials take them seriously and deal with them on the basis of equality and honesty. To be blunt, it needs to be recognized that diplomacy based on falsehoods and façades is counterproductive and indeed venomous for any alliance.

There is a precedent for this putative initiative. During the Cold War, the very public debate over burden sharing was forever being argued among members of the Western alliance[25] and at least one analyst has called for its return.[26] The threat posed by the Warsaw Pact had the effect of focusing Western politicians' minds on a daily basis to the fact that money not spent or wasted by an ally would have to be compensated by others. In this zero-sum financial environment, therefore, waste or inaction, both real and alleged, were called out in NATO councils and leaked with great regularity to the press. With the immediacy of the overt threat from the Warsaw Pact long vanished, the burden-sharing debate among NATO countries has devolved into meaningless obsessions over percentages of GDP dedicated to defense,[27] as opposed to a more constructive discussion about the viability of producing predictable defense outcomes.[28] In light of Russian president Vladimir Putin's more aggressive stance, it is long past time for the alliance to return to its Cold War practice of focusing on the *outcomes* of allies' defense institutions. Higher defense spending among nations, *ipso facto*, does not necessarily translate into higher and improved defense outputs. If even the relatively reformed Polish defense institution has difficulty to plan new capabilities in a coherent fashion,[29] additional funding is unlikely to produce greater defense outcomes. But money wasted on bloated bureaucracies, excess infrastructure, and barely deployable forces not only does not deter, but can provide an illusion of defense capabilities when hardly any exist.

Thus, Eastern political and defense officials need to become more discerning and demanding in the quality and effectiveness of advice and assistance that purport to introduce Western democratic defense governance concepts. Proper deep diagnostics, and not endless assessments that go unactioned, are needed, with the understanding that existing concepts, assumptions, and logic must be reviewed and replaced in a brutally mutually exclusive manner. These governments need to adopt as a priority reforming their respective defense institutions.[30] And Western defense and political officials need to operationalize the reality that institutional reform requires stronger political oversight and commitment. One would think that a cadre of better-informed policy oversight and content program managers should be able quickly to see the futility of simply providing carte blanche advice and assistance on a repetitive basis with little or no effect. Equally, officials managing these projects need to be better informed to be able to ascertain whether the advice/assistance *methodologies* are effective, or better yet, whether actual causation has been properly determined. As President Putin's recent actions in Europe have demonstrated, the Euro-Atlantic community is likely never going to be isolated from a turbulent world. It is time to complete the integration of Eastern and Central European defense institutions into the Western fold and work collectively to retire permanently the adjectival form of "legacy" that continues to be used in this context.

Partnership Action Plan on Defence Institution Building (PAP-DIB)

(7 June 2004)

"10 Commandments"

Précis

(1) Develop effective and transparent arrangement for the democratic control of defence activities.

(2) Develop effective and transparent procedures to promote civilian participation in developing defence and security policy.

(3) Develop effective and transparent legislative and judicial oversight of the defence sector.

(4) Develop effective and transparent arrangements and procedures to assess security risks and national defence requirements.

(5) Develop effective and transparent measures to optimise the management of defence ministries.

(6) Develop effective and transparent arrangements and practices to ensure compliance with internationally accepted norms and practices established in the defence sector, including export controls.

(7) Develop effective and transparent personnel structures and practices in the defence force.

(8) Develop effective and transparent financial, planning, and resource allocation procedures in the defense area.

(9) Develop effective, transparent and economically viable management of defence spending, taking into account macro-economic affordability and sustainability.

(10) Develop effective and transparent arrangements to ensure effective international co-operation and good neighbourly relations in defence and security matters.

The PAP-DIB was agreed by nations at the Istanbul Summit, Brussels, Press Release (2004)096, 28 June 2004, point 28.

Appendix 2

U.S. Code Title 22 Security Assistance to Select Countries in Central and Eastern Europe, Fiscal Years 1999–2013

	IMET totals	FMF totals
Albania		
IMET and Emergency Draw-Downs	$15,360,000	
Foreign Military Finance Waived		$62,006,000
Armenia		
IMET and Emergency Draw-Downs	$7,175,000	
Foreign Military Finance Waived		$44,497,000
Azerbaijan		
IMET and Emergency Draw-Downs	$9,172,000	
Foreign Military Finance Waived		$44,497,000
Bosnia and Herzegovina		
IMET and Emergency Draw-Downs	$14,550,000	
Foreign Military Finance Waived		$83,131,000
Bulgaria		
IMET and Emergency Draw-Downs	$26,040,000	
Foreign Military Finance Waived		$150,282,000
Croatia		
IMET and Emergency Draw-Downs	$8,763,000	
Foreign Military Finance Waived		$30,358,000
Czech Republic		
IMET and Emergency Draw-Downs	$30,255,000	
Foreign Military Finance Waived		$140,821,000
Estonia		
IMET and Emergency Draw-Downs	$18,233,000	
Foreign Military Finance Waived		$74,566,000

	IMET totals	FMF totals
Georgia		
IMET and Emergency Draw-Downs	$19,002,000	
Foreign Military Finance Waived		$209,914,000
Hungary		
IMET and Emergency Draw-Downs	$27,701,000	
Foreign Military Finance Waived		$104,531,000
Latvia		
IMET and Emergency Draw-Downs	$18,414,000	
Foreign Military Finance Waived		$74,409,000
Lithuania		
IMET and Emergency Draw-Downs	$18,336,000	
Foreign Military Finance Waived		$79,052,000
Macedonia		
IMET and Emergency Draw-Downs	$12,001,000	
Foreign Military Finance Waived		$104,844,000
Moldova		
IMET and Emergency Draw-Downs	$13,402,000	
Foreign Military Finance Waived		$18,854,000
Montenegro		
IMET and Emergency Draw-Downs	$2,143,000	
Foreign Military Finance Waived		$5,891,000
Poland		
IMET and Emergency Draw-Downs	$36,203,000	
Foreign Military Finance Waived		$467,249,000
Romania		
IMET and Emergency Draw-Downs	$26,387,000	
Foreign Military Finance Waived		$215,345,000
Serbia		
IMET and Emergency Draw-Downs	$4,786,000	
Foreign Military Finance Waived		$7,205,000
Slovkia		
IMET and Emergency Draw-Downs	$16,178,000	
Foreign Military Finance Waived		$78,541,000
Slovenia		
IMET and Emergency Draw-Downs	$13,044,000	
Foreign Military Finance Waived		$29,339,000

	IMET totals	FMF totals
Ukraine		
IMET and Emergency Draw-Downs	$30,893,000	
Foreign Military Finance Waived		$106,619,000
Totals:	$368,038,000	$2,131,951,000
Combined totals:		$2,499,989,000

Source: US Defense Security Cooperation Agency, Foreign Military Sales, Foreign Military Construction Sales and Other Security Cooperation Historical Facts (Washington, DC, 30 September 2013).

Appendix 3

Cultural Tools and Country Comparisons

	Estonia	Latvia	Lithuania	Ukraine	Bulgaria	Czech Rep.	Hungary	Poland	Romania	Slovakia	Croatia	Serbia	Slovenia	US
Power distance	40	44	42	92	63	49	38	61	85	100	73	86	73	40
Individualism	60	70	60	25	28	61	87	64	28	54	33	25	27	91
Masculinity	30	9	19	27	39	58	92	66	41	100	40	43	19	62
Uncertainty avoidance	60	63	65	95	74	63	71	82	79	41	80	92	88	46
Pragmatism	82	69	82	55	72	73	60	31	53	81	58	52	49	26
Indulgence	16	13	16	18	16	29	31	29	20	28	33	28	48	68

Definitions

Power distance: This dimension deals with the fact that all individuals in societies are not equal—it expresses the attitude of the culture toward these inequalities among us. Power distance is defined as the extent to which the less powerful members of institutions and organizations within a country expect and accept that power is distributed unequally.

Individualism: The fundamental issue addressed by this dimension is the degree of interdependence a society maintains among its members. It has to do with whether people's self-image is defined in terms of "I" or "We." In individualist societies, people are supposed to look after themselves and their direct family only. In collectivist societies, people belong to "in groups" that take care of them in exchange for loyalty.

Masculinity: A high score (masculine) on this dimension indicates that the society will be driven by competition, achievement, and success, with success being defined by the winner/best in field—a value system that starts in school and continues throughout organizational behavior.

Uncertainty avoidance: The dimension Uncertainty Avoidance has to do with the way that a society deals with the fact that the future can never be known: should we try to control the future or just let it happen? This ambiguity brings with it anxiety, and different cultures have learnt to deal with this anxiety in different ways. The extent to which the members of a culture feel threatened by ambiguous or unknown situations and have created beliefs and institutions that try to avoid these is reflected in the UAI score.

Pragmatism: This dimension describes how people in the past as well as today relate to the fact that so much that happens around us cannot be explained. In societies with a normative orientation, most people have a strong desire to explain as much as possible. In societies with a pragmatic orientation, most people don't have a need to explain everything, as they believe that it is impossible to understand fully the complexity of life. The challenge is not to know the truth but to live a virtuous life.

Indulgence: One challenge that confronts humanity, now and in the past, is the degree to which little children are socialized. Without socialization we do not become "human." This dimension is defined as the extent to which people try to control their desires and impulses, based on the way they were raised. Relatively weak control is called "indulgence" and relatively strong control is called "restraint." Cultures can, therefore, be described as indulgent or restrained.

Source: Geert Hofstede, *Culture's Consequences: Comparing Values, Behaviors, Institutions and Organizations across Nations*, 2nd edn (Thousand Oaks: Sage Publications, 2001) and https://geert-hofstede.com/

Notes

Preface

1   Edward Lucas, "Europe's New Frontier," in *Frontline Allies: War and Change in Central Europe: U.S.-Central Europe Strategic Assessment Group Report* (Warsaw: Center for European Policy Analysis, November 2015), 19.

Introduction

1   Slovakia, *The White Paper on Defence of the Slovak Republic* (Bratislava: Ministry of Defense, 2013), 16, 18.

2   Charlemagne: "Defenceless? Austerity is Hollowing Out Europe's Armies," *The Economist,* December 21, 2013, 82.

3   Curt Gasteyger, "The Remaking of Eastern Europe's Security," *Survival* 33, no. 2 (March/April 1991): 111.

4   The abbreviated Partnership Action Plan on Defense Institution Building is found in Appendix 1.

5   For a concise, but informative, historical analysis of the role of the Polish officer in society, see Andrew A. Michta, *The Soldier-Citizen: The Politics of the Polish Army after Communism* (New York: St. Martin's Press, 1997), 23–45.

6   See Zoltan D. Barany, *The Future of NATO Expansion: Four Case Studies* (Cambridge: Cambridge University Press, 2003), 167–168.

7   David Yost, *NATO's Balancing Act* (Washington, DC: United States Institute of Peace, 2014), *passim.*

8   Anton A. Bebler, "The Regionwide Perspective on Post-Communist Civil-Military Relations," in *Civil-Military Relations in Post-Communist States: Central and Eastern Europe in Transition*, ed. Anton A. Bebler (Westport, CN: Praeger, 1997), 76.

9   See Kathleen J. McInnis and Nathan J. Lucas, "What is 'Building Partner Capacity?': Issues for Congress," R44313 (Washington, DC: Congressional Research Service, December 18, 2015), 38–39.

10 The International Institute for Strategic Studies, *The Military Balance 2015* (London: Routledge, February 2015), *passim.*

11 David B. Ralston, *Importing the European Army: The Introduction of European Military Techniques and Institutions into the Extra-European World, 1600–1914* (Chicago: University of Chicago Press, 1900).

12 "The 2014 defeat of the Iraqi security forces (ISF) by ISIS is the most recent reminder of the limits of U.S. security assistance when the broader political and sectarian challenges undermine the capabilities and will of partner security forces." Dafna H. Rand and Stephen Tankel, *Security Cooperation and Assistance: Rethinking the Return on Investment* (Washington, DC: Center for a New American Security, August 2015), 9.

13 Rand and Tankel argue that short-term security assistance objectives have overtaken the US government's efforts to promote accountable governance and the rule of law. Ibid., 9–10.

14 Willard C. Frank, Jr., and Philip S. Gillette, *Soviet Military Doctrine from Lenin to Gorbachev, 1915–1991* (Westport, CT; Greenwood Press, 1990); William H. Mott, IV, *Soviet Military Assistance: An Empirical Perspective* (Westport, CT; Greenwood Press, 2001).

15 Dicke, Hendrickson, and Kutz argue that the lack of implementation of the 2010 Bulgarian defense white paper was due to corruption (see Bulgaria, *White Paper on Defence and the Armed Forces of the Republic of Bulgaria*, Sofia: Ministry of Defense, 2010). Not to ignore the issue of corruption, it is not clear whether it occurred to these knowledgeable analysts that the lack of implementation of this document could be simply due to bureaucratic inertia and incompetence. See Rachel A. Dicke, Ryan C. Hendrickson, and Steven Kutz, "NATO's Mafia Ally: The Strategic Consequences of Bulgarian Corruption," *Comparative Strategy* 33, no. 3 (2014): 287–298.

16 Theo Farrell and Terry Terriff, eds., *The Sources of Military Change, Culture, Politics, Technology* (Boulder, CO: Lynne Reiner, 2002), 6.

17 Chris Donnelly, "Civil-Military Relations in the New Democracies," in *Army and State in Postcommunist Europe*, eds. David Betz and John Löwenhardt (London: Frank Cass, 2001), 8.

18 Betz introduces a useful hierarchy of policy: general policy (formulated by government); executive policy (the implementation of policy done in coordination with experts); and administrative policy. David J. Betz, *Civil-Military Relations in Russia and Eastern Europe* (New York: Routledge Curzon, 2004), 71.

19 David S. Pion-Berlin, "Political Management of the Military in Latin America," *Military Review* 85, no. 1 (January–February 2005): 21.

20 See Reka Szemerkenyi, "Central European Civil-Military Reforms at Risk," *Adelphi Paper* 306 (London: The International Institute for Strategic Studies, 1996).

21 Ryzard Kapuscinski, *Shah of Shahs* (London: Quartet Books, Ltd., 1985), 58.

22 To which this author contributed.

23 Emily Goldman and Leslie Eliasen, eds., *Adaptive Enemies, Reluctant Friends: The Impact of Diffusion on Military Practice* (Stanford: Stanford University Press, 2003), 8.

24 See Virginia Aksan, *Ottoman Wars, 1700–1870: An Empire Besieged* (New York: Longman Publishing Group, 2007).

25 Goldman and Eliasen, eds., *Adaptive Enemies, Reluctant Friends*, 9.

26 See E. H. Schein, *Organizational Culture and Leadership*, 3rd edn (Hoboken, NJ: Jossey-Bass, 2005).

27 Richard L. Millet, *Searching for Stability: The U.S. Development of Constabulary Forces in Latin America and the Philippines* (Fort Leavenworth: Combat Studies Institute Press, 2010), 117.

28 Ralston, *Importing the European Army*, 173.

29 This is a term that is bantered around in NATO fora and circles often without a proper definition. To wit: "These efforts aim at achieving intellectual interoperability. In order to succeed in building a common security and defence culture, a greater common understanding of concepts related to security, defence, and defence reform are required." See "NATO-led team helps build intellectual interoperability in Georgia," Brussels, NATO, March 15, 2009. http://www.nato.int/cps/en/natohq/news_52912.htm?selectedLocale=en (accessed May 20, 2016).

30 David Betz, John Löwenhardt, and Hew Strachan, "Conclusion," in *Army and State in Postcommunist Europe,* 147.

31 Anthony Forster, Timothy Edmunds, and Andrew Cottey, eds., "Introduction," in *Challenge of Military Reform in Postcommunist Europe: Building Professional Armed Forces* (London: Palgrave Macmillan, 2003), 8.

Chapter 2

1 Emily Goldman and Leslie Eliasen, eds., *Adaptive Enemies, Reluctant Friends: The Impact of Diffusion on Military Practice* (Stanford: Stanford University Press, 2003), 397.

2 Mikhail Tsypkin, "Soviet Military Culture and the Legacy of the War," in *Histories of the Aftermath: The Legacies of the Second World War in Europe,* eds. Frank Biess and Robert G. Moeller (New York: Berghahn Books, 2010), 270.

3 James J. Schneider, "The Origins of Soviet Military Science," *Journal of Soviet Military Studies* 2, no. 4 (1989): 492.

4 For one of the very few published descriptions and insightful analysis of a Soviet-type ministry of defense, see David J. Betz, *Civil-Military Relations in Russia and Eastern Europe* (New York: Routledge Curzon, 2004), 72–73.

5 Aghasi Yenokyan, "Country Study: Armenia," in *Defense Institution Building: Country Profiles and Needs Assessments for Armenia, Azerbaijan, Georgia, and Moldova: Background Materials,* eds. Philipp H. Fluri and Viorel Cibotaru (Geneva: Geneva Centre for the Democratic Control of Armed Forces, 2008), 28.

6 This is no small challenge to ensuring mutual understanding. That said, even many excellent Western analysts of post-communist defense institutions fail to recognize this important distinction. See, for example, Natalie Mychajlyszyn, "Civil-Military Relations in Post-Soviet Ukraine: Implications for Domestic and Regional Stability," *Armed Forces and Society* 28, no. 3 (Spring 2002): 465.

7 Christopher Donnelly, *Red Banner: The Soviet Military System in Peace and War* (Coulsdon, Surrey: Jane's Information Group, 1988), 106.

8 See, for example, in the case of Moldova, Trevor Waters, "The Republic of Moldova: Armed Forces and Military Doctrine," *Journal of Slavic Military Studies* 11, no. 2 (1998): 88–89.

9 For an excellent treatment of the Western concept of command, see Richard E. Simpkin, *Race to the Swift: Thoughts on Twenty-First Century Warfare* (London: Brassey's, 1985), 227–240.

10 Timothy Edmunds, Andrew Cottey, and Anthony Forster, eds., "Introduction," in *Civil-Military Relations in Post-Communist Europe: Reviewing the Transition* (London: Routledge, 2006), 3.

11 John Erickson, "The Soviet Military System: Doctrine, Technology and 'Style'," in *Soviet Military Power and Performance,* eds. John Erickson and E.J. Feuchtwanger (Hamden, CT: Archon Book, 1979), 37.

12 Ibid., 32.

13 Chris Donnelly, "The Soviet Soldier: Behaviour, Performance, Effectiveness," in *Soviet Military Power and Performance,* 115.

14 Norman Stone, "The Historical Background of the Red Army," in *Soviet Military Power and Performance,* 14.

15   Erickson, "The Soviet Military System," 38:

> While the "large military system"; (LMS) may be put through its paces, difficulties arise at lower levels, particularly with the sub-unit, where the dichotomy between centralised direction and a show of personal initiative is at its sharpest. Two examples must suffice—that of a battalion commander who followed "the book" but took 40 minutes to "consider" his decisions and issue the requisite orders, thus leaving only 50 minutes to complete the approach march, deploy, and attack (all manifestly impossible); and that of a motor-rifle battalion commander who failed to bring in helicopters for fire support because "the plan did not call for this".

16   Donnelly, "The Soviet Soldier," 116.

17   Lester W. Grau, *The Bear Went over the Mountain: Soviet Combat Tactics in Afghanistan* (Washington, DC: National Defense University Press, 1996), 101.

18   Soldiers were essentially seen as being expendable. Tsypkin, "Soviet Military Culture," 277–278.

19   See David M. Glantz, *Soviet Military Deception in the Second World War* (London: Frank Cass, 1989).

20   "In brief, this is a 'battlefield philosophy,' with its emphasis on manage-limitation and counterforce (to use Western terms): the Soviet command puts its trust in fire-power and sought from the earliest days of the strategic weapons programme to maximise this. Nor, as we shall see, did they lose sight of numerical solutions." Erickson, "The Soviet Military System," 25.

21   Paul Adair, *Hitler's Greatest Defeat: The Collapse of Army Group Centre, June 1944* (London: Weidenfeld Military, 1994).

22   Schneider, "The Origins of Soviet Military Science," 498.

23   Graham H. Turbiville, Jr., "Sustaining Theater Strategic Operations," *Journal of Soviet Military Studies* 1, no. 1 (1988): 81–107.

24   John Hemsley, "The Soviet Ground Forces," in *Soviet Military Power and Performance*, 66–67.

25   Stone, "The Historical Background of the Red Army," 14–15.

26   James Sherr, "Ukraine: Reform in the Context of Flawed Democracy and Geopolitical Anxiety," in *Civil-Military Relations in Post-Communist Europe*, 158–158.

27   Larry L. Watts, "Democratic Civil Control of the Military in Romania: An Assessment as of October 2001," in *Civil-Military Relations in Post-Cold War Europe*, ed. Graeme P. Herd (Camberley: Conflict Studies Research Centre, 2001), 32.

28   Alex Alexiev, "The Romanian Army," in *Communist Armies in Politics*, ed. Jonathan R. Adelman (Boulder, CO: Westview Press, 1982), 156–157.

29   Watts, "Democratic Civil Control of the Military in Romania," 36.

30   See Jerzy J. Wiatr, *The Soldier and the Nation: The Role of the Military in Polish Politics, 1918–1985* (Boulder, CO: Westview Press, 1988).

31   See Kieran Williams, "Lustration as the Securitization of Democracy in Czechoslovakia and the Czech Republic," *Journal of Communist Studies and Transition Politics* 19, no. 4 (December 2003): 1–24; Pal Dunay, "Building Professional Competence in Hungary's Defence: Slow Motion," in *The Challenge of Military Reform in Post-Communist Europe: Building Professional Armed Forces*, eds. Anthony Forster, Timothy Edmunds, and Andrew Cottey (London: Palgrave Macmillan, 2002), 71; Reka Szemerkenyi, "Central European Civil-Military Reforms at Risk," *Adelphi Paper* 40 (London: The International Institute for Strategic Studies, 1996).

32   Bradley R. Gitz, *Armed Forces and Political Power in Eastern Europe: The Soviet/ Communist Control System* (New York: Greenwood Press, 1992), 8–9.

33   For an excellent treatment of the transition to democracy and the challenges faced by these ministries of defense, particularly in Poland and Hungary, see Betz, *Civil-Military Relations in Russia and Eastern Europe*, 74–76.

34   Andrew Michta, *The Soldier-Citizen: The Politics of the Polish Army After Communism* (New York: St Martin's Press, 1997), 85.

35   Dunay, "Building Professional Competence in Hungary's Defence," 63.

36   Gitz, *Armed Forces and Political Power in Eastern Europe*, 68.

37   Larry Watts, "The Transformation of Romanian Civil-Military Relations: Enabling Force Projection," in *Civil-Military Relations in Post-Communist Europe*, 95.

38   Alexiev, "The Romanian Army," 156–159.

39   Gitz, *Armed Forces and Political Power in Eastern Europe*, 67–68.

40   Marian Zulean, "Professionalisation of the Romanian Armed Forces," in *Civil-Military Relations in Post-Communist Europe*, 116.

41   Alexiev, "The Romanian Army," 156–157.

42   *Warsaw Pact Wartime Statutes: Instruments of Soviet Control* (Washington, DC: Central Intelligence Agency, Center for the Study of Intelligence and Historical Collections Division, 2011).

43   Marybeth Peterson Ulrich, "Professionalisation of the Slovak Armed Forces," in *The Challenge of Military Reform in Post-Communist Europe*, 56.

44   Gitz, *Armed Forces and Political Power in Eastern Europe*, 69.

45   Dunay, "Building Professional Competence in Hungary's Defence," 70.

46   For an excellent treatment of how Soviet thinking was played out in operational planning, see Donnelly, *Red Banner*, 261–267.

47   See Andrzej Korbonski, "The Polish Army"; Jiri Valenta and Condoleezza Rice, "The Czechoslovak Army"; Alex Alexiev, "The Romanian Army," in *Communist Armies in Politics*, 116, 140, 154, respectively.

48   T.S. Szayna and F.S. Larrabee, *East European Military Reform after the Cold War: Implications for the United States* (Santa Monica, CA: RAND, 1995), 6.

49   Jeffrey Simon, *NATO and the Czech and Slovak Republics: Comparative Study in Civil-Military Relations* (Lanham: Rowman & Littlefield, 2004), 220.

50   Gitz, *Armed Forces and Political Power in Eastern Europe*, 107–108.

51   Ibid., 110.

52   Zulean, "Professionalisation of the Romanian Armed Forces," 116.

53   Ibid., 118.

54   Gitz, *Armed Forces and Political Power in Eastern Europe*, 110.

55   The country's formal nomenclature changed over the years. The 1946 Constitution designated the country as the Federal People's Republic of Yugoslavia. This changed with the ratification of the 1963 Constitution and the country became the Socialist Federal Republic of Yugoslavia. For the sake of brevity and clarity, this work will simply use the generic term "Yugoslavia."

56   Without doubt, the most comprehensive study of the JNA in English is found in James Gow, *Legitimacy and the Military: The Yugoslav Crisis* (New York: St. Martin's Press, 1992).

57   Robin Allison Remington, "Armed Forces and Society in Yugoslavia," in *Political-Military Systems: Comparative Perspectives*, ed. Catherine McArdle Kelleher (Beverley Hills: Sage, 1974), 167.

58 Robert W. Dean, "The Yugoslav Army," in *Communist Armies in Politics*, 85.

59 See, for example, Mensur Seferovic, ed., *Total National Defense in Theory and Practice* (Belgrade: Narodna Armija, 1975), *passim*.

60 See Bojan Dimitrijevic, "The Mutual Defense Aid Program in Tito's Yugoslavia, 1951–1958, and Its Technical Impact," *Journal of Slavic Military Studies* 10, no. 2 (1997): 19–33; "Military Assistance Agreement Between the United States and Yugoslavia," November 14, 1951, U.S. Department of State, *Treaties and Other International Agreements (TIAS)*, 2349; 2 UST 2254.

61 Adam Roberts, *Nations in Arms: The Theory and Practice of Territorial Defense* (New York: Praeger Publishers, 1976), 147.

62 See Horst Menderhausen, *Territorial Defense in NATO and Non-NATO Europe*, R-1184-ISA (Santa Monica: RAND, 1973), 85.

63 See *The Military Balance 1991–1992* (London: The International Institute for Strategic Studies, 1991), 96–97.

64 Dimitrijevic, "The Mutual Defense Aid Program in Tito's Yugoslavia," 22–23.

65 Ibid., 26–28.

66 Robert Niebuhr, "Death of the Yugoslav People's Army and the Wars of Succession," *Polemos*, no. 13/14 (January 2004): 93.

67 Robert Dean, "Civil-Military Relations in Yugoslavia, 1971–1975," *Armed Forces and Society* 3, no. 1 (November 1976): 39.

68 In the autonomous provinces of Vojvodina and Kosovo, there were Territorial Defense headquarters, but they fell under the command of the Serbian Territorial Defense Headquarters in Belgrade. Note that the Territorial Defense organization in Kosovo was effectively dismantled by the federal government in 1981 following the initiation of civil unrest by the Albanian majority. See Gow, *Legitimacy and the Military*, 64–72.

69 See *The Military Balance 1991–1992*, 96.

70 Menderhausen, *Territorial Defense in NATO and Non-NATO Europe*, 86.

71 Ibid.

72 See Alex J. Bellamy, "A Revolution in Civil-Military Affairs: The Professionalisation of Croatia's Armed Forces," in *The Challenge of Military Reform in Post-Communist Europe*, 168–169; Zoltan D. Barany, *The Future of NATO Expansion: Four Case Studies* (Cambridge: Cambridge University Press, 2003), 112.

73 Miroslav Hadzic, *The Yugoslav People's Army: The Role of the Yugoslav People's Army* (Aldershot: Ashgate Publishing Limited, 2002), 208.

74 Sector for Manning, Mobilization and Systems Issues, General Staff of the Armed Forces of Yugoslavia, "Order on Authorities of the Organizational Units of the General Staff of the Armed Forces of Yugoslavia," Belgrade, March 20, 2002 (translated text).

75 Roberts, *Nations in Arms*, 158.

76 James Gow, "Professionalisation and the Yugoslav Army," in *The Challenge of Military Reform in Post-Communist Europe*, 185.

77 For the best treatment of the role played by Territorial Defense Forces in the Yugoslav Wars, see Branka Magas and Ivo Zanic, eds., *The War in Croatia and Bosnia-Herzegovina, 1991–1995* (London: Frank Cass, 2001).

78 Remington, "Armed Forces and Society in Yugoslavia," 172, 188.

79 Dean, "Civil-Military Relations in Yugoslavia, 1971–1975," 46. This is an excellent contemporary analysis of the rising political influence enjoyed by the JNA and necessitated by the centrifugal political and ethnic forces growing within the federation.

80　See Roberts, *Nations in Arms*, 179, for an explanation of the provisions of the 1974 Constitution as regards national command structures and authorities, which interestingly did not specify or define either's subordination to the other by clearly placing them both under the commander-in-chief.

81　Seferovic, *Total National Defense in Theory and Practice*, 41–83.

82　Roberts, *Nations in Arms*, 155.

83　Dean, "The Yugoslav Army," 88.

84　A. Ross Johnson, *The Role of the Military in Communist Yugoslavia: An Historical Sketch*. P-6070 (Santa Monica, CA: RAND Corporation, January 1978), 7–8.

85　Specifically, Articles 51 and 52 of the 1969 Defense Act. See Roberts, *Nations in Arms*, 177.

86　Ibid., 178.

87　Anton Bebler, "Democratic Control of Armed Forces in Slovenia," in *Democratic Control of the Military in Postcommunist Europe: Guarding the Guards*, eds. Andrew Cottey, Timothy Edmunds, and Anthony Forster (New York: Palgrave, 2002), 163.

88　Centar za strategijska istraživanja GŠ JNA, Savezni sekretiajat za narodnu odbranu, *Strategija oružane borbe* (Beograd: Vojna Štramparija, 1983), 138–153. I am indebted to Svetožar Braković for sharing his JNA manuals and discussing them with me.

89　Davor Marijan, "The Yugoslav National Army Role in the Aggression against the Republic of Croatia from 1990 to 1992," *National Security and the Future* 3–4, no. 2 (2001): 145.

90　James Horncastle, "Reaping the Whirlwind: Total National Defense's Role in Slovenia's Bid for Secession," *Journal of Slavic Military Studies* 26, no. 3 (2013): 533.

91　Charles R. Patrick, "Tactics of the Serb and Bosnian-Serb Armies and Territorial Militia," *Journal of Slavic Military Studies* 7, no. 1 (1994): 20.

92　Lieutenant General Dusan Kveder, "Territorial War: The New Concept of Resistance," *Foreign Affairs* 32, no. 1 (October 1953): 93.

93　Patrick, "Tactics of the Serb and Bosnian-Serb Armies and Territorial Militia," 20–21.

94　Niebuhr, "Death of the Yugoslav People's Army and the Wars of Succession," 93.

95　Ibid., 29.

96　See Gow, "Professionalisation and the Yugoslav Army," 184.

97　Patrick, "Tactics of the Serb and Bosnian-Serb Armies and Territorial Militia," 25; 19.

98　For a comprehensive perspective on the lead up to and the campaign for independence, see Janez Jansa, *The Making of the Slovenian State, 1988–1992: The Collapse of Yugoslavia* (Ljubljana: Mladinska Knjiga Publishing House, 1994).

99　*Yugoslavia's Armed Forces* (Belgrade: Narodna Armija, 1980), 122–143.

100　Dimitrijevic, "The Mutual Defense Aid Program in Tito's Yugoslavia," 28.

101　Richard C. Herrick, "The Yugoslav People's Army: Its Military and Political Mission" (MA thesis, Naval Postgraduate School, Monterey, CA), 16.

102　See Savo Drljevic, "The Role of Geo-Political, Socio-Economic, and Military-Strategic Factors," in *The Yugoslav Concept of General People's Defense* (Belgrade: Medjunarodna politika, 1970), 216.

103　Milojica Pantelic, "The System and Organization of National Defense," *Yugoslav Survey* 10, no. 2 (May 1969): 6.

104　See Glen E. Curtis, ed., *Yugoslavia: A Country Study* (Washington, DC: Federal Research Division, Library of Congress, December 1992), 252.

105   Roberts, *Nations in Arms,* 195, and Anton Bebler, "The Yugoslav Crisis and
       the 'Yugoslav People's Army,'" *Zürcher Beiträge zur Sicherheitspolitik und
       Konfliktforschung,* Heft. nr. 23 (1992): 10–11.

106   In 1971, Serbs made up 40 percent of population of the Yugoslav Federation, but
       they provided over 60 percent of the officer corps. Roberts, *Nations in Arms,* 200.

107   Timothy Edmunds, "Civil-Military Relations in Serbia-Montenegro: An Army in
       Search of a State," *European Security* 14, no. 1 (2005): 117.

108   Hadzic, *The Yugoslav People's Army,* 208, 221.

109   Ibid., 221.

110   Max Hastings, *Armageddon: The Battle for Germany, 1944–1945* (New York: Knopf,
       2004).

111   FM 3–24 (MCWP 3–33.5), *Army Field Manual 3–24: Counterinsurgency.* See James A.
       Russell, *Innovation, Transformation, and War: Counterinsurgency Operations in Anbar
       and Ninewa Provinces, Iraq, 2005–2007* (Stanford: Stanford University Press, 2011).

112   See Thomas-Durell Young, *Multinational Land Formations and NATO: Reforming
       Practices and Structures* (Carlisle Barracks, PA, Strategic Studies Institute, 1997),
       25–26.

113   For an excellent treatment of how contemporary European armies evolved into
       employing a common planning method, see Anthony King, *The Transformation
       of Europe's Armed Forces: From the Rhine to Afghanistan* (Cambridge: Cambridge
       University Press, 2011), 115–118.

114   Supreme Headquarters Allied Powers Europe, *Comprehensive Operations Planning
       Directive,* September 10, 2010. NATO UNCLASSIFIED, Releasable to PfP/EU.

115   For the US Army's approach to MDMP, see FM-5, *The Operations Process,* March
       2010, annex B (MDMP) and C (Troop Leading Procedures). The Canadian Armed
       Forces' process is found in Canada, Canadian Forces Joint Publication 5.0, *The
       Canadian Forces Operational Planning Process,* April 2008, see chapters 4 and 5.
       A description of the approach of the British Army can be found in J. E. Passmore,
       RE, "Decision Making in the Military," *The British Army Review* no. 126 (Winter
       2001–2002): 43–49.

116   For a fascinating comparison between the US and Soviet/Russian armies' concepts
       of operational planning, see Andrei V. Demurenko and Timothy L. Thomas,
       "Toward Joint Planning and Conduct of Operations: A Russian-US Comparison,"
       Journal of Slavic Military Studies 6, no. 2 (1993): 208–220.

117   Cf., *The Military Balance 1991–1992,* 96–97.

118   I am indebted to my friend and colleague Major General Walter Holmes, Canadian
       Army (Ret), for allowing me to use this chart that he developed and used in
       numerous communist legacy defense institutions to explain this important
       differentiation. Of note, he was the last commanding officer of Allied Command
       Europe Mobile Force (Land).

119   As a result of continuous operations with task-organized units, the alliance's
       understanding of "interoperability" has become more nuanced. For instance,
       NATO now includes in the definition of interoperability references to
       "compatibility," "commonality," "force interoperability," "interchangeability,"
       "military interoperability," and "standardization." Cf., the 2000 and 2013 versions
       of *NATO Glossary of Terms and Definitions* (English and French), Allied
       Administrative Publication (AAP)-6, published by the NATO Standardization
       Agency, Brussels.

120   David M. Glantz, "Military Training and Education Challenges in Poland, the Czech Republic, and Hungary," *Journal of Slavic Military Studies* 11, no. 3 (1998): 27. Italics added.

Chapter 3

1   For a description of this naïve thinking, see Robert Kagan, *The Return of History and an End of Dreams* (New York: Alfred A. Knopf, 2008), 6–10.

2   Congressman Lee Hamilton noted many of the early skeptics of PfP were Central and Eastern European officials. See his editorial "NATO's Partnership for Peace: Already a Success," *The Christian Science Monitor*, September 28, 1995.

3   See Zoltan D. Barany, *The Future of NATO Expansion: Four Case Studies* (Cambridge: Cambridge University Press, 2003), 30–31.

4   Michael H. Clemmesen, "Integration of New Alliance Members: The Intellectual-Cultural Dimension," *Defense Analysis* 15, no. 3 (December 1999): 261–272 and Marybeth Peterson Ulrich, *Democratizing Communist Militaries: The Case of the Czech and Russian Armed Forces* (Ann Arbor: The University of Michigan Press, 2000), 108–153.

5   This debate is well explained and documented in Thomas S. Szayna, *NATO Enlargement 2000–2015: Determinants and Implications for Defense Planning and Shaping*. MR-1243-AF (Santa Monica, CA: RAND, 2001), 5–26. For a detailed description and analysis by the officials involved in the withdrawal of Soviet/Russian forces from Czechoslovakia, Poland, Hungary, and Germany, see Svetozar Nadovic, Hartmut Foertsch, Imre Karacsony, and Zdzislaw Ostrowski, *The Great Withdrawal: Withdrawal of the Soviet-Russian Army from Central Europe, 1990–1994* (Bratislava: Ministry of Defense of the Slovak Republic, 2005).

6   For a superb and exhaustive review of the debate behind the alliance's transformation and early debate over expansion, see Barany, *The Future of NATO Expansion*, 10–25.

7   See David S. Yost, *NATO Transformed: The Alliance's New Roles in International Security* (Washington, DC: United States Institute of Peace Press, 1999).

8   For an excellent treatment on peacekeeping operations as a focus of Western policy of engaging reforming communist legacy defense institutions, see Andrew Cottey and Anthony Forster, "Reshaping Defence Diplomacy: New Roles for Military Cooperation and Assistance," *Adelphi Paper* 365 (London: The International Institute for Strategic Studies, 2004), 52–58.

9   A senior Hungarian defense official admitted to the author in 1990 of such discussions to which he was present following the fall of the communist government and the election of the Antall government in May 1990. Also see "East German Ministry of State Security, 'US and NATO Military Planning on Mission of V Corps/US Army During Crises and in Wartime'" (excerpt), December 16, 1982, History and Public Policy Program Digital Archive, BStU, Berlin, ZA, HVA, 19, 126–359. Translated from German by Bernd Schaefer, available in original language at the Parallel History Project. http://digitalarchive.wilsoncenter.org/document/112680 (accessed May 20, 2016).

10   Press Communiqué S-1(91)86, Issued by the Heads of State and Government participating in the meeting of the North Atlantic Council in Rome, November 8, 1991, §11.

11 "Partnership for Peace: Framework Document," Issued by the Heads of State and Government participating in the meeting of the North Atlantic Council, Brussels, NATO Headquarters, January 10–11, 1994. For an officially sanctioned explanation of the program and its rationales, see Nick Williams, "Partnership for Peace: Permanent Fixture or Declining Asset?" *Survival* 38, no. 1 (Spring 1996): 98–110.

12 See Reka Szemerkenyi, "Central European Civil-Military Reforms at Risk," *Adelphi Paper* 306 (London: The International Institute for Strategic Studies, 1996), 66–68.

13 From January to May 1995, the first round of this process was organized for fourteen participating partner countries: Albania, Bulgaria, Czech Republic, Estonia, Finland, Hungary, Latvia, Lithuania, Poland, Romania, Slovakia, Slovenia, Sweden, and Ukraine. See Anthony Cragg, "The Partnership for Peace Planning and Review Process," *NATO Review* 43, no. 6 (November 1995): 23–25.

14 Timothy Edmunds, *Security Sector Reform in Transforming Societies: Croatia, Serbia, and Montenegro* (Manchester: Manchester University Press, 2007), 195.

15 Basic document of the Euro-Atlantic Partnership Council, May 30, 1997.

16 "Study on NATO Enlargement," Brussels, North Atlantic Treaty Organization, September 3, 1995. For an analysis of this policy document, see Andreas Behnke, *NATO's Security Discourse after the Cold War: Representing the West* (London: Routledge, 2013), 103–106.

17 For a dated, yet informative, analysis of the enlargement debate, see Sean Kay, "NATO Enlargement: Policy, Process, and Implications," in *America's New Allies: Poland, Hungary, and the Czech Republic in NATO*, ed. Andrew A. Michta (Seattle: University of Washington Press, 1999), 149–182.

18 Membership Action Plan (MAP), approved by the Heads of State and Government participating in the meeting of the North Atlantic Council, April 24, 1999.

19 Prague Summit Declaration, Issued by the Heads of State and Government participating in the meeting of the North Atlantic Council in Prague on November 21, 2002, Press Release (2002) 127, § 7.

20 Intensified Dialogue was initially created in 1996 to establish the basis for detailed consultations between allies and partners before the Membership Action Plan was created. It was revived in 2005 to manifest a heightened level of discussions with partners (i.e., Ukraine and Georgia) after the second tranche of states were admitted to the alliance in 2004.

21 Videlicet: "enhance the personnel management policy compliant to the NATO requirements and standards." See Latvia, *Report on the State Defence Policy and Armed Forces Development* (Riga: Ministry of Defence, 2004), 40.

22 Willem Matser and Christopher Donnelly, "Security Sector Reform and NATO Enlargement: Success Through Standardization of Standards?" in *Towards Security Sector Reform in Post Cold War Europe: A Framework for Assessment*, eds. Wilhelm N. Germann and Timothy Edmunds (Baden-Baden: Nomos Verlagsgesellschaft, 2003), 145–146.

23 Carl Ek, "NATO Common Funds Burdensharing: Background and Current Issues," 7-5700, RL30150 (Washington, DC: Congressional Research Service, February 15, 2012).

24 For a comprehensive and critical assessment of early US policy and programs in support of democratization and reform of Central and Eastern European communist legacy defense institutions, see Peterson Ulrich, *Democratizing Communist Militaries*, 49–66.

25 *Public Law 102–228.*

26 See United States Government Accountability Office, *NATO Partnerships: DOD Needs to Assess U.S. Assistance in Response to Changes to the Partnership for Peace Program*, Joseph A. Christoff, GAO Report 10–1015 (Washington, DC: Government Printing Office, September 2010), 4–5.

27 Cottey and Forster, "Reshaping Defence Diplomacy," 11.

28 See Malcolm Haworth, "Foreword," in *Democratic Control of the Military in Postcommunist Europe: Guarding the Guards*, eds. Andrew Cottey, Timothy Edmunds, and Anthony Forster (New York: Palgrave, 2002), vii; ix.

29 The Nordic Initiative is an arrangement among Nordic nations to coordinate and combine efforts in the delivery of assistance to countries in the Western Balkans with the objective to further regional stability and peace. See Amadeo Watkins, *Security Sector Reform and Donor Assistance in Serbia: Complexity of Managing Change* (Shrivenham: Defense Academy of the United Kingdom, September 2010), 22.

30 For a comprehensive list of US Security Assistance and Security Cooperation programs, see Dafna H. Rand and Stephen Tankel, *Security Cooperation and Assistance: Rethinking the Return on Investment* (Washington, DC: Center for a New American Security, August 2015), 5 (figure 1).

31 These documents were leaked in November 1997 and reported in the press. See Kay, "NATO Enlargement," 166–167.

32 Andrew A. Michta, "Introduction," in *America's New Allies*, 8–9.

33 For example, read then-Brigadier-General Von Kirchbach's account of taking command of the NVA's 9th Armored Division upon unification in October 1990. He was given the task of integrating elements of the division into the Bundeswehr. Hans-Peter von Kirchbach et al., *Abenteuer Einheit: Zum Aufbau der Bundeswehr in den neuen Ländern* (Frankfurt am Main: Report Verlag, 1992), *passim*.

34 Bradley R. Gitz, *Armed Forces and Political Power in Eastern Europe: The Soviet/Communist Control System* (New York: Greenwood Press, 1992), 8–9.

35 Pál Dunay, "The Half-Hearted Transformation of the Hungarian Military," in *Civil-Military Relations in Post-Communist Europe: Reviewing the Transition*, eds. Timothy Edmunds, Andrew Cottey, and Anthony Forster (London: Rutledge, 2006), 18.

36 Christian O. Millotat, "The *Bundeswehr* in the New Federal States: Aspects of the Development of Home Defense Brigade, 38: Sachen-Anhalt," *Defense Analysis* 9, no. 3 (1993): 311–318.

37 Cf., "In this context, the GDR is the one Warsaw Pact state capable of maintaining a stable economy whilst ensuring the costs of continuous military modernization." Douglas A. MacGregor, "The GDR: A Model Mobilisation," in *NATO-Warsaw Pact Force Mobilization*, ed. Jeffrey Simon (Washington, DC: National Defense University Press, 1988), 181–204.

38 Millotat, "The *Bundeswehr* in the New Federal States," 312.

39 Ibid., 313.

40 See Christopher Donnelly, *Red Banner: The Soviet Military System in Peace and War* (Coulsdon, Surrey: Jane's Information Group, 1988), 108–109.

41 For treatment of the Russian practice of *dedovshchina*, see Douglas J. Brown, "'Dedovshchina': Caste Tyranny in the Soviet Armed Forces," *Journal of Soviet Military Studies* 5, no. 1 (1992): 53–79.

42 Clemmesen, "Integration of New Alliance Members," 261–263.

43 Aleksandr Golts, "Russia: Military Reforms Meaningless Unless Accompanied by Educational Reforms," *Yezhednevnyy Zhurnal*, September 7, 2010.

44 Albeit dated, Glantz's critique of this institution is representative of the curriculum and general educational approach briefed to this author in Warsaw in May 2012. See David M. Glantz, "Military Training and Education Challenges in Poland, the Czech Republic, and Hungary," *Journal of Slavic Military Studies* 11, no. 3 (1998): 35–38.

45 Merab Mamardashvili quoted in *The Economist*, August 21–27, 2010, 40.

46 Milanovic is an economist at the City University of New York. His blog, "globalinequality" can be found at http://glineq.blogspot.com and is cited by David Brooks, "The Legacy of Fear," *The New York Times*, November 10, 2015.

47 Geert Hofstede, *Culture's Consequences: Comparing Values, Behaviors, Institutions and Organizations across Nations*, 2nd edn (Thousand Oaks: Sage Publications, 2001), *passim*; Geert Hofstede, Gert Jan Hofstede, and Michael Minkov, *Cultures and Organizations: Software of the Mind*, 3rd edn (New York: McGraw-Hill, 2010), *passim*.

48 The degree to which less powerful members of a culture both accept and expect an inequality of power distribution.

49 The degree to which a member of a culture accepts, or rejects, uncertainty/ambiguity.

50 Jaroslav Naď, Marian Majer, and Milan Šuplata, *75 Solutions for Slovakia's Defence* (Bratislava: Central European Policy Institute, c. 2015), 2.

51 Emily Goldman and Leslie Eliasen, eds., *Adaptive Enemies, Reluctant Friends: The Impact of Diffusion on Military Practice* (Stanford: Stanford University Press, 2003), 391.

52 For a treatment of this concept, see Peter Katzenstein, ed., *The Culture of National Security* (New York: Columbia University Press, 1996). For an excellent, albeit incomplete, series of recent surveys of the strategic cultures of European countries, see Heiko Biehl, Bastian Giegerich, and Alexandra Jonas, eds., *Strategic Cultures in Europe: Security and Defence Policies across the Continent*, in *Schriftenreihe des Zentrums für Militärgeschichte und Sozialwissenschaften der Bundeswehr* 13 (Wiesbaden: Springer VS, 2013).

53 Jan Jires, "Czech Republic," in *Strategic Cultures in Europe*, 69.

54 Dunay, "The Half-Hearted Transformation of the Hungarian Military," 21.

55 Charles M. Perry and Dimitris Keridis, *Defense Reform, Modernization, and Military Cooperation in Southeastern Europe* (Herndon, VA: Brassey's Inc., 2004), 2.

56 For an excellent treatment of the challenges of the lack of a strategic culture in Ukraine, see Natalie Mychajlyszen, "The Euro-Atlantic Strategic Culture: Democratic Civil-Military Relations, and Ukraine," in *The Evolution of Civil-Military Relations in East-Central Europe and the Former Soviet Union*, eds. Natalie Mychajlyszyn and Harald von Riekhoff (Westport, CT: Praeger, 2004), 191–209.

57 See Mikhail Tsypkin, "Soviet Military Culture and the Legacy of the War," in *Histories of the Aftermath: The Legacies of the Second World War in Europe*, eds. Frank Biess and Robert G. Moeller (New York: Berghahn Books, 2010), 279–283.

58 T. Csiki and P. Talas, "Can We Identify a Coherent Strategic Culture in Hungary?" in *Strategic Cultures in Europe*, 165.

59 Timothy Edmunds, Andrew Cottey, and Anthony Forster, "Introduction," in *Civil-Military Relations in Post-Communist Europe*, 5–6.

60 See Thomas C. Bruneau and Richard B. Goetze, "Ministries of Defense and Democratic Control," in *Who Guards the Guardians and How: Democratic Civil-Military Relations*, eds. Thomas C. Bruneau and Scott D. Tollefson (Austin: University of Texas Press, 2006), 71–98.

61 Dunay, "The Half-Hearted Transformation of the Hungarian Military," 21.

62 Philipp Fluri and Hari Bucur-Marcu, *Partnership Action for Defence Institution Building: Country Profiles and Need Assessments for Armenia, Azerbaijan, and Georgia, and Moldova* (Geneva: Geneva Centre for the Democratic Control of Armed Forces, 2007), 11.

63 Poland, *White Book on National Security of the Republic of Poland* (Warsaw: National Security Bureau, 2013).

64 David J. Betz, *Civil-Military Relations in Russia and Eastern Europe* (New York: Routledge Curzon, 2004), 128. For background on these bodies as they exist in Poland, Hungary, and Ukraine, see 128–132; 143–146.

65 For example, laws on "defense planning" that exist in a number of these countries (e.g., Georgia and Ukraine) are formulaic and almost exogenous to the realities of defense planning.

66 Natalie Mychajlyszyn, "Civil-Military Relations in Post-Soviet Ukraine: Implications for Domestic and Regional Stability," *Armed Forces and Society* 28, no. 3 (Spring 2002): 459–560.

67 Kristina Soukupova, "The Influence of Civil-Military Relations on the Implementation of Network Enabled Capabilities as a Transformation Driver and Security Sector Consolidation Catalyst in the Czech Republic" (PhD dissertation, King's College London, 2010), 7.

68 The best example of this practice is the Serbian Army of 13,250 personnel organized into thirty-five battalions. See The International Institute for Strategic Studies, *The Military Balance 2015* (London: Routledge, February 2015), 131.

69 James Sherr, "Ukraine: Reform in the Context of Flawed Democracy and Geopolitical Anxiety," in *Civil-Military Relations in Post-Communist Europe*, 160.

70 I am indebted to my colleague Dr Kristina Soukupova for raising to my attention this linguistic and conceptual point.

71 Glantz, "Military Training and Education Challenges in Poland, the Czech Republic, and Hungary," 33.

72 Szemerkenyi, "Central European Civil-Military Reforms at Risk," 17.

73 A representative example of this is found in Armenia, *The Military Doctrine of the Republic of Armenia* (Yerevan: Ministry of Defense, 2007), in which is expressed a "defense strategy" for the country. The point is not to grade this doctrine, but rather simply to demonstrate that there remains a continued lack of consistent usage of important terms which, to this writer's mind, implies a continued gap in conceptual understanding.

74 Edmunds, Cottey, and Forster, "Introduction," 6.

75 Anthony Cottey, Timothy Edmunds, and Anthony Forster, "The Second Generation Problematic: Rethinking Democracy and Civil-Military Relations," *Armed Forces and Society* 29, no 1 (Fall 2002): 31–56.

76 To their credit, Bellamy and Edmunds acknowledge, too, that these nations have not successfully made the full transition to Western norms: "the international community has shown little sensitivity to the structural impediments to reform described earlier. This has resulted in unrealistic expectations, and in the past, at least, the articulation of inappropriate and ineffective policies." Alex J. Bellamy and Timothy Edmunds, "Civil-Military Relations in Croatia: Politicisation and Politics of Reform," in *Civil-Military Relations in Post-Communist Europe*, 89.

77 Ibid., 77.

78 Larry Watts, "Reforming Civil-Military Relations in Post-Communist States: Civil Control vs. Democratic Control," *Journal of Political and Military Sociology* 30, no. 1 (Summer 2002): 51–52, 56.

79   James Sherr, "Hungary: A Corner Turned?" in *The Evolution of Civil-Military Relations in East-Central Europe and the Former Soviet Union*, 65.

80   Pal Dunay, "Building Professional Competence in Hungary's Defence: Slow Motion," in *The Challenge of Military Reform in Post-Communist Europe: Building Professional Armed Forces*, eds. Anthony Forster, Timothy Edmunds, and Andrew Cottey (London: Palgrave Macmillan, 2002), 76.

Chapter 4

1   James Sherr, "Ukraine: Reform in the Context of Flawed Democracy and Geopolitical Anxiety," in *Civil-Military Relations in Post-Communist Europe: Reviewing the Transition*, eds. Timothy Edmunds, Andrew Cottey, and Anthony Forster (London: Rutledge, 2006), 158–159.

2   To wit: Admiral of the Fleet Ivan Isakov, Marshal Ivan Bagramyan, Marshal of Aviation Sergei Khudyakov, and Chief Marshal of Armored Forces Hamazasp Babadzhanian. I am indebted to Ara Mesrobyan of the Armenian Ministry of Defense for his extensive and detailed knowledge of Armenian military history.

3   Sir Garry Johnson, "Security Sector Reform in the Southern Caucasus," in *Security Sector Governance in Southern Caucasus: Challenges and Visions*, eds. Anja H. Ebnöther and Gustav E. Gustenau (Geneva: Geneva Centre for the Democratic Control of Armed Forces, 2004), 53.

4   As argued by Gayane Novikova and Sergey Sargsyan, "Armenia," in *Security Sector Reform in Countries of Visegrad and Southern Caucasus: Challenges and Opportunities*, ed. Marian Majer (Bratislava: Centre for European and North Atlantic Affairs (CENAA), 2013), 16.

5   Georgia enjoys one of the most transparent ministries of defense in the region and is supported by a vibrant community of think tanks and NGOs focused on national defense and security issues. One of the best detailed descriptions and analysis of the formation of the Georgian Ministry of Defense and its armed forces is found in David Darchiashvili, "Defense Reform and the Caucasus: Challenges of Institutional Reform during Unresolved Conflict," *Mediterranean Quarterly* 20, no. 3 (Summer 2009): 19–39.

6   See Stephen F. Jones, "Adventurers or Commanders? Civil-Military Relations in Georgia Since Independence," in *Civil-Military Relations in the Soviet and Yugoslav Successor States*, eds. Constantine P. Danopoulos and Daniel Zirker (Boulder, CO: Westview Press, 1996), 35–52.

7   For an excellent examination of the birth and early years of the Ukrainian armed forces, see Sergey Denisentsev, "The Soviet Inheritance of Ukrainian Armed Forces," in *Brothers Armed: Military Aspects of the Crisis in Ukraine*, eds. Colby Howard and Ruslan Pukhov (Minneapolis: East View Press, 2014), 25–56.

8   Roy Allison, "Armed Forces in Successor Soviet States," *Adelphi Paper* 280 (London: The International Institute for Strategic Studies, 1993), 42.

9   Leonid I. Polyakov, *U.S.-Ukraine Military Relations and the Value of Interoperability* (Carlisle Barracks, PA: Strategic Studies Institute, December 2004), 57–63.

10   James Sherr, "Civil-Democratic Control of Ukraine's Armed Forces: To What End? By What Means?" in *Army and State in Postcommunist Europe*, eds. David Betz and John Löwenhardt (London: Frank Cass, 2001), 67; 76 (n. 1).

11 For a dated, but extremely informative, treatment of the early development of the armed forces of the Baltic States, see Albert M. Zaccor, "Problems in the Baltic Armed Forces," *Journal of Slavic Military Studies* 8, no. 1 (1995): 53–72.

12 "Treaty of Peace with Finland Signed in Paris," February 10, 1947, *United Nations Treaty Series* 48, 203 ff. For background on Estonia's connection to Finnish defense expertise, see Holger Mölder, "The Development of Military Cultures," in *Apprenticeship, Partnership, Membership: Twenty Years of Defence Development in the Baltic States*, eds. Tony Lawrence and Tomas Jermalavičius (Tallinn: International Centre for Defence Studies, 2013), 105–106.

13 See Eric Männik, "Development of the Estonian Defence: Finnish Assistance," *Baltic Defence Review* 1, no. 7 (2002): 34–42.

14 Michael H. Clemmesen, "Baltic States and Different Territorial Defence Models: A Discussion," *Baltic Defense Review* 2, no. 4 (2002): 115–121.

15 Albert M. Zaccor, "Guerrilla Warfare on the Baltic Coast: A Possible Model for Baltic Defense Doctrines Today?" *Journal of Slavic Military Studies* 7, no. 4 (1994): 682–702.

16 For an excellent contemporary analysis of the state of development of these forces, see Piotr Szymanski, "The Baltic States' Territorial Defence Forces in the Face of Hybrid Threats," *OSW/Commentary*, no. 165, March 19, 2015.

17 As officially defined by the Estonian Parliamentary, Total Defense consists of: "(1) military defence, (2) civilian sector support to military defence, (3) international activities, (4) the internal security effort, (5) securing critical infrastructure, and (6) psychological defence." Kadi Salu and Erick Männik, "Estonia," in *Strategic Cultures in Europe: Security and Defence Policies across the Continent, Schriftenreihe des Zentrums für Militärgeschichte und Sozialwissenschaften der Bundeswehr* 13, eds. Heiko Biehl, Bastian Giegerich, and Alexandra Jonas (Wiesbaden: Springer VS, 2013), 105.

18 See Milton Paul Davis, "An Historical and Political Overview of the Reserve and Guard Forces of the Nordic Countries at the Beginning of the Twenty-first Century," *Baltic Security and Defence Review* 10 (2008): 171–201.

19 This arguement is addressed well by Harald von Riekhoff, "Civil-Military Relations in the Baltic States," in *The Evolution of Civil-Military Relations in East-Central Europe and the Former Soviet Union*, eds. Natalie Mychajlyszyn and Harald von Riekhoff (Westport, CT: Praeger, 2004), 106–107.

20 Lithuania, *Lithuanian Defence Policy: White Paper* (Vilnius: Ministry of National Defence, 2006), 17.

21 The decision by all three defense institutions not to make any substantive changes to their territorial defense forces was likely not met with universal approval by NATO nations. See Szymanski, "The Baltic States' Territorial Defence Forces:" 5.

22 See Trevor Taylor, "The Functions of a Defence Ministry," in *Managing Defence in a Democracy*, eds. Laura R. Cleary and Teri McConville (New York: Routledge, 2006), 92–104.

23 *Marele Stat Major,* or "Main Staff," in the case of Moldova.

24 Harald von Riekhoff, "Introduction," in *The Evolution of Civil-Military Relations in East-Central Europe and the Former Soviet Union*, 11–12.

25 Kęstutis Paulauskas, "The Baltic Quest to the West: From Total Defence to 'Smart Defence' (and Back?)," in *Apprenticeship, Partnership, Membership*, 55–56.

26 Jan Arveds Trapans, "Professionalisation of the Armed Forces in Central and Eastern Europe: The Case of Latvia," in *The Challenge of Military Reform in Post-Communist*

Europe: Building Professional Armed Forces, eds. Anthony Forster, Timothy Edmunds, and Andrew Cottey (London: Palgrave Macmillan, 2002), 87.

27 Leonid A. Karabeshkin, "The Ongoing Transformation of the Estonian Defence Forces," in *Democratic Civil-Military Relations: Soldiering in 21st Century Europe*, ed. Sabine Mannitz (London: Routledge, 2012), 130.

28 See James S. Corum, *Development of the Baltic Armed Forces in Light of Multinational Deployments* (Carlisle Barracks, PA: The Strategic Studies Institute, August 2013), 34–38.

29 Von Riekhoff, "Civil-Military Relations in the Baltic States," 123, 124–127.

30 The fall 2010 decision to abandon the newly created Joint Operations Command that was just reaching Full Operational Capacity being an excellent case in point—and a painful one. The author was the program manager who assisted the Ukrainian General Staff to create the command based on various Western concepts. Its creation was the result of early reform efforts following the Orange Revolution. See Ukraine, *The White Book 2006, Defence Policy of Ukraine* (Kyiv: Ministry of Defense, Zapovit Publishing House, 2007), 110, and M. Kutsyn, "Guidelines of the State Programme of the Ukrainian Armed Forces Development during 2006–2011: The Joint Operational Command," Defense and Security Policy Center, Kyiv, *Defense Bulletin*, No. 5, 2010: 51–53.

31 Natalie Mychajlyszyn, "Civil-Military Relations in Post-Soviet Ukraine: Implications for Domestic and Regional Stability," *Armed Forces and Society* 28, no 3 (Spring 2002): 462, 474 (n. 32).

32 For a somewhat dated, but still accurate, general treatment of Ukrainian security and defense structures, see Natalie Mychajlyszen, "The Euro-Atlantic Strategic Culture: Democratic Civil-Military Relations, and Ukraine," in *The Evolution of Civil-Military Relations in East-Central Europe and the Former Soviet Union*, 197–202.

33 See Ukraine, *White Book 2010, Armed Forces of Ukraine* (Kyiv: Ministry of Defense, 2011), 67 (Annex 2) for an organization chart of the ministry of defense.

34 See Ukraine, *Reforms Initiatives Overview* (Kyiv: Ministry of Defense, Projects Reforms Office, October 2015).

35 See the organizational structure of the ministry of defense in *Programul de Dezvoltare Strategică al Ministerului Apără pentru perioada 2012–2014* (Chişinu, 2012), 6.

36 Georgia, *Georgia National Security Concept* (Tbilisi, 2011), 15.

37 Robert L. Larsson, "The Enemy Within: Russia's Military Withdrawal from Georgia," *Journal of Slavic Military Studies* 17, no. 3 (2004): 410.

38 David Darchiashvili, "Georgian Defense Policy and Military Reform," in *Statehood and Security: Georgia after the Rose Revolution*, eds. Bruno Coppieters and Robert Legvold (Cambridge, MA: MIT Press, 2005), 124–125, 127.

39 Georgia, Ministry of Defense, "Georgia: Advancing Towards NATO," brochure 2007, and Darchiashvili, "Georgian Defense Policy and Military Reform," in *Statehood and Security*, 146–147.

40 See "Civil service system already introduced in defense ministry of Armenia," Mediamax, February 18, 2010, http://www.mediamax.am/en/news/interviews/82/ (accessed May 20, 2016).

41 Betz's observation that the Ukrainian defense institution has produced sophisticated policy is simply unconvincing. The ineffectualness of plans, such as the lauded Program on the Armed Forces Reform and Development until 2005, is addressed quite critically *infra* under Defense Planning Techniques. See David J. Betz, *Civil-Military Relations in Russia and Eastern Europe* (New York: Routledge Curzon, 2004), 152–153.

42 For a very good comparative and critical analysis of the three states' evolution in their respective security and defense thinking, see Erik Männik, "The Evolution of Baltic Security and Defence Strategies," in *Apprenticeship, Partnership, Membership,* 13–44.

43 Armenia, *Strategic Defense Review, 2011–2015,* Public Release (Yerevan: Ministry of Defense, c. 2011), 7–8.

44 Paulauskas, "The Baltic Quest to the West," 74–76; 59. For instance, Latvia acknowledged the need for such a policy change even prior to formal admittance into the alliance. See Latvia, *Report on the State Defence Policy and Armed Forces Development* (Riga: Ministry of Defence, 2004), 18.

45 As regards the functioning of the Lithuanian Ministry of Defense, see Vaidotas Urbelis and Tomas Ubronas, "The Challenges of Civil-Military Relations and Democratic Control of Armed Forces: The Case of Lithuania," in *Democratic Control of the Military in Postcommunist Europe: Guarding the Guards,* eds. Andrew Cottey, Timothy Edmunds, and Anthony Forster (London: Palgrave, 2002), 117–118.

46 See Georgia, *Strategic Defence Review, 2013–2016* (Tbilisi: Ministry of Defence, 2013), 22 and 23, for the structures of the ministry of defense and joint staff, respectively.

47 See http://www.mil.am/en/pn (accessed May 20, 2016).

48 Ben Lombardi, "Ukrainian Armed Forces: Defence Expenditure and Military Reform," *Journal of Slavic Military Studies* 14, no. 3 (2001): 32.

49 Mychajlyszyn, "Civil-Military Relations in Post-Soviet Ukraine," 463.

50 Euroasianet.org, October 23, 2013, http://www.eurasianet.org/node/67660 (accessed May 20, 2016).

51 John Colston, Philipp Fluri, and Sergei Piroshkov, eds., *Security Sector Legislation of Ukraine* (Geneva: Geneva Center for Civil Control of Armed Forces, 2006).

52 That said, Betz is spot-on in stating that this (alleged) expertise came at the expense of preservation of old thinking. Betz, *Civil-Military Relations in Russia and Eastern Europe,* 45.

53 Georgia, *Strategic Defence Review, 2013–2016,* 4.

54 Tengiz Pkhaladze and Alexander Rondeli, "Georgia," in *Security Sector Reform in Countries of Visegrad and Southern Caucasus,* 41–42.

55 Ukraine, *The White Book 2006.*

56 For an excellent discussion of this policy/financial disconnect in Ukrainian defense planning, see Deborah Sanders, "Ukraine's Military Reform: Building a Paradigm Army," *Journal of Slavic Military Studies* 21, no. 4 (2008): 607–611.

57 Sherr, "Civil-Democratic Control of Ukraine's Armed Forces," 72.

58 To understand the state of the defense institution's inability to conduct even rudimentary planning, see the highly complex, confusing, and stilted "strategic planning" process in the ministry of defense authored by then Deputy Minister of Defense H. Pedchenko, "Strategic Planning in Ukraine: Content and Challenges Related to its Realization in the Ministry of Defense of the [*sic*] Ukraine," Defense and Security Policy Centre, Kyiv, *Defense Bulletin* No. 5, 2010: 4–5.

59 Albeit dated, this study provides one of the very few analyses of the defense budgeting system in Azerbaijan and it observes, *inter alia,* that transparency is lacking. Tamara Pataraia and Tata Makhatadze, "Defence Institution Building in Azerbaijan," in *Partnership Action for Defence Institution Building: Country Profiles and Need Assessments for Armenia, Azerbaijan, and Georgia, and Moldova,* eds.

Philipp Fluri and Hari Bucur-Marcu (Geneva: Geneva Centre for the Democratic Control of Armed Forces, 2007), 33, 34.

60 Ibid., 37.

61 International Crisis Group, "Azerbaijan: Defense Sector Management and Reform," *Europe Briefing* No. 50, October 29, 2008: 14.

62 For Latvia, the decision was made to introduce the new method by 1999. See Latvia, *Report on the State Defence Policy and Armed Forces Development*, 43–44. For an explanation of Estonia's planning method, see Lt-Col Veiko Palm, Director of Defence Planning Department, Ministry of Defence, "Defence Planning in Estonia: Some Practical Aspects of PPBES," Tallinn, n.d.

63 Kristine Rudzite-Sejskala, "Financing Defence," in *Apprenticeship, Partnership, Membership*, 178.

64 Paulauskas, "The Baltic Quest to the West," 77.

65 Lithuania, "Guidelines of the Minister of National Defence for 2009–2014" (Vilnius: Ministry of National Defence, February 29, 2008), 25.

66 Estonia, *National Defence Development Plan, 2013-2022*, Tallinn: Ministry of Defense, n.d.

67 Estonia, National Audit Office, *Effectiveness of Formation, Maintenance and Replenishment of Resources Required for Increasing Military Capability and Mobilisation of Defence Forces from 2009–2012* (summary of report), Tallinn, May 30, 2013.

68 Roman Mileshko, "The Evolution of the Defense Budget Process in Ukraine, 1991–2006" (MA thesis, Naval Postgraduate School, Monterey, CA, 2006), 70–71.

69 There is very little written in Western languages that address these Ukrainian-unique processes, let alone the assumptions upon which they are based. In the Ukrainian language there is M. Neckhayev, "The System of Joint Strategic Planning of Resource Support to the National Security in the Military Sphere," Ye. F. Shelest, "'Resource'— The Information-Analytical System for Support to the Defense Planning," and O. F. Zaskoka, "On the Reforming of the System of Manning in the Armed Forces of Ukraine," *Science and Defense: Scientific-Theoretic and Scientific-Practical Journal* no. 3 (2005): 9–15, 16–22, 23–29, respectively.

70 Vitaliy Kosianchuk, "Cobb-Douglas production function as an approach for better resource allocation in the Ukrainian Armed Forces" (MA thesis, Naval Postgraduate School, Monterey, CA, 2013), 27, 3.

71 See E. Sheltes, "Comment of the Chairman of the Center for Defence and Security Policy," Center for Defense and Security Policy, Kyiv, *Defense Bulletin*, No. 5, 2010: 14.

72 Iryna Bystrova, "Defense Planning in the Ministry of Defense of Ukraine: Decade of Attempts and Mistakes" (MA thesis, Naval Postgraduate School, Monterey, CA, June 2015).

73 See Antje Fritz, "Security Sector Governance in Georgia (I): Status," in *From Revolution to Reform: Georgia's Struggle with Democratic Institution Building and Security Sector Reform*, eds. Philipp H. Fluri and Eden Cole (Vienna: Bureau for Security Policy at the Austrian Ministry of Defence, National Defence Academy, and Geneva Centre for the Democratic Control of Armed Forces in cooperation with PfP-Consortium of Defence Academies and Security Studies Institutes, July 2005), 66–67.

74 Georgia, *Manual Planning and Control: PPBS/FMS* (Tbilisi: Ministry of Defense, March 9, 2007).

75 Theona Akubardia, "Security and Defence Policy Development," in *Democratic Control over the Georgian Armed Forces Since the August 2008 War*, ed. Tamara

Pataraia (Geneva: Geneva Centre for the Democratic Control of Armed Forces, 2010), 17.

76 Georgia, *Strategic Defence Review, 2013–2016*, 7–8.

77 David Darchiashvili, "Striving for Effective Parliamentary Control Over the Armed Forces of Georgia," in *Civil-Military Relations in Europe: Learning from Crisis and Institutional Change*, eds. Hans Born, Marina Caparini, Karl W. Haltiner, and Jürgen Kuhlmann (New York: Routledge, 2006), 84–88.

78 *24 Saati* (Tbilisi), June 26, 2007, quoting David Smith, cited in David Darchiashvili, *Security Sector Reform in Georgia 2004–2007* (Tbilisi: Caucasus Institute for Peace, Democracy, and Development, 2008), 22 (fn. 65).

79 Viorel Cibotaru, "Defence Reform in Moldova," in *Defense Institution Building: Country Profiles and Needs Assessments for Armenia, Azerbaijan, Georgia, and Moldova*, 77–78.

80 Aghasi Yenokyan, "Country Study: Armenia," in *Defense Institution Building: Country Profiles and Needs Assessments for Armenia, Azerbaijan, Georgia, and Moldova*, 20; 26.

81 Darchiashvili, "Defense Reform and the Caucasus," 134.

82 Pataraia and Makhatadze, "Defence Institution Building in Azerbaijan," 33.

83 Betz, *Civil-Military Relations in Russia and Eastern Europe*, 99.

84 Sherr, "Ukraine: Reform in the Context of Flawed Democracy and Geopolitical Anxiety," 159–160.

85 Yenokyan, "Country Study: Armenia," 10, 17.

86 Cibotaru, "Defence Reform in Moldova," 86.

87 See Ronald D. Asmus, *A Little War That Shook the World: Georgia, Russia, and the Future of the West* (New York: Palgrave Macmillan, 2010).

88 Sintija Oškalne, "Supreme Command and Control of the Armed Forces: The Roles of Presidents, Parliaments, Governments, Ministries of Defence and Chiefs of Defence," in *Apprenticeship, Partnership, Membership*, 124–135.

89 Karabeshkin, "The Ongoing Transformation of the Estonian Defence Forces," 130–133.

90 Martin Hurt, "Lessons Identified in Crimea: Does Estonia's National Defence Model Meet our Needs?" *Policy Paper* (Tallinn: International Centre for Defence Studies, April 2014), 6.

91 Constitution of the Republic of Latvia, Articles 42, 43, and 44.

92 Oškalne, "Supreme Command and Control of the Armed Forces," 136–151.

93 Vaidotas Urbelis, "Lithuania's Strategic Culture," *Lithuanian Annual Strategic Review 2006* (Vilnius: Strategic Research Center, 2007): 201.

94 Ibid., 160.

95 Vytautas Jokubauskas, "The Financing and Personnel of the Lithuanian Army," *Lithuanian Strategic Review 2014–2015* 13 (2015): 160.

96 Edmunds refers to this practice as having, *de facto*, created "two-tire" armed forces practiced by all post-communist defense institutions. This was envisaged to create centers of reform within these armed forces in periods of financial austerity. Timothy Edmunds, "NATO and its New Members," *Survival* 45, no. 3 (Autumn 2003): 158.

97 International Crisis Group, "Azerbaijan," 16.

98 Ibid., 1.

99 Azerbaijan's 2010 Military Doctrine. Cited by Novikova and Sargsyan, "Armenia," 12 (n.8).

100   Denisentsev, "The Soviet Inheritance of Ukrainian Armed Forces," 25–56.

101   Yenokyan, "Country Study: Armenia," 18.

102   Kamal Makili-Aliyev, "Azerbaijan," in *Security Sector Reform in Countries of Visegrad and Southern Caucasus*, 31.

103   Latvia's ambitious objectives to develop its logistics structures and procedures in anticipation of alliance membership are detailed in Latvia, *Report on the State Defence Policy and Armed Forces Development*, 32–34.

104   O. Ostapets, "Guidelines of the State Programme of the Ukrainian Armed Forces Development during 2006–2011: Outsourcing in the Ukrainian Armed Forces," Defense and Security Policy Center, Kyiv, *Defense Bulletin*, No. 5, 2010: 17.

105   Ukraine, *White Book 2014, Armed Forces of Ukraine* (Kyiv: Ministry of Defense, 2015), 11–12.

106   This lacuna is being addressed by NATO with the donation of supply management software. See North Atlantic Treaty Organization, "NATO's Practical Support to Ukraine," *Fact Sheet*, Brussels, February 2015.

107   See organizational charts of these organizations in Ukraine, *White Book 2014*, 73–74.

108   There is little formally published on the activities of the Volunteers and civil society's efforts to support the defense of Ukraine. First-hand reports from soldiers at the front are numerous and explicit in their praise of Volunteers and criticism of the defense institution and particularly senior military officials. See, for example, "Ukrainian Soldier Speaks—This is our Stalingrad: What it's Like to Serve on the War's Front Line," August 7, 2015, https://medium.com/@warisboring/ukrainian-soldier-speaks-this-is-our-stalingrad-81bd54cde6d2#.44x1drfqw (accessed May 20, 2016).

109   *The Times* (London), February 24, 2015.

110   International Crisis Group, "Azerbaijan," 12.

111   Pkhaladze and Rondeli, "Georgia," 38.

112   Julie A. George and Jeremy M. Teigen, "NATO Enlargement and Institution Building: Military Personnel Policy Challenges in the Post-Soviet Context," *European Security* 17, no. 2–3 (2008): 339–366.

113   Cibotaru, "Defence Reform in Moldova," 89.

114   For an excellent briefing of an ambitious, but equally sobering final assessment of one such a program in support of the Ukrainian armed forces, see MPRI, "NCO Professional Development Program; Ukrainian Armed Forces: Final Program Brief," July 2009.

115   *Frontline Allies: War and Change in Central Europe: U.S.-Central Europe Strategic Assessment Group Report* (Warsaw: Center for European Policy Analysis, November 2015), 7.

116   Denisentsev, "The Soviet Inheritance of Ukrainian Armed Forces," 55.

117   Armenia, *Strategic Defense Review, 2011–2015*.

Chapter 5

1   Reka Szemerkenyi, "Central European Civil-Military Reforms at Risk," *Adelphi Paper* 306 (London: The International Institute for Strategic Studies, 1996), 40–41.

2   Anthony Cottey, Timothy Edmunds, and Anthony Forster, "The Second Generation Problematic: Rethinking Democracy and Civil-Military Relations," *Armed Forces and Society* 29, no 1 (Fall 2002): 31–56.

3   Paul Dunay, "Civil-Military Relations in Hungary: No Big Deal," in *Democratic Control of the Military in Postcommunist Europe: Guarding the Guards*, eds. Andrew Cottey, Timothy Edmunds, and Anthony Forster (London: Palgrave, 2002), 83–84.

4   For instance, Bulgaria's first Individual Partnership Program was approved in November 1994 and the first PARP cycle started in February 1995. Charles M. Perry and Dimitris Keridis, *Defense Reform, Modernization, and Military Cooperation in Southeastern Europe* (Herndon, VA: Brassey's Inc., 2004), 71.

5   Kristina Soukupova, "The Influence of Civil-Military Relations on the Implementation of Network Enabled Capabilities as a Transformation Driver and Security Sector Consolidation Catalyst in the Czech Republic" (PhD dissertation, King's College London, 2010), 6.

6   For example, Poland's defense budget for 2014 is $9.5 billion, which has grown by an impressive 7 percent from 2012, which is close to 2 percent of GDP. Most importantly, the percentage of the budget that is directed to capital investment is envisaged to increase from 15 to 33 percent. This constitutes a political and financial commitment to defense that is all but unmatched in the region, with the possible exception of Estonia. See "Flexing Its Muscles," *The Economist*, August 17–23, 2013, 44–45.

7   Italics added. See James S. Corum, "The Security Concerns of the Baltic States as NATO Allies," *The Letorte Papers*, Carlisle Barracks, PA, Strategic Studies Institute, August 2013, vii.

8   Poland, *White Book on National Security of the Republic of Poland* (Warsaw: The National Security Bureau, 2013), 49. One source calculated that from 1989 until 2009, some 67,000 soldiers and civilians served abroad on UN, NATO, OSCE, and EU operations. Quoted by Marek Pietras, "Poland's Participation in NATO Operations," in *NATO's European Allies: Military Capability and Political Will*, eds. Janne Haaland Matlary and Magnus Petersson (New York: Palgrave Macmillan, 2013), 210.

9   German defense and military officials have been remarkably quiet about their experience of employing inherited NVA equipment. What is known is that equipment which was kept following unification was extensively modernized and critical safety systems were introduced to bring the kit to Western standards. That said, this legacy kit has all been retired from the Bundeswehr.

10   Lukas Dycka and Miroslav Mares, "The Development and Future of Fighter Planes Acquisition in Countries of the Visegrad Group," *Journal of Slavic Military Studies* 25, no. 4, (2012): 544–546, 555.

11   *15 Years in NATO* (Warsaw: Ministry of National Defense Republic of Poland, 2014), 16.

12   Remigiusz Wilk, "Polish F-16s Deploy for First Time Ever Combat Operation," *IHS Jane's 360*, July 7, 2016. http://www.janes.com/article/62046/polish-f-16s-deploy-for-first-ever-combat-operation.

13   Peter Polbielski, *Report No. 08: Transform or Modernize: Why Polish Military Transformation Matters* (Washington, DC: Center for European Policy Analysis, October 26, 2006).

14   See Zoltan D. Barany, *The Future of NATO Expansion: Four Case Studies* (Cambridge: Cambridge University Press, 2003), 173.

15   See various years of *The Military Balance* (London: The International Institute for Strategic Studies), annual publication.

16   Private correspondence with Thomas Szayna, RAND, Santa Monica, CA, and Larry Watts, Bucharest, Romania.

17 See Emilian Kavalski, "We Are the Hawks of Freedom: Bulgaria's Good Fishing in the Muddy Waters of the Gulf," *Journal of Slavic Military Studies* 19, no. 1 (2006): 33–55.

18 See Tsonsho Draganski, "Accumulate Battle Experience," Bulgarian Army webpage, February 15, 2013.

19 Contained in the Garret report. See Barany, *The Future of NATO Expansion*, 81.

20 For an excellent and in-depth treatment of the difficult evolution of the Polish and Hungarian ministries of defense after independence, see David J. Betz, *Civil-Military Relations in Russia and Eastern Europe* (New York: Routledge Curzon, 2004), 84–90.

21 See Barany, *The Future of NATO Expansion*, 71–73, for an insightful discussion of the challenges of creating a ministry of defense and developing civilian defense expertise in Slovakia.

22 Jan A. Trapans, "Democracy and Defence in Latvia: Thirteen Years of Development: 1991–2004," in *Civil-Military Relations in Post-Communist Europe: Reviewing the Transition*, eds. Timothy Edmunds, Andrew Cottey, and Anthony Forster (London: Routledge, 2006), 53.

23 Szemerkenyi, "Central European Civil-Military Reforms at Risk," 48.

24 Agnieszka Gogolewska, "Problems Confronting Civilian Democratic Control in Poland," in *Civil-Military Relations in Europe: Learning from Crisis and Institutional Change*, eds. Hans Born, Marina Caparini, Karl W. Haltiner, and Jürgen Kuhlmann (New York: Routledge, 2006), 102.

25 For a description of the struggle for ascendency of civilian control via civil ministries in Poland and Hungary, see Betz, *Civil-Military Relations in Russia and Eastern Europe*, 90–93.

26 For a background of these early efforts to establish the Slovak defense institution, see Jeffrey Simon, *NATO and the Czech and Slovak Republics: Comparative Study in Civil-Military Relations* (Lanham: Rowman and Littlefield, 2004), 147–148, 162–163.

27 See Barany, *The Future of NATO Expansion*, 72–77 and Simon, *NATO and the Czech and Slovak Republics*, 244.

28 "Frequently, the responsibility for fulfilling a task is not combined with sufficient powers and adequate financial means to achieve them. Moreover, communication between the MoD and the FS is inadequate and in many areas the division of powers is unclear." Maria Vlachova, "Professionalisation of the Army of the Czech Republic," in *The Challenge of Military Reform in Post-Communist Europe: Building Professional Armed Forces*, eds. Anthony Forster, Timothy Edmunds, and Andrew Cottey (London: Palgrave Macmillan, 2002), 40–41.

29 The most detailed, if not comprehensive, account of the "birth" of the Czech defense institution is provided in Simon, *NATO and the Czech and Slovak Republics*, *passim*.

30 David J. Betz, "Civil-Military Relations in the Czech Republic: Ambivalent Reformers, Immature Structures," in *The Evolution of Civil-Military Relations in East-Central Europe and the Former Soviet Union*, eds. Natalie Mychajlyszyn and Harald von Riekhoff (Westport, CT: Praeger, 2004), 47.

31 Lefebvre argues that in the latter part of the 1990s, the Czech Republic started to develop a strategic culture. Such an argument, in light of the evidence to the contrary, is not convincing. Surely evidence of a prevailing strategic culture should be manifested in no small degree in defense policy coherence. Cf., Stéphane Lefebvre. "The Czech Republic and National Security, 1993–1998," *Journal of Slavic Military Studies* 23, no. 2 (2010): 367–369.

32 Simon, *NATO and the Czech and Slovak Republics*, 31, 35–36.

33 Gogolewska, "Problems Confronting Civilian Democratic Control in Poland," 101.

34 Andrew A. Michta, *The Soldier-Citizen: The Politics of the Polish Army after Communism* (New York: St. Martin's Press, 1997), 50–53.

35 See http://www.army.cz/en/armed-forces/organisational-structure/general-staff/organisational-structure-of-the-general-staff-114454/ (accessed May 22, 2016).

36 Guidance is to be provided via the annual issuance of the *Defense Planning Guidance* document. George Cristian Maior and Mihaela Matei, "Bridging the Gap in Civil-Military Relations in Southeastern Europe: Romania's Defense-Planning Case," *Mediterranean Quarterly* 14, no. 2 (Spring 2003): 71–72.

37 Romania, General Staff, "Strategy of Transformation of Romanian Armed Forces," signed by state secretaries for Euro-Atlantic Integration and Defense Policy, and Armament, and Chief of General Staff, approved by the Secretary General of the Ministry of National Defense, Bucharest, 2007.

38 Law on Defense Planning, No. 473 of November 4, 2004; repeals Government Ordinance No.52/1998 on national defense planning, *Monitorul Oficial*, Bucharest, No. 525, October 25, 2000.

39 Mary Borissova, "Politicians, Experts and Democracy. Civil–Military Relations in Central and Eastern Europe: The Case of Bulgaria," *European Security* 15, no. 2 (2006): 199.

40 Gogolewska, "Problems Confronting Civilian Democratic Control in Poland," 101.

41 Following the end of the Cold War, Congress changed existing legislation related to the applicability of those foreign individuals who could attend education and training (both in the United States and via education/training teams) under the provision of the Department of States International Education and Training program to apply to civilian defense officials. U.S. Code 22, Chapter 32, Subchapter II, Part V, § 2347. See as well, John A. Cope, "International Military Education and Training: An Assessment," *McNair Paper 14* (Washington, DC: Institute for National Strategic Studies, October 1995).

42 Defense Resource Management Study Program, *2010 Annual Report*, Irregular Warfare Division, Office of the Secretary of Defense, Cost Assessment and Program Evaluation, Washington, DC, 2010.

43 Gogolewska, "Problems Confronting Civilian Democratic Control in Poland," 112.

44 Tomasz Paszewski, "Can Poland Defend Itself?," *Survival* 58, no. 2 (April–May 2016): 126–127.

45 Pal Dunay, "Building Professional Competence in Hungary's Defence: Slow Motion," in *The Challenge of Military Reform in Post-Communist Europe: Building Professional Armed Forces*, eds. Anthony Forster, Timothy Edmunds, and Andrew Cottey (London: Palgrave Macmillan, 2002), 63.

46 Simon, *NATO and the Czech and Slovak Republics*, 35.

47 Soukupova, "The Influence of Civil-Military Relations on the Implementation of Network Enabled Capabilities as a Transformation Driver and Security Sector Consolidation Catalyst in the Czech Republic," 146.

48 Zoltan Barany, "Hungary: An Output on the Troubled Periphery," in *America's New Allies: Poland, Hungary, and the Czech Republic in NATO*, ed. Andrew A. Michta (Seattle: University of Washington Press, 1999), 92.

49 Szemerkenyi, "Central European Civil-Military Reforms at Risk," 31.

50 Without any doubt, the best and very early excoriation of the dismal record of PPBS in Central and Eastern Europe can be found in ibid., 30–32.

51 Ibid., 34.

52 Simon, *NATO and the Czech and Slovak Republics*, 200.

53 Slovakia, *The White Paper on Defence of the Slovak Republic* (Bratislava: Ministry of Defense, 2013), 16–17, 18, 39.

54 For historical background and context, see Marian Majer, "Slovakia," in *Security Sector Reform in Countries of Visegrad and Southern Caucasus: Challenges and Opportunities*, ed. Marian Majer (Bratislava: Centre for European and North Atlantic Affairs [CENAA], 2013), 106–108.

55 Jaroslav Naď, Marian Majer, and Milan Šuplata, *75 Solutions for Slovakia's Defence* (Bratislava: Central European Policy Institute, c. 2015), 4.

56 Slovakia, *White Paper*, 17, 39. Like its 2010 Bulgarian counterpart, the 2013 Slovak defense white paper is one of the most honest and introspective reviews of a defense institution in all of Central and Eastern Europe. That said, the recommendation that a solution to its planning conundrum is in the adoption of a long-term defense plan is unlikely to provide the policy and planning answers that the organization so desperately needs. Likewise, the assertion (63) that "The purposefulness and functionality of defence planning will be enhanced by the stability of financial resources in the years ahead" will likely prove an illusion as sensible planning must assume both best- and worst-case scenarios. Cf., Bulgaria, *White Paper on Defence and the Armed Forces of the Republic of Bulgaria* (Sofia: Ministry of Defense, 2010), *passim*.

57 Marie Vlachova, "Defense Reform in the Czech Republic," in *Post-Cold War Defense Reform: Lessons Learned in Europe and the United States*, eds. Istvan Gyarmati and Theodor Winkler (Washington, DC: Brassey's, Inc., 2002), 400–401.

58 Soukupova, "The Influence of Civil-Military Relations on the Implementation of Network Enabled Capabilities as a Transformation Driver and Security Sector Consolidation Catalyst in the Czech Republic," 160.

59 Czech Republic, *The White Paper on Defense* (Prague: Ministry of Defense, DPC, 2011), 54.

60 Szemerkenyi, "Central European Civil-Military Reforms at Risk," 31.

61 Betz, "Civil-Military Relations in the Czech Republic," 51.

62 Mihály Zambori, "Economically Viable Management and Defence Spending," in *Defence Institution Building: A Sourcebook in Support of the Partnership Action Plan (PAP-DIB)*, eds. Wim F. Van Eekelen and Philipp H. Fluri (Vienna: Landesverteidigungsakademie, 2006), 275–294.

63 Hungary, *Hungary's National Security Strategy* (Budapest: Ministry of Foreign Affairs, 2012) and Hungary, *Hungary's National Military Strategy* (Budapest: Ministry of Defense, 2012), respectively.

64 Tamás Csiki, "Lessons Learnt and Unlearnt. Hungary's 15 years in NATO," in *Newcomers No More? Contemporary NATO and the Future of the Enlargement from the Perspectives of "Post-Cold War" Members*, eds. Robert Czulda and Marek Madej (Warsaw: International Relations Research Institute, 2015), 68, 64.

65 Szemerkenyi, "Central European Civil-Military Reforms at Risk," 35.

66 Jozsef Paor, "The Resource, Cost and Budget Planning Sub-Systems in the Defense Planning Process," in *Planning, Programming, Budgeting, Evaluation System: Benefits and Challenges*, Workshop unfolded during the postgraduate course in Planning Programming Budgeting System, ed. Maria Constantinescu, Regional Department of Defense Resources Management Studies (Bucharest: National Defense University "Carol I" Publishing House, 2010), 59.

67 Hungary was the principal laggard in mind as argued by Celeste A. Wallander, "NATO's Price: Shape Up or Ship Out," *Foreign Affairs* 81, no. 6 (November–December 2002): 2–8. For further debate on the issue of the state of unpreparedness of new NATO members to meet their obligations, see Barany, *The Future of NATO Expansion*, 26–29.

68 Bulgaria, Council of Ministers, "Programme for the Development of the Defence Capabilities of the Bulgarian Armed Forces 2020," Sofia, approved September 30, 2015, 37.

69 Dimitar Dimitrov, "Military Reform and Budgeting for Defence in Bulgaria (1989–2000)," in *Army and State in Postcommunist Europe*, eds. David Betz and John Löwenhardt (London: Frank Cass, 2001), 126, 128.

70 Larry L. Watts, "Stressed and Strained Civil-Military Relations in Romania, but Successfully Reforming," in *Civil-Military Relations in Europe: Learning from Crisis and Institutional Change*, eds. Hans Born, Marina Caparini, Karl W. Haltiner, and Jürgen Kuhlmann (New York: Routledge, 2006), 26.

71 Oana-Raluca Manole, "PPBES Process Overview: Considerations Regarding Its Implementation and Use," in *Planning, Programming, Budgeting, Evaluation System: Benefits and Challenges*, 36.

72 Szemerkenyi, "Central European Civil-Military Reforms at Risk," 35–36.

73 Ratislav Kacer, MoD state secretary, cited by Marybeth Peterson Ulrich, "Professionalisation of the Slovak Armed Forces," in *The Challenge of Military Reform in Post-Communist Europe: Building Professional Armed Forces*, eds. Anthony Forster et al. (London: Palgrave Macmillan, 2002), 54.

74 Szemerkenyi, "Central European Civil-Military Reforms at Risk," 8.

75 Dunay, "Civil-Military Relations in Hungary," 70.

76 Paul Latawski, "Democratic Control of Armed Forces in Postcommunist Poland: The Interplay of History, Political Society, and Institutional Reform," in *Democratic Control of the Military in Postcommunist Europe*, 30, 30–36, for detailed discussion of how changes to the constitution to clarify these passages were debated.

77 Gogolewska, "Problems Confronting Civilian Democratic Control in Poland," 99–100.

78 Poland, *White Book on National Security*, 47–48, 204, 245.

79 Andrew A. Michta, "Polish Hard Power: Investing in the Military as Europe Cuts Back," in *A Hard Look at Hard Power: Assessing the Defense Capabilities of Key U.S. Allies and Security Partners*, ed. Gary J. Schmitt (Carlisle Barracks, PA: U.S. Army War College Press, July 2015), 154.

80 Szemerkenyi, "Central European Civil-Military Reforms at Risk," 6.

81 For a description of Poland's dualistic governance structure, see Marcin Terlikowski, "Poland," in *Strategic Cultures in Europe: Security and Defence Policies across the Continent, Schriftenreihe des Zentrums für Militärgeschichte und Sozialwissenschaften der Bundeswehr* 13, eds. Heiko Biehl, Bastian Giegerich, and Alexandra Jonas (Wiesbaden: Springer VS, 2013), 276–277.

82 Borissova, "Politicians, Experts and Democracy," 196–197.

83 Republic of Bulgaria, *Defence and Armed Forces Act*, Promulgated SG No. 5/12.05.2009, effective 12.05.2009. Specifically, Article 16.2 vests in the National Assembly the powers of declaring martial law, or an emergency situation, upon a proposal of the president, or the Council of Ministers. Although broad circumstances of the declaration of martial law, or an emergency situation, were established in Articles 20, 109, and 122, the possibility of the president and Council of Ministers

disagreeing over whether the actual situation would require the declaration of martial law or an emergency situation seems not to be addressed.

84   Liubomir K. Topaloff, "Bulgaria," in *Strategic Cultures in Europe*, 50.

85   Tomas Zipfel, "The Politics and Finance of Civil-Military Reform in the Czech Republic," in *Army and State in Postcommunist Europe*, 102.

86   Borissova, "Politicians, Experts and Democracy," 197, 202–204.

87   Michael H. Clemmesen, "Integration of New Alliance Members: The Intellectual-Cultural Dimension," *Defense Analysis* 15, no. 3 (December 1999): 269.

88   Peterson Ulrich, "Professionalisation of the Slovak Armed Forces," 56.

89   Vlachova, "Professionalisation of the Army of the Czech Republic," 46.

90   Supreme Headquarters Allied Powers Europe, *Comprehensive Operations Planning Directive (COPD)*, September 10, 2010, NATO UNLASSIFIED, Releasable to PfP/EU; and, Simon Geza and Muzaffer Duzenli, "The Comprehensive Operations Planning Directive," *NATO Rapid Deployable Corps—Italy*, Issue 14, www.nato.int/nrdc-it/magazine/2009/0914/0914g.pdf. For an excellent historical and analytical treatment of NATO's concept of operational planning procedures, see Anthony King, *The Transformation of Europe's Armed Forces: From the Rhine to Afghanistan* (Cambridge: Cambridge University Press, 2011), 114–118, 141–142.

91   See Maria Wagrowska, "The Polish Soldier between National Traditions and International Projection," in *Democratic Civil-Military Relations: Soldiering in 21st Century Europe* (New York: Routledge, 2012), 196–197.

92   Perry and Keridis, *Defense Reform, Modernization, and Military Cooperation in Southeastern Europe*, 110.

93   Dunay, "Building Professional Competence in Hungary's Defence," 71.

94   See Gregory W. Pedlow, ed., *NATO Strategy Documents, 1949–1969* (Mons: Supreme Headquarters Allied Powers Europe, Historical Division, 1997).

95   Beata Gorka-Winter, "Poland," in *Security Sector Reform in Countries of Visegrad and Southern Caucasus*, 93.

96   Videlicet, Article 1 of Constitution of the Czech Republic; Constitutional Act of Law No. 110/1998 Collection, of April 22, 1998, on Security of the Czech Republic. See http://www.psp.cz/cgi-bin/eng/docs/laws/1998/110.html; http://www.psp.cz/cgi-bin/eng/docs/laws/1993/1.html. Moreover, this interpretation is supported by the constitution and the constitutional act by the Law on the Armed Forces 219/1999 Collection, which in Head III, Paragraph 9, states: "(1) The core function of the armed forces is to prepare for the defense of the Czech Republic against external offences." Note that subsequent policy documents now describe territorial defense within its proper NATO context of collective defense. See Czech Republic, *Defence Strategy of the Czech Republic: A Responsible State and a Reliable Ally* (Prague: Ministry of Defence, 2012), 7 (point 13).

97   This tension between the National Security Bureau and the ministry of defense is explained very well in Paszewski, "Can Poland Defend Itself?," 125–127.

98   Ibid., 121–124.

99   Poland, *Vision of the Armed Forces of the Republic of Poland—2030* (Warsaw: Ministry of Defense, Department of Transformation, May 2008), 14–15.

100   Adam Slodczyk, "Challenges in Logistic Support for Polish Armed Forces," Strategy Research Project, U.S. Army War College, March 10, 2010, 5.

101   For a dated, but informative, review of initial efforts on the part of the Czech Army to initiate elements of Western logistics concepts and organization, see Stéphane

Lefebvre, "The Army of the Czech Republic: A Status Report," *Journal of Slavic Military Studies* 8, no. 4 (1995): 731.

102   Zoltan Szenes, "The Implications of NATO Expansion for Civil-Military Relations in Hungary," in *Army and State in Postcommunist Europe*, 91.

103   Watts, "Stressed and Strained Civil-Military Relations in Romania," 23.

104   Gogolewska, "Problems Confronting Civilian Democratic Control in Poland," 110.

105   Dunay, "Building Professional Competence in Hungary's Defence," 70.

106   See Kieran Williams, "Lustration as the Securitization of Democracy in Czechoslovakia and the Czech Republic," *Journal of Communist Studies and Transition Politics* 19, no 4 (December 2003): 1–24.

107   See Dunay, "Building Professional Competence in Hungary's Defence," 71, Lavinia Stan, "Lustration in Romania: The Story of a Failure," *Studia Politica* 6, no. 1 (2006): 135–156, Szemerkenyi, "Central European Civil-Military Reforms at Risk," 40.

108   Betz, "Civil-Military Relations in the Czech Republic," 49.

109   See Barany, *The Future of NATO Expansion*, 69.

110   Dunay, "Building Professional Competence in Hungary's Defence," 71.

111   Ibid., 4.

112   Peterson Ulrich, "Professionalisation of the Slovak Armed Forces," 56.

113   Vlachova, "Professionalisation of the Army of the Czech Republic," 37–40.

114   Ibid., 40.

115   Perry and Keridis, *Defense Reform, Modernization, and Military Cooperation in Southeastern Europe*, 106. For HRM challenges faced by the defense institution after democratization, see Larry L. Watts, "Democratic Civil Control of the Military in Romania: An Assessment as of October 2001," in *Civil-Military Relations in Post-Cold War Europe*, ed. Graeme P. Herd (Camberley: Conflict Studies Research Centre, 2001), 23–24.

116   For an informative review of the challenges facing Slovak HRM policy and strategy, see Jaroslav Nekoranec and Eva Revayova, "Strategic Management of Human Resource [*sic*] and the Slovak Armed Forces," *Journal of Defense Resources Management* 5, no. 1 (2014): 51–58.

117   Watts, "Democratic Civil Control of the Military in Romania," 14.

118   http://www.airforce-technology.com/news/newsromanian-air-force-selects-lockheed-f-16-fighting-falcon-aircraft-4267921 (accessed July 28, 2016).

119   See Georgi Tzvetkov, "Defense Policy and Reforms in Bulgaria since the End of the Cold War: A Critical Analysis," *Connections: The Quarterly Journal* 13, no. 2 (Spring 2014): 72 (n.22).

120   See Bulgaria, *White Paper*, 16–18, which attempted to lay out a reform program to end these dangerous imbalances.

Chapter 6

1   Note that although Kosovo declared its independence from the Republic of Serbia on February 17, 2008, and indeed, a number of NATO members have recognized its independence (to include the United States), it has not to date created a de jure defense institution. Given this fact, and the modest development of its Ministry of the Security Force—in 2014, it was announced that the ministry would transition to a formal ministry of defense and create its own army (see *Defense*

News, March 6, 2014)—it will not be assessed in this analysis. Moreover, the work will concentrate on the institutional developments in Serbia and Montenegro subsequent to the dissolution of the State Union in 2006. For an excellent analysis of the tortured evolution of the Yugoslav defense institution and JNA (in its various manifestations, i.e., *Vojska Jugoslavije* and *Vojska Srbije i Crne Gore*) from 1990 to 2006, see Timothy Edmunds, *Security Sector Reform in Transforming Societies: Croatia, Serbia, and Montenegro*(Manchester: Manchester University Press, 2007), 83–111, 152–181.

2   Timothy Edmunds, *Security Sector Reform in Transforming Societies: Croatia, Serbia, and Montenegro* (Manchester: Manchester University Press, 2007), 85, 153.

3   Anton Bebler, "Democratic Control of Armed Forces in Slovenia," in *Democratic Control of the Military in Postcommunist Europe: Guarding the Guards*, eds. Andrew Cottey, Timothy Edmunds, and Anthony Forster (London: Palgrave, 2002), 160–161.

4   The JNA began its support for UN peacekeeping operations in the UN Emergency Force in 1956 in the Sinai and ended in 1991 with the deployment of military observers to the UN Iran-Iraq Military Observer Group and UN Angola Verification Mission I. See Serbia, *White Paper on Defence of the Republic of Serbia* (Belgrade: Ministry of Defense, Strategic Planning Department, Defence Policy Sector, 2010), 141–142.

5   John Zametica, "The Yugoslav Conflict," *Adelphi Paper* 270 (London: The International Institute for Strategic Studies, 1992), 40.

6   See Anton Bebler, "'The Yugoslav Crisis and the 'Yugoslav People's Army'", *Zürcher Beiträge zur Sicherheitspolitik und Konfliktforschung*, Heft. nr. 23 (1992): 12–19 for an excellent and revealing discussion of the communist "soul" of the JNA.

7   Miroslav Hadzic, *The Yugoslav People's Army: The Role of the Yugoslav People's Army* (Aldershot: Ashgate Publishing Limited, 2002), 208.

8   "Prior to 1989, Romania's hyper-centralised communist dictatorship was considered the most oppressive in Europe." Larry L. Watts, "Stressed and Strained Civil-Military Relations in Romania, but Successfully Reforming," in *Civil-Military Relations in Europe: Learning from Crisis and Institutional Change*, eds. Hans Born, Marina Caparini, Karl W. Haltiner, and Jürgen Kuhlmann (New York: Routledge, 2006), 21.

9   Robert Dean, "Civil-Military Relations in Yugoslavia, 1971–1975", *Armed Forces and Society* 3, no. 1 (November 1976): 46.

10   Anton Grizold, "Civil-Military Relations in Slovenia," in *Civil-Military Relations in Post-Communist States: Central and Eastern Europe in Transition*, ed. Anton A. Bebler (Westport, CT: Praeger, 1997), 104.

11   Robert Niebuhr, "Death of the Yugoslav People's Army and the Wars of Succession," *Polemos*, Issue 13/14 (January 2004): 98.

12   Grizold, "Civil-Military Relations in Slovenia," 102.

13   See, for example, a description of this still present problem in the case of Slovenia in Anton Alex Bebler, "Civil-Military Relations in Slovenia," in *Civil-Military Relations in the Soviet and Yugoslav Successor States*, eds. Constantine P. Danopoulos and Daniel Zirker (Boulder, CO: Westview Press, 1996), 208–210.

14   For a superb analysis of this conflict and why the JNA performed so badly, see Robert Niebuhr, "War in Slovenia: Doctrine and Defeat," *Journal of Slavic Military Studies* 19, no. 3 (2006): 489–513.

15 "Even in times of the former Yugoslavia, civil society in Slovenia was known for its sensitivity to interference by the armed forces in civil affairs. Equally, it was sensitive to occasional attempts to militarise society." Marjan Malesic, "Executive Decisions and Division: Disputing Competences in Civil-Military Relations in Slovenia," in *Civil-Military Relations in Europe: Learning from Crisis and Institutional Change*, eds. Hans Born, Marina Caparini, Karl W. Haltiner, and Jürgen Kuhlmann (New York: Routledge, 2006), 130.

16 Bebler, "Democratic Control of Armed Forces in Slovenia," 167.

17 Resolution 713 (1991) Adopted by Security Council at its 3009th meeting, September 25, 1991, in Snezana Trifunovska, ed., *Yugoslavia through Documents: From ts Creation to its Dissolution* (Dordrecht: Martinus Nijhoff Publishers, 1994), 349–350. Note that the arms embargo was only lifted on October 1, 1996, well after the signing of the Dayton Peace Accords which were effected via UN Security Council Resolution 1021, November 22, 1995, http://www.un.org/press/en/1996/19961001. sc6274.html (accessed December 11, 2016).

18 Charles M. Perry and Dimitris Keridis, *Defense Reform, Modernization, and Military Cooperation in Southeastern Europe* (Herndon, VA, Brassey's Inc., 2004), 9.

19 Osterman cites that from 1997 until 2014, some 4,700 personnel served on deployments, some of which have been demanding operations, i.e., Iraq and Afghanistan. For perspective, the size of the Slovenian armed forces in October 2014 was 7,214 personnel. See Andrej Osterman, "Republic of Slovenia in NATO: Slovenian Armed Forces Ten Years Later," *Contemporary Military Challenges* 16, no. 3 (October 2014): 49–51.

20 In spring 1990, the JNA secretariat transferred heavy weapons from the Territorial Defense Force to JNA control. Edmunds, *Security Sector Reform in Transforming Societies*, 124.

21 Zlatko Isakovic and Constantine P. Danopoulos, "In Search of Identity: Civil-Military Relations and Nationhood in the Former Yugoslav Republic of Macedonia (FYROM)," in *Civil-Military Relations in the Soviet and Yugoslav Successor States*, 180–181.

22 Perry and Keridis, *Defense Reform, Modernization, and Military Cooperation in Southeastern Europe*, 203.

23 "Bosnia and Herzegovina emerged from a four-year war as a destroyed and poor country. The war damage is estimated to amount to over 200 billion US dollars." See Bisera Turković, "Civil-Military Relations in Bosnia and Herzegovina," in *The Evolution of Civil-Military Relations in South East Europe: Continuing Democratic Reform and Adapting to the Needs of Fighting Terrorism*, eds. Philipp H. Fluri et al. (Heidelberg: Physica-Verlag, 2005), 81.

24 For a comprehensive treatment of the Defence Reform Commission, see Rohan Maxwell and John Andreas Olsen, "Destination NATO: Defence Reform in Bosnia and Herzegovina, 2003–13," *Whitehall Papers* 80 (London: Royal United Services Institute, 2013), 29–88.

25 Vanja Rokvic, Zoran Jeftic, and Zeljko Ivanis, "Civil-Military Relations and Democratic Control over the Armed Forces in the Republic of Serbia," *Armed Forces and Society* 38, no. 4 (2012): 680.

26 Jim Seroka, "Serbian National Security and Defense Strategy: Forever Wandering in the Wilderness?" *Journal of Slavic Military Studies* 23, no. 3 (September 2010): 442.

27 Perry and Keridis, *Defense Reform, Modernization, and Military Cooperation in Southeastern Europe*, 258.

28 That said, there are a number of important *lacunae* in current policies; for example, the precise nature of the armed force's responsibilities in support of civil authorities, the employment of the armed forces in support of domestic counterterrorism operations, or conducting combat operations abroad. See Branimir Furlan, "Civilian Control and Military Effectiveness: Slovenian Case," *Armed Forces and Society* 39, no. 3 (2012): 440.

29 Islam Yusufi, "Macedonia," in *Security Policies in the Western Balkans*, eds. Miroslav Hadžić, Milorad Timotić, and Predrag Petrović (Belgrade: Center for Civil-Military Relations, 2010), 98, 114. Specifically, the Defense Strategy and the White Paper on Defense.

30 See Furlan, "Civilian Control and Military Effectiveness," 444–445.

31 Igor Kotnik, "Professionalization of the Slovenian Armed Forces—A Goal or a Path?," *Contemporary Military Challenges* 17, no. 4 (December 2015): 13.

32 For an excellent treatment of this subject in Serbia, see Edmunds, *Security Sector Reform in Transforming Societies*, 102–106.

33 The rebirth of the Serbia defense institution was hardly a quick and easy passage. The plebiscite by Montenegro to dissolve the State Union in June 2006 hit the Federal Ministry of Defense hard as it was one of the few truly federal ministries. In consequence, upon the dissolution of the State Union, the Serbian defense institution was in a prolonged state of *jus nullius*, during a critical period when a policy framework should have been taking hold.

34 Svetlana Djurdjevic-Lukic, "Defence Reform in Serbia/Serbia and Montenegro: Hampering Exceptionalism," in *Security Sector Reform in the New Partnership for Peace Members: Bosnia-Herzegovina, Montenegro, Serbia*, eds. Philipp H. Fluri and George Katsirdakis (Geneva: The Geneva Centre for the Democratic Control of Armed Forces, 2007), 130 (n.15).

35 See Republic of Serbia, "Defence Reform—Current Results," Bucharest, Southeast Europe Clearinghouse meeting, December 2006, 1.

36 To the credit of the Federal Republic of Yugoslavia's Ministry of Defense, at least the function and purpose of ministerial guidance were defined in an open-source document. "Ministerial Guidance defines objectives, tasks and priorities in planning and provides guidelines for organisational changes, personnel project, development, modernisation and equipment of the SMAF as well as financing of the defence [*sic*] in 2006." See Serbia and Montenegro, *Ministerial Guidance for the Year 2006* (Belgrade: Federal Ministry of Defense, Sector for Defense Policy, 2006), 5.

37 See LTC Katarina Štrbac, Ministry of Defense, Department of Strategic Planning, "Ministerial Guidance 2007," Belgrade, briefing, c. March 2007.

38 It needs to be stated, equally, that while the development of a policy framework has presented challenges to the Serbian defense institution, it has been able to produce insightful and remarkably candid self-assessments which rival, or exceed, similar efforts in NATO countries. Specifically, the 2006 SDR observed the following regarding the ministry of defense:

- too many organisational units at the Ministry of Defence;
- relatively huge size of the MOD and its subordinated establishments;
- organisation of the military health service, logistic and education is not adequate for needs of the system and does not [have] enough of the state's resources [*sic*];
- a number of military institutions, which are being funded from the budget, should earn their income and distribute it by themselves;

- insufficient usability of the IT to accelerate and increase the quality of work, and
- unfavourable personnel structure.

Serbia, *Strategic Defense Review: Final* (Belgrade: Ministry of Defense, July 2006), III–8.

39 For an excellent discussion on the development of policy framework in Croatia, see Edmunds, *Security Sector Reform in Transforming Societies*, 67–70.

40 Timothy Edmunds, "Defence Reform in Croatia and Serbia-Montenegro," *Adelphi Paper* 360 (London: The International Institute for Strategic Studies, 2003), 9. Note absolute numbers were relatively high. A Croatian defense official stated to the author that approximately 1,500 JNA officers transferred to the incipient Croatian armed forces. Ethnic representation in the JNA's officer corps in both numbers and percentage of population can be found from official declassified sources. Bebler, "The Yugoslav Crisis and the 'Yugoslav People's Army'," 14–17.

41 Edmunds, *Security Sector Reform in Transforming Societies*, 56.

42 James Horncastle, "Croatia's Bitter Harvest: Total National Defence's Role in the Croatian War of Independence," *Small Wars and Insurgencies* 26, no. 5 (2015): 751–752.

43 Zvonimir Mahecic, "Croatia," in *Security Policies in the Western Balkans*, 61.

44 For a superb précis of the challenges of defense reform in Croatia during this era, see Alex J. Bellamy and Timothy Edmunds, "Civil-Military Relations in Croatia: Politicization and Politics of Reform," *European Security* 14, no. 1 (March 2005): 71–93.

45 Mladen Staničić, *The Evolution of Civil-Military Relations in South East Europe: Continuing Democratic Reform and Adapting to the Needs of Fighting Terrorism*, eds. Philipp H. Fluri et al. (Heidelberg: Physica-Verlag, 2005), 130.

46 Edmunds, *Security Sector Reform in Transforming Societies*, 134–135.

47 Mahecic, "Croatia," in *Security Policies in the Western Balkans*, 64.

48 Milan Jazbec, "Defence Reform in the Western Balkans: The Way Ahead," *Policy Paper* (Geneva: General Centre for the Democratic Control of Armed Forces, April 2005), 10–11. Scott Vesel seconded the need for this important reform in "Croatia: Analysis of the Stability Pact Self-Assessment Studies," in *Defence and Security Sector Governance and Reform in South East Europe*, eds. Eden Cole, Timothy Donais, and Philipp H. Fluri (Baden-Baden: Nomos, 2004), 57.

49 See the organizational chart of the general staff in Serbia, *White Paper on Defence of the Republic of Serbia*, 47.

50 See, for example, the organizational chart of the Montenegrin Ministry of Defense at http://www.odbrana.gov.me/en/organisation (accessed May 22, 2016).

51 While the title *collegium* is eschewed, there is the practice of using boards or committees, some of which, as it was related to this author, function as *collegia* in all but name.

52 A perhaps intriguing point of enquiry might be to assess the Macedonian case to ascertain how well these directors of staff are functioning and whether there remains a need for *collegia*, or are they anachronistic? One suspects that the answer would depend on whether these directors have full power similar to their counterparts in NATO nations' defense institutions.

53 See Zoltan D. Barany, *The Future of NATO Expansion: Four Case Studies* (Cambridge: Cambridge University Press, 2003), 110–111.

54 Republic of Serbia, *Strategic Defense Review*, 2006, IV–6.

55 See Serbia and Montenegro, *White Paper on Defense of the State Union of Serbia and Montenegro* (Belgrade: Ministry of Defence, Sector for Defence Policy, 2005), point 5.2.2.

56 Republic of Montenegro, *Strategic Defense Review 2010* (Podgorica: Ministry of Defense, June 2010), 25–26.

57 As one of the provisions with the 2013 SDR. See Republic of Montenegro, *Strategic Defense Review 2013* (Podgorica: Ministry of Defense, July 2013), 45–46.

58 Edmunds, "Defence Reform in Croatia and Serbia-Montenegro," 16.

59 Alex J. Bellamy and Timothy Edmunds, "'Civil-military Relations in Croatia: Politicisation and Politics of Reform'", in *Civil-Military Relations in Post-Communist Europe: Reviewing the Transition*, eds. Timothy Edmunds, Andrew Cottey, and Anthony Forster (London: Rutledge, 2006), 80.

60 Croatia, *Strategic Defence Review* (Zagreb: Ministry of Defence, 2005), 38.

61 Vlada Republike Hrvatske, *Strateški pregled odbrane* (No. 73/2013), July 25, 2013, 19.

62 See H. Vetschera and M. Damian, "Security Sector Reform in Bosnia and Herzegovina: The Role of the International Community," *International Peacekeeping* 13, no. 1 (2006): 40.

63 See Turković, "Civil-Military Relations in Bosnia and Herzegovina," 89.

64 Transition Management Group, *Defence Reform in BiH—An Executive Overview*, Sarajevo, NATO HQ Sarajevo, June 26, 2007.

65 "Decision Establishing the Defence Reform Commission," Sarajevo, Office of the High Representative, May 9, 2003.

66 Defense Reform Commission, *AFHIM: A Single Military Force for the 21st Century*, Sarajevo, September 2005.

67 Private Office of the Secretary General, "Presentation Document of Bosnia and Herzegovina," SG(2007)0045, January 22, 2007, NATO UNCLASSIFIED, annex, 6.

68 Vetschera and Damian, "Security Sector Reform in Bosnia and Herzegovina," 33–35.

69 To wit, Security Policy was adopted in February 2006, but it was preceded by Defense Policy in May 2001; while a Military Strategy was published in May 2009, a Military Doctrine was released in November 2003, and a Defense White Paper was published in June 2005. This is yet another clear example of conceptual incoherence caused when importing exogenous "models." See the chart and subsequent discussion in Kenan Dautovic, "Bosnia and Herzegovina," in *Security Policies in the Western Balkans*, 36–37.

70 Gülnur Aybet, "NATO Conditionality in Bosnia and Herzegovina: Defense Reform and State Building," *Problems of Post-Communism* 57, no. 5 (September–October 2010): 26–32.

71 Hrvatske, *Strateški pregled odbrane*, 14.

72 The author had the benefit of a tour of the *Triglav 11* in Luka Bar, Montenegro, in June 2011 shortly after its commissioning. Although hardly a blue-water warship, it was assessed by a retired RCN captain as possessing modern sensors, light weapons, superb (largely German) machinery and electrical systems, and frankly a professional crew—clearly, the result of careful and insightful planning, program management, and leadership.

73 See Furlan, "Civilian Control and Military Effectiveness," 442.

74 Slovenia, *Defence Sector Strategic Review 2009 (DSSR): Summary of Key DSSR 2009 Conclusions*, No. 800-1/2009-189 (Ljubljana: Ministry of Defence, October 14, 2009), 42.

75   Viktor Potocnik, "Slovenian Armed Forces Size and Character," *Contemporary Military Challenges* 17, no. 4 (December 2015): 32.

76   See, *Defence White Paper of Bosnia and Herzegovina* (Sarajevo: Ministry of Defense, June 2005), 24.

77   Amadeo Watkins, *Security Sector Reform and Donor Assistance in Serbia: Complexity of Managing Change* (Shrivenham, Defense Academy of the United Kingdom, September 2010), 9.

78   Islam Yusufi, "Republic of Macedonia: Defence Sector Assessment," in *Security Sector Governance in the Western Balkans: Self-Assessment Studies on Defence, Intelligence, Police and Border Management Reform*, eds. Anja H. Ebnöther, Philipp H. Fluri, and Predrag Jurekovic (Geneva: Geneva Centre for the Democratic Control of Armed Forces, 2007), 149.

79   Robert M. McNab, "Implementing Program Budgeting in the Serbian Ministry of Defense," *Public Budgeting and Finance* 31, no. 2 (Summer 2011): 217, 221.

80   "[W]hile applying scarce defence resources in an efficient and cost effective manner to address those military tasks most critical to the security of the State." See *Defence White Paper of Bosnia and Herzegovina*, 25.

81   Macedonia, *White Paper on Defence* (Skopje: Ministry of Defense, December 2012), 30–31.

82   Political-Military Steering Committee on Partnership for Peace, "Report of the Seventh Meeting of the Defence Review Group, Belgrade," PFP/SC-N(2006)0072, December 20, 2006, annex 1, 1–3.

83   *Croatian Armed Forces Long-Term Development Plan 2006–2015*, Zagreb, June 2006; adopted in the Croatian Parliament on July 7, 2006, published in the Official Gazette, No. 81 of July 19, 2006.

84   Bellamy and Edmunds, "Civil-Military Relations in Croatia," 73.

85   Hrvatske, *Strateški pregled odbrane*, 13.

86   See Barany, *The Future of NATO Expansion*, 110.

87   Bebler, "Civil-Military Relations in Slovenia," 201.

88   See Furlan, "Civilian Control and Military Effectiveness," 442.

89   Edmunds, "Defence Reform in Croatia and Serbia-Montenegro," 16.

90   Edmunds, *Security Sector Reform in Transforming Societies*, 59.

91   Andreja Bogdanovski, "Macedonia," in *Almanac on Security Sector Oversight in the Western Balkans: 2012*, eds. Franziska Klopfer and Douglas Cantwell with Miroslav Hadžić and Sonja Stojanović (Belgrade/Geneva: Belgrade Center for Security Policy and Geneva Centre for the Democratic Control of Armed Forces, 2012), 133, 135–136.

92   For a rather comprehensive list of "documents" which must be approved by the president, see Macedonia, *White Paper on Defence*, 24–25.

93   Bellamy and Edmunds, "Civil-Military Relations in Croatia: Politicisation and Politics of Reform," 77.

94   Edmunds, *Security Sector Reform in Transforming Societies*, 55–56.

95   Bellamy and Edmunds, "Civil-Military Relations in Croatia," 77.

96   Edmunds, "Defence Reform in Croatia and Serbia-Montenegro," 17.

97   Vesel, "Croatia: Analysis of the Stability Pact Self-Assessment Studies," 56–57.

98   "The main problem of the executive is opaque jurisdiction between the Office of the President and the Government, i.e., the Prime Minister." Staničić, "The Evolution of Civil-Military Relations in South East Europe: The Case of Croatia," 119. See also Republic of Croatia, "Annual Exchange on Defense Planning 2007," according to Vienna Document of 1999; § 15.2.1, 14.

99   Serbia, *Law on the Serbian Armed Forces*, 116/2007, October 30, 2007, cf., Articles 17, 18, and 19.

100 Filip Ejdus, "State Building and Image of the Democratic Soldier in Serbia," in *Democratic Civil-Military Relations: Soldiering in 21st Century Europe*, ed. Sabine Mannitz (New York: Routledge, 2012), 227–228.

101 See Vetschera and Damian, "Security Sector Reform in Bosnia and Herzegovina," 34.

102 Ibid., 28.

103 Niebuhr, "Death of the Yugoslav People's Army and the Wars of Succession," 93.

104 For a description of MPRI's activities in Croatia, see Edmunds, *Security Sector Reform in Transforming Societies*, 191–193.

105 The total size of the entire armed forces is, as of 2015, 2080 personnel, divided among the army, navy, and air force. See *The Military Balance 2015* (London: The International Institute for Strategic Studies, February 2015), 117.

106 Montenegro, *Strategic Defense Review 2013*, 13 (point 4.1.1).

107 The CHOD during this period, LTG Zdravko Ponos (2006–2008), was remarkably Western-oriented and made many valiant attempts to drive the Serbian armed forces beyond its comfortable legacy practices and assumptions and adopt Western concepts. He left office before he was able to realize these ambitious objectives. See *New York Times*, October 20, 2008, Seroka, "Serbian National Security and Defense Strategy," 448–450.

108 Notwithstanding the claims by the ministry of defense of this reform, specifics were not forthcoming. Republic of Serbia, "Defence Reform," Southeast Europe Clearinghouse meeting, n.d., 3.

109 Interview with Land Force Commander, Lieutenant-General Ljulsa Dikovic in "Change of Pace, Country Briefing: Serbia," *Janes Defence Weekly*, September 7, 2011, 26.

110 Law on National Defense, Article 14.3; Law of Serbian Armed Forces, Article 19.3.

111 See Charles R. Shrader, *The Muslim-Croat Civil War in Central Bosnia: A Military History, 1992–1994* (College Station: Texas A&M University Press, 2003), 17–18.

112 "The existing armed forces structure [of Croatia] has been oriented towards developing and maintaining territorial-based self-defense capabilities." Croatia, *Strategic Defence Review* (Zagreb: Ministry of Defense, November 10, 2005), 15.

113 Ibid., 15, 17.

114 Hrvatske, *Strateški pregled odbrane 2013*, 30.

115 See interview with former Serbian Minister of Defense Dragan Šutanovac, who discusses these challenges in "Change of Pace, Country Briefing: Serbia," 34.

116 Edmunds, *Security Sector Reform in Transforming Societies*, 85.

117 Slovenia, *Defence Sector Strategic Review 2009 (DSSR)*, 11–15.

118 Slovenia, Ministry of Defense, "Resolution on General Long-Term Development and Equipping Programme of the Slovenian Armed Forces up to 2025," *Official Gazette of the Republic of Slovenia* no. 99/2010 (Ljubljana, December 7, 2010): 24.

119 Slovenia, *Annual Report of the Ministry of Defence for 2013*, No. 0100-127/2013-34 (Ljubljana: Ministry of Defense, May 27, 2014), 89.

120 Slovenia, *Defence Sector Strategic Review 2009 (DSSR)*, 11.

121 Edmunds, *Security Sector Reform in Transforming Societies*, 173.

122 See, for example, the excellent recounting of the challenges faced by the US Army when it adopted a profession force following the Vietnam War in James Kitfield,

Prodigal Soldiers: How the Generation of Officers Born of Vietnam Revolutionized the American Style of War (New York: Simon & Schuster, 1995).

123 Tobias Pietz, "Demobilizing and Retraining for the Future: The Armed Forces in Serbia and Montenegro," *Brief 31* (Bonn: International Center for Conversion, July 2005), 4.

124 Government of Macedonia, "Annual National Programme of the Republic of Macedonia for NATO Membership 2006/2007," Skopje, 2006, §413.

125 Bellamy and Edmunds, "Civil-Military Relations in Croatia," 86.

126 For a general discussion on HRM in this document, see 37–40.

127 Edmunds, "Defence Reform in Croatia and Serbia-Montenegro," 40. One suspects that an analysis of similar data for the other five countries would show similar worrying trends.

128 Edmunds, "Defence Reform in Croatia and Serbia-Montenegro," 9.

129 See Croatia, *Strategic Defence Review,* 2005, 33.

130 Edmunds, *Security Sector Reform in Transforming Societies,* 70.

131 See Furlan, "Civilian Control and Military Effectiveness," 441.

132 Neil Grayston, "Democratic Control of the Armed Forces of Slovenia: A Progress Report," in *Civil-Military Relations in Post-Cold War Europe,* ed. Graeme P. Herd (Camberley: Conflict Studies Research Centre, 2001), 9.

133 *Defence White Paper of Bosnia and Herzegovina,* 28.

134 For a superb recounting of the challenges of personnel management with the merging of the three Entity armed forces, see Maxwell and Olsen, "Destination NATO," 57–63.

135 Kotnik, "Professionalization of the Slovenian Armed Forces," 15.

136 Ljubica Jelusic, "Continuity, Restructuring, or Development from Scratch? Dilemmas of Slovenian Defense Reform, 1991–2001," in *Post-Cold War Defense Reform: Lessons Learned in Europe and the United* States, eds. Istvan Gyarmati and Theodor Winkler (Washington, DC: Brassey's, Inc., 2002), 128. Note that Dr. Jelusic was minister of defense from 2008 to 2011.

Chapter 7

1 Anthony Cottey, Timothy Edmunds, and Anthony Forster, "The Second Generation Problematic: Rethinking Democracy and Civil-Military Relations," *Armed Forces and Society* 29, no. 1 (Fall 2002): 31–56.

2 Alex J. Bellamy and Timothy Edmunds, "Civil-Military Relations in Croatia: Politicisation and Politics of Reform" in *Civil-Military Relations in Post-Communist Europe: Reviewing the Transition,* eds. Timothy Edmunds, Andrew Cottey, and Anthony Forster (London: Routledge, 2006), 89.

3 Jeffrey Simon, *NATO and the Czech and Slovak Republics: Comparative Study in Civil-Military Relations* (Lanham: Rowman and Littlefield, 2004), 7.

4 Bengt Abrahamsson, *Military Professionalization and Political Power* (Beverly Hills: Sage Publications, 1972), 151–163.

5 David M. Glantz, "Military Training and Education Challenges in Poland, the Czech Republic, and Hungary," *Journal of Slavic Military Studies* 11, no. 3 (1998): 4. Italics in the original.

6 Christopher Donnelly, *Red Banner: The Soviet Military System in Peace and War* (Coulsdon, Surrey: Jane's Information Group, 1988), 135–137.

7   For example, see Thomas S. Szayna, "Slovak Civil-Military Relations: A Balance Sheet after Nine Years of Independence," in *Civil-Military Relations in Post-Cold War Europe*, ed. Graeme P. Herd (Camberley: Conflict Studies Research Centre, 2001), 46.

8   The claim that in 1998 the Bulgarian Ministry of Defense established a functioning defense planning directorate is problematic and is an example of the lack of understanding and appreciation of the challenge faced by legacy ministries of defense to seize and effectively control the defense budget in accordance with policy. See Piotr Dutkiewicz and Plamen Pantev, "Postcommunist Civil-Military Relations in Bulgaria," in *The Evolution of Civil-Military Relations in East-Central Europe and the Former Soviet Union*, eds. Natalie Mychajlyszyn and Harald von Riekhoff (Westport, CT: Praeger, 2004), 148–149.

9   For example, "For the period following 2018 and up until 2024, we envisage a gradual increase of [*sic*] the defense spending, depending on the growth of the economic capacity of our country, in accordance with the decisions made at the NATO Summit in Wales (2014)." Bulgaria, Council of Ministers, "Programme for the Development of the Defence Capabilities of the Bulgarian Armed Forces 2020," Sofia, approved September 30, 2015, 32.

10   See the discussion on the weaknesses of the Georgian Law on Defense Planning, No. 4130, April 28, 2006, in Teona Akubardia, "Overview of the Legislation Facilitating the Civil Democratic Oversight of Armed Forces in Georgia," in *Democratic Control over the Georgian Armed Forces since the August 2008 War*, ed. Tamara Pataraia (Geneva: Geneva Centre for the Democratic Control of Armed Forces, 2010), 26–27.

11   Reka Szemerkenyi, "Central European Civil-Military Reforms at Risk," *Adelphi Paper* 306 (London: The International Institute for Strategic Studies, 1996), 17.

12   David Darchiashvili, *Security Sector Reform in Georgia, 2004–2007* (Tbilisi: Caucasus Institute for Peace, Democracy, and Development, 2008), 61.

13   See Ariel Cohen and Robert Hamilton, *The Russian Military and the Georgian War: Lessons and Implications* (Carlisle Barracks, PA: Strategic Studies Institute, June 2011).

14   Timothy Phillips, *Beslan: The Tragedy of School No.1* (London: Granta, 2008).

15   Rudolf Joo, "The Democratic Control of Armed Forces," *Chaillot Papers* 23 (Paris: Institute for Security Studies, February 1996), 15.

16   Paul Latawski, "Professionalisation of the Polish Armed Forces: 'No Room for Amateurs and Undereducated Soldiers'," in *The Challenge of Military Reform in Post-Communist Europe: Building Professional Armed Forces*, eds. Anthony Forster et al. (London: Palgrave Macmillan, 2002), 24.

17   Jan Arveds Trapans, "Professionalisation of the Armed Forces in Central and Eastern Europe: The Case of Latvia," in *The Challenge of Military Reform in Post-Communist Europe*, 92.

18   "To copy one of the old members [of NATO] (or even worse, the lowest common denominator) is not likely to bring enough momentum for the reforms to succeed. Copying is likely only to produce superficial and anachronistic copies that mirror any weakness of the original. It is therefore absolutely necessary that supporting states stop advising new states to copy their system." Michael H. Clemmesen, "Integration of New Alliance Members: The Intellectual-Cultural Dimension," *Defense Analysis* 15, no. 3 (December 1999): 263.

19   See the recommendations from the US Kievenaar report on the Lithuanian armed forces that were offered obviously without consideration of their financial costs

in Harald von Riekhoff, "Civil-Military Relations in the Baltic Republics," in *The Evolution of Civil-Military Relations in East-Central Europe and the Former Soviet Union*, 119.

20 Ionel Nicu Sava, "Civil-Military Relations, Western Assistance and Democracy in South East Europe," G-125 (Sandhurst: Conflict Studies and Research Centre, August 2003), 17.

21 Bellamy and Edmunds, "Civil-Military Relations in Croatia," 80.

22 Timothy Edmunds, "Security Sector Reform: Concepts and Implementation," in *Towards Security Sector Reform in Post Cold War Europe: A Framework for Assessment*, eds. Wilhelm N. Germann and Timothy Edmunds (Baden-Baden: Nomos Verlagsgesellschaft, 2003), 25.

23 Koenraad Van Brabant, "Value-for-Money? The Overall Record of Technical Assistance for Institutional and Governance Reform," International Peacebuilding Advisory Team, Effective Advising in Complex and Fragile Situations, *Working Paper 1* (Geneva, n.d.), 9.

24 For instance, Croatia was the early recipient of such expertise in the form of the Office of the Secretary of Defense's Kievenaar report, which formulaically advocated the adoption of, *inter alia*, a National Security Strategy and National Military Strategy. See Charles M. Perry and Dimitris Keridis, *Defense Reform, Modernization, and Military Cooperation in Southeastern Europe* (Herndon, VA: Brassey's Inc., 2004), 193.

25 To wit: "The development of a National Security Strategy and National Military Strategy, using a transparent inter-ministerial approach compatible with other Euro-Atlantic defense establishments, will serve as the foundation for subsequent defense reforms. Therefore, the development of these national security documents should be the first modernization initiative undertaken by the Moldovan Government." See "The Republic of Moldova Defense Assessment," prepared by the Office of the Assistant Secretary of Defense for International Security Affairs and the United States European Command, October 8, 2004, 154–155. One can find the same message (essentially all but verbatim) in, for instance, the report provided to the Slovak Republic. See Simon, *NATO and the Czech and Slovak Republics*, 208.

26 *U.S. Code, Title 50*, Chapter 44, § 3043, Annual National Security Report.

27 Robert M. Gates, *Duty: Memoirs of a Secretary at War* (New York: Alfred A. Knopf, 2014), 144.

28 The process employed was so exogenous to Czech governance that when there was an attempt to coordinate two documents with other ministries, "Eventually everyone just got tired and bored with it." David J. Betz, "Civil-Military Relations in the Czech Republic: Ambivalent Reformers, Immature Structures," in *The Evolution of Civil-Military Relations in East-Central Europe and the Former Soviet Union*, 51–52.

29 Georgia, *National Military Strategy 2005* (Tbilisi: Ministry of Defense, 2005), 8. Note that this objective remains in current policy. See Georgia, *Minister's Vision 2013–2014* (Tbilisi: Ministry of Defense, 2013), 3.

30 Theona Akubardia, "Security and Defence Policy Development," in *Democratic Control over the Georgian Armed Forces since the August 2008 War*, ed. Tamara Pataraia (Geneva: Geneva Centre for the Democratic Control of Armed Forces, 2010), 12.

31 See C. Vance Gordon and Wade Hinkle, *Best Practices in Defense Resource Management*. IDA Document D-4137 (Washington, DC: Institute for Defense Analysis, January 2011), B-1 thru B-5.

258   *Notes*

32   Jerry McCaffery and L. R. Jones, *Budgeting and Financial Management in the Federal Government* (Charlotte, NC: Information Age Publishing, 2001), 258–259.

33   "As a starting point, no real progress toward savings will be possible without reforming our budgeting practices and assumptions." Eisenhower Library (Defense Spending), Remarks as Delivered by Secretary of Defense Robert M. Gates, Abilene, KS, Saturday, May 8, 2010.

34   It is unfortunate to learn that the US Department of Defense is assisting the Afghan government to develop a PPBS for its ministry of defense. Clearly, a better case of providing a country with an atomic clock when a semireliable Timex would certainly be more than sufficient would be difficult to find. It is disheartening to read of the challenges facing the ministry of defense and its American advisors as they could have profited from greater experience gained from Central and Eastern Europe as the challenges they face are generally the same that still plague defense institution throughout the region. See US Department of Defense, "Report on Progress toward Security and Stability in Afghanistan," Report to Congress in accordance with sections 1230 and 1231 of the National Defense Authorization Act (NDAA) for Fiscal Year 2008 (P.L. 110–181), as amended, to include reports in response to section 1221 of the NDAA for Fiscal Year 2012 (P.L. 112–81), and sections 1212, 1223, and 1531(d) of the NDAA for Fiscal Year 2013 (P.L. 112–239), Washington, November 2013, 36–38.

35   This work is not the place to argue against this methodology at great length. However, what is surprising is that NATO nations' officials and even the International Staff have encouraged the adoption of this methodology by reforming countries, absent any understanding or knowledge of its effectiveness. One of the most influential writers on strategic planning, admittedly from a business perspective (which in the case of PPBS only recommends more his relevance), Mintzberg, writes that the development and implementation of PPBS constitutes one of the greatest efforts and failure of all time in the area of public finance. Henry Mintzberg, *The Rise and Fall of Strategic Planning: Reconceiving Roles for Planning, Plans, Planners* (New York: Free Press, 1994), 19. A leading expert on public finance at the time of the development of PPBS for the US Department of Defense, Aaron Wildavsky, writes that "PPBS has failed everywhere and at all times." See *The Politics of the Budgetary Process* (New York: Little, Brown, 1984), 121. He continues, "Nowhere has PPBS (1) been established (2) influenced government decisions (3) according to its own principles. The program structures do not make sense to anyone. They are not, in fact, used to make decisions of any importance."

36   As one respected US defense analyst put it: "PPBS is inappropriate for these countries, in part, because it 'helps' them solve problems that do not exist in their system and never will."

37   Georgia presents an excellent example of this disconnect. See Akubardia, "Overview of the Legislation Facilitating the Civil Democratic Oversight of Armed Forces in Georgia," 31–32.

38   Robert M. McNab, "Implementing Program Budgeting in the Serbian Ministry of Defense," *Public Budgeting and Finance* 31, no. 2 (Summer 2011): 225. More specifically, the Serbian programming structure matches the defense institution's structures: army, air force and air defense, training command, central administration, and the general staff.

39   In spring 2011, the Bulgarian minister of defense announced that the Bulgarian Navy would support operations in Libya using its "high readiness" frigate. Due

to the centralization of funding, it took the navy two weeks to deploy the vessel, yet another example of the disconnect between policy and defense outcomes with the usual bottleneck being the PPBS system. See *Dnevnik* (Sofia), March 29, 2011.

40 In the case of Bulgaria:

> In 2000, the MoD introduced a new resource management system under which it must submit a draft budget to the Ministry of Finance to be incorporated into the government budget approved by the National Assembly. *Fully compatible with NATO-standard planning procedures, the system manages a six-year cycle of planning, programming, and budgeting with an annual review in mid cycle.* (emphasis added)

Perry and Keridis, *Defense Reform*, 53–54.

41 Maria Vlachova and Stefan Sarvas, "Democratic Control of Armed Forces in the Czech Republic: A Journey from Social Isolationism," in *Democratic Control of the Military in Postcommunist Europe: Guarding the Guards*, eds. Andrew Cottey, Timothy Edmunds, and Anthony Forster (London: Palgrave, 2002), 55:

> In 1993, the Czech Republic became the first Central and Eastern European country to introduce the American-designed system of management of public funds that is used worldwide in various areas of the public sector. Although the country gained a system designed to provide both efficiency and transparency in the allocation of funds, problems in the management and control of military spending continue to exist.

42 In practically all defense institutions in Central and Eastern Europe in which this author has conducted assessments and provided advice, those with dominant PPBS methods had underperforming cost models.

43 For example, apropos the Canadian experience see R. V. Segsworth, "P.P.B.S. and Policy Analysis: The Canadian Experience," *International Review of Administrative Sciences* 38, no. 4 (December 1972): 419–425.

44 See Frank Boland, "Capability Development," briefing (Brussels: Defense Policy and Planning Division, NATO International Staff, January 27, 2014).

45 Specifically, Slovenia, Ministry of Defense, "Resolution on General Long-Term Development and Equipping Programme of the Slovenian Armed Forces up to 2025," *Official Gazette of the Republic of Slovenia* no. 99/2010 (Ljubljana, December 7, 2010).

46 Serbia, *White Paper on Defence of the Republic of Serbia* (Belgrade: Ministry of Defense, Strategic Planning Department, Defence Policy Sector, 2010), 128–129.

47 For example, see information on Exercise LOGEX 2013 at http://www.nspa.nato.int/en/news/news-20130214.htm

48 *The New York Times*, June 4, 2016.

49 See MPRI, "NCO Professional Development Program; Ukrainian Armed Forces: Final Program Brief," Kyiv, July 2009.

50 One finds this interpretation even in the literature. To wit: "The absence of NCOs continues to be a major weakness in command and control structures." Marybeth Peterson Ulrich, "Professionalisation of the Slovak Armed Forces," in *The Challenge of Military Reform in Post-Communist Europe*, 56.

51 To their credit, Russian defense officials reduced their PME structure from sixty-five military higher education institutions to ten in 2008, augmented by a renovated

training system. Its results can be easily seen in Crimea and Eastern Ukraine from 2014 onwards. See Andrei Makarychev and Alexander Sergunin, "Russian Military Reform: Institutional, Political, and Security Implications," *Defense and Security Analysis* 29, no. 4 (December 2013): 359.

52   Albeit somewhat dated, Edmunds's 2007 accurate description of the unreformed and expansive Serbian Military Academy (not to mention the National Defense Academy) in the Topcider quartier of Belgrade was validated by this author as late as in March 2014. See Timothy Edmunds, *Security Sector Reform in Transforming Societies: Croatia, Serbia, and Montenegro* (Manchester: Manchester University Press, 2007), 175.

53   James Sherr, "Civil-Democratic Control of Ukraine's Armed Forces: To What End? By What Means?" in *Army and State in Postcommunist Europe*, eds. David Betz and John Löwenhardt (London: Frank Cass, 2001), 74.

54   See Zoltan D. Barany, *The Future of NATO Expansion: Four Case Studies* (Cambridge: Cambridge University Press, 2003), 81–82, 166–167. It should be noted that in both cases, there was a British/Dutch staff training program in the Slovak Defense College and a Romanian-British Regional Training Center located in Bucharest. Both conducted Western-oriented staff courses.

55   Poland, *White Book on National Security of the Republic of Poland* (Warsaw: The National Security Bureau, 2013), 48.

56   Beata Gorka-Winter, "Poland," in *Security Sector Reform in Countries of Visegrad and Southern Caucasus: Challenges and Opportunities*, ed. Marian Majer (Bratislava: Centre for European and North Atlantic Affairs (CENAA), 2013), 95–96.

57   Otto Kalo and Andras Racz, "'Hungary," in *Security Sector Reform in Countries of Visegrad and Southern Caucasus: Challenges and Opportunities*, 76.

58   Mary Borissova, "Politicians, Experts and Democracy. Civil–Military Relations in Central and Eastern Europe: The Case of Bulgaria," *European Security* 15, no. 2 (2006): 202.

59   See Dutkiewicz and Pantev, "Postcommunist Civil-Military Relations in Bulgaria," 149–150.

60   Barany, *The Future of NATO Expansion*, 209–210, acknowledged in 2002 the lack of suitable instructors. In the ensuing years, very little progress had been made as observed by this author during his numerous visits to G. S. Rakovski Defense Academy.

61   Keagle argues the need for faculty members of PME institutions to have, *inter alia*, a teaching tour of up to five years with the possibility of promotions and selection for competitive assignments as their counterparts in the armed forces. Not a bad model, except that faculty in legacy PME institutions typically are assigned to these posts as junior officers and remain there for the rest of their professional lives, which, in itself, inhibits the introduction of new faculty and those with recent operational experience. James M. Keagle, "A Special Relationship: U.S. and NATO Engagement with the Partnership for Peace to Build Partner Capacity Through Education," *Connections* 11, no. 2 (Fall 2012): 71.

62   As argued by change management experts of the school of positive deviance who are skeptical of employing "best practices" to solve institutional and social problems. See Richard Pascale, Jerry Sternin, and Monique Sternin, *The Power of Positive Deviance: How Unlikely Innovators Solve the World's Toughest Problems* (Cambridge, MA: Harvard Business Press, 2010).

63   "The legacy of suppression of any critical thinking in education is also still echoing throughout the Czech educational system, and the military education is unfortunately one of the most resistant to change. As a result, although the number

of experts is growing slowly, they are all heavily influenced by the 'old cadres' and thus subscribe to very similar views." Kristina Soukupova, "The Influence of Civil-Military Relations on the Implementation of Network Enabled Capabilities as a Transformation Driver and Security Sector Consolidation Catalyst in the Czech Republic" (PhD dissertation, King's College London, March 2010), 264.

64   Edmunds reinforces the essentiality of the political nature of defense reform in his analysis of assistance techniques delivered to reform the Ministry of Defense of Serbia and Montenegro, circa 2004. See Edmunds, *Security Sector Reform in Transforming Societies*, 200–221, 253.

65   John P. Kotter and Dan S. Cohen, *Heart of Change: Real Life Stories of How People Change Their Organization* (Cambridge, MA: Harvard Business Press, 2012), 2–3.

66   Cezar Vasilescu, "The Advantages and Disadvantages of Implementing the Planning, Programming, Budgeting and Execution System (PPBES)," in *Planning, Programming, Budgeting, Evaluation System: Benefits and Challenges*, ed. Maria Constantinescu, Workshop unfolded during the postgraduate course in Planning Programming Budgeting System, Regional Department of Defense Resources Management Studies (Bucharest: National Defense University "Carol I" Publishing House, 2010), 116.

67   McNab, "Implementing Program Budgeting in the Serbian Ministry of Defense," 217, 226.

68   One innovative attempt to open communication in the Bulgarian defense institution (2011–2013) was Minister of Defense Anyu Angelov's use of Facebook.

69   Christopher C. Locksley, "Concept, Algorithm, Indecision: Why Military Reform Has Failed in Russia since 1992," *Journal of Slavic Military Studies* 14, no. 1 (2001): 21.

70   Kotter and Cohen, *Heart of Change, passim.*

71   Christopher Donnelly, "Reform Realities," in *Post-Cold War Defense Reform: Lessons Learned in Europe and the United States*, eds. Istvan Gyarmati and Theodor Winkler (Washington, DC: Brassey's, Inc., 2002), 40.

72   For a description of the modest assets and activities of the International Staff, see Jos Boonstra, "NATO's Role in Democratic Reform," *Working Paper* 38 (Madrid: FRIDE, May 2007), 11–13.

73   Mr Frank Boland, then the director of Planning, Defence Policy and Planning Division of the International Staff, was described as "fearsome" to Baltic defense planners prior to admission. See Kęstutis Paulauskas, "The Baltic Quest to the West: From Total Defence to 'Smart Defence' (and Back?)," in *Apprenticeship, Partnership, Membership: Twenty Years of Defence Development in the Baltic States*, eds. Tony Lawrence and Tomas Jermalavičius (Tallinn: International Centre for Defence Studies, 2013), 66.

74   Kotter and Cohen, *Heart of Change*, 142–143.

75   See Watkins's excellent analysis of how donor assistance should be vectored in legacy defense institutions, as well as ministries of internal affairs. Amadeo Watkins, *Security Sector Reform and Donor Assistance in Serbia: Complexity of Managing Change* (Shrivenham: Defense Academy of the United Kingdom, September 2010), 17.

76   "Changes in the personnel management system must, in most cases, be forced upon the military structures, ensuring that promotion stops being guided mainly by seniority and influenced by nepotism. It must depend on active leadership in training as well as on proven moral courage to fight the wide-spread routine, low-level, laissez-faire service corruption." Clemmesen, "Integration of New Alliance Members," 264.

77   Holger Mölder, "The Development of Military Cultures," in *Apprenticeship, Partnership, Membership*, 108. This skepticism aside, Mölder makes a strong point that "Estonia has taken its commitments to NATO very seriously. Despite its strong commitment to the Nordic model of military culture and suspicions of the European model, Estonia continues to support the transformation of NATO and the EU's CSDP in promoting cooperative security approaches for the current security environment."

78   Note that Estonian stockpiles are in locations used during the Soviet period, and therefore, one could assume that Russian officials are quite aware of their respective locations. See Martin Hurt, "Lessons Identified in Crimea: Does Estonia's National Defence Model Meet Our Needs?" *Policy Paper* (Tallinn: International Centre for Defence Studies, April 2014), 4–5.

79   Paulauskas, "The Baltic Quest to the West," 74.

80   Igor Kotnik, "Professionalization of the Slovenian Armed Forces—A Goal or a Path?" *Contemporary Military Challenges* 17, no. 4 (December 2015): 12, 15.

Chapter 8

1   Reka Szemerkenyi, "Central European Civil-Military Reforms at Risk," *Adelphi Paper* 306 (London: The International Institute for Strategic Studies, 1996), 72–73.

2   As persuasively argued by Marybeth Peterson Ulrich, *Democratizing Communist Militaries: The Case of the Czech and Russian Armed Forces* (Ann Arbor: The University of Michigan Press, 2000), 180–181.

3   David B. Ralston, *Importing the European Army: The Introduction of European Military Techniques and Institutions into the Extra-European World, 1600–1914* (Chicago: University of Chicago Press, 1990), 174.

4   Jan Arveds Trapans, "Democracy and Defence in Latvia: Thirteen Years of Development: 1991–2004," in *Civil-Military Relations in Post-Communist Europe: Reviewing the Transition*, eds. Timothy Edmunds, Andrew Cottey, and Anthony Forster (London: Rutledge, 2006), 53.

5   Andrew Cottey, Timothy Edmunds, and Anthony Forster, "The Second Generation Problematic: Rethinking Civil-Military Relations and Democracy," *Armed Forces and Society* 29, no. 1 (Fall 2002): 36–37.

6   As opined by the editorial board of the *New York Times*, some $93 billion has been spent on reconstruction and security programs in Afghanistan but these efforts have been plagued by failures in execution and management.

> The Pentagon has proceeded with the purchase of aircraft costing $771.8 million (including 30 Russian helicopters) despite the fact that just 7 of 47 Afghan pilots assigned to their air force unit are fully qualified to fly counterterrorism missions, which is the primary objective. The unit has a quarter of the 806 personnel needed to operate at full strength, and there is no plan for reaching that goal. It will take the air unit at least 10 years to perform critical maintenance and logistics tasks independently, in part because of the difficulty of finding recruits who are literate and don't have criminal records.

See "The Afghan Legacy," *New York Times*, July 5, 2013.

7   Jeffrey Marshall, *Skin in the Game: Partnership in Establishing and Maintaining Global Security and Stability* (Washington, DC: National Defense University Press, 2011), xiv:

> Currently, U.S. partner capability- and capacity-building is inefficient. There are too many authorities, funding mechanisms often are too inflexible, and planning and execution are fragmented. We need to streamline this process and make it much more effective and responsive if we want to rapidly adapt to changing situations and requirements. We also need to establish capability organizations that can effectively work with our partners, develop clear, concise plans, and successfully implement them in a timely manner.

Alas, all too true, but Marshall fails to explain how these authorities should be rationalized and funding made more flexible and blithely assumes that current organizational structures are immutably fit for purpose.

8   For example, Expanded-International Military Education and Training. See Andrew Cottey and Anthony Forster, "Reshaping Defence Diplomacy: New Roles for Military Cooperation and Assistance," *Adelphi Paper* 365 (London: The International Institute for Strategic Studies, 2004), 9–10.

9   For example, Section 1206 funding. See Nina Serafino, *Security Assistance Reform: "Section 1206" Background and Issues for Congress*, RS22855 (Washington, DC: Congressional Research Service, 2010).

10   Section 543 of the Foreign Assistance Act of 1961, as amended, states that IMET programs shall, *inter alia*, "1) encourage effective and mutually beneficial relations, and increased understanding between the United States and foreign countries in furtherance of the goals of international peace and security; 2) improve the ability of participating countries to use their resources with maximum effectiveness, thereby contributing to greater self-reliance."

11   David E. Thaler, Michael J. McNerney, Beth Grill, Jefferson P. Marquis, and Amanda Kadlec, *From Patchwork to Framework: A Review of Title 10 Authorities for Security Cooperation* (Santa Monica, CA: RAND, 2016), 25.

12   US Government Accountability Office, *NATO Partnerships: DoD Needs to Assess U.S. Assistance in Response to Changes in the Partnership for Peace Program*, by Joseph A. Christoff, GAO-10-1015 (Washington, DC: September 2010), 5.

13   Marshall, *Skin in the Game*, xv–xvi:

> While DOD and the Department of State (DOS) recognize the importance of building partner capability and have budgeted considerable funds for it, their efforts are hindered by suboptimal and obsolete processes, budgeting, authorities, and organizational structures. We still have not recognized that we need to change how we do business if we are going to engage our partners effectively and work with them to build capacity.

14   Peterson Ulrich claims that the US Department of State failed to take the lead, allowing the Department of Defense to take and keep the policy initiative. See Peterson Ulrich, *Democratizing Communist Militaries*, 56–57.

15   Catherine Dale, "Clarifying the Concept of 'Partnership' in National Security," R42516 (Washington, DC: Congressional Research Service, May 4, 2012), 2.

16   See Malcolm Haworth, "The Role of Western Assistance and Cooperation: The Case of the UK," in Andrew Cotty, Timothy Edmunds, and Anthony Forster, "Civil-Military

Relations and Defence Planning: Challenges for Central and Eastern Europe in the New Era." ESRC "One Europe or Several" Programme, *Working Paper* 09/00, 2000, 16.

17 For a very frank discussion on the challenges confronting the International Staff in providing useful feedback to MAP and PfP countries from officials who played essential roles during those years, see Willem Matser and Christopher Donnelly, "Security Sector Reform and NATO Enlargement: Success Through Standardization of Standards?" in *Towards Security Sector Reform in Post Cold War Europe: A Framework for Assessment*, eds. Wilhelm N. Germann and Timothy Edmunds (Baden-Baden: Nomos Verlagsgesellschaft, 2003), 149–151.

18 Dafna H. Rand and Stephen Tankel, *Security Cooperation and Assistance: Rethinking the Return on Investment* (Washington, DC: Center for a New American Security, August 2015), 22.

19 An important point underscored in Walter L. Perry, Stuart E. Johnson, Stephanie Pezard, Gillian S. Oak, David Stebbins, and Chaoling Feng, *Defense Institution Building: An Assessment* (Santa Monica, CA: RAND, 2016), 127.

20 For instance, See US Government Accountability Office, *NATO Partnerships, passim*, and Dale, "Clarifying the Concept of 'Partnership' in National Security."

21 For a very practical treatment of this issue, see Foreign and Commonwealth Office, "Assisting Host Country Militaries: Assessing Lessons from NATO, EU and Member State Experience," Conference Report, WP 1296 (Wilton Park, December 4–6, 2013), 12.

22 Peterson Ulrich, *Democratizing Communist Militaries*, 58, 186.

23 David J. Betz, *Civil-Military Relations in Russia and Eastern Europe* (New York: Routledge Curzon, 2004), 85.

24 An exception to this dreary reality is the programs offered by the Baltic Defence College in Tartu, Estonia.

25 The document appears at Appendix 1.

26 Jos Boonstra, "NATO's Role in Democratic Reform," *Working Paper* 38 (Madrid: FRIDE, May 2007), 10.

27 US Government Accountability Office, *NATO Partnerships*, 48.

28 See Zoltan D. Barany, *The Future of NATO Expansion: Four Case Studies* (Cambridge: Cambridge University Press, 2003), 163–165.

29 "The NATO Defence Planning Process" (Brussels: NATO Headquarters, November 11, 2014), http://www.nato.int/cps/en/natolive/topics_49202.htm (accessed July 26, 2016).

30 Rand and Tankel, "Security Cooperation and Assistance," 16.

31 See James R. Locher III, *Victory on the Potomac: The Goldwater-Nichols Act Unifies the Pentagon* (College Station: Texas A & M University Press, 2002).

32 For the politically painful effort to create a national command capability, see Thomas-Durell Young, "Post-unification German Military Organisation: The Struggle to Create National Command Structures," in *Germany at Fifty-Five: Berlin ist nicht Bonn?*, ed. James Sperling (New York: Manchester University Press, 2004), 325–347.

33 "This Foreign Military Sales (FMS) requirement will support the Georgian Armed Forces (GAF) and the Ministry of Defense (MOD) in learning and understanding methodologies utilized to establish and develop systems; functions and procedures in key areas of personnel management; intelligence; strategic planning and execution; command and control support systems; training and doctrine; logistics systems; defense planning; resource management; acquisition methodology and installation master planning. Program Manager's expertise requirements can be found at

"Georgia Defense Transformation Services," 4.8.1., Solicitation, Offer and Award, Solicitation, No. W91ORB-10-R-0055, issued by US Army RDECOM CONTR CTR, June 21, 2010."

34   For example, in Croatia: see Timothy Edmunds, *Security Sector Reform in Transforming Societies: Croatia, Serbia, and Montenegro* (Manchester: Manchester University Press, 2007), 194, as well as in Romania, see Charles M. Perry and Dimitris Keridis, *Defense Reform, Modernization, and Military Cooperation in Southeastern Europe* (Herndon, VA: Brassey's Inc., 2004), 129(n. 3).

35   Alex J. Bellamy and Timothy Edmunds, "'Civil-Military Relations in Croatia': Politicisation and Politics of Reform," in *Civil-Military Relations in Post-Communist Europe*, 80.

36   Deborah Avant, *The Market for Force: The Consequences of Privatizing Security* (New York: Cambridge University Press, 2005), 107. Avant documents in great detail the history of MPRI's involvement in Croatia, 98–113.

37   Michael. H. Clemmesen, "Supporting States Advice and Defence Development," *Baltic Defence Review* no. 4 (2000): 9–10.

38   Peterson Ulrich, *Democratizing Communist Militaries*, 67–68.

39   Ingrid Olstad Busterud, "Defense Sector Reform in the Western Balkans: Different Approaches and Different Tools," *European Security*, published online: March 11, 2014, http://www.tandfonline.com/doi/abs/10.1080/09662839.2014.893428, 7, 13 (accessed November 20, 2016).

40   Eric Petersen, "The Kosovo Protection Corps," *CESS Occasional Paper* (September 2005), 5.

41   For a comprehensive, but disappointingly uncritical, description of the combatant commands and their roles in executing Security Cooperation and Security Assistance programs, see Derek S. Reveron, *Exporting Security: International Engagement, Security Cooperation, and the Changing Face of the U.S. Military* (Washington, DC: Georgetown University Press, 2010), 79–100.

42   Marshall, *Skin in the Game*, xiv.

43   See US Government Accountability Office, *International Military Education and Training: Agencies Should Emphasize Human Rights Training and Improve Evaluations*, by Charles Michael Johnson, Jr., GAO Report 12-123 (Washington, DC: Government Printing Office, 2011).

44   Duncan L. Clarke, Daniel B. O'Connor, and Jason D. Ellis, *Send Guns and Money: Security Assistance and U.S. Foreign Policy* (Westport, CT: Praeger, 1997), 20–22.

45   Alex J. Bellamy and Timothy Edmunds, "Civil-Military Relations in Croatia," 86.

46   Peterson Ulrich, *Democratizing Communist Militaries*, 156–157.

47   Recently promulgated US policy has finally acknowledged these policy shortcomings and has attempted to address this gap. Whether the US armed forces can fulfill this new direction remains to be seen. US Department of Defense, Defense Institution Building (DIB), DoD Directive 5205.82 (Washington, DC, January 27, 2016), 6.

48   Thaler et al., *From Patchwork to Framework*, 4.

49   This method is succinctly explained in Perry et al., *Defense Institution Building*, 60–62. Marshall is to be credited for identifying this as a problem that needs to be addressed. Regrettably he fails to articulate in any detail as how this might be accomplished. Marshall, *Skin in the Game*, 48.

50   Jan Arveds Trapans, "Professionalisation of the Armed Forces in Central and Eastern Europe: The Case of Latvia," in *The Challenge of Military Reform in Post-*

Communist Europe: Building Professional Armed Forces, eds. Anthony Forster, Timothy Edmunds, and Andrew Cottey (London: Palgrave Macmillan, 2002), 92.

51 Rand and Tankel, "Security Cooperation and Assistance," 18–19.

52 Marshall, *Skin in the Game*, 31.

53 See Kim Campbell, Project Rapporteur, *All Elements of National Power Moving toward a New Interagency Balance for US Global Engagement* (Washington, DC: Atlantic Council, 2014).

54 On this point, Marshall would appear to contradict himself. "Capability-building requires a dedicated *organization* to plan and execute. Without planners who understand capability-building authorities, funding mechanisms, and processes, we will not generate effective plans." How can one argue that these commands are optimal for capacity-building if they lack the necessary personnel? Marshall, *Skin in the Game*, 17.

55 Thaler et al., *From Patchwork to Framework*, 11–12.

56 US Senate, Committee on Foreign Relations, *Embassies as Command Posts in the Anti-Terror Campaign*, Committee Print 109–52 (Washington, DC: Government Printing Office, 2006), 11. http://frwebgate.access.gpo.gov/cgi-bin/getdoc.cgi?dbname=109_cong_senate_committee_prints&docid=f:31324.pdf (accessed November 20, 2017).

57 Rand and Tankel, "Security Cooperation and Assistance," 21–22.

58 US Office of the Secretary of Defense, Department of Defense, *Foreign Area Officer Program Report for Fiscal Year 2011* (Washington, DC: US Department of Defense, October 4, 2012).

59 *Interagency Evaluation of the Section 1206 Global Train and Equip Program*, Washington DC, US Department of Defense and US Department of State, 2009, 32. https://oig.state.gov/system/files/129491.pdf (accessed November 20, 2016).

60 An important point acknowledged by Perry et al. in relation to US policy and management of DIB. Yet, the authors of this report fail to acknowledge the reality that arguing for "greater coordinating" will not solve the inherent problem of the lack of effective "unity of command." One official with authority and responsible for reforming these institutions is clearly needed, and it is doubtful that such an official would have the bureaucratic strength needed to bring unity to these disparate efforts if their authority is limited solely to Department of Defense programs. See Perry et al., *Defense Institution Building*, 123–126.

61 Peterson Ulrich, *Democratizing Communist Militaries*, 183.

62 US Senate, Committee on Armed Services, Subcommittee on Emerging Threats, "Department of Defense Security Cooperation and Assistance Programs and Authorities," Hearings, 114th Congress, March 9, 2016; and US House of Representatives, Committee on Armed Services, "Examining DOD Security Cooperation: When It Works and When It Doesn't," Hearings, 114th Congress, October 21, 2015. http://www.armed-services.senate.gov/hearings/16-03-09-department-of-defense-security-cooperation-and-assistance-programs-andauthorities (accessed November 20, 2016).

Chapter 9

1 I am indebted to my colleague Dr Jaan Murumets for raising this important point through using this accurate analogy.

2   A problem identified by Chris Donnelly as early as 1996/7. See Christopher Donnelly, "Defense Transformation in the New Democracies: Framework for Tackling the Problem," *NATO Review* 45, no. 2 (January 1997): 15–19.

3   See, for example, the excellent report that addresses the Slovak defense institution's problems with such solutions as increasing defense expenditures, binding procurement plan, longer-term defense plans, and so on. Jaroslav Naď, Marian Majer, and Milan Šuplata, *75 Solutions for Slovakia's Defence* (Bratislava: Central European Policy Institute, c. 2015), 4.

4   Reka Szemerkenyi, "Central European Civil-Military Reforms at Risk," *Adelphi Paper* 306 (London: The International Institute for Strategic Studies, 1996).

5   Harald von Riekhoff, "Introduction," in *The Evolution of Civil-Military Relations in East-Central Europe and the Former Soviet Union*, eds. Natalie Mychajlyszyn and Harald von Riekhoff (Westport, CT: Praeger, 2004), 13.

6   Slovenia, Ministry of Defense, "Resolution on General Long-Term Development and Equipping Programme of the Slovenian Armed Forces up to 2025," *Official Gazette of the Republic of Slovenia*, No. 99/2010, Ljubljana, December 7, 2010, 28.

7   Slovenia, *Annual Report of the Ministry of Defence for 2013*, No. 0100-127/2013-34 (Ljubljana: Ministry of Defense, 27 May 2014), 83.

8   Bulgaria, Council of Ministers, "Programme for the Development of the Defence Capabilities of the Bulgarian Armed Forces 2020," Sofia, approved September 30, 2015, 32.

9   Branimir Furlan, "Civilian Control and Military Effectiveness: Slovenian Case," *Armed Forces and Society* 39, no. 3 (2012): 434–449.

10   As argued persuasively by Diane de Gramont, *Beyond Magic Bullets in Governance Reform* (Washington, DC: Carnegie Endowment for International Peace, 2014), 14–16.

11   Koenraad Van Brabant, "Value-for-Money? The Overall Record of Technical Assistance for Institutional and Governance Reform," International Peacebuilding Advisory Team, Effective Advising in Complex and Fragile Situations, *Working Paper* 1 (Geneva, n.d.), 11–12.

12   As argued by change management experts of the school of positive deviance who are skeptical of employing "best practices" to solve institutional and social problems. See Richard Pascale, Jerry Sternin, and Monique Sternin, *The Power of Positive Deviance: How Unlikely Innovators Solve the World's Toughest Problems* (Cambridge, MA: Harvard Business Press, 2010).

13   An important point that argues against the possible utility of formulaic assessments that only looks at structures and the presence of procedures. See, for example, Hari Bucur-Marcu, *Defense Institution Building Self-Assessment Kit* (Geneva: Geneva Center for Democratic Control Armed Forces, 2010). *Pace*, this author has been equally guilty of authoring precisely these types of reports.

14   Michael Oakeshott, *Rationalization in Politics and Other Essays* (Indianapolis: Liberty Fund, 1991), 15.

15   Perry et al. have found that the Department of State is currently rather weak in this general area. See Walter L. Perry, Stuart E. Johnson, Stephanie Pezard, Gillian S. Oak, David Stebbins, and Chaoling Feng, *Defense Institution Building: An Assessment* (Santa Monica, CA: RAND, 2016), 116.

16   William Easterly, *The Tyranny of Experts: Economists, Dictators, and the Forgotten Rights of the Poor* (New York: Basic Books, 2013), 6.

17   Ibid., 10.

18   Cf., Dafna H. Rand and Stephen Tankel, *Security Cooperation and Assistance: Rethinking the Return on Investment* (Washington, DC: Center for a New American Security, August 2015), 22, who argue that the development of measures of effectiveness is challenging. Perhaps, but not in the case of NATO nations' armed forces, there the issue is simply one of intensifying an existing practice and raising shortcomings within existing political fora.

19   Jeffrey Marshall, *Skin in the Game: Partnership in Establishing and Maintaining Global Security and Stability* (Washington, DC: National Defense University Press, 2011), 71–72.

20   Emily Goldman and Leslie Eliasen, eds., *Adaptive Enemies, Reluctant Friends: The Impact of Diffusion on Military Practice* (Stanford: Stanford University Press, 2003), 372.

21   As currently written and interpreted, Title 10 U.S.C. §1051 authority has been limited to expenses incurred by partner ministry of defense personnel and cannot be used to sponsor the participation of officials from other ministries.

22   See US Department of Defense, Defense Institution Building (DIB), DoD Directive 5205.82 (Washington, DC, January 27, 2016), 5.

23   For an excellent discussion of these bodies in these countries, see Harald von Riekhoff, "Civil-Military Relations in the Baltic Republics," in *The Evolution of Civil-Military Relations in East-Central Europe and the Former Soviet Union*, 121–122.

24   "NATO Secretary General Calls for 'Smart Defence' at Munich Conference," February 5, 2011, http://www.nato.int/cps/en/natohq/news_70327.htm (accessed November 20, 2016).

25   The literature on burden-sharing during the Cold War is anything short of being vast. A good treatment can be found in Simon Duke, *The Burdensharing Debate* (New York: Saint Martin's Press, 1993).

26   Alexander Mattelaer, "Revisiting the Principles of NATO Burden-Sharing," *Parameters* 46, no. 1 (Spring 2016): 25–34.

27   See then-secretary of defense Robert Gates's valedictory strong public rebuke to NATO allies for their meagre defense budgets. *New York Times*, June 10, 2011.

28   Hillison develops a strong argument that new NATO members have not been generally guilty of taking a free ride. But he measures, *inter alia*, GDP percentages allocated to defense and their deployments in support of NATO and US campaigns. He does not consider, however, the net "burden" that accrues to the collective when defense institutions go unreformed. Joel R. Hillison, *Stepping Up: Burdensharing by NATO's Newest Members* (Carlisle Barracks, PA: Strategic Studies Institute and U.S. Army War College Press, November 2014).

29   "Polish Military Modernization: The Road Ahead," *Intelligence Brief* No. 2 (Warsaw: Center for European Policy Analysis, September 2015), 8.

30   Anthony Forster, "Introduction," in *The Challenge of Military Reform in Post-Communist Europe: Building Professional Armed Forces*, eds. Anthony Forster, Timothy Edmunds, and Andrew Cottey (London: Palgrave Macmillan, 2002), 1.

Bibliography

Official documents

Armenia. *The Military Doctrine of the Republic of Armenia*. Yerevan: Ministry of Defense, 2007.

Armenia. *Strategic Defense Review, 2011–2015*. Public Release. Yerevan: Ministry of Defense., n.d. (c. 2011).

Azerbaijan *National Security Concept of the Republic of Azerbaijan*. Approved by Instruction No. 2198 of the President of the Republic of Azerbaijan, Baku, May 23, 2007.

Bosnia-Herzegovina. *AFHIM: A Single Military Force for the 21st Century*. Sarajevo: Defense Reform Commission, September 2005.

Bosnia-Herzegovina. *Defence White Paper of Bosnia Herzegovina*. Sarajevo: Ministry of Defense, June 2005.

Bulgaria. *Military Doctrine of the Republic of Bulgaria*. Sofia: Council of Ministers, 2002.

Bulgaria. *National Security Concept of the Republic of Bulgaria*. Sofia: Council of Ministers, 2002.

Bulgaria. "Policy Framework of the Strategic Defense Review." Adopted by the National Assembly. Sofia: Council of Ministers, March 25, 2004.

Bulgaria. "Programme for the Development of the Defence Capabilities of the Bulgarian Armed Forces 2020." Sofia: Council of Ministers, September 30, 2015.

Bulgaria. *Strategic Defence Review*. Sofia: Council of Ministers, 2004.

Bulgaria. "Updated Plan for [the] Organizational Build-up and Modernization of the Armed Forces." Sofia: Council of Ministers, March 2008.

Bulgaria. *White Paper on Defence and the Armed Forces of the Republic of Bulgaria*. Sofia: Ministry of Defense, 2010.

Croatia. *Croatian Armed Forces Long-Term Development Plan 2006–2015*. Adopted in the Croatian Parliament on July 7, 2006, published in the Official Gazette, No.81, July 19, 2006. Zagreb: Ministry of Defense, June 2006.

Croatia. *Strategic Defence Review*. Zagreb: Ministry of Defence, November 10, 2005.

Croatia. *Strategic Defence Review*. Zagreb: Ministry of Defence, July 25, 2013.

Czech Republic. *Defence Strategy of the Czech Republic: A Responsible State and a Reliable Ally*. Prague: Ministry of Defence, 2012.

Czech Republic. *Defense White Paper*. Prague: Ministry of Defense, 2011.

Estonia. *Effectiveness of Formation, Maintenance and Replenishment of Resources Required for Increasing Military Capability and Mobilisation of Defence Forces from 2009–2012* (Summary of Report). Tallinn: National Audit Office, May 30, 2013.

Estonia. *National Defence Development Plan, 2013–2022*. Tallinn: Ministry of Defense, n.d.

Estonia. *National Defence Strategy of Estonia*. Tallinn: Ministry of Defense, 2011.

Estonia. *National Security Concept of Estonia*. Adopted by the Riigikogu, Tallinn, May 12, 2010 (unofficial translation).

Georgia. *Law on Defense Planning.* No. 4130, April 28, 2006.

Georgia. *Minister's Vision, 2013–2014.* Tbilisi: Ministry of Defense, 2013.

Georgia. *National Military Strategy 2005.* Tbilisi: Ministry of Defence, 2005.

Georgia. *National Security Concept of Georgia.* Tbilisi, 2011.

Georgia. *Strategic Defence Review, 2007.* Tbilisi: Ministry of Defence, 2007.

Georgia. *Strategic Defence Review, 2013–2016.* Tbilisi: Ministry of Defence, 2013.

Hungary. *Hungary's National Military Strategy.* Budapest: Ministry of Defence, 2012.

Hungary. *Hungary's National Security Strategy.* Budapest: Ministry of Foreign Affairs, 2012.

Latvia. *Report on the State Defence Policy and Armed Forces Development.* Riga: Ministry of Defence, 2004.

Latvia. *The State Defence Concept.* Riga: Ministry of Defence, May 10, 2012.

Lithuania. *Defence Policy of Lithuania.* Vilnius: Ministry of National Defense, April 7, 2014.

Lithuania. "Guidelines of the Minister of National Defence for 2009–2014." Vilnius, Ministry of National Defence, February 29, 2008.

Lithuania. "Guidelines of the Minister of National Defence for 2016–2021." Vilnius, Ministry of National Defence, December 29, 2015.

Lithuania. *Military Strategy of the Republic of Lithuania.* No. V-1305. Vilnius, November 22, 2012.

Lithuania. *Military Strategy of the Republic of Lithuania.* No. V-252. Vilnius, March 17, 2016.

Lithuania. "Resolution amending the Seimas of the Republic of Lithuania Resolution on the Approval of the National Security Strategy." No. XI-2131, June 26, 2012.

Lithuania. *White Paper: Lithuanian Defence Policy.* Vilnius: Ministry of National Defence, 2006.

Macedonia. *White Paper on Defence.* Skopje: Ministry of Defense, December 2012.

Moldova. *Concepției Reformei Militare.* Chișinu: Monitorul Oficial Nr. 117, No. 975, August 15, 2002.

Moldova. *Programul de Dezvoltare Strategică al Ministerului Apără pentru perioada 2012–2014.* Chișinu, 2012.

Moldova. *Raportul Ministerului Apărării: cu privire la implementarea politicilor de apărare în anul 2013.* Chișinu, 2013.

Montenegro. *Strategic Defense Review of Montenegro.* Podgorica: Ministry of Defense, June 2010.

Montenegro. *Strategic Defense Review of Montenegro.* Podgorica: Ministry of Defense, July 2013.

Poland. *Defense Strategy of the Republic of Poland: Sector Strategy of the National Security Strategy of the Republic of Poland.* Warsaw: Ministry of National Defense, 2009.

Poland. *Strategy of Development of the National Security System of the Republic of Poland 2022.* Warsaw: Council of Ministers, April 9, 2013.

Poland. *Vision of the Polish Armed Forces 2030.* Warsaw: Ministry of National Defense, Department of Transformation, May 2008.

Poland. *White Book on National Security of the Republic of Poland.* Warsaw: National Security Bureau, 2013.

Poland. *White Paper.* Warsaw: Ministry of National Defense, 2001.

Romania. Law on Defense Planning, No. 473 of November 4, 2004; repeals Government Ordinance No.52/1998 on national defense planning, *Monitorul Oficial*. Bucharest, No. 525, October 25, 2000.

Romania. *Military Strategy of Romania*. Bucharest: Ministry of National Defense, 2005.

Romania. *National Security Strategy of Romania*. Bucharest: Supreme Council of National Defense, April 17, 2007.

Romania. *The National Security Strategy of Romania: The European Romania, the Euro-Atlantic Romania: For a Better Life in a Democratic, Safer and More Prosperous Country*. Bucharest: Presidency, April 17, 2006 (N.B.: English translation is dated 2007).

Romania. "Strategy of Transformation of Romanian Armed Forces." Signed by State Secretaries for Euro-Atlantic Integration and Defense Policy, and Armament, and Chief of General Staff; approved by the Secretary General of the Ministry of National Defense. Bucharest: General Staff, 2007.

Serbia. *Strategic Defense Review: Final*. Belgrade: Ministry of Defense, July 2006.

Serbia. *White Paper on Defence of the Republic of Serbia*. Belgrade: Ministry of Defense, Strategic Planning Department, Defence Policy Sector, 2010.

Slovakia. *Defense Strategy of the Slovak Republic*. Bratislava: Ministry of Defense, May 25, 2001.

Slovakia. *The White Paper on Defence of the Slovak Republic*. Bratislava: Ministry of Defense, 2013.

Slovenia. *Annual Report of the Ministry of Defence for 2013*. No. 0100-127/2013-34. Ljubljana: Ministry of Defense, May 27, 2014.

Slovenia. *Defence Sector Strategic Review 2009 (DSSR): Summary of Key DSSR 2009 Conclusions*. No. 800-1/2009-189. Ljubljana: Ministry of Defence, October 14, 2009.

Slovenia. "Resolution on General Long-Term Development and Equipping Programme of the Slovenian Armed Forces up to 2025." *Official Gazette of the Republic of Slovenia*. No. 99/2010. Ljubljana: Ministry of Defense, December 7, 2010.

Ukraine. *Reforms Initiatives Overview*. Kyiv: Ministry of Defence, Projects Reforms Office, October 2015.

Ukraine. *White Book 2006, Defence Policy of Ukraine*. Kyiv: Ministry of Defence, Zapovit Publishing House, 2007.

Ukraine. *White Book 2010, Armed Forces of Ukraine*. Kyiv: Ministry of Defense, 2011.

Ukraine. *White Book 2011, Armed Forces of Ukraine*. Kyiv: Ministry of Defense, 2012.

Ukraine. *White Book 2014, Armed Forces of Ukraine*. Kyiv: Ministry of Defense, 2015.

United States. Central Intelligence Agency. *Balkan Battlegrounds: A Military History of the Yugoslav Conflict, 1990–1995*. Volume I. Washington, DC, May 2002.

United States Defense Security Cooperation Agency. *Foreign Military Sales, Foreign Military Construction Sales and Other Security Cooperation Historical Facts*. Washington, DC, September 30, 2013.

United States Department of Defense. "Defense Institution Building (DIB)." DoD Directive 5205.82. Washington, DC, January 27, 2016.

United States Department of State. "Military Assistance Agreement Between the United States and Yugoslavia," November 14, 1951. *Treaties and Other International Agreements (TIAS)*, 2349; 2 UST 2254.

United States Government Accountability Office. *NATO Partnerships: DOD Needs to Assess U.S. Assistance in Response to Changes to the Partnership for Peace Program*, by Joseph A. Christoff. GAO Report 10–1015. Washington, DC: Government Printing Office, September 2010.

Theses and dissertations

Bystrova, Iryna. "Defense Planning in the Ministry of Defense of Ukraine: Decade of Attempts and Mistakes." MA Thesis. Monterey, CA: Naval Postgraduate School, June 2015.

Herrick, Richard C. "The Yugoslav People's Army: Its Military and Political Mission." MA Thesis. Monterey, CA: Naval Postgraduate School, September 1980.

Kosianchuk, Vitaliy. "Cobb-Douglas Production Function as an Approach for Better Resource Allocation in the Ukrainian Armed Forces." MA Thesis. Monterey, CA: Naval Postgraduate School, June 2013.

Mileshko, Roman. "The Evolution of the Defense Budget Process in Ukraine, 1991–2006." MA Thesis. Monterey, CA: Naval Postgraduate School, June 2006.

Soukupova, Kristina. "The Influence of Civil-Military Relations on the Implementation of Network Enabled Capabilities as a Transformation Driver and Security Sector Consolidation Catalyst in the Czech Republic." PhD Dissertation. London: King's College, March 2010.

Stan, Ramona. "Romania's Experiences with Defense Reform since the December 1989 Revolution and the Dimensions of Civil-Military Relations Viewed as a Trinity." MA Thesis. Monterey, CA: Naval Postgraduate School, March 2007.

Monographs

Adelman, Jonathan R., ed. *Communist Armies in Politics*. Boulder, CO: Westview Press, 1982.

Allison, Roy. "Armed Forces in Successor Soviet States." *Adelphi Paper* 280. London: The International Institute for Strategic Studies, 1993.

Avant, Deborah. *The Market for Force: The Consequences of Privatizing Security*. New York: Cambridge University Press, 2005.

Barany, Zoltan D. *The Future of NATO Expansion: Four Case Studies*. Cambridge: Cambridge University Press, 2003.

Bebler, Anton A., ed. *Civil-Military Relations in Post-Communist States: Central and Eastern Europe in Transition*. Westport, CT: Praeger, 1997.

Behnke, Andreas. *NATO's Security Discourse after the Cold War: Representing the West*. London: Routledge, 2013.

Betz, David J. *Civil-Military Relations in Russia and Eastern Europe*. New York: Routledge Curzon, 2004.

Betz, David and John Löwenhardt, eds. *Army and State in Postcommunist Europe*. London: Frank Cass, 2001.

Biehl, Heiko, Bastian Giegerich, and Alexandra Jonas, eds. *Strategic Cultures in Europe: Security and Defence Policies across the Continent. Schriftenreihe des Zentrums für Militärgeschichte und Sozialwissenschaften der Bundeswehr*, Vol. 13, Wiesbaden: Springer VS, 2013.

Boonstra, Jos. "NATO's Role in Democratic Reform." *Working Paper* 38, Madrid, FRIDE, May 2007.

Born, Hans, Marina Caparini, and Philipp Fluri, eds. *Security Sector Reform and Democratic Transitional Societies*. Baden-Baden: Nomos Verlagsgesellschaft, 2002.

Born, Hans, Marina Caparini, Karl W. Haltiner, and Jürgen Kuhlmann, eds. *Civil-Military Relations in Europe: Learning from Crisis and Institutional Change*. New York: Routledge, 2006.

Callaghan, Jean and Mathias Schönborn, eds. *Warriors in Peacekeeping: Points of Tension in Complex Cultural Encounters: A Comparative Study Based on Experiences in Bosnia*. Münster: LIT Verlag, 2004.

Clarke, Duncan L, Daniel B. O'Connor, and Jason D. Ellis. *Send Guns and Money: Security Assistance and U.S. Foreign Policy*. Westport, CT: Praeger, 1997.

Cleary, Laura R. and Teri McConville, eds. *Managing Defence in a Democracy*. New York: Routledge, 2006.

Colston, John and Philipp Fluri, eds. *Defence Co-operation between NATO and its Partners: Visions of the Future*. Geneva: Geneva Center for the Control of Armed Forces, 2007.

Colston, John, Philipp Fluri, and Sergei Piroshkov, eds. *Security Sector Legislation of Ukraine*. Geneva: Geneva Center for Civil Control of Armed Forces, 2006.

Constantinescu, Maria, ed. *Planning, Programming, Budgeting, Evaluation System: Benefits and Challenges*. Workshop unfolded during the postgraduate course in Planning Programming Budgeting System. Bucharest: National Defense University "Carol I" Publishing House, 2010.

Coppieters, Bruno and Robert Legvold, eds. *Statehood and Security: Georgia after the Rose Revolution*. Cambridge, MA: MIT Press, 2005.

Corum, James S. *Development of the Baltic Armed Forces in Light of Multinational Deployments*. Carlisle Barracks, PA: The Strategic Studies Institute, August 2013.

Corum, James S. "The Security Concerns of the Baltic States as NATO Allies." In *The Letorte Papers*. Carlisle Barracks, PA: Strategic Studies Institute, August 2013.

Cottey, Andrew and Anthony Forster. "Reshaping Defence Diplomacy: New Roles for Military Cooperation and Assistance." *Adelphi Paper* 365. London: The International Institute for Strategic Studies, 2004.

Cottey, Andrew, Timothy Edmunds, and Anthony Forster. "Civil-Military Relations and Defence Planning: Challenges for Central and Eastern Europe in the New Era." ESRC "One Europe or Several" Programme, *Working Paper* 09/00, 2000.

Cottey, Andrew, Timothy Edmunds, and Anthony Forster, eds. *Democratic Control of the Military in Postcommunist Europe: Guarding the Guards*. London: Palgrave, 2002.

Czulda, Robert and Marek Madej. *Newcomers No More? Contemporary NATO and the Future of the Enlargement from the Perspectives of "Post-Cold War" Members*. Warsaw: International Relations Research Institute, 2015.

Dale, Catherine. "Clarifying the Concept of 'Partnership' in National Security." R42516. Washington, DC: Congressional Research Service, May 4, 2012.

Danopoulos, Constantine P. and Daniel Zirker, eds. *Civil-Military Relations in the Soviet and Yugoslav Successor States*. Boulder, CO: Westview Press, 1996.

Darchiashvili, David. *Security Sector Reform in Georgia, 2004–2007*. Tbilisi: Caucasus Institute for Peace, Democracy, and Development, 2008.

"Defence Reform in the Baltic States." Conference papers, Riga, Latvia. Geneva: Geneva Center for Democratic Control of Armed Forces, June 17–18, 2003.

de Gramont, Diane. *Beyond Magic Bullets in Governance Reform*. Washington, DC: Carnegie Endowment for International Peace, 2014.

Dunigan, Molly. *Victory for Hire: Private Security Companies' Impact on Military Effectiveness*. Stanford: Stanford University Press, 2011.

Easterly, William. *The Tyranny of Experts: Economists, Dictators, and the Forgotten Rights of the Poor*. New York: Basic Books, 2013.

Ebnöther, Anja H. and Gustav E. Gustenau. *Security Sector Governance in Southern Caucasus: Challenges and Visions*. Geneva: Geneva Centre for the Democratic Control of Armed Forces, 2004.

Ebnöther, Anja H., Philipp H. Fluri, and Predrag Jurekovic, eds., *Security Sector Governance in the Western Balkans: Self-Assessment Studies on Defence, Intelligence, Police and Border Management Reform*. Geneva: Geneva Centre for the Democratic Control of Armed Forces, 2007.

Eden Cole, Timothy Donais, and Philipp H. Fluri, eds. *Defence and Security Sector Governance and Reform in South East Europe*. Baden-Baden, Nomos, 2004.

Edmunds, Timothy. "Defence Reform in Croatia and Serbia-Montenegro." *Adelphi Paper* 360, London: The International Institute for Strategic Studies, 2003.

Edmunds, Timothy. *Security Sector Reform in Transforming Societies: Croatia, Serbia, and Montenegro*. Manchester: Manchester University Press, 2007.

Edmunds, Timothy, Andrew Cottey, and Anthony Forster, eds. *Civil-Military Relations in Post-Communist Europe: Reviewing the Transition*. London: Rutledge, 2006.

Erickson, John and E.J. Feuchtwanger, eds. *Soviet Military Power and Performance*. Hamden, CT: Archon Book, 1979.

Farrell, Theo and Terry Terriff, eds. *The Sources of Military Change, Culture, Politics, Technology*. Boulder, CO: Lynne Reiner, 2002.

Fluri, Philipp and Hari Bucur-Marcu. *Partnership Action for Defence Institution Building: Country Profiles and Need Assessments for Armenia, Azerbaijan, and Georgia, and Moldova*. Geneva: Geneva Centre for the Democratic Control of Armed Forces, 2007.

Fluri, Philipp H. and Viorel Cibotaru, eds. *Defense Institution Building: Country Profiles and Needs Assessments for Armenia, Azerbaijan, Georgia, and Moldova: Background Materials*. Geneva: Geneva Centre for the Democratic Control of Armed Forces, 2008.

Fluri, Philipp H. and Eden Cole, eds., *From Revolution to Reform: Georgia's Struggle with Democratic Institution Building and Security Sector Reform*, Vienna: Bureau for Security Policy at the Austrian Ministry of Defence; National Defence Academy, and Geneva Centre for the Democratic Control of Armed Forces in co-operation with PfP-Consortium of Defence Academies and Security Studies Institutes, July 2005.

Fluri, Philipp H. and George Katsirdakis, eds. *Security Sector Reform in the New Partnership for Peace Members: Bosnia-Herzegovina, Montenegro, Serbia*. Geneva: Geneva Centre for the Democratic Control of Armed Forces, 2007.

Fluri, Philipp H., Gustav E. Gustenau, and Plamen I. Pantev, eds. *The Evolution of Civil-Military Relations in South East Europe: Continuing Democratic Reform and Adapting to the Needs of Fighting Terrorism*. New York: Physica-Verlag, 2005.

Forster, Anthony. *Armed Forces and Society in Europe*. New York: Palgrave MacMillan, 2006.

Forster, Anthony, Timothy Edmunds, and Andrew Cottey, eds. *The Challenge of Military Reform in Post-Communist Europe: Building Professional Armed Forces*. London: Palgrave Macmillan, 2002.

Frontline Allies: War and Change in Central Europe: U.S.-Central Europe Strategic Assessment Group Report. Warsaw: Center for European Policy Analysis, November 2015.

Germann, Wilhelm N. and Timothy Edmunds, eds. *Towards Security Sector Reform in Post Cold War Europe: A Framework for Assessment*. Baden-Baden: Nomos Verlagsgesellschaft, 2003.

Gheciu, Alexandra. *NATO in the "New Europe": The Politics of International Socialization after the Cold War*. Stanford: Stanford University Press, 2005.

Gitz, Bradley R. *Armed Forces and Political Power in Eastern Europe: The Soviet/Communist Control System*. New York: Greenwood Press, 1992.

Goldman, Emily and Leslie Eliasen, eds. *Adaptive Enemies, Reluctant Friends: The Impact of Diffusion on Military Practice*. Stanford: Stanford University Press, 2003.

Gow, James. *Legitimacy and the Military: The Yugoslav Crisis*. New York: St. Martin's Press, 1992.

Grattan, Robert F. *Strategic Review: The Process of Strategy Formulation in Complex Organisations*. Farnham, Surrey: Gower Publishing Limited, 2011.

Gyarmati, Istvan and Theodor Winkler, eds. *Post-Cold War Defense Reform: Lessons Learned in Europe and the United States*. Washington, DC: Brassey's, Inc., 2002.

Hadžić, Miroslav. *The Yugoslav People's Army: The Role of the Yugoslav People's Army*. Aldershot: Ashgate Publishing Limited, 2002.

Hadžić, Miroslav, Milorad Timotić, and Predrag Petrović, eds. *Security Policies in the Western Balkans*. Belgrade: Center for Civil-Military Relations, 2010.

Herd, Graeme P., ed. *Civil-Military Relations in Post-Cold War Europe*. Camberley, England: Conflict Studies Research Centre, 2001.

Hillison, Joel R. *Stepping Up: Burdensharing by NATO's Newest Members*. Carlisle Barracks: Strategic Studies Institute and U.S. Army War College Press, November 2014.

Howard, Colby and Ruslan Pukhov. *Brothers Armed: Military Aspects of the Crisis in Ukraine*. Minneapolis: East View Press, 2014.

Hurt, Martin. "Lessons Identified in Crimea: Does Estonia's National Defence Model Meet Our Needs?" *Policy Paper*. Tallinn: International Centre for Defence Studies, April 2014.

International Crisis Group. "Azerbaijan: Defense Sector Management and Reform." *Europe Briefing* no. 50, October 29, 2008.

Jansa, Janez. *The Making of the Slovenian State, 1988–1992: The Collapse of Yugoslavia*. Ljubljana: Mladinska Knjiga Publishing House, 1994.

Jazbec, Milan. "Defence Reform in the Western Balkans: The Way Ahead." *Policy Paper*. Geneva: Geneva Centre for the Democratic Control of Armed Forces, April 2005.

Johnson, A. Ross. "The Role of the Military in Communist Yugoslavia: An Historical Sketch." P-6070. Santa Monica, CA, RAND Corporation, January 1978.

Joo, Rudolf. "The Democratic Control of Armed Forces." *Chaillot Papers 23*. Paris: Institute for Security Studies, February 1996.

Kernic, Franz, Paul Klein, and Karl Haltiner, eds. *The European Armed Forces in Transition: A Comparative Analysis*. New York: Peter Lang, 2005.

King, Anthony. *The Transformation of Europe's Armed Forces: From the Rhine to Afghanistan*. Cambridge: Cambridge University Press, 2011.

Klopfer, Franziska and Douglas Cantwell, with Miroslav Hadžić and Sonja Stojanović, eds. *Almanac on Security Sector Oversight in the Western Balkans: 2012*. Belgrade/Geneva: Belgrade Center for Security Policy and Geneva Centre for the Democratic Control of Armed Forces, 2012.

Lawrence, Tony and Tomas Jermalavičius, eds. *Apprenticeship, Partnership, Membership: Twenty Years of Defence Development in the Baltic States*, Tallinn: International Centre for Defence Studies, 2013.

Magas, Branka and Ivo Zanic, eds. *The War in Croatia and Bosnia-Herzegovina, 1991–1995*. London: Frank Cass, 2001.

Majer, Marian, ed. *Security Sector Reform in Countries of Visegrad and Southern Caucasus: Challenges and Opportunities*. Bratislava: Centre for European and North Atlantic Affairs (CENAA), 2013.

Mannitz, Sabine, ed. *Democratic Civil-Military Relations: Soldiering in 21st Century Europe*. London: Routledge, 2012.

Marshall, Jeffrey. *Skin in the Game: Partnership in Establishing and Maintaining Global Security and Stability*. Washington, DC: National Defense University Press, 2011.

Matlary, Janne Haaland and Magnus Petersson, ed. *NATO's European Allies: Military Capability and Political Will*. New York: Palgrave Macmillan, 2013.

Maxwell, Rohan and John Andreas Olsen. "Destination NATO: Defence Reform in Bosnia and Herzegovina, 2003–13." *Whitehall Papers* 80. London: Royal United Services Institute, 2013.

McInnis, Kathleen J. and Nathan J. Lucas. "'What is 'Building Partner Capacity?' Issues for Congress." R44313. Washington, DC: Congressional Research Service, December 18, 2015.

Menderhausen, Horst. "Territorial Defense in NATO and Non-NATO Europe." R-1184-ISA. RAND: Santa Monica, CA, 1973.

Michta, Andrew A., ed. *America's New Allies: Poland, Hungary, and the Czech Republic in NATO*. Seattle: University of Washington Press, 1999.

Mychajlyszyn, Natalie and Harald von Riekhoff, eds. *The Evolution of Civil-Military Relations in East-Central Europe and the Former Soviet Union*. Westport, CT: Praeger, 2004.

Naď, Jaroslav, Marian Majer, and Milan Šuplata. *75 Solutions for Slovakia's Defence*. Bratislava: Central European Policy Institute, c. 2015.

Nadovic, Svetozar, Hartmut Foertsch, Imre Karacsony, and Zdzislaw Ostrowski. *The Great Withdrawal: Withdrawal of the Soviet-Russian Army from Central Europe, 1990–1994*. Bratislava: Ministry of Defense of the Slovak Republic, 2005.

Pataraia, Tamara, ed. *Democratic Control over the Georgian Armed Forces since the August 2008 War*. Geneva: Geneva Centre for the Democratic Control of Armed Forces, 2010.

Perry, Charles M. and Dimitris Keridis. *Defense Reform, Modernization, and Military Cooperation in Southeastern Europe*. Herndon, VA: Brassey's Inc., 2004.

Perry, Walter L., Stuart E. Johnson, Stephanie Pezard, Gillian S. Oak, David Stebbins, and Chaoling Feng. *Defense Institution Building: An Assessment*. Santa Monica, CA: RAND, 2016.

Perry, Walter L., et al. *The Warsaw Initiative Fund Program: An Assessment*. FOUO. Santa Monica, CA: RAND, May 2013.

Peterson Ulrich, Marybeth. *Democratizing Communist Militaries: The Case of the Czech and Russian Armed Forces*. Ann Arbor: The University of Michigan Press, 2000.

Pietz, Tobias. "Demobilizing and Retraining for the Future: The Armed Forces in Serbia and Montenegro." *Brief 31*. Bonn: International Center for Conversion, July 2005.

"Polish Military Modernization: The Road Ahead." *Intelligence Brief* No. 2. Warsaw: Center for European Policy Analysis, September 2015.

Ralston, David B. *Importing the European Army: The Introduction of European Military Techniques and Institutions into the Extra-European World, 1600–1914*. Chicago: University of Chicago Press, 1990.

Rand, Dafna H. and Stephen Tankel. "Security Cooperation and Assistance: Rethinking the Return on Investment." Washington, DC, Center for a New American Security, August 2015.

Reveron, Derek S. *Exporting Security: International Engagement, Security Cooperation, and the Changing Face of the U.S. Military.* Washington, DC: Georgetown University Press, 2010.

Roberts, Adam. *Nations in Arms: The Theory and Practice of Territorial Defense,* New York: Praeger Publishers, 1976.

Sava, Ionel Nicu. "Civil-Military Relations, Western Assistance and Democracy in South East Europe." G-125. Sandhurst: Conflict Studies and Research Centre, August 2003.

Schmitt, Gary J., ed. *A Hard Look at Hard Power: Assessing the Defense Capabilities of Key U.S. Allies and Security Partners.* Carlisle Barracks, PA: U.S. Army War College Press, July 2015.

Seferovic, Mensur, ed. *Total National Defense in Theory and Practice.* Belgrade: Narodna Armija, 1975.

Sequin, Barre R. "Why Did Poland Choose the F-16s?" *Occasional Papers Series* No. 11. Garmisch-Partenkirchen: George C. Marshall Center, June 2007.

Shrader, Charles R. *The Muslim-Croat Civil War in Central Bosnia: A Military History, 1992–1994.* College Station: Texas A&M University Press, 2003.

Simon, Jeffrey. *Hungary and NATO: Problems in Civil-Military Relations.* Lanham, MD: Rowman and Littlefield Publishers, Inc., 2003.

Simon, Jeffrey. *NATO and the Czech and Slovak Republics: Comparative Study in Civil-Military Relations.* Lanham: Rowman & Littlefield, 2004.

Simon, Jeffrey. *NATO Enlargement and Central Europe: A Study in Civil-Military Relations.* Washington: National Defense University Press, 1996.

Simon, Jeffrey, ed. *NATO-Warsaw Pact Force Mobilization.* Washington, DC: National Defense University Press, 1988.

Soukupova, Kristina. *Bringing Peace and Democracy to Troubled Places: The Case of Macedonia.* Saarbrücken: LAP Lambert Academic Publishing, 2004.

Szayna, Thomas S. *NATO Enlargement 2000–2015: Determinants and Implications for Defense Planning and Shaping.* MR-1243-AF. Santa Monica, CA: RAND, 2001.

Szayna T. S. and F. S. Larrabee. *East European Military Reform after the Cold War: Implications for the United States.* Santa Monica, CA: RAND, 1995.

Szemerkenyi, Reka. "Central European Civil-Military Reforms at Risk." *Adelphi Paper* 306. London: The International Institute for Strategic Studies, 1996.

Szymanski, Piotr. "The Baltic States' Territorial Defence Forces in the Face of Hybrid Threats." *OSW/Commentary,* No. 165, March 19, 2015.

Thaler, David E., Michael J. McNerney, Beth Grill, Jefferson P. Marquis, and Amanda Kadlec. *From Patchwork to Framework: A Review of Title 10 Authorities for Security Cooperation.* Santa Monica, CA: RAND, 2016.

Trapans, Jan and Philipp Fluri, eds. *Defence and Security Sector Governance and Reform in South East Europe: Insights and Perspectives. Volume I and II Albania, Bulgaria, Croatia, FYROM Macedonia, Moldova, Romania.* Geneva: Geneva Centre for the Democratic Control of Armed Forces, 2003.

Trifunovska, Snezana, ed. *Yugoslavia through Documents: From its Creation to its Dissolution.* Dordrecht: Martinus Nijhoff Publishers, 1994.

Van Brabant, Koenraad. "Value-for-Money? The Overall Record of Technical Assistance for Institutional and Governance Reform." International Peacebuilding Advisory Team, Effective Advising in Complex and Fragile Situations. *Working Paper* 1. Geneva, n.d.

Van Eekelen, Wim F. and Philipp H. Fluri, eds. *Defence Institution Building: A Sourcebook in Support of the Partnership Action Plan (PAP-DIB)*. Vienna: Landesverteidigungsakademie, 2006.

Vashakmadze, Mindia. *The Legal Framework of Security Sector Governance in Georgia*. Geneva: Geneva Centre for the Democratic Control of Armed Forces, 2014.

von Kirchbach, Hans-Peter, et al. *Abenteuer Einheit: Zum Aufbau der Bundeswehr in den neuen Ländern*. Frankfurt am Main: Report Verlag, 1992.

Watkins, Amadeo. *Security Sector Reform and Donor Assistance in Serbia: Complexity of Managing Change*. Shrivenham: Defense Academy of the United Kingdom, September 2010.

Yost, David. *NATO Transformed: The Alliance's New Roles in International Security*. Washington, DC: United States Institute of Peace Press, 1998.

Zametica, John. "The Yugoslav Conflict." *Adelphi Paper* 270. London: The International Institute for Strategic Studies, 1992.

Articles

Aybet, Gülnur. "NATO Conditionality in Bosnia and Herzegovina: Defense Reform and State Building." *Problems of Post-Communism* 57, no. 5 (September–October 2010): 20–34.

Atkinson, Carol. "Constructivist Implications of Material Power: Military Engagement and the Socialization of States, 1972–2000." *International Studies Quarterly* 50 (2006): 509–537.

Barany, Zoltan. "Democratic Consolidation and the Military: The East European Experience." *Comparative Politics* 30, no. 1 (October 1997): 21–43.

Bayliss, Thomas. "Presidents versus Prime Ministers: Shaping Executive Authority in Eastern Europe." *World Politics* 48, no. 3 (April 1996): 297–323.

Bebler, Anton. "The Yugoslav Crisis and the 'Yugoslav People's Army'." *Zürcher Beiträge zur Sicherheitspolitik und Konfliktforschung* 23, (1992).

Borissova, Mary. "Politicians, Experts and Democracy. Civil–Military Relations in Central and Eastern Europe: The Case of Bulgaria." *European Security* 15, no. 2 (2006): 191–212.

Busterud, Ingrid Olstad. "Defense Sector Reform in the Western Balkans: Different Approaches and Different Tools." *European Security* (published online: March 11, 2014), http://www.tandfonline.com/doi/abs/10.1080/09662839.2014.893428 (accessed November 20, 2016)

Carnovale, Marco. "NATO Partners and Allies: Civil-Military Relations and Democratic Control of the Armed Forces." *NATO Review* 45, no. 2 (March 1997): 32–35.

Castagner, Marc-Olivier. "Discursive Fields and Military Transformations: Poland and the Baltic States as Legitimate Members of NATO." *The Journal of Power Institutions in Post-Soviet Societies*, Issue 14/15 (2013), http://pipss.revues.org/4004 (accessed June 2, 2016)

Clemmesen, Michael H. "Integration of New Alliance Members: The Intellectual-Cultural Dimension." *Defense Analysis* 15, no. 3 (December 1999): 261–272.

Clemmesen, Michael H. "Supporting States Advice and Defence Development." *Baltic Defence Review* no. 4 (2000): 7–12.

Cottey, Andrew, Timothy Edmunds, and Anthony Forster. "The Second Generation Problematic: Rethinking Civil-Military Relations and Democracy." *Armed Forces and Society* 29, no. 1 (Fall 2002): 31–56.

Darchiashvili, David. "Defense Reform and the Caucasus: Challenges of Institutional Reform during Unresolved Conflict." *Mediterranean Quarterly* 20, no. 3 (Summer 2009): 19–39.

Dean, Robert W. "Civil-Military Relations in Yugoslavia, 1971–1975." *Armed Forces and Society* 3, no. 1 (November 1976): 17–58.

Dicke, Rachel A., Ryan C. Hendrickson, and Steven Kutz. "NATO's Mafia Ally: The Strategic Consequences of Bulgarian Corruption." *Comparative Strategy* 33, no. 3 (July 2014): 287–298.

Dimitrijevic, Bojan. "The Mutual Defense Aid Program in Tito's Yugoslavia, 1951–1958, and its Technical Impact." *Journal of Slavic Military Studies* 10, no. 2 (1997): 19–33.

Dycka, Lukas and Miroslav Mares. "The Development and Future of Fighter Planes Acquisition in Countries of the Visegrad Group." *Journal of Slavic Military Studies* 25, no. 4 (2012): 533–557.

Edmunds, Timothy. "Civil-Military Relations in Serbia-Montenegro: An Army in Search of a State." *European Security* 14, no. 1 (2005): 115–135.

Edmunds, Timothy. "NATO and its New Members." *Survival* 45, no. 3 (Autumn 2003): 145–165.

Furlan, Branimir. "Civilian Control and Military Effectiveness: Slovenian Case." *Armed Forces and Society* 39, no. 3 (2012): 434–449.

George, Julie A. and Jeremy M. Teigen. "NATO Enlargement and Institution Building: Military Personnel Policy Challenges in the Post-Soviet Context." *European Security* 17, nos. 2–3 (2008): 339–366.

Gheciu, Alexandra. "Security Institutions as Agents of Socialization? NATO and the 'New Europe.'" *International Organization* 59, no. 4 (Autumn, 2005): 973–1012.

Glantz, David M. "Accomplishments, Strengths, and Weaknesses of the US Military (Security) Assistance Program." *Journal of Slavic Military Studies* 11, no. 4 (1998): 1–71.

Glantz, David M. "Military Training and Education Challenges in Poland, the Czech Republic, and Hungary." *Journal of Slavic Military Studies* 11, no. 3 (1998): 1–55.

Glantz, David M. "Military Training and Education Challenges in Poland, the Czech Republic, and Hungary: Conclusions and Recommendations." *Journal of Slavic Military Studies* 12, no. 1 (1999): 1–12.

Hendrickson, Ryan C. "NATO's Visegrad Allies: The First Test in Kosovo." *Journal of Slavic Military Studies* 13, no. 2 (June 2000): 25–38.

Heard, Graeme P. and Tom Tracy. "Democratic Civil-Military Relations in Bosnia and Herzegovina." *Armed Forces and Society* 32, no. 4 (July 2006): 549–565.

Horncastle, James. "Croatia's Bitter Harvest: Total National Defence's Role in the Croatian War of Independence." *Small Wars and Insurgencies* 26, no. 5 (2015): 744–763.

Horncastle, Jamie. "A House of Cards: The Yugoslav Concept of Total National Defence and its Critical Weakness." *Macedonian Historical Review* 2 (2011): 285–302.

Horncastle, James. "Reaping the Whirlwind: Total National Defense's Role in Slovenia's Bid for Secession." *Journal of Slavic Military Studies* 26, no. 3 (2013): 528–550.

Jokubauskas, Vytautas. "The Financing and Personnel of the Lithuanian Army." *Lithuanian Annual Strategic Review 2014–2015* 13 (2015): 147–170.

Kotnik, Igor. "Professionalization of the Slovenian Armed Forces—A Goal or a Path?" *Contemporary Military Challenges* 17, no. 4 (December 2015): 11–25.

Kris, Zdenek. "Army and Politics in the Czech Republic Twenty Years after the Velvet Revolution." *Armed Forces and Society* 36, no. 4 (2010): 627–646.

Kriz, Zdenek. "Czech Military Transformation: Towards a Military Typical of a Consolidated Democracy?" *Journal of Slavic Military Studies* 23, no. 4 (2010): 617–629.

Larsson, Robert L. "The Enemy Within: Russia's Military Withdrawal from Georgia." *Journal of Slavic Military Studies* 17, no. 3 (2004): 405–424.

Lefebvre, Stéphane. "The Czech Republic and National Security, 1993–1998." *Journal of Slavic Military Studies* 23, no. 2 (2010): 328–369.

Leonard, Thomas M. "NATO Expansion: Romania and Bulgaria within the Larger Context." *East European Quarterly* 33, no. 4 (2000): 517–544.

Locksley, Christopher C. "Concept, Algorithm, Indecision: Why Military Reform has Failed in Russia since 1992." *Journal of Slavic Military Studies* 14, no. 1 (2001): 1–26.

Lombardi, Ben. "Ukrainian Armed Forces: Defence Expenditure and Military Reform." *Journal of Slavic Military Studies* 14, no. 3 (2001): 31–68.

Maior, George Cristian and Mihaela Matei. "Bridging the Gap in Civil-Military Relations in Southeastern Europe: Romania's Defense-Planning Case." *Mediterranean Quarterly* 14, no. 2 (Spring 2003): 60–76.

Makarychev, Andrei and Alexander Sergunin. "Russian Military Reform: Institutional, Political, and Security Implications." *Defense and Security Analysis* 29, no. 4 (December 2013): 356–364.

Marijan, Davor. "The Yugoslav National Army [sic] Role in the Aggression against the Republic of Croatia from 1990 to 1992." *National Security and the Future* 3–4, no. 2 (2001): 143–178.

Mattelaer, Alexander. "Revisiting the Principles of NATO Burden-Sharing." *Parameters* 46, no. 1 (Spring 2016): 25–34.

Mcauliffe, Amy. "Poland, Trying to Punch above its Weight Class in NATO." *Journal of Slavic Military Studies* 13, no. 4 (2000): 1–28.

McNab, Robert M. "Implementing Program Budgeting in the Serbian Ministry of Defense." *Public Budgeting and Finance* 31, no. 2 (Summer 2011): 216–230.

Millotat, Christian O. "The *Bundeswehr* in the New Federal States: Aspects of the Development of Home Defense Brigade, 38: Sachen-Anhalt." *Defense Analysis* 9, no. 3 (1993): 311–318.

Mychajlyszyn, Natalie. "Civil-Military Relations in Post-Soviet Ukraine: Implications for Domestic and Regional Stability." *Armed Forces and Society* 28, no. 3 (Spring 2002): 455–479.

Nikolić, Nebojša. "Culture of Career Development and Ranking and Selection of Military Officers." *Western Balkans Security Observer*, no. 14 (July–September 2009): 120–141.

Niebuhr, Robert. "Death of the Yugoslav People's Army and the Wars of Succession." *Polemos*, no. 13/14 (January 2004): 91–105.

Niebuhr, Robert. "War in Slovenia: Doctrine and Defeat." *Journal of Slavic Military Studies* 19, no. 3 (2006): 489–513.

Parchomenko, Walter. "The State of Ukraine's Armed Forces and Military Reform." *Journal of Slavic Military Studies* 13, no. 3 (2000): 63–86.

Paszewski, Tomasz. "Can Poland Defend Itself?" *Survival* 58, no. 2 (April–May 2016): 117–133.

Patrick, Charles R. "Tactics of the Serb and Bosnian-Serb Armies and Territorial Militia." *The Journal of Slavic Military Studies* 7, no. 1 (1994): 16–43.

Peyrouse, Sébastien. "The Central Asian Armies Facing the Challenge of Formation." *The Journal of Power Institutions in Post-Soviet Societies*, Issue 11 (2010). http://pipss.revues.org/index3776.html (accessed June 2, 2016).

Potocnik, Viktor. "Slovenian Armed Forces Size and Character." *Contemporary Military Challenges* 17, no. 4 (December 2015): 27–46.

Remington, Robin Allison. "Armed Forces and Society in Yugoslavia." In *Political-Military Systems: Comparative Perspectives*, ed. Catherine McArdle Kelleher, 163–189. Beverley Hills: Sage, 1974.

Rokvic, Vanja, Zoran Jeftic, and Zeljko Ivanis. "Civil-Military Relations and Democratic Control over the Armed Forces in the Republic of Serbia." *Armed Forces and Society* 38, no. 4 (2012): 675–694.

Sanders, Deborah. "Ukraine's Military Reform: Building a Paradigm Army." *Journal of Slavic Military Studies* 21, no. 4 (2008): 599–614.

Sava, Constantin. "Main State Bodies Providing Transparency of Security and Defence Planning in Romania." In *Transparency in Defence Policy, Military Budgeting and Procurement*, edited by Todor Tagarev, 129–137. Geneva: Geneva Center for the Control of Armed Forces, 2002.

Schneider, James J. "The Origins of Soviet Military Science." *Journal of Soviet Military Studies* 2, no. 4 (1989): 491–519.

Sedelius, Thomas and Olga Mashtaler. "Two Decades of Semi-Presidentialism: Issues of Intra-Executive Conflict in Central and Eastern Europe 1991–2011." *East European Politics* 29, no. 2 (2013): 109–134.

Seroka, Jim. "Serbian National Security and Defense Strategy: Forever Wandering in the Wilderness?" *Journal of Slavic Military Studies* 23, no. 3 (September 2010): 438–460.

Tsypkin, Mikhail. "Soviet Military Culture and the Legacy of the War." In *Histories of the Aftermath: The Legacies of the Second World War in Europe*, edited by Frank Biess and Robert G. Moeller, 269–286. New York: Berghahn Books, 2010.

Turbiville, Graham H., Jr., "Sustaining Theater Strategic Operations." *Journal of Soviet Military Studies* 1, no.1 (1988): 81–107.

Tzvetkov, Georgi. "Defense Policy and Reforms in Bulgaria since the End of the Cold War: A Critical Analysis." *Connections: The Quarterly Journal* 13, no. 2 (Spring 2014): 65–78.

Vetschera, H. and M. Damian. "Security Sector Reform in Bosnia and Herzegovina: The Role of the International Community." *International Peacekeeping* 13, no. 1 (2006): 28–42.

Waters, Trevor. "The Republic of Moldova: Armed Forces and Military Doctrine." *Journal of Slavic Military Studies* 11, no. 2 (1998): 80–97.

Watts, Larry. "Reforming Civil-Military Relations in Post-communist States: Civil Control vs. Democratic Control." *Journal of Political and Military Sociology* 30, no. 1 (Summer 2002): 51–70.

Zaccor, Albert M. "Guerrilla Warfare on the Baltic Coast: A Possible Model for Baltic Defense Doctrines Today?" *Journal of Slavic Military Studies* 7, no. 4 (1994): 682–702.

Zaccor, Albert M. "Problems in the Baltic Armed Forces." *Journal of Slavic Military Studies* 8, no. 1 (1995): 53–72.

Zagorcheva, Dessie P. "The Evolution of Democratic Civil-Military Relations in Bulgaria." *Journal of Slavic Military Studies* 15, no. 1 (2002): 29–56.

Index

Made in the USA
Las Vegas, NV
09 December 2021